PARTITION

Also by Barney White-Spunner

Horse Guards

Of Living Valour

PARTITION

*The story of Indian independence and
the creation of Pakistan in 1947*

BARNEY WHITE-SPUNNER

**SIMON &
SCHUSTER**

London · New York · Sydney · Toronto · New Delhi

A CBS COMPANY

First published in Great Britain by Simon & Schuster UK Ltd, 2017
A CBS COMPANY

1 3 5 7 9 10 8 6 4 2

Simon & Schuster UK Ltd
1st Floor
222 Gray's Inn Road
London WC1X 8HB

www.simonandschuster.co.uk
www.simonandschuster.com.au
www.simonandschuster.co.in

Simon & Schuster Australia, Sydney
Simon & Schuster India, New Delhi

The author and publishers have made all reasonable efforts
to contact copyright-holders for permission, and apologise
for any omissions or errors in the form of credits given.
Corrections may be made to future printings.

A CIP catalogue record for this book
is available from the British Library

Hardback ISBN: 978-1-4711-4800-2
eBook ISBN: 978-1-4711-4802-6

Typeset in Sabon by M Rules
Printed and bound by CPI Group (UK) Ltd, Croydon, CR0 4YY

MIX
Paper from
responsible sources
FSC® C020471

Simon & Schuster UK Ltd are committed to sourcing paper
that is made from wood grown in sustainable forests and support the Forest
Stewardship Council, the leading international forest certification organisation.
Our books displaying the FSC logo are printed on FSC certified paper.

Dedicated to all those who lost their lives
in India and Pakistan in 1947

Contents

LIST OF MAPS AND ILLUSTRATIONS

MAPS

All maps © ML Design

Pages 4–5: India, 1947

Page 208: Punjab, August 1947

Page 274: Bengal, 1947

Page 304: Kashmir, 1947

ILLUSTRATIONS

Plate Section One

Page 1: © Imperial War Museums (HU 87259) (top); © Imperial War Museums (HU 87261) (bottom).

Page 2: © William Vandivert/The LIFE Picture Collection/ Getty Images (top, bottom).

Page 3: © Associated Newspapers/REX/Shutterstock (top left); © National Army Museum (top right); source unknown (bottom).

Page 4: © Mansell/The LIFE Picture Collection/Getty Images) (top); source unknown (bottom).

Page 5: From the private collection of Major General Syed Ali Hamid (top); source unknown (bottom).

Page 6: Source unknown (top left); © Imperial War Museums (TR 842) (top right); © Margaret Bourke-White/The LIFE Picture Collection/Getty Images) (middle left); Wikipedia/Government of India (middle right); © Keystone/Hulton Archive/Getty Images (bottom left); source unknown (bottom right).

Page 7: © *India Times* (top); © AP/REX/Shutterstock (bottom).

Page 8: From the private collection of Major General Syed Ali Hamid (top, middle); source unknown (bottom).

Plate Section Two

Page 1: © Gamma-Keystone via Getty Images (top); © AP/REX/Shutterstock (bottom).

Page 2: Source unknown (top left); © Henry Bush/Associated Newspapers/REX/Shutterstock (top right); source unknown (bottom left, bottom right).

Page 3: Courtesy of Robert Beaumont.

Page 4: © Francis Tuker (top); © AP/REX/Shutterstock (bottom).

Page 5: © Uncredited/AP/REX/Shutterstock (top); © Universal History Archive/UIG via Getty Images) (bottom).

Page 6: © Keystone-France/Gamma-Keystone via Getty Images (top); © Margaret Bourke-White/The LIFE Picture Collection/Getty Images (bottom).

Page 7: © Universal History Archive\UIG/REX/Shutterstock (top); © Margaret Bourke-White/The LIFE Picture Collection/Getty Images (bottom).

Page 8: © National Portrait Gallery, London (top left); © Max Desfor/AP/REX/Shutterstock (top right, bottom).

Notes on the Text

Place names. I have written place names as they were in 1947, so Bombay instead of Mumbai, Cawnpore instead of Kanpur, Ferozepore instead of Firozpur. I appreciate that there are some people who might be offended by this, as that in most cases these are the anglicised versions of the original Indian names. However, given that I am quoting contemporary accounts, it would not make sense to change them.

Language and terminology. Similarly I have throughout used the language and terminology common in 1947. Again this will seem anachronistic, even offensive, to some but it is logical given that I am trying to understand how people thought seventy years ago. The term 'classes', for example, to denote the various different racial and religious groups from which the British Indian Army was recruited, will grate with some readers, but it was the way in which those who divided that army thought.

Money. The currency across India in 1947 was the rupee, usually written as Rs, which is the convention I have followed in this book. The rupee was pegged to the pound sterling at the rate of Rs 13 to £1, so a rupee was worth a bit less than two shillings in old British money. A rupee was divided into 16 annas, so an anna was worth about one old-style British penny. The rupee coins had the King Emperor's head on one side and a prowling tiger on the reverse. Pakistan continued to use Indian currency throughout 1947.

In 1947, rupees were often expressed, as they still are today in

India, Pakistan and Bangladesh, as lakhs, which is 100,000, or as a crore, which is 10,000,000.

Style of address. Indian titles and honorifics are as confusing as British ones. I have tended to avoid them throughout so that Nehru is just Nehru, rather than Pandit Nehru, Pandit being a term of respect for a learned person; Patel plain Patel, rather than Sardar Patel, where Sardar means a chief or leader, and Mountbatten simply Mountbatten, rather than Rear Admiral Viscount Mountbatten of Burma. It is tempting to refer to V. P. Menon by his honorific Rao Bahadur, which means Most Honourable, and which was awarded formally as a title together with a badge, but instead, for the sake of consistency, I have referred to him throughout just as V. P. Menon and Krishna Menon, unsurprisingly, as Krishna Menon to avoid confusion.

Indian Words. There are, obviously, a lot of Indian words and expressions in the text. Anything in italics is explained in the glossary on page 359.

Preface

In 2008 I was the military commander of British and Coalition troops in Basrah and the three other provinces designated by the Coalition Authority in Baghdad as constituting the South Eastern Sector of Iraq. It was a time of some confusion. British troops had been withdrawn from Basrah city the previous summer. We were now based at Basrah airport, with insufficient numbers to do much more than protect the airport and unable to exercise much influence on the immediate area and very little on the outlying provinces. When we asked London for instructions we were told that our job was to stay put, ostensibly to help reopen the airport but in effect simply to be a continuing British presence to bolster an American effort that would be seen to be weakened morally, if not practically, should we withdraw. It was a strange strategy that did not convince many, least of all the Iraqis. British soldiers are at their best in such awkward situations but even their patience was tried by being restricted to guarding a perimeter while being subjected to periodic rocket attacks.

We had become a presence that supposedly conveyed international influence but in effect could be said to have damaged the United Kingdom's standing in the world. We had stayed on too long and with insufficient strength to do anything. We made this point to the then prime minister, Gordon Brown. I grew to respect his personal integrity and concern but his government struck us as having a weak team of strategic advisers. Ultimately, by developing a plan to deploy soldiers directly with the Iraqi Army, we were able to help them reoccupy Basrah and thus drive out the Iranian-backed militias that had been making life for Basrawis so miserable. But it was a difficult operation during which we lost the initiative. We then regained it and the British Army can look with some pride on the fact that Basrah is today the most peaceful part of Iraq, although that must remain a relative judgement given that the country as a whole is fragmenting.

But why had we stayed on so long in Basrah when it had become counter to our interests? Why hadn't we left when we had originally intended, that is, within eighteen months of the 2003 invasion? It was not as if we were overseeing the reconstruction of the Basrah economy or its infrastructure, which had been so badly damaged by a combination of Saddam's general disinterest and occasional vindictiveness. Basrah in 2008 suffered from the same power shortages, lack of proper sewerage and mass unemployment as it had in 2003, despite all the effort that had been made to get London to take an interest in its development.

The British Army's experience in Iraq, and later in Afghanistan, also led many of us to think about how previous British armies would have coped and, in particular, how the whole mechanism of Imperialism had worked. We had been reared on the exploits of the British Indian Army, and their legacy was difficult to avoid in Iraq. We compared ourselves to them, generally unfavourably, and asked whether there were lessons to be learned from how they had organised and conducted themselves. Equally interesting was how the British administration had worked in the Empire; how had we managed to run huge economies like India while now we seemed unable to get the power stations working in Basrah?

Yet as we looked deeper we began to see cracks in the model of British India. The British Indian Army had undoubtedly been a most impressive if surprisingly delicate machine, yet the much-vaunted administration of the Raj did not seem to have achieved that much. The Indian peasant in 1932 had the same income and standard of living as when the Mughal Emperor Akbar died in 1605, just after the East India Company was founded in 1599. Was what we went through in Basrah actually just a repeat, albeit on a very small scale, of the same old British pattern of being unable to leave when it would have been in our and India's best interests to do so? Staying on in Iraq achieved very little for our national interest but, more seriously, had our inability to leave India led to two of the worst losses of life in the twentieth century – the Bengal famine of 1942–44 and Partition in 1947? And the great British Indian Army, designed specifically to keep internal order, and which had accomplished such an extraordinary victory over the Japanese in 1944, had then seemed powerless to act. Why?

What we were trying to do in Iraq was obviously on a totally different scale to India and, as such, the two are incomparable. Yet Basrah seemed to me to be a microcosm of the same issue, namely that Britain has long intervened overseas, as have many nations, usually for reasons of profit and occassonaly for prestige, sometimes unwillingly, and then been unable to leave – at great cost to itself and the local people. This year, 2017, is the seventieth anniversary of Indian independence, the birth of Pakistan and the end of the Raj. It is timely to re-examine exactly what happened in 1947.

I have written this book from a soldier's perspective. It does not purport to be a full history of Indian Independence and the birth of Pakistan. Such a study would be a lifetime's work, fill many volumes and is correctly best left to professional historians. Rather what I have attempted to do, as someone who has played a small part in British interventions around the world, is to explore the thinking of and pressures on the politicians, administrators and soldiers of seventy years ago, and the effect their subsequent actions had on the people of the Indian subcontinent. Inevitably, given my background, I have a better understanding of the British players in this tragedy than I do of their Indian and Pakistani counterparts. Neither am I an apologist for Empire. That is not my role, but what is both terrible and fascinating to explore is what happened when that extraordinarily thin crust, which represented law and order under the Raj, collapsed into holocaust.

This has been an absorbing book to write, but it is only fair to warn the reader that it is also a violent and shocking story, as it must be when so many people died in such terrible circumstances; from the outset you will be confronted by scenes that may make you shudder. I have told it month by month, following the sequence of events as people experienced them at the time, dipping back where necessary to explain the history behind them.

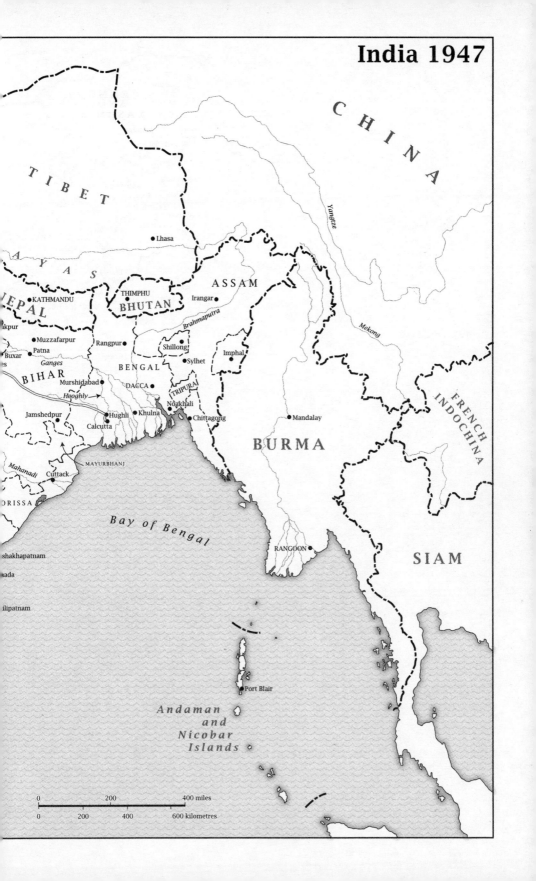

India 1947

CHINA

TIBET

Lhasa

ASSAM

Irangar

BHUTAN

THIMPHU

NEPAL

KATHMANDU

Muzzafarpur

Rangpur

Shillong

Imphal

Patna

BENGAL

Sylhet

Buxar

Ganges

BIHAR

Murshidabad

DACCA

Brahmaputra

Hooghly

TRIPURA

Jamshedpur

Hughli

Khulna

Noakhali

Calcutta

Chittagong

Mandalay

Mahanadi

MAYURBHANJ

Cuttack

BURMA

ORISSA

Bay of Bengal

shakhapatnam

RANGOON

SIAM

ada

FRENCH INDOCHINA

ilipatnam

Yangtze

Mekong

Port Blair

Andaman
and
Nicobar
Islands

0	200	400 miles
0	200	400	600 kilometres

1. JANUARY

THE END OF THE RAJ

*'I see with worry and dismay the rising tide of ruin
which is engulfing this great country of India'*

(A. P. HUME – Indian Civil Service)

Field Marshal Lord Archibald Wavell, Viceroy of India and ruler of half a billion souls, had returned to Delhi from London at the end of December 1946 as bitter a man as his even temper and undemonstrative character would allow. Reserved, almost taciturn, Wavell had been appointed viceroy in October 1943, having previously been commander-in-chief in India, a post to which he had been transferred, having been sacked by Churchill as commander-in-chief Middle East in 1941. There was an element of the consolation prize in his being made viceroy, Churchill having previously toyed with making him Governor General of Australia. It was a curious way of selecting the incumbent of the most important post in the Empire. The two men detested each other. Wavell thought Churchill was a blundering amateur strategist and blamed him for the diversion of British forces from North Africa to Greece, which resulted in the German breakthrough in early 1941. After his first year as viceroy Wavell's opinion had not changed, describing Churchill's government as 'negligent, hostile and contemptuous'.[1] For his part Churchill thought Wavell was the epitome of the cautious, unimaginative general, unwilling to take risks, and in turn blamed him for the failure to retake Tobruk. Once Wavell became viceroy, Churchill corresponded with him directly just twice between October 1943 and June 1944, once demanding to know why Gandhi had not yet died.[2] He described Wavell, inappropriately, as a 'contemptible self-seeking advertiser' and 'talked about the handicap India is to defence'.[3]

Despite Churchill's antipathy, Wavell turned out to be as successful a wartime viceroy as the extraordinary circumstances allowed. Almost his first act was to visit Bengal, where the most terrible famine of the twentieth century had been raging since 1942, and to divert army resources from the campaign against the Japanese in Burma to bring what relief was still possible at that late stage; over 1 million people had already starved to death. Although not from the Indian Army himself,[4] Wavell had considerable experience of India, having spent thirteen years of his life there – two and a half as a child, five years as a young officer and six years as commander-in-chief of the Indian Army and then viceroy. Consequently he knew the country well and had a deep affection for it in that slightly paternalistic manner so characteristic of the Raj. He was generally well liked and respected within the admittedly narrow circle of the administrative classes in India. On New Year's Day he dined with the Royal Scots Fusiliers, a British regiment stationed near Delhi. Captain Shahid Hamid, an Indian officer on the staff of Field Marshal Claude Auchinleck, the commander-in-chief, remembers him 'looking cheerful in spite of the very heavy burden which he is carrying. He is a great man. He is straight and honest. Even Gandhi, whom Wavell regards as an unscrupulous old hypocrite, cannot fool him'.[5]

Yet the circumstances that January were very different to those wartime years and the problems Wavell faced were in many ways more intractable than ending the Bengal famine or mobilising India to defeat Japan. His job now was to bring to an end ninety years of direct British rule in India, and to hand over power to representatives of an Indian people bitterly divided between the majority Hindus, led by the Congress Party, and the minority Muslims led by the All-India

Muslim League who were demanding their own jurisdiction, termed Pakistan, but it was not clear what form that jurisdiction would take. Neither did he have the support he felt he should have in London. Although Churchill had been defeated in the July 1945 general election, Wavell found he was getting on no better with the new Labour prime minister, Clement Attlee. Handling the subtleties of politicians was not one of Wavell's strengths. Attlee's Cabinet were not, he felt, demonstrating 'sufficient directness of purpose'.[6] He had gone to London in December 1946 with an Indian delegation comprising of Hindu, Muslim and Sikh representatives but the negotiations had proved fruitless. Their immediate problem was to make the putative Constituent Assembly work, a body that could, should the Muslim League support it, have come up with a plan for the handover of power. Wavell had told the Cabinet that if it did not, then 'we should not be able to enforce British rule in India beyond 31st March 1948'. He advised abandoning the four southern provinces[7] and conducting a gradual evacuation of the British community rather like a military withdrawal. The Cabinet had debated his recommendations on New Year's Eve. They did see merit in announcing a date by which the Raj would end but thought the rest of Wavell's plan too drastic and too military. Wavell had few supporters in the Cabinet. They thought him defeatist. Ernest Bevin, the Foreign Secretary, told Attlee on New Year's Day that he should be recalled and replaced by 'somebody with courage who would, even if he were the last man left there would come out with dignity and uphold the British Empire'.[8] Attlee, who knew India quite well and had served on the 1927 Simon Commission, agreed that Wavell had 'a defeatist mind'. He had kept him hanging around in London throughout December although he did graciously lend him his aeroplane so the viceroy could be back in Delhi for Christmas. Bevin went on to say that the Cabinet themselves were badly divided. Sir Stafford Cripps, a veteran negotiator of the handover of power, was 'so pro Congress' that 'a balanced judgment is not being brought to bear on the importance of the Muslim world' while A. V. Alexander, who had recently assumed the Defence portfolio, was 'too pro Muslim'.[9]

However calm he may have appeared to young Captain Hamid at that New Year's Day dinner, and however dignified he was as he knighted Reginald Savory, the Adjutant General of India, before they sat down to eat, Wavell was, as he himself admitted, very tired. It had been 'rather an unhappy year. It is a great strain on a small man to do a job which is too big for him, if he feels it is too big'.[10] The issue was not just the apparent intractability of the opposing Indian parties, or the failure of any British initiative to achieve a solution that was mutually acceptable, but that law and order were beginning to break down across the vast subcontinent. What had started as an anti-British movement, a nationalist campaign that had initially encompassed all religions and 'classes', as the Raj referred to the different Indian ethnic and religious groups, orchestrated by Congress against British unwillingness to hand over power, had become a violent conflict between Hindus and Sikhs on the one hand, and Muslims on the other, which now teetered on the brink of becoming civil war.

Murder and arson were a daily occurrence, and there had been several major outbreaks of violence. In August 1946, Calcutta, the capital of Bengal, had seen three days of Hindu versus Muslim rioting which had left approximately 5,000 dead and 10,000 injured, in what came to be known as the 'Great Calcutta Killings'.[11] The Muslim League had announced that they would declare 16 August a public holiday to celebrate their withdrawal from the Congress-dominated Interim Government. Muhammad Ali Jinnah, the League's dynamic leader and 'Sole Spokesman'[12] had also declared it to be 'Direct Action Day' although neither he nor the Muslim Premier of Bengal, Huseyn Suhrawardy, had specified exactly what that meant. Unruly mobs in Calcutta, Muslim and Hindu *goondas* needed little encouragement to interpret it in their own way and it took the army four days to restore order. The journalist Nikhil Chakravarty could not recall having seen so much devastation. He remembered hundreds of people lying dead in the street, the bodies shrinking in the terrible Bengal summer heat and the stomach-churning stink. He saw an old Muslim laundryman in a good neighbourhood being beaten up by well-to-do Hindus who all knew him well – but now he represented to them a species that must go.[13]

One of the most feared Hindu gang leaders was Gopal 'Patha' Mukherjee. He was, recalled Andrew Whitehead, who interviewed him afterwards, 'an unlikely retired gang leader. He is positively beatific, with his thick, black-rimmed spectacles, long white hair tied up on top of his head'. Yet his gang of 800 murdered hundreds of Muslims. Gopal saw it as his duty. 'It was a very critical time for the country', he told Whitehead. 'We thought if the whole area became Pakistan there would be more torture and repression.' If one Hindu was murdered he instructed his boys to kill ten Muslims in retaliation. They used all sorts of weapons – 'small knives, big choppers, sticks, rods, guns and pistols. During the Second World War the American Army were in Calcutta. If you gave them Rs 250 or a bottle of whisky, they would give you a pistol and a hundred cartridges'. One day Gopal killed four Muslims himself in one go.[14]

What was so shocking was the 'unbridled savagery with homicidal maniacs let loose to kill and kill and maim and burn' wrote General Sir Francis Tuker, who witnessed much of it. The worst butchery was in the south of the city. As the soldiers moved in they had to clear over 150 corpses from one crossroads so that they could get their vehicles past. In one bustee, or slum, area they found a house with fifteen bodies in the first room and twelve in the second. They came across a rickshaw stand where not only the passengers but also the wretched pullers had all been cut down. Many of the bodies were horribly mutilated. The majority of those killed in Calcutta were Hindus. A favourite trick of the Muslim goondas was to tie people to a pole with their hands behind their backs and then bore a small hole in their foreheads so that they bled slowly to death through their brains. Hardened soldiers of the York and Lancaster Regiment who had fought through the campaigns against the Japanese were sick on the spot.[15]

Phillips Talbot, a hardened American journalist, was in Calcutta at the time. He wrote to Walter Rogers at the Institute of Current World Affairs:

It would be impossible to describe everything we saw. In street after street rows of shops had been stripped to the walls. Tenements and business buildings were burned out and their contents strewn over the pavements. A pall of smoke hung over many blocks, and buzzards sailed in great, leisurely circles. Most overwhelming were the neglected human casualties; fresh bodies, bodies grotesquely bloated in the tropical heat, slashed bodies, bodies bludgeoned to death, bodies piled on push carts, bodies caught in drains, bodies stacked high in vacant lots, bodies, bodies, bodies.[16]

Naffese Chohan, aged fifteen and safely at home miles away in the Punjab, heard a violent knocking at the door in the middle of the night. It was her cousin, who was like a brother to her. He 'had a good education, in an "English" school and spoke English well'. He had been working in Calcutta. Now he stood outside the door of their house just with the clothes he was wearing and without shoes. Her mother asked what on earth had happened. 'Don't ask', he replied, but soon the story emerged. He said there had been 'killing and blood everywhere'. It would soon, he warned, come to the Punjab, but the old people did not believe him.[17]

The Great Calcutta Killings were just the beginning. The trouble in Bengal then spread outside Calcutta itself, to the rural areas of Chittagong, Tippera and Noakhali in eastern Bengal where Muslim gangs under Ghulam Sarwar went round Hindu villages demanding forcible conversion of Hindus and butchering those who refused. Congress was blamed for exaggerating the numbers killed, which were fewer than in Calcutta but nevertheless significant.

Jharna Chowdhury was nine years old at the time. One morning in the middle of October 1946 she remembered 'hundreds of people came to our house with flaming torches. They were shouting Allah-o-Akbar. Then they set the house on fire. We fled and laid in a nearby garden. There were so many attackers . . .' but what shocked her was that among them she saw people from her own village, neighbours whom she had known all her life. It was a pattern that would be repeated many times across India in the coming year.[18]

Chandra Pal had been working away from home. He returned to find that his 'parents' house had been attacked and looted but luckily lives were spared. But our neighbours' houses, the big zamindars' (landowners) houses and those of big business families – those houses had been looted like anything; people had been massacred and their women taken away'. This was to be another disturbing aspect of the trouble that lay ahead. Pal also thought that 'the rioters wanted vengeance against those with money and power', and certainly the majority of the big landowners in Bengal were Hindus.[19]

'Many people jumped into ponds to save themselves', remembered M. K. Majumdar, a retired schoolteacher. 'They tried to hide under the water hyacinths. But the attackers killed them with fishing spears.'[20] For weeks afterwards Hindu men were forced to offer *namaz,* ritual Muslim prayers, and adopt Muslim names. The fate of the abducted women was particularly grim. Ashoka Gupta, married to a judge, recalled one man approaching her in tears. His wife was being carried off and raped every night by the same group of men and he was helpless to stop them.

The ageing Gandhi took it on himself to tour the area in a peace pilgrimage. Ashoka Gupta also remembers his arrival. He came by boat and crowds turned out to cheer him, both Hindu and Muslim. Abdul Rauf, a local Muslim, was initially impressed by him. 'He was wearing two pieces of khadi (homespun) cloth and there was a watch at his waist. He took support from the shoulders of two women.' But the Muslims soon got rather fed up with him. They noticed he seemed dependent on milk from his accompanying goat; one night a group of them kidnapped the goat and barbecued it.[21]

Worst came in Bihar, the neighbouring province to Bengal, where about 8,000 Muslims were massacred in October by Hindu gangs, a death toll promptly exaggerated to 20,000 by the Muslim League. One of the most shocking incidents occurred at the Garhmukteshwar Fair on 6 to 7 November. The fair was a traditional rural gathering on the banks of the River Ganges. Although primarily a Hindu festival, many Muslims went as traders. On the evening of 6 November, a shout went up that a Muslim had insulted a Hindu woman, a Jat.

Almost immediately, and in a move that many considered premeditated although nothing substantial has ever been proved, gangs of Jats moved in and killed every Muslim man, woman and child in the most appalling fashion.

> Pregnant women were ripped up, their unborn babies torn out and infants' brains bashed out on walls and on the ground. There was rape, and women and children were seized by the legs by burly fiends and torn apart. Most were killed with spears but some of the killings were by strangulation. The murderers' women stood about, laughing with glee, egging on their men folk.[22]

The next day the Jat gangs moved from the fairground on the Ganges into the town of Garhmukteshwar itself, repeating their savagery. What was most shocking about this whole dreadful incident was that the Garhmukteshwar police, all Hindu, did absolutely nothing to stop it. The army reckoned at least 2,000 Muslims had been killed over the two days.

Most worrying of all for Wavell and the government in Delhi was the possibility of a major breakdown of order in the Punjab. If India was described as the jewel in the crown of the British Empire, then the Punjab was the brightest part of that jewel. Not only did its population produce nearly half the manpower for the Indian Army but it was also India's most fertile province. Its agricultural land, watered by the five rivers from which it takes its name, and an elaborate and effective canal system, produced almost one third of India's wheat as well as 10 per cent of its cotton and rice. Its capital at Lahore was one of the great cities of Asia, a former Mughal capital with a sophisticated and cosmopolitan society. Yet the Punjab also had a delicate balance of communities. The Muslims were narrowly in the majority, forming 57 per cent of the population of approximately 25 million, but were concentrated mostly in the west. East of Lahore, centred on their holy city of Amritsar, were 5 million Sikhs who, although only 20 per cent of the population, exercised a disproportionate influence. Originally a religious sub-sect of Hinduism, they had emerged in the seventeenth century as a 'distinct and militant community as a result of the proselytising zeal of the Moghul emperor Aurangzeb'.[23] Sikh organisation and military prowess had enabled them to rule the Punjab as a separate kingdom under Maharajah Ranjit Singh as the Mughal Empire declined. Conquered by the British in a series of wars in the 1840s, they had subsequently been among the Raj's most loyal supporters, and were to form a major part of the Indian Army after the Mutiny in 1857. In January 1947, the Punjab was ruled by a coalition government, much to the fury of the Muslim League who felt the majority of Muslims in the province should have entitled them to power. On 24 January they urged their supporters to 'smash the ministry' and their newspaper *Dawn* started printing quotations from the Holy Qur'an on its front pages.[24] The Punjab's population was polarising rapidly. People were becoming passionately and ostentatiously Muslim or Hindu.

In what the British referred to with some understatement as 'Viceroy's House', the enormous palace in Delhi designed by Edwin Lutyens, with its staff of over a thousand, including one man whose job was simply to pluck chickens and another to make butter pats, Wavell was beginning to realise that the machinery of the Raj was falling apart. It had only ever been at best skin deep, able to rule India and maintain law and order when not challenged. The war had masked its decline but now the police, never the strongest of the Raj's institutions, was collapsing and the Indian Civil Service overwhelmed by the scale of the problem and unsure how much authority they still held. 'I see with sorrow and dismay the rising tide of ruin which is engulfing this great country of India', A. P. Hume, an ICS officer of nineteen years standing, had written to his father at the end of 1946. 'The administrative machinery has already broken down in large areas, and justice and orderly government are being submerged in a morass of corruption, incompetence and misrepresentation of the truth.' His father had, unhelpfully, forwarded the letter to Attlee. Even Sir Olaf Caroe, one of the most experienced and able, if controversial, provincial governors, had written that 'the administration is running down, crime is going up and revenue not coming in'.[25]

The only branch of government Wavell knew he could rely on was the army, nearly half a million men of the Indian Army and 30,000 British troops still positioned strategically in mobile brigades around India. The Labour government was not impressed with the Indian Army's 'complete lack of leadership', which Bevin believed would 'cause the disaster that will overtake the British Empire'.[26] Even allowing for Bevin's tendency to overstate his case, it was strong criticism, but it was the army that Wavell might ultimately have to rely on. In late 1946 he had asked Auchinleck, the commander-in-chief in India and responsible for all the Indian armed forces, to conduct an exercise to establish how prepared the army was to deal with a complete breakdown. The results of Exercise Embrace were used to draw up plans to deal with an 'open insurrection'.[27] In the cool of early January, when the weather in Delhi was still bearable, Wavell realised that he was not only presiding over the end of the Raj but that he could end up doing so amid the most terrible violence.

The India that Wavell ruled in 1947 as the King Emperor's representative was the second-largest country in the world by population. Of its 400 million people, 300 million lived in eleven provinces directly under British rule. Three of these were the great provinces of Bombay, Madras and Bengal, which had grown from being the earliest trading posts and later administrative centres of the East India Company; all British territory in southern India was divided between Bombay and Madras. It was, though, Bengal that had long presented the British with their greatest challenges in India. Conquered in stages during the seventeenth and eighteenth centuries, with its principal city of Calcutta on the Hooghly river, it was vital to British trade partly as a place where vessels engaged in the China trade could cross-load and partly for its own rich resources such as jute; Bengal would dominate the world jute trade well into the twentieth century.

Calcutta had been the logical place for the East India Company and later the British Raj to base their government until in 1911 it was decided to move to the more central Delhi, the old Moghul capital. Yet Bengal was also a difficult province to administer. It was over-populated, with the majority of the population living in miserably poor rural villages. It was also, like the Punjab, divided between Muslims and Hindus. In 1905, with Bengal's population topping 80 million, Lord Curzon, viceroy since 1899, decided the province should be partitioned for ease of administration, and with some political benefits from the British perspective, creating a separate Muslim-dominated East Bengal and a Hindu-dominated West Bengal. The resulting outcry from the Hindu population and the rising Indian nationalist movement made this plan unsustainable and in 1911 it was reversed. The two halves of Bengal were reunited but two new Hindu-dominated provinces, which had previously been incorporated in West Bengal, were created. The first, Bihar, included Orissa, and, secondly, North Bengal became a separate province as Assam.

West of Bihar and Orissa, the British ruled the vast plains of Central India from two provinces, the United Provinces with its capital at Lucknow to the north and the Central Provinces, established in 1861 to rule the land taken from the Marathas, with its capital at Nagpur, to the south. Both these provinces had Hindu majorities, albeit with sizeable pockets of Muslims. There were then two provinces to the north and west. The first, Sind, was the low-lying area where the Indus river system empties into the Indian Ocean, with its principal port and city at Karachi. Sind had been conquered by troops of the East India Company under Lord Napier in 1843, giving rise to Napier's famous quip 'Peccavi' ('I have sinned'), which, in all its classical glibness, seems to summarise so much of the British attitude to ruling India. Originally administered as part of Bombay, in 1936 Sind became a separate province. It was predominantly Muslim, but had a sizeable Hindu mercantile community and many low-caste Hindu workers. North of Sind, and bordering Afghanistan as its name suggests, the North West Frontier Province, with its capital at Peshawar, had been established in 1901 to administer the bandit lands, police the ill-defined Afghan border and to keep some sort of order among the Pathan tribes who lived along it. It was the

North West Frontier that was to dominate so much of British India's strategic thinking and give rise to the popular image of the Raj.

These eleven provinces only covered part of the vast territory that comprised British India. Approximately one third of it remained under its traditional rulers, families who had made treaties with the Raj and who were allowed to continue to administer their territories as many had done for centuries. There were 562 of these 'Princely states' with a combined population of just under 100 million. They ranged from enormous territories such as Hyderabad, dominating central southern India, and the size of Italy, with a population of 16 million, to pieces of land that were really no more than large country estates. Some of these were ethnically and religiously coherent, with rulers and population coming from the same stock, such as the ancient Hindu Rajput states, while others had a ruling family whose religion was different from the majority of their population. The Nizam of Hyderabad, for example, reputedly the world's richest and meanest man, was a Muslim but the vast majority of his subjects were Hindus; in Jammu and Kashmir a Hindu maharajah ruled a state that was 75 per cent Muslim. It was a tension that was to cause considerable problems later in the year.

Wavell was, like so many of his British contemporaries, devoted to India and genuinely thought that he was putting Indian interests first. In that curiously patriarchal manner, so patronising to Indians and yet so natural to a class of British soldiers and administrators who had been brought up to rule an empire, Wavell believed that it was people like him who understood the 'real India'. They had soldiered with her sons, lived in her remote villages and in her hills and thought they knew her best interests better than the wily, urban politicians of Congress and the Muslim League. They certainly thought they knew India better than the Labour politicians at home who seemed obsessed with Britain's domestic problems, and with Palestine. It was an attitude summarised so well by one of the brightest of the British officials in India, Loftus Tottenham, who thought that 'to contemplate handing over the people of India in the name of democracy to be governed by an oligarchy of people who are more oppressive and more selfish than anything you can conceive is really funny ... If it weren't tragic'.[28]

That many individual British officials were so well intentioned towards India would certainly contribute to the quite remarkable lack of antagonism between Britain and the future nations of India, Pakistan and Bangladesh. It was, however, a misunderstanding that was to have catastrophic consequences and to lead to a degree of complacency that would contribute to the tragedies of the coming August.

It was also a misunderstanding that had marked the Raj since its inception following the terrible violence of 1857. The Indian Mutiny, or the First War of Independence as some historians refer to it, was notable for two things. First, it took the British almost entirely by surprise and, secondly, for the murderous violence shown first by the mutinous Indian soldiers, the sepoys, and subsequently by the British in their subjugation of the uprising. It had been caused, ostensibly, by conditions in the army, traditionally because the sepoys had been issued with cartridges that were greased with pigs' fat. In fact, the real grievance was a change in the soldiers' pay and conditions, a reduction in their *batta*, the money they drew for being in the field, but this was really a reflection of a breakdown of trust between the British officers in the East India Company's service and their men, as the Company's army changed from an army of expansion to an army of occupation. Deeper than this ran dissatisfaction at the British ignoring long-established Indian interests and at their forsaking the easy relationships and mutual respect, which had allowed them to be so successful in the eighteenth century, and replacing it with a more distant attitude of racial and religious superiority.

It was the Mutiny that led in 1858 to the East India Company losing its remit to govern India, which was assumed by the British crown. A Secretary of State for India was established as a Cabinet post in Westminster and the governor general in Calcutta added the honorific 'Viceroy' to his title, becoming the monarch's representative. He had a Legislative Council of twelve, half of whom were to be non-official posts, which acted like a Cabinet. There was also a major overhaul of the Indian Army. The main recruiting effort was switched from Bengal and Oudh, where the mutinous Brahmins had largely come from, to the Punjab, which had remained loyal, and to the Jats, Sikhs, Punjabi Muslims, Garwahlis, Gurkhas and Marathas. They would henceforth form the main 'classes' from which the Indian Army was recruited. One British regiment was now brigaded with two Indian regiments or battalions, thus ensuring a core of British troops throughout India, and all artillery was to be kept in British hands. The poor communications and transport system, which had meant that the Mutiny took fourteen months to suppress due to the East India Company's inability to concentrate and move their soldiers, was radically overhauled, with a railway grid now laid out so that troops could move rapidly around the country. The princes, who had largely remained loyal throughout the Mutiny, were rewarded by being drawn closer into the Raj, no longer merely living in uneasy coexistence but becoming an active part of its structure of governance with a complex hierarchy of privileges. Over the coming ninety years, many of the princes came to believe that supporting the Raj was the most effective method of safeguarding their interests.

Yet although the British learned the military lessons of the Mutiny, and learned them well so that the Indian Army grew to be a reliable and efficient body that would serve the Raj loyally until its very last days, they failed to understand the deeper lessons. Although it is fair to argue that the Mutiny was not a national war of independence, it being largely restricted to the north and east and there being few Indians at the time who would have described themselves as being members of an Indian nation, it was undeniably a major revolt against British rule. However it is judged, the Mutiny should have made the British realise that large parts of their regime were both insensitive and unwanted, and that an objective study of British interests in India, which were ultimately largely commercial, should have led to an appreciation that they could best be safeguarded by greater Indian participation in government. But this was the age of Imperialism when Europeans, and the British in particular, thought it their duty and their right to govern less civilised countries. 'Hardly any Victorian doubted that the British could govern India much better than anyone else and that British rule was for India's good',[29] wrote Philip Mason. Curzon thought of the British role as being like 'the prolonged trusteeship for a ward in court' rather than as any preparation for ultimate self-government,[30] although there were those who thought like Evan Maconachie, who retired from the Indian government in 1921, that it was absurd that a race like the British should

> claim superiority to peoples that gave the world a Buddha, an Asoka and an Akbar, religions, and philosophies that embrace every religion that has ever existed, an epic literature perhaps unrivalled, and some of the greatest masterpieces in the realm of human art. It is absurd to suppose that a handful of foreigners from across the sea can continue to rule indefinitely over hundreds of millions of Orientals on the patriarchal lines pursued.[31]

But men like him were in the minority.

There was a strong racial undertone to this imperial self-confidence. While it was acknowledged that one of the causes of the Mutiny had been a lack of engagement with leaders of Indian society, efforts such as having Indians on the Viceroy's Legislative Council were really only window-dressing. Queen Victoria's 1858 proclamation notwithstanding, the Raj operated on a strictly racist basis, with Indians excluded from British clubs and institutions and from any really effective role in government save in the Princely states. From 1857 until 1909, in what has been described as the Imperial Heyday, the Raj ruled India with minimal Indian participation despite a few Indians being a little grudgingly admitted to the ranks of the Indian Civil Service, and making very little progress towards addressing the issues that had caused the terrible events of 1857. This was the age of maharajahs and elephants, of tiger hunts and magnificent state gatherings, the famous durbars. It was an age when the viceroy's train had ten carriages and its own staff of 142, and when ten coolies arrived in the vicereine's sitting room because she said she thought a chair should be moved. It was the age that gave the Raj its enduring glamorous image and which encouraged so many young British men to serve it.

The Indian reaction to the failure of the revolt was very different. The typical British officer saw it as a rude interruption to the logical progress of their civilising influence, soon solved by tightening their monopoly of force, and they believed British rule would last indefinitely. The Indian reaction, both Hindu and Muslim, was, by way of contrast, initially one of intellectual reflection. How had the Mutiny failed? How had hundreds of millions of Indians failed to dislodge a tiny number of foreigners and had to suffer so much indignity in the process? Many of the rebels had been Muslim sepoys, and as far as there had been any figurehead it was the King of Delhi, the descendant of the Muslim Mughal emperors who had been the last rulers of anything approaching a united India before the British conquests. The Muslim reaction was to question why God had allowed them to be defeated and to ask whether it was because they had drifted away from true Islam. A group of scholars in Deoband founded the Darul Uloom School, dedicated to ensuring rigorous adherence to the correct path, in their case Hanafi Sunnism, and to oppose the corrupting influence of the British. The Deobandi movement, which is still so important in Islam today, not least in the United Kingdom, believed that Hindus and Muslims should unite in opposing the British and many of them would oppose the Muslim League's calls for Pakistan.[32]

The Hindu reaction was rather different. Up until the Mutiny it could be argued that although Hinduism ordered almost every part of Indian life, it had not been connected to nationalism. That was to change. Much as the Muslims went back to their religious routes, prominent Hindu scholars like the Gujarati Brahmin Swami Dayananda, who founded the Arya Samaj movement, looked to the Vedas, the original Hindu scriptures, for inspiration. He argued that Hindus had also drifted too far from their routes and advocated returning to the religion's absolutely pure form, rejecting all later additions such as caste and the seclusion of widows. He developed a particular following in the Punjab where his intolerance of other faiths, particularly Islam, would have repercussions later in 1947. More generally, however, Hindu scholars looked at the West and saw that there was nothing to stop them adapting what was successful and attractive in Western learning and lifestyle while still retaining the core elements of Hinduism, including caste. It was 'the dhoti at ease, the western suit on duty'[33] approach, an important result of which was the enthusiastic uptake across India of Western education.

Yet these movements would take time to progress and the lack of any strong Indian reaction in the years following 1857 served only to strengthen the Raj's self-confidence. They now formalised and strengthened a system of governance that, however impressive the quality of its servants, was to prove of questionable relevance to the majority of the Indian population. Each province was run by a governor, answerable to the viceroy who supervised a series of districts. In the larger provinces these districts were grouped into divisions so, for example, the United Provinces had forty-eight districts divided into nine divisions. The size of each district varied considerably, but a typical one would be about the size of several English counties and have a population of about 1 million. An official with three different functions ran a district. He was first the deputy commissioner, charged with local administration such as public health and education; secondly he was the district magistrate, responsible for law and order, with a large measure of control over the police and also required to spend a considerable amount of time hearing court cases. Thirdly, he was also the Collector, responsible for gathering the land tax; for revenue purposes a district was subdivided into a number of *tahsils*, themselves comprising of collections of villages, with the village headman being required to pay the land tax to the local *tahsildar*.

The men who came to staff this system were the Indian Civil Service, perhaps one of the most successful British public institutions ever created for the quality and commitment of its staff, although ultimately one of the most frustrated. Typically ICS men were recruited from the British public school system via university, usually Oxford or Cambridge, on a fiercely competitive basis; the ICS demanded a higher pass mark in its examinations than its British equivalent. Its recruits had not only to master Indian law and languages, but also to be hardy outdoor types who could spend hours in the saddle and who were happy to live much of the year in a tent as they toured their vast districts. They also had to be prepared to dedicate themselves to a lonely and sometimes dangerous career when they would go months without seeing another European and where family life was difficult. If they were successful they could end up as the governor of a province or as a member of the Viceroy's Executive Council, knighted and with a generous pension; if they were unlucky they would die of malaria. These were the men who, like Wavell, developed a particular love of India and whose work on her culture and her history showed a dedication far beyond what their career demanded. There were never very many of them, their numbers restricted by a parsimonious budget; by the end of 1919, when the ICS had largely recovered after the First World War, there were only 760 British ICS officers, a tiny number compared with the 13,500-odd British officers who served in the British Indian Army. Admittedly the ICS would have considered many Indian Army officers of insufficient quality to join their ranks, although every Indian Army officer was required to speak a local language and had a natural understanding of local affairs from interaction with his soldiers.

This lack of numbers, and the bewildering variety of their responsibilities, meant that it was impossible for ICS officers ever to be on top of their briefs, a problem compounded by the curiously illogical system of government they had to implement. The governors and administrators of the East India Company had, when drawing up Indian law and practice, relied heavily on the Mughal system of land tenure they had inherited. Successive early nineteenth-century governor generals, such as Cornwallis and Dalhousie, had added to this what they undoubtedly thought to be the best parts of British landowning practice, effectively consolidating the rights of the landlords. The result was that by the second half of the nineteenth century the Indian landowning system – and the vast majority of the population relied on the land for their livelihood – was largely feudal with a highly developed landlord and tenant structure. With this system came inherent indebtedness because it gave the peasant land rights against which he could borrow, and, given the frequent shortages created by an unpredictable climate and an ever-increasing population, most peasants found they borrowed regularly and on disadvantageous terms. The result was that those who thrived were the landlords, the zamindars, and the moneylenders, the *bania*. It was a system the British introduced because they were themselves the greatest *bania*, said both Indian and British critics,[34] and the so-called reforms of Cornwallis and Dalhousie had in fact led to the peasants being worse off.

The British legal system that formed the basis of the Indian legal code was equally perplexing. Even the great Governor General Warren Hastings thought it a 'monstrous injustice that Indians should be subjected to laws designed for quite different social conditions' and Macaulay wrote that 'All the injustice of former oppressors, Asiatic and European, appeared as a blessing when compared to the justice of the Supreme Court'.[35] By the 1930s it had become 'systemized perjury', thought Penderel Moon, one of the more thoughtful members of the ICS, with a procedure far too complex for litigants to follow in a language that they did not understand and with lawyers who were generally corrupt.[36] It was also a system that, because it had got rid of the old Mughal practice of village elders, the panchayats, deciding on minor cases, meant the courts were flooded with petty personal quarrels. In 1942 in the Punjab alone, with a population of just 25 million people, 277,004 cases were brought to court. Those incredibly well-trained and motivated ICS men would consequently spend long hours hearing evidence on cases that were almost totally irrelevant to maintaining law and order and on which they were highly unlikely to be able to reach a satisfactory judgement.

It did, however, serve to show that the British system of government, however thinly spread and however unintelligible to the average Indian farmer, was fair, and even the most trenchant nationalist critics of the Raj would admit that the ICS was fairly incorruptible, something worthy of comment in India prior to 1947.

Inder Malhotra, the well-known journalist and later editor of both the *Statesman* and *The Times of India*, and who was seventeen in 1947, summed it up when he said that there were 'some odd bad hats amongst the Brits – but by and large they were seen as just and impartial'.[37]

Yet the real problem with the officers of the ICS, enthusiastic and dedicated as they were, was that the way they operated meant they only ever scratched the surface of India. Apart from the sterility of their time in court, much of an ICS officer's working life was spent in touring his district. He would ride round the villages, holding council under banyan trees, assessing land for revenue purposes and settling disputes so long as he could understand what they were about. It was personally fulfilling work in many ways, and no doubt reminded them of life in the rural idylls of the classics, which had formed such a large part of their education. They saw themselves as the moral upholders of an oppressed peasantry, with a duty to protect them from moneylender and landlord, but, despite Gandhi's warming exhortations, the peasantry remained largely irrelevant to India's politics and anyway their very state was the result of British policy in the first place. These extraordinarily able men would have been more profitably employed in the cities, engaging with India's rising middle classes and producing proper development plans rather than in assessing liability for a land tax that fell disproportionately on the already indebted rural poor.

It was this lack of development that is probably the most difficult legacy of the Raj to justify. Unpopular as it was when a much-respected ICS officer and Indian historian, W. H. Moreland, produced the figures, the average Indian income per head in 1932 was shown to be the same as it had been in 1605 under Akbar. When compared to the comparable growth in the quality of life in Great Britain, and allowing for relative increases in population, India had stood still. The English population had in fact increased eight times over the period while India's had increased just under four times but per capita GDP in Great Britain had grown six times.[38] Even as late as 1944 half the population of India was under twenty years old, which is a damning comment on the lack of improvement in life expectancy under the Raj.[39]

A look at the government of India's revenue and expenditure for 1934 explains why – 26 per cent of its revenue went to the military, 14 per cent to the railways, 10 per cent to the police and jails and 6 per cent to government and administrative expenses including 3 per cent to official pensions. By contrast 1 per cent was spent on public health, 1 per cent on agricultural development and only 6 per cent on education. In revenue terms, revenue from income tax was only 7 per cent, compared to 45 per cent in Great Britain, with India's revenue coming largely from indirect taxes, which again fell most heavily on the poor. Customs duties produced 23 per cent, the salt tax 3 per cent and the hated land tax, whose collection preoccupied the ICS, produced only 15 per cent, about the same income the government earned from the railways. The continuous land tax reassessments conducted by the ICS touring officers had in fact raised it to roughly 25 per cent of disposable assets by the mid-1930s, with every holding above one acre or producing over 20 rupees liable to pay.[40] It was onerous, unpopular and unfair.

There had of course been some development. The Indian government was justifiably proud of its canals, which had made a major difference to the productivity of the Punjab, and of the railways. Yet the railways were laid out primarily so that troops could be moved quickly, and were also something of a cash cow for their British backers. Each investor was guaranteed a 5 per cent coupon regardless of how much money the railways actually made, any deficit being made up from government revenue, which meant that unsurprisingly the railways made a loss until 1900, effectively being subsidised by the wretched payers of the land tax. However, the general population did benefit from them; by 1930 there were 41,500 miles of railway along which 620 million passengers and 85 million tons of freight travelled every year.[41]

Part of the problem was that the Indian government had an inadequate economic planning capacity. The senior ICS men who staffed the viceroy's ministries had been trained on tour in the provinces, assessing land disputes or bringing troublesome border tribes to order. They had little notion of making capital available to fund development or of how to increase industrialisation and they did not really think it was their job to do so anyway. By 1931 there were only three industries employing more than 200,000 people: jute, cotton and coal mining, and still only 9,206 factories across the whole of India.[42] Many of these were in the Princely states where the rulers were more sensitive to the importance of financial incentives and tax breaks. S. Moolgaonkar, a Tata executive, recalled that virtually the entire cement industry was located in the Princely states as the Indian government would not give it any financial support in the British provinces, something he, like many, ascribed to a desire to protect imported cement supplies from Britain. 'The Brits imported everything', he complained, 'even the man hole covers'.[43]

It was trade that had brought the East India Company to India in the late sixteenth century, originally to acquire saltpetre (for gunpowder), cotton, silk and spices. Later, as the Indian trade became less profitable, Bengal became the base from which they could trade opium to China in return for tea. Under the Raj, India was to become one of the most important markets for British manufactures. Although India came to be seen as the prop of the British Empire, and strategically important as an end in itself, it was trade that still underpinned Britain's interest. Up until the First World War India bought most of its iron, steel, coal and heavy machinery from Britain. It also bought cotton cloth, something that it could easily have manufactured; in 1914 Indians bought the staggering total of 3,000-million yards of British spun cloth, or approximately a hundred yards per person.[44] Britain also benefited enormously in terms of the balance of payments advantages, also known as the multilateral system of settlements, from India exporting goods such as jute, tea and leather worldwide while firmly 'Buying British' for imports. As competition to British commercial dominance grew from Europe and the United States, Indian exports allowed Britain to buy more from these countries than she was selling to them thereby masking a weakness in the British economy that would not become apparent until the First World War.

By the 1930s the younger ICS officers, many of whom now had a smattering of economics as well as the almost mandatory Latin and Greek, were finding the Delhi government's inability to fund development frustrating and embarrassing. In 1944 Norval Mitchell, a dedicated ICS man who had been seconded to the Maratha state of Kolhapur, was desperate to fund a dam on part of the Panchganga river system which would have substantially improved the productivity of the local farmers. Try as he might, and however detailed the financial plans he submitted, no official in Delhi would sanction a project that could not show at least a 3 per cent return in its first year, something that was clearly impossible. Mitchell's dam was not built until after independence. There was not, he believed, a single official in Delhi who understood the employment of capital nor who would accept any of the states taking on debt.[45]

Indian nationalism took its time to get organised after 1857 but began to assert itself more strongly from the early twentieth century. The very strong Hindu opposition to Curzon's division of Bengal in 1905 was the first time it started to be effective but it would take nearly fifty years to achieve its aim of full independence for the country. The Raj responded to its challenge grudgingly and in a series of four blocks of measures, each of which, until 1947, were inadequate to satisfy nationalist demands or to secure a permanent way forward. The first measures, the Morley-Minto Reforms, named after the Secretary of State and Viceroy respectively, came in 1909. There had been for some time Legislative Councils advising both the viceroy and the provincial governors although these were composed entirely of nominated members, a large part of whom were officials. The 1909 reforms introduced an elected element to these councils, albeit based on a very limited and selective franchise. Critically, the reforms introduced a separate electorate for Muslims.

The next set of reforms came after the First World War, the 1919 Montagu-Chelmsford Reforms, but it was these measures, and the events that surrounded them, that would prove to be the turning point. Up until 1919 it may have been possible to find a solution in

India that preserved some sort of mutually beneficial link to Great
Britain, much as Canada and Australia had done as dominions, and
could have satisfied nationalist aspirations; after 1919 it was to prove
impossible. The reason for this lies in the expectation created by
both British politicians and world events during the First World War.
The 1909 reforms had led Indians to believe that they were a step
towards assuming their own government, an attitude strengthened
by a statement in Parliament by Edwin Montagu, Secretary of State
for India, on 20 August 2017, that the government's policy was the
'gradual development of self-governing institutions, with a view to
the progressive realization of responsible government in India as an
integral part of the Empire'.[46] Indians also thought they deserved this
because of their unstinting support of the British war effort despite
it being at best peripheral to Indian interests. The Indian Army had
grown to 1.2 million men, all volunteers, 800,000 of whom were
combatants. These men had been incompetently managed in France
and subsequently took heavy casualties in Mesopotamia. India also
contributed £100 million as a one-off grant to Westminster in 1914,
followed by generous annual payments, funded by increasing taxes.
British troop levels in India were reduced to 15,000, and despite
there having been some nationalist violence in the pre-war years,
particularly in Bengal, there was no attempt to take advantage of
Britain's unpreparedness.

The First World War also led many Indians to question British
moral superiority. Here was the nation they had long been taught
to revere as the ultimate in civilisation locked in a bitter struggle
with other European powers, accusing each other of atrocities and
coming near to defeat. The Russian Revolution showed that it was
possible to challenge the existing order successfully while the entry
into the war by the United States promised international emphasis
on Woodrow Wilson's Fourteen Points and their call for national
self-determination. Indian Muslims were also deeply disturbed
by their troops fighting the Turks, whose sovereign, the Ottoman
Sultan, was still regarded as the Caliph. Britain's answer that all
these aspirations would be dealt with 'after the war' was accepted

but when that answer came it was thought to be inadequate and ungrateful.

There is something illogical and self-defeating in much of the British government's colonial policy in the years immediately following the end of the First World War. In Ireland, a country the Indian nationalists watched carefully, correctly seeing many similarities to their own situation, the unnecessarily violent British overreaction to the 1916 Irish nationalist uprising meant that any hope of a peaceful move to home rule was almost impossible and led instead to a violent war of independence. In India the Montagu-Chelmsford package promised much, Montagu even describing Gandhi as a 'pure visionary'[47] but delivered far less than was expected. In fact constitutionally the reforms were quite far-reaching. They contained two major provisions. The first was to create a system of shared power in the provinces, termed 'dyarchy'. The provincial Legislative Councils were expanded, their franchise widened considerably, and they were given powers under ministers to deal with public health, education and local government, what became known as the 'transferred subjects'. The governor, answering to the viceroy, continued to exercise powers for law and order and finance, the so-called 'reserved subjects'. In the central government, now in Delhi, two new bodies were created, a Council of State and a Legislative Assembly to replace the old Legislative Council, and although the Viceroy's Executive Council remained appointed by the Secretary of State, it was now to have three as opposed to a single Indian member. It could have been seen as a progressive series of measures that established an assembly, a legislature, and an executive, but in fact the former had little control over the latter; the Council of State and the central Legislative Assembly still contained a significant number of officially nominated members and the viceroy had the power to reject any legislation he regarded as unnecessary. The system of 'dyarchy', with power divided between the central government and the provinces, would also lead to a monumental confusion as to who was responsible for what, which would soon have tragic consequences.

Yet what really caused resentment was not the reforms themselves but the accompanying Rowlatt Acts. Although there had been very little violence in India during the war, there was still some, largely a hangover from Hindu opposition to the partition of Bengal. During the war India had been subject to the Defence of India Act which had given the government wide internal security powers. Now this was no longer applicable, a prominent judge, Mr Justice Rowlatt, was asked to advise on what alternative measures should be put in place. He recommended two bills: the first would allow judges to try political cases without juries while the second permitted internment without trial. Despite being opposed by every Indian member of the Executive Council, they became law on the vote of the official majority. Congress, ably orchestrated by Gandhi, mobilised opposition and rioting broke out across India but particularly badly in the Punjab, the province that had suffered most from increased taxation and recruitment during the war. It had also suffered terribly from outbreaks of plague and then flu in 1917–18. During early April the violence escalated, with attacks on banks, post offices and the railways.

The government's response was uncompromising. On 13 April 1919, martial law was imposed on the Punjab. Brigadier General Reginald Dyer, commanding the brigade responsible for the Sikh holy city of Amritsar, deployed about a hundred soldiers from the Gurkha and Baluch regiments to deal with a gathering, belatedly declared illegal, of approximately 20,000 people in a confined space called the Jallianwalla Bagh, an area of rough ground close to the Golden Temple, surrounded by buildings and with only two very narrow exits. The large crowds were there because Amritsar was packed due to the annual Baisakhi horse fair. Dyer first blocked the entrances and then ordered his troops to fire into the crowd without warning. His men fired 1,650 rounds in ten minutes. The terrified crowd could not escape and were mown down in what became a confined killing ground. You can still see the bullet holes in the walls.

At least 379 people were killed and a further 1,000 wounded. When later asked why he had blocked the entrances so people could not disperse he replied that the shooting was not intended to disperse the crowd but to punish them for disobedience. One macabre advantage of the lack of access was that Dyer could not use the armoured car he had brought along, which, with its turret-mounted machine gun, would have greatly increased the casualty toll. In the days after the massacre, Indians were forced into humiliating gestures, being made to crawl down a street where a European woman had been molested, with British soldiers posted at either end to ensure that they did so, and subjected to indiscriminate physical punishment from the police. Public flogging was instituted.

It is difficult to exaggerate the effect of the Jallianwalla Bagh massacre. Of all the many terrible events of Empire, it ranks as one of the worst. Even Churchill, usually so determined in his defence of authority, said, 'It was an extraordinary event, a monstrous event, an event which stands in singular and sinister isolation'.[48] Dyer was sacked, his conduct condemned in the House of Commons and he was sent home from India, but the damage was done. Indian opinion was incensed that he still received a vote in his favour in the House of Lords and a fund set up in appreciation of his services. Although a commission was created to investigate his actions he was never prosecuted, instead just found guilty of a mistaken notion of duty. Of all the events of that immediate post-war period, it is the Amritsar Massacre that did the most to destroy trust and the reputation of the Raj. Instead of being thanked and recognised for their part in a war in which they had little direct interest, Indians had been subject to repressive legislation and then seen their people mown down when they had gathered to protest about it. Dyer's conduct, so untypical of a British army and particularly a British Indian army specifically constituted and trained to maintain law and order with a minimum of violence, is a testament to the brutalising effect of the war. In Delhi, as in Dublin, a political solution had suddenly become much more difficult.

The aftermath of Amritsar was an inevitable strengthening of Indian nationalism. Congress, orchestrated by Gandhi, realised that they must develop an all-India campaign to get rid of the British and to establish home rule, Swaraj. At a conference in Lucknow in 1916, Congress had agreed with the Muslim League that they would work together, in return for which Congress reaffirmed the 1909 provision that there would be a separate Muslim electorate and a reserved allocation of Muslim seats in the various representative bodies. Consequently during the 1920s and early 1930s the emphasis was very much on getting rid of the Raj rather than on inter-communal issues. Gandhi realised that taking on the Raj by force would not be successful and was in any case inimical to his own strong belief in non-violence. Instead he developed his satyagraha campaign, which broadly meant using non-cooperation, civil disobedience and peaceful protest. Gandhi also needed to widen the support for independence from the rather narrow group of middle-class Hindus who constituted the Congress leadership to make it a mass movement. Satyagraha was not that successful in practical terms but morally and psychologically it left the British government floundering. Through a series of non-cooperation protests, hunger strikes and jail sentences interspersed with dialogue, Gandhi made the unshakeable case that the Raj was unjustified and must go. British reaction was generally clumsy. In 1927 they appointed Sir John Simon to head a commission to report on the effects of the Montagu-Chelmsford Reforms ten years on. Simon's team were entirely British and reported solely to the Westminster Parliament; predictably Gandhi organised for it to be boycotted.

More positively, in 1926, Lord Irwin became viceroy. He managed to persuade reluctant politicians in London to say that the goal of British policy was for India to gain Dominion status. He and Gandhi achieved an understanding and in March 1931 they signed a joint agreement that led to a round table conference in London to work out how this might be achieved. The round table conference in the end achieved very little but the very fact that it took place showed that there was a split emerging in British opinion. The Raj itself, its officials and its rigid, almost racist society in India was only grudgingly coming to terms with acknowledging that ultimately Indians had a right to independence, whereas in the British Isles attitudes had moved more quickly. In many areas of life Indians and Indian culture were becoming accepted and welcomed, helped by the obvious bravery of Indian soldiers in the First World War. As early as 1892, when no Indians even had the vote in India, Dadabhai Naoroji had been elected as Member of Parliament for Finsbury, despite Lord Salisbury's assertion that, 'However far we have advanced in overcoming prejudices, I doubt we have yet got to that point when a British constituency will take a black man to represent them'.[49] K. S. Ranjitsinhji captained Sussex and played for England. Sophia Duleep Singh, daughter of the eponymous maharajah, was a prominent member of the suffragette movement at a time when even extending the franchise to all men in India was considered laughable. Indian food became universally popular in the early 1930s, due to Mulk Raj Anand's curry cookbook and Uday Shankar dazzled London audiences dancing with Anna Pavlova at the Royal Opera House in 1923. Here was a society that now saw Indians as friends and equals and it was the Raj itself that seemed to be an anachronism. The well-known Indian novelist Kushwant Singh summed it up when he said that: 'Most Indians who had Brit friends met them in England not India'. It became apparent to most British voters that Indian independence was not only inevitable but also desirable.

India also became less important to British commerce after the First World War. It was still importing £185 million worth of woven cloth from British mills in 1928 but this now represented only 29 per cent of total cloth imports, the rest mostly coming from other Asian countries. In 1929 India imported 3,645 British cars but 7,943 from the United States, and Britain was buying more from India – over 200,000 tons of jute and 300 million pounds of tea.[50] The British stranglehold on India's balance of payments was gradually reducing, and there had been at least some British recognition of the unfairness of the previous system. A tariff board was created in 1923, in 1925 the cotton excise was abolished, and measures introduced to protect Indian manufacturers from cheap Japanese imports.

Reducing commercial pressure, Indian nationalist agitation and changing British attitudes combined to influence the British government to move, albeit grudgingly, towards home rule – the Swaraj that Gandhi and the Congress Party were demanding. The resulting 1935 Government of India Act was, like the Montagu-Chelmsford Reforms, both a success in that it introduced significant improvements in self-government but a failure in that it omitted any clear commitment to actual independence. Its first major provision was to introduce a strong federal system. The provinces were reorganised into the eleven that Wavell now ruled and given significant autonomy. Provincial governments were to be elected by a franchise that increased from 6 to 30 million people, and also included women for the first time, although property qualifications meant few could actually vote. These provincial governments assumed full powers for everything except defence and foreign affairs, which remained with a 'strong centre' in Delhi. It was a sensible outcome in many ways, which recognised the wide diversity of the country but it was also to cause confusion since British governors remained in place with their staffs and with powers to intervene but it was not always clear who was in charge; this was soon to prove catastrophic in Bengal. It also meant that in reality power remained in Delhi. The allocation of seats to Muslims was also confusing, with Muslims over-represented in the United Provinces but insufficiently in the Punjab.

The second major change was that the Princely states, that one third of India still governed by its hereditary rulers, were included in the constitution in much the same way as the British-administered provinces. The princes controlled one third of the seats in the Lower House in the Central Assembly and two fifths in the Upper House, effectively giving them a power bloc, which although it roughly corresponded with the size of their population was seen as disproportionate and unreasonable by a democratic Congress. They regarded it as the Raj trying to influence the shape of the future India as a conservative nation.

The Muslim League viewed the 1935 Act rather differently. They saw it as being the work of Congress and, although the federal principle was intended to allay Muslim fears, in fact it had the opposite effect. The League supposed that they might gain power in Sind, the North West Frontier Province, Punjab and Bengal, all provinces where Muslims constituted the largest electorate, but in the resulting elections, which took place in 1937, Congress swept the board. In five out of the eleven provinces they won a clear majority. In the North West Frontier Province their Muslim allies prevented the League from taking power; in Bengal there was a Muslim ministry but anti-League and in the Punjab, with its Muslim majority, a coalition government of various agricultural interests. Only in Sind and Assam in the far north-east was there a League ministry. It was the League's reaction to these disappointments, and to Congress' insistence that it spoke for all Indians regardless of religion, that was to energise Muhammad Ali Jinnah and eventually make the events of 1947 inevitable.

Despite Congress misgivings about working with the British, they set about forming ministries and started the work of provincial government. From 1937 to late 1939 was one of the more peaceful periods India had known in twenty years. Had world events taken a different course it is possible that the 1935 Act would have formed the basis, in time, for a more satisfactory handover of power but the declaration of war in 1939 was to prove as decisive for India as it was for Europe. On 3 September 1939, the viceroy, Lord Linlithgow, declared India to be at war and assumed special powers, something he did without consulting either Congress or the League. Congress asked the viceroy, not unreasonably as the party with the largest pan-Indian electorate, what British war aims were and what guarantees could be given of Indian independence afterwards. Linlithgow's replies were vague, only promising discussions on 'Dominion status' after the hostilities were over. It was not enough. Memories of Indian sacrifice in the First World War were fresh and on 15 November 1939 all the Congress ministries resigned.

Yet Congress was slow to take advantage of the British in their hour of need. Many sympathised with British war aims and were strongly anti-Fascist. This was, however, soon to change. In 1940, Churchill, a strong opponent of Indian independence and who had opposed the 1935 Act, became prime minister. In 1941 he and

President Roosevelt made the Atlantic Charter declaration that said all peoples had a right to choose their own government. However, Churchill said that it did not apply to India, which 'was quite a separate problem'.[51] Churchill's intransigence over India, which he still saw through the eyes of a young cavalry officer who had served there in the late 1890s, was to be a major factor in Congress' subsequent actions. Then in February 1942 Singapore fell to the Japanese, followed by the humiliating British retreat through Burma. Not only were the mighty British on the run from an Asiatic power but it also looked as if the Japanese would invade India.

From August 1942 two major movements came to dominate Indian life. On 7 August, after their meeting in Bombay, Congress' attitude changed. Urged on by Gandhi, they now launched a major civil disobedience movement, 'Quit India'. This was to prove fairly ineffective in practical terms but it was a major distraction to the British war effort. It failed because Linlithgow quickly jailed the Congress leadership, taking them out of the political debate at a critical time and allowing Jinnah to consolidate the position of the Muslim League. The second movement was the British mobilising India to a war footing, increasing the army from 175,000 to over 2 million. This was far more than just a recruiting exercise. The previous rather delicate balance of 'classes' that the army had used to structure itself was now impossible to maintain and, with rapid mechanisation, there was a mass modernisation that exposed Indians from all areas and backgrounds to trades and experiences that would previously have been foreign to them. Indians also worked alongside a new class of British soldiers, men who had not been brought up in the stifling attitudes of the Raj, and who treated them as equals. Indian industry received a huge boost from the war economy, resulting in higher employment and wages. India's war effort proved to be exceptional, and however much criticism Wavell, Auchinleck (the commander-in-chief) and Linlithgow earned from subsequent events, the effort that put the 14th Army into the field so that it could drive the Japanese out of Burma and lead to their ultimate defeat should never be underestimated.

Yet the war years in India were overshadowed by something much more terrible and destructive. The Bengal famine of 1942–4 killed six times as many human beings as all the other British Empire losses in the Second World War. The actual number who died is unclear and was subject to endless revision as the figures were used to justify differing political positions. The 1943 Famine Enquiry originally estimated 1.5 million while most later estimates, allowing for subsequent deaths from disease resulting from malnutrition, have calculated nearer 3 million.[52] The famine showed clearly both how the British administration in India had only ever been skin deep and just how inadequate and demoralised it had become by the early 1940s. It must remain one of the most shaming events in the whole history of Empire.

Famines were certainly not new in India and had occurred regularly in the second half of the nineteenth century. The worst were in 1876–8, mainly in Bombay, Madras and Hyderabad, when up to 5 million people died, and the awful famines of 1898–1902 when the toll may have been as high as 19 million. Although it is less straightforward to apportion blame then, when the government had poor communications and little transport, it is nevertheless hard to empathise with the veteran district officer who blamed the 1899 famine in Gujarat on the Gujurati being a 'soft man ... unused to privation, accustomed to earn his food easily' and 'who seldom worked at all in the hot weather'.[53] Equally many dedicated and selfless British officials lost their lives from disease as they struggled to provide relief; Central India remains dotted with their graves. But what makes the 1942–4 famine so terrible is that it took place when it was in the government's power to prevent it and when the supply of food was a critical part of the war effort. In Great Britain an elaborate system of rationing had been introduced and a Ministry of Food set up as early as 1936; the Atlantic convoys that helped keep Britain fed took much of the nation's resources. Yet nobody thought of establishing a food department in famine-prone India until 1942 by which time it was too late. 'Starvation, death and pestilence have been known to follow in the wake of victorious tyrants over running foreign territory but in the present instance, however, this gigantic tragedy is being enacted whilst a well established government is functioning', complained K. C. Neogy, a member of the Bengal Assembly for a rural district near Dacca, who will later feature significantly in this story.[54]

What is even worse about the Bengal famine (1942–4) is that it was caused not by a shortage of food but by an inability to ensure it was fairly distributed. The food situation had always been precarious in India – Kipling famously wrote that the life of the Indian peasant was 'a long drawn out question between a crop and a crop' – but it was particularly so in Bengal. Sir Jogendra Singh, Member for Education, Health and Lands on the Viceroy's Executive Council, said that prior to the famine he estimated that even before the war only 39 per cent of Bengalis were well nourished; 41 per cent were poorly nourished and 20 per cent had insufficient food.[55] The reason for this was that half the farming families in rural Bengal owned less than two acres and were dependent on agricultural wages to have enough money to eat; many were also already indebted to their landlords.

The Bengal climate supports three rice harvests a year. The *boro* or *rabi*, sown in November and harvested in the early spring; the *aus*, sown in the spring and harvested in the early autumn and the *aman*, sown in May and harvested in the late autumn. Of the three it is the *aman* that is by far the most important, accounting for 73 per cent of total production. In 1942 the *aman* was damaged by a series of cyclones, and the subsequent heavy rain caused some disease although the harvest was still 83 per cent of 1941 levels. However, at the same time grain supplies from Burma were cut off by the Japanese occupation. These were not actually that significant, being somewhere between 100,000 and 200,000 tons, but taken together with the crop damage this started a scare in a population already worried about the Japanese advance. The government didn't help by evacuating the productive coastal areas in case of invasion, and confiscating fishing boats so they would not be used by the enemy, reducing the availability of fish, a critical source of protein. They also took over some land for the army and brought extra labour to Calcutta for war industries. None of these factors had a significant effect on the overall supply of grain but they did cause nervousness and encourage hoarding. The price of grain started to rise. Throughout 1942 the price of rice doubled from about 6 rupees per maund[56] to 14 rupees by December but worse was to come. Between January and August 1943 it had risen to 37 rupees, a six-fold increase in eighteen months. Actual stocks remained fragile but were not significantly reduced. Food stocks in 1943 were in fact 11 per cent higher than they had been in 1941 and, even allowing for the wartime influx of refugees and the army, the population had not increased by more than 9 per cent.[57] But the rural poor could not afford to buy rice and the governments in Delhi and Bengal appeared incapable of introducing a system of price control or rationing that would have allowed them to do so or given them the minimum to survive.

The effect in the villages of rural Bengal was catastrophic. The average agricultural worker held very small stocks. In some areas unscrupulous landlords insisted on buying these at a price they dictated on pain of eviction; the evil Indian landlord has become as much a historical truism as the arrogant British official. But there were also acts of village charity and mutual support. However, once any surplus had gone, families 'resorted to selling the few possessions they had – first their domestic utensils and ornaments, then parts of their dwellings such as doors, windows and corrugated iron sheets, trade implements, clothes and domestic animals if they had any to more fortunate neighbours at cut throat prices'.[58] By June 1943 the situation had become desperate. Children were being sold partly so they didn't have to be fed but also to raise money. Murder was common to seize hoarded stocks. But for most the only solution was to leave and head for the cities. 'Under the scorching rays of the summer sun a strange silence is enveloping villages', noted one observer.[59] The Tinkori family were typical. Forced to sell their stocks and possessions at an artificially low price to their landlord, Ganga Singh, they eventually couldn't afford to buy seed. Already in debt they were unable to pay rent and were evicted and their land given to a friend of the estate accountant. So under cover of darkness:

[Tinkori] put his bundle of household goods on his head and, with his wife Toti and his daughter Chandi walked out along the road. After a long and melancholy journey the family entered the outskirts of the town where large numbers of straw huts and clay caves stood like rubbish heaps of piles of manure. Tinkori and his family settled down in a small clearing by a ditch among the heaps of humanity.[60]

Even if they made it to the cities there was little relief available. Camps were set up around Calcutta but could only take 55,000 people, a tiny proportion of the requirement. By August 1943 about 2,000 people were dying on the streets of Calcutta every week although Leo Amery, Secretary of State for India, was insisting in Westminster that it was only 1,000.[61] 'In a city like Calcutta dead bodies are lying on the road', said Bankin Mukherjee in a speech on 6 November. 'A child dies in agony in the lap of its mother while the mother leaves it behind.'[62] Wavell, on his first visit after he had taken over as viceroy in October 1943, wrote that he had seen a 'destitute woman and several destitute children' in a bazaar near Contai. 'The children were sucking water out of a bucket in which an old gur bag had been placed.'[63] A 'mental demoralization' took control of the victims. 'Children, reduced to skin and bone, had got into the habit of feeding like dogs. You tried to give them a decent meal but they would break away and start wandering about and eat filth.'[64] By October any form of mutual respect had vanished. 'The villagers are themselves getting callous about it. One [village] head is quoted as saying about those dying "what does it matter – they are the useless ones".'[65]

What is so shocking about the famine is not just the appalling death toll but the official reaction. An equally strange hopelessness seems to have gripped the governments both in Delhi and Calcutta. The Bengal government was a coalition. Khwaja Nazimuddin, the premier, and Huseyn Suhrawardy, the Minister for Supply, were both Muslim politicians but not supporters of the League. They were technically responsible for food supplies and were roundly blamed by the British governor, Sir Jack Herbert, for not doing enough. Yet the problem was clearly one that called for intervention and assistance, something that the 1935 Act had foreseen when it made provision for the governor to assume control in an emergency. Herbert, however, confined himself to hand-wringing. As well as blaming Nazimuddin's ministry, he blamed Delhi, writing to Linlithgow, the viceroy, in July 1943, that 'unless the food situation is taken in hand efficiently ... and that can only be done by the central government, a position will be reached in which I cannot guarantee the indispensable requirements of the war effort'.[66] He went on to say that as Bengal had been allocated an inadequate quota under Delhi's 'Revised Basic Plan' for food redistribution across India, then he 'must disown all responsibility for the deterioration of the position in Bengal'.

Linlithgow in turn blamed Herbert. 'I am forming the strong impression that Herbert has no real control of what is going on. I am told that his cabinet meetings consist very often of little more than an interminable and rather muddled homily by the Governor,' he complained to Leo Amery but he did nothing about it even when Herbert went down with appendicitis.[67] While this high-powered war of elegant words continued, the junior officials began to fall out under the strain. Leonard George Pinnell, the competent director of Civil Supplies in Bengal and J. R. Blair, the chief secretary, both resigned in August. On 10 August, Mr Justice Biswas, a High Court judge, took the unusual step of telling the *Hindustan Times* that the present situation was 'due to the stupid and scandalous bungling of the powers that be ... the government seem to remain undecided about the course they should adopt'.[68] Debates were held on whether to introduce price controls as early as March 1943 but it was decided that it was too difficult. Seizing stocks at a fixed price was also ruled out as being too coercive. Officials were told to just buy what they could at market rates, thus pushing prices even higher.

Linlithgow himself did little more than blame the war. He appears to have only visited Bengal once, and then in disguise, during the whole of the famine period. His officials in Delhi, although they looked at diverting food supplies from the rest of India, again engaged in a war of words with Calcutta. Major General Wood, a competent man who had impressed in several roles, told the Bengal government that they could not expect any more help 'until Bengal's hidden stocks are prised loose'.[69] It was not until Wavell arrived in October 1943 that things started to improve. His first act as viceroy was to tour Bengal and within a week he had deployed the army, despite its priority being clearing the Japanese from Burma. By January 1944 he had established 347 civil emergency hospitals and 18 large military hospitals and deployed 1,700 extra public health staff. He found the 'Bengal administration a mass of corruption and dishonesty from top to bottom' and 'that the pilfering and misappropriation of food grains was now on such a scale as to make relief measures largely ineffective'.[70] He was unimpressed with Thomas Rutherford, who had finally taken over from Herbert, and thought him 'not up to a hard day's work'.[71] The army found it disturbing work. 'We were with 8 battalions diverted en route to the front', recorded D. K. Palit, later a highly decorated Indian general but then a junior officer in the Baluch Regiment. 'The people were very affected – grievously affected. We stayed 4–5 months; our soldiers ended up cooking for the people. We felt the famine was an act of man.'[72]

By January 1944, Wavell thought that the worst of the crisis was passing, although deaths from disease caused by persistent malnutrition would continue to kill large numbers of people for the next year. He now turned his attention to pressing Churchill and the London government to divert shipping so that India could build up a reserve of grain. Churchill's refusal to release Allied shipping from the war to transport grain to Bengal had become a major issue by mid-1943. In September 1943, Linlithgow had pressed, rather ineffectively, for the import of 1.5 million tons but the Cabinet had agreed only to 500,000 tons over the following six months. Very little of this had started to arrive, with Churchill adamantly maintaining that it was not a priority, and that shipping was urgently required elsewhere. Wavell now took up the fight and was much more direct. 'I warn with all seriousness that if they refuse our demands they are risking a catastrophe', he told Amery on 9 February 1944, and, not for the last time, threatened to resign. Churchill still prevaricated, although a disastrous bout of Indian weather in March did make him ask the Americans what ships they could spare. They refused to provide any but by that stage supplies were beginning to drift in. By June 350,000 tons of wheat had arrived with a further 400,000 committed and with the harvests now looking better, Wavell finally agreed that supplies could be at a safe level.[73]

Churchill's refusal to release shipping has been blamed for causing more deaths in Bengal. In fact the issue was something of a red herring given that there were adequate stocks and that the problem was one of distribution and price. Even had 1.5 million tons arrived in 1943 it would not have reached those who needed it. Rutherford complained to Wavell on 4 November that eighty wagons of corn had arrived in Dacca but as no one had made any arrangements for distribution, it was beginning to rot.[74] Yet what Churchill's attitude did show was an apparent lack of concern for India and reinforced the view that he regarded Indian lives as in some way inferior to British ones. His attitude, although not that widely known at the time due to wartime censorship, seemed typical of a British administration now not only callous but also hopelessly inefficient. Wavell summed it up when he complained to Amery after his first visit to Bengal that:

> In the old days the senior members of the ICS were to some extent public figures ... regarded as ministerial. They held themselves morally and personally responsible for the welfare of the people in their charge. And would not have tolerated in Calcutta, than you would in London, the disgraceful episode of the destitutes. The officials do not seem to me to be conscious of the disgrace brought upon the administration.[75]

The Bengal famine was, he concluded later, 'One of the greatest disasters that has befallen any people under British rule and damage to our reputation here is incalculable'.[76]

Why had it all gone so wrong? The answer lies back in the early

1920s, in the gradual lack of moral confidence that crept into the
ICS, in the various Acts that had resulted in no one really knowing
where power and responsibility lay and in the British insistence on
staying on long past when they should have handed over power
and gone. Although the 1935 Act had supposedly done away with
'dyarchy' – that system of dual control that dated from the 1919
Montagu-Chelmsford Reforms – it had still left a muddle. Who was
in charge in Bengal? Was it the inadequate Jack Herbert, unwell and
incapable of grip, and his vestige of a British administration, or was it
Nazimuddin's ministry? The active Non-Mohammedan member for
Dacca Division (Rural), Mr. K. C. Neogy, went on to say that it was
the unclear division of responsibility between the various branches
of government that had made dealing with the famine so difficult.[77]
And who was there at a more junior level who could oversee those
poor rural areas where so many died and which traditionally were
the preserve of the ICS District Officers?

W. H. Saumarez Smith joined the ICS from Cambridge in 1934.
On his application form he was asked to list his preferred province
for his first posting. He listed all nine – Sind and Orissa were not then
separate provinces but created under the 1935 Act – with the Punjab
first and Bengal last. He was promptly posted to Bengal on the not
unreasonable basis that no other candidates had mentioned it. It had
always been an unpopular posting, partly because of its hothouse
climate and partly because there had been a terrorist campaign that
had seen six senior British officials murdered between 1930 and
1933 and the governor narrowly escaping an assassination attempt.[78]
It was hardly surprising that, with the lack of ICS officers and the
added pressures of the war, the system creaked a bit but 'there was',
wrote Sir Frederick Burrows, Governor of Bengal in 1947, 'during
the famine an almost complete breakdown of the administrative
machine'.[79]

But more telling is reading between the lines of Linlithgow's,
Amery's and Herbert's letters. There is a refusal to accept responsibility, a feeling that it is all too difficult to deal with and a naive hope
that everything will turn out to be all right, which is symptomatic of

a system that has lost its bite. Would the great early administrators of the East India Company have behaved in the same way? Would Clive or Hastings have contented themselves with drafting elegant memoranda? One suspects not. The Raj had lost its ability to govern. Gandhi wrote, in his direct, polite but biting prose, to Linlithgow as he left India. 'Of all the high functionaries I have had the honour of meeting, none has been the cause of such deep sorrow to me as you have been. I hope and pray that God will some day put it into your heart to realize that you, a representative of a great nation, have been led into a grievous error.'[80]

The war would end well for the Raj. Through 1944 and 1945 General Bill Slim's 14th Army swept the Japanese out of Burma and retook Rangoon. Allied forces under Mountbatten (as Supreme Allied Commander South East Asia), working in conjunction with American forces in the Pacific, led to Japan's surrender on 15 August 1945. It was in many ways a triumph for India and Indian arms but any euphoria was short-lived. Wavell had now to turn his attention to demobilising the 2 million men and women in the armed forces, and to the handover of power, relying on a British administrative class who realised there was no future for them in India.

There had been some moves towards trying to advance the transfer of power during the war before the Quit India movement started. Churchill had, grudgingly, and under pressure from the Americans and his Labour coalition allies, sent out Sir Stafford Cripps in March 1942, just after Rangoon fell when it became clear that a superhuman Indian war effort would now be necessary. Although Cripps was a strong supporter of Congress – he and Nehru were both upper-class socialists – his mission was a failure. He did not get on with Gandhi, who famously described his report as being 'a postdated cheque on a failing bank'.[81] Cripps's mission left bitterness and confusion and led directly to the Congress meeting in Bombay in the summer of 1942 at which Quit India was launched. Soon after the Raj locked up the Congress leadership who would spend the rest of the war in jail, except for Gandhi whom Wavell released in mid-1944. Churchill had said in Westminster that the failure of Quit India had shown Congress' powerlessness,[82] but now the war was over Wavell was about to discover just how much support they commanded.

Wavell flew back to London in March 1945, spending three difficult months being kept hanging around by Churchill as he tried to get his authority to start a new political approach. Even at this late stage, when it had become clear to most people that the Raj must end, Churchill seems to have harboured notions that a grateful India would reject Congress and return happily to live under their British masters. Wavell returned to Delhi in June 1945 and released the remaining Congress leadership from jail. He invited them to Simla, the hill station where the government retreated during the summer from the unrelenting heat of Delhi, to see whether it was possible to establish a way forward. Wavell proposed a simple sharing of power in the Assembly on a communal basis but the conference failed because of disagreement over who could represent Muslims. Congress, increasingly seeing itself as a pan-Indian party, claimed it could speak for all Indians while Jinnah insisted that only the League could nominate Muslim candidates; he strongly objected to the inclusion of Maulana Azad, a Muslim and previous Congress president, as a Congress nominee.

Two things then happened on 15 August that changed the course of events. First, in July 1945 the Labour Party had scored a convincing and unexpected win in the British general election. In the King's Speech on 15 August, the new prime minister, Clement Attlee, published that the government 'would do their utmost to promote, in conjunction with the leaders of Indian opinion, the early realization of self-government in India'.[83] Wavell subsequently announced elections for that autumn. The same day victory was declared over Japan.

There had been no elections in India for nine years and the results were now very different from 1937. Jinnah had not wasted the wilderness years for Congress when its leadership had been jailed. A revitalised League won all Central Assembly seats reserved for Muslims with 86 per cent of the vote. In the provinces they won 428 of the 492 Muslim seats and 79 per cent of the Muslim vote. They formed the government in Bengal and Sind. Congress formed the government in eight provinces, including the North West Frontier Province and Assam, with the Punjab again governed by a coalition, but it was undoubtedly a triumph for Jinnah. The League had fought the elections on the issue of Pakistan. The question now was how could it be delivered, coupled with a growing realisation that the British might, finally, be leaving.

With India becoming increasingly polarised between two competing communities, Attlee dispatched a Cabinet Mission consisting of Cripps again, with Alexander, the defence secretary, and the rather marginal figure of Lord Frederick Pethick-Lawrence, the seventy-two-year-old new Secretary of State for India, to attempt to find a solution. Wavell was not at all sure he wanted them, mindful of Cripps's previous failure, and the mission did tend rather pointedly to ignore the opinions of the British Indian establishment. On 5 May they held a second conference at Simla. The plan that emerged was to some extent a statement of the obvious. It concluded that India must attain independence 'in the short-est time and with the least danger of internal disturbance and conflict', but it did manage to achieve some sort of consensus on the form this might take.

The Cabinet Mission Plan, as it was always known, effectively recommended a federal India, with a strong 'centre' responsible for defence, foreign affairs and communications but with respective communal differences accounted for by provincial governments. There were three groups of provinces. In Group A were the five Hindu majority provinces; in Group B the Punjab, North West Frontier Province and Sind and in Group C Bengal and Assam. The idea was that all powers beyond those reserved for the centre should be exercised by the elected provincial governments. A province could, after ten years, vote to call for a reconsideration of its status.

The League assumed this implied that the provinces would be compulsorily 'grouped' to give a Muslim bloc in the north-west and north-east; in other words they would, by virtue of the Muslim majorities in the Group B and C provinces, effectively control all five. Congress, on the other hand, thought it implied something looser. They wanted the provinces to be able to opt out, arguing that although there may be a numerical Muslim majority in the Group B and C provinces, this did not imply that the League commanded it. It was the old argument that Congress spoke for all Indians regardless of religion. They also argued that they spoke for the Sikhs who would inevitably find themselves under permanent Muslim governance.

Part of the Cabinet Mission Plan also recommended establishing a Constituent Assembly, elected by the provincial legislatures, whose job would be to turn the plan into an actual constitution and that, while this was going on, an Interim Government should be set up. For a short period it looked as if the plan might just work. Jinnah accepted it on 6 June but, encouraged by Gandhi, Congress prevaricated. Perversely, they accepted the long-term constitutional arrangements but rejected the idea of an Interim Government. A deeply frustrated Wavell and the Cabinet Mission then announced, on 16 June, that they were setting it up anyway and would invite ministers to participate on the basis of six from Congress, five from the League, one Sikh, one Parsee and one Christian. Again, for a few days, it looked as if both Congress and the League might accept this but once again Gandhi argued that Congress must have the right to nominate a Muslim; they could not accept Jinnah's claim that only the League represented India's Muslims.

Elections for the Constituent Assembly took place in July. Congress won 205 seats and the League 73. But it was to little effect. Jinnah thought he had been double-crossed by both Congress and Wavell. At the end of July the League met in Bombay and withdrew their previous support for the plan in its entirety. 'This day', he said, 'we bid goodbye to constitutional methods'.[84] He called the Direct Action Day in Calcutta, and by the autumn of 1946 both sides were as far apart as ever despite the Interim Government actually forming without any League participation on 2 September. Those few months – July to September 1946 – were to prove decisive. Was it then that Congress concluded they could not work with Jinnah and decided on the path leading to the coming tragedy? The League did finally take up its five places in the Interim Government in October but refused to cooperate with Congress.

In December, in an attempt to break the deadlock and breathe some life back into what was seen by many as a perfectly sensible plan, Wavell led the delegation to London. They made little progress. Unblocking the Constituent Assembly was the immediate issue now confronting him in the cool of January 1947 but he was always haunted by the fear that India would break down, that the Raj would lose control and end in chaos. In 1946 there had been 1,629 strikes involving the loss of 12 million man-days.[85] Already, as demobilisation took longer than expected, there had even been trouble in the armed forces. In January that year the Royal Air Force had 'mutinied' in Karachi, a protest that quickly spread across India. It wasn't a violent mutiny, more a series of sit-down protests at how long it was taking to get wartime airmen home, and it petered out after ten days. There were few immediate repercussions, but Wavell blamed the RAF for encouraging the more serious Indian Navy Mutiny in February.

On 18 February 1946 the sailors on HMIS (His Majesty's Indian Ship) *Talwar* went on strike over their conditions, complaining about the food. Admiral Chatterji, later chief of the Naval Staff but then a junior officer in Karachi, thought the mutiny was really caused by bad officers although Commander King, who commanded *Talwar* was, he felt, a decent man. But like many he felt the deeper reason was because the whole process of demobilisation was proceeding too slowly and being badly managed. There were, he thought, a lot of bored sailors who wanted to go home.[86] The mutiny quickly spread from the ship to the Bombay shore establishments and had to be put down by force. The mutineers fired on a Mahratta battalion sent in to disarm them and it took two more battalions and a squadron of RAF Mosquitos before they surrendered. Congress sent Sardar Vallabhbhai Patel to negotiate with them. He asked for clemency, which was agreed.

In Karachi, mutineers turned a ship's guns onto an army barracks but in the end were quite quickly disarmed by a British infantry battalion of the Black Watch. The local Indian naval commander had imaginatively told them they could all go on leave so they wouldn't technically be on duty and therefore liable to court martial but they refused. Ultimately there were few casualties, Congress did not support the mutineers and in practical terms neither mutiny amounted to much. Later in May the police in Bihar also mutinied, again requiring British troops to intervene. The British establishment was becoming alarmed.

The British were also dealing with an Indian Army whose wartime experience had changed it from the carefully recruited 'class'-based army of 1939 where soldiers had been selected according to religion, caste and often the district where they lived. It was also an army that regarded the British rather differently. D. K. Palit recalled that before the war there was no social mixing between British and Indians; he was never asked into the houses of any of the British officers he served with in his battalion. 'That all changed in the war', he recalled, 'lots of Brits came who were not stuck in a colonial time warp. They couldn't give a damn who we were as long as we did the job'.[87]

Many of those 'Brits' were fairly shocked at what they found in India. Clive Branson, an articulate and brave soldier who would be killed in Burma, recalled how on arriving in Bombay in 1942 'everyone was filled with amazement at the appalling conditions in which the people live ... after 175 years of Imperialism ... the conditions are a howling disgrace. The slogan among the British Other Ranks of "India for the Indians" is universally popular'. Branson was a member of the Communist Party, so possibly coming at things from a certain perspective, but his father had been an Indian Army officer and his views were shared by many.

By the end of the war there were very few of the 'old' Indian Army officers left serving with their regiments and during 1946 occasional agitation had developed among Indian soldiers. Muslim soldiers were affected by British policy in Palestine, which they thought unfair, and regiments returning from Indonesia had seen the independence struggle there against the Dutch. Seemingly small things, such as a tactless issue of free cigarettes to British troops but not to Indian, became major issues, blown up in the press. Lieutenant General Sir Francis Tuker, already feeling uncomfortable at having to stand up in a Bren-gun carrier during the VJ Day celebrations in Delhi in March 'like some sort of carnival float' was even more uncomfortable when he was showered with bricks as the procession passed through Connaught Circus.[88]

Another sensitive issue was what to do about the Indian National Army, the INA. This was the organisation, founded by Subhas Chandra Bose in 1943, which had recruited Indian soldiers captured during the Japanese victories in 1942, and from the large Indian civilian population in Burma, to fight against the Raj alongside the Japanese. Militarily it had been something of a distraction and Bose himself had been killed in August 1945 but the very existence of the INA had made a significant political statement and attracted Congress support. The immediate issue that confronted Wavell was what to do about INA prisoners. Were they to be treated harshly as traitors, which is what both the Indian and British officers of the Indian Army who had fought against them demanded but which would have made them into nationalist martyrs, or were they to be quietly ignored? It was to prove a much more difficult issue than anyone had anticipated.

And could he continue to rely on the rapidly dwindling ranks of the ICS? By 1947 ICS officers fell into three categories. There were those long-term, loyal servants of India, who saw themselves as part of the Indian government of whatever persuasion it might be. They were men like Norval Mitchell, posted in 1946 to be chief secretary to Sir Olaf Caroe in the North West Frontier Province, who had made his commitment to India back in the 1920s, and John Christie, soon to join the viceroy's staff and who was in India because he and his family saw it as home. Many of these men had already been working for Indians, the second category of ICS officers, those Indians who had been recruited alongside the British, albeit in much smaller numbers. They were men like Sir Chandulal Trivedi,

Governor of Orissa, who would play such an important role in the coming months, as would V. P. Menon, the reforms commissioner to the viceroy, who had started life as a railway stoker, and to whom the Raj would become much indebted. These were the men who would soon be the backbone of the government of the new India.

The third category were those British who saw the end of the Raj as the end of their service. Many had already started to leave after the war and understandably there were few new recruits joining from Great Britain. Sir John Colville, Governor of Bombay, estimated on 20 January that 70 per cent of his ICS officers and 90 per cent of his police officers were leaving.[89] There had also been a perceptible decline in commitment among some British ICS officers during the last decade. Norval Mitchell, happily married to an American wife, was horrified at the amount of adultery he found among the ICS and European community at his first station of Nagpur. It seemed to him that the chief occupations of most of his brother officers were 'adultery and bridge'.[90] He was equally shocked by the amount of time the police spent investigating it. Others lost their moral focus. Mitchell became enraged in Kolhapur at his senior officer, the Resident – an officer from the Indian Political Service, the select sub-group of the ICS who managed the Raj's affairs with the Princely states – whose own preoccupation was rebuilding his house from public funds. It had probably always gone on but for Mitchell it felt like a terrible betrayal at a time when the future of the whole service was unsure.

Many of those who served in the 1930s and 1940s also found they didn't like it. Kushwant Singh, that bemused and not unsympathetic observer of the Raj, thought that British nostalgia for India was a figment of their imagination, as they all seemed to hate it while they were there.[91] Even the Indophile Mitchell admitted that he found the Central Provinces 'extremely depressing, extremely hot and extremely dirty'.[92] 'Going there with me in 1943 were about one hundred young men who felt much, and knew as little, as I did and hated the place', wrote Paul Scott as he joined the Indian Army; 'we had no sense of having arrived at the splendid and glittering heart of the British Empire'.[93] Scott actually came to love India but many did not.

It was perhaps the inevitable result for a class who had tried to isolate themselves, impose their own views and morality, warts and all, and lost the easy relationship their East India Company forebears had originally enjoyed in the happier times before the Mutiny.

Tired, demoralised, lacking support, with an apparently intractable political situation, increasing violence and with a crumbing country, January 1947 was not a happy month for Wavell. On 17 January he wrote to Attlee saying that he was 'very sorry that the Cabinet had not been able to give him a more definite policy' and that all he could do 'at present is to draw up plans for an emergency withdrawal'.[94] On 21 January he established an Emergency Planning Committee tasked with preparing plans to evacuate the 100,000 British and European civilians and 63,000 British military and British serving with the Indian Armed Forces. It was not what Attlee wanted to hear. Then on 24 January it looked as if the Punjab would erupt. The premier, Malik Sir Khizar Hayat Tiwana, supported by Sir Evan Jenkins, the British governor, moved against the RSS (the Rashtriya Swayamsevak Sangh) and the League National Guards, the paramilitary groups respectively representing the Muslim and Hindu communities, whom he correctly felt were causing disturbances. For a tense week there was the threat of major violence until Khizar, under pressure from Delhi, backed down.

Wavell's problem was that he knew India too well, was almost too accommodating and, after eight long years of war and political infighting, lacked the necessary energy. Wavell collected other men's poetry. Clement Attlee wrote his own. On 31 January he sent Wavell a letter. 'I think', he wrote, 'you may agree that the time has come to make a change in the viceroyalty.'[95]

A VICTORY FOR CONGRESS?

'We no longer have any real power to control events ... if we stay we may become involved in a situation like Palestine'

(WAVELL)

Wavell was not alone in feeling worn out by the beginning of February. On 1 February Muhammad Ali Jinnah announced that the Muslim League would play no further part in the Constituent Assembly. The League's Working Committee had met the day before in Karachi, the day Attlee wrote to Wavell telling him he was being replaced, and formally resolved that the Constituent Assembly should be dissolved and that the Cabinet Mission Plan had 'definitively and finally failed'.[1] It seemed to Congress as if a resolution was as far away as ever. Their leadership, the heirs apparent to the new independent nation of India, was equally as tired and frustrated as the sacked viceroy. Gandhi was seventy-eight and Vallabhbhai Patel seventy-two; Jawaharlal Nehru was admittedly only fifty-eight but he, like many senior Congress leaders, had spent much of the last twenty-five years in jail and had suffered illness and bereavement. They were beginning to wonder if they would ever achieve their goal.

The founders of Congress, the creators of the independence movement that resolved that the Raj must end, had died many years before. The reaction of both Hindus and Muslims to the failure of the 1857 Mutiny had been one of intellectual reflection, a soul-searching as to why the British had prevailed. The Hindus looked back to their religious root, to their original scriptures, the Vedas and to the later Upanishads for guidance on how society should react. The Muslims looked naturally to the Holy Qur'an and the Hadiths. Movements like the Deobandis thought their failure was because they had drifted too far from the original teaching of the Prophet. Yet this period of spiritual reflection, and subsequent lack of political organisation and action, did not last long.

Three factors would ensure that within thirty years, by 1885, Indian opposition to the Raj would take a much stronger form. The first of these was education. The East India Company had realised in the 1830s, well before the Mutiny, that they would need a pool of local people with the necessary skills to run their administration as their territory and remit expanded. In January 1857 the University of Calcutta was founded as a multi-disciplinary, secular body and although its original governance was exclusively British, by 1890 it had its first Indian vice chancellor, Gooroodas Banerjee, a High Court judge. In July 1857 Bombay University followed, modelled on London University and with two departments – arts and medicine. Finally Madras University was founded the same year. Indians now had an opportunity to update themselves with Western scientific and medical progress but they could also appreciate English values, language and culture away from the stifling world of the military or bureaucracy. There turned out to be a huge interest in the English language and English literature, which seems quite odd in a country like India with its own rich literary tradition, but less surprising when taken in the context of not only wanting to understand the Raj but also to be able to secure junior jobs in its administration. Alongside the universities there was a mass founding of schools and colleges, mostly based on a British model, often complete with impractical British-type school uniforms, quaint traditions and an emphasis on the classics. Some of these were more Anglo-Indian than Indian, and were sometimes quite racist in their attitude, but slowly this began to change.

These schools and universities not only allowed intellectual Indians of different backgrounds to mix in a way that had previously been difficult but they also exposed them to the values of patriotism and enterprise, ironically at the core of the Imperial British education system. These were precisely the ideas and approach that educated Indians needed to articulate protest. As importantly, it was difficult to read Shakespeare and Shelley, and to listen to British lecturers extolling the virtues of British freedom without questioning why that was not also being extended to the Raj's Indian subjects. The Indian universities were also remarkably freethinking, encouraging ideas and experimentation without the domination of the Church, which was still such a strong influence in many European universities.

This study of British culture had a twofold effect. It gave some Indians a deep understanding and appreciation of elements of British culture, such as the English language, which has lasted to today. Rather as many British became fascinated with Indian culture, so the process worked in reverse. V. P. Menon summed it up when he said to a BBC interviewer in 1964, 'Culturally we were [your] product. All our leaders were absolutely saturated with British culture'.[2] Even Gandhi was a London-trained lawyer; so was Nehru, the father of modern India, a qualification he had gained after Harrow and Cambridge.

The second major influence on the formation of Congress was the emergence of an Indian middle class, a new phenomenon to the Raj and one with which they felt distinctively uncomfortable. Whereas they understood the princes and their courts, who would invite them to do agreeable things such as shoot tigers, and they had based their whole system of government on the flawed concept of protecting the peasant farmers, they never really understood the commercial urban class that gained strength in the second half of the nineteenth century and from which Congress would initially draw its support. These were the graduates of the new universities, the men who made money from the law or commerce, and who saw themselves as the leaders of a future India rather than the princes who had been discredited, in their eyes, during the Mutiny.

Thirdly, although the Mutiny cannot be seen as a national movement, it did make people start thinking about India as a nation. Part of the reason that the East India Company was able to dominate India relatively easily in the eighteenth century was the lack of an effective central power to oppose them. The Mughal emperors, who had invaded India in the sixteenth century, had never succeeded in integrating it as one country. Through a series of treaties with the powerful Rajput and Maratha rulers who dominated Central India, they had achieved some sort of partial unity, but it was liable to constant uprisings and civil war. In the seventeenth century Sivaji, a charismatic leader and effective military commander, had led a major Maratha revolt; the Sikhs had been growing in strength in the Punjab and states like Hyderabad were virtually independent. There was no unifying language, no universal religion, the Mughals were Muslim but most of their subjects Hindu. The Mutiny had taken the aged King of Delhi, the last vestige of the Mughal monarchy, as their figurehead but he had never been more than that. Now, post-1857, there was a desire to see India as one nation, to look back before the Mughals, even to the great King Ashoka, who ruled most of what is today India, Pakistan and Bangladesh in the third century BC and whose lion symbol is now the national emblem of modern India.

The issue that brought these three influences together was the Ilbert Bill introduced by the liberal Viceroy Lord Ripon in 1883. This was a simple legislative reform, which would have allowed Indian judges to try Europeans in certain criminal cases, occasioned because Indians were now rising up the junior levels of the Indian legal structure. The Raj exploded in fury at the prospect of such an insult. Ripon, a fair-minded reformist but lacking resolve, backed down, and the bill was shelved. It was now the turn of the Indian political class to explode. In 1885 came the first meeting of the Indian National Congress in Bombay. From its initial seventy members its numbers quickly spread, its popularity sending a message in itself. By 1900, despite some tacit support from Ripon's successor, it became the vehicle to oppose the Raj and demand greater Indian representation and ultimately independence.

Although Congress would later inevitably become closely associated with Hinduism, that was never its intention. Hinduism is not a
religion that easily allows itself to be used as a political force, being
more a way of life, and Congress insisted, as it still does today, that
it spoke for all Indians, the claim that Jinnah would find so hard
to accept. In its early days the Congress movement was dominated
by two great thinkers, both of whose legacies would translate into
the various wings of the party that now debated where to go in the
depressing early days of February 1947.

The first of these was Gopal Krishna Gokhale. He was the
epitome of the new Indian, born in 1866 to a not-very-well-off
Brahmin family of the Chitpavan Brahmin sub-caste, in what is
today Maharashtra, and was educated at Elphinstone College and
then Bombay University. He secured a job as a junior civil servant in
Bombay and rose to be on the Governor General's Council. He was
a keen Anglophile, a disciple of John Stuart Mill and Burke, whose
approach was to work with the British to achieve first social reform
and then self-government. His famous line was that if the British ever
left India the Indians would call them back before they reached the
Red Sea.[3] He became president of Congress in 1903 when he also
founded the Servants of India, a society dedicated to furthering education. He was, in many ways, the Raj's ideal nationalist – reasoned,
conciliatory, and easy to deal with; he was made a Companion of
the Indian Empire, one of the Raj's highest honours. Gokhale visited
Ireland and corresponded widely across the English-speaking world.
In 1909 he was instrumental in the Morley-Minto Reforms. Yet he
was a convinced nationalist and an influential mentor to Gandhi,
whom he visited in Africa, and to both Nehru, who particularly
admired his Westernised, constitutionalist approach, and to Jinnah.

Gokhale's conciliatory, gradual way of doing things was in
marked contrast to that of the other great nationalist leader, Bal
Gangadhar Tilak. Ten years older than Gokhale, he was also a
Maharashtra Chitpavan Brahmin, and another early product of
the new education, eventually qualifying as a lawyer but whereas
Gokhale became an admirer of British culture, Tilak came to

despise it. The Chitpavans had previously enjoyed some status in the Maratha states, something they saw as having been reduced with the coming of the British. Tilak's reaction to his education was to look back to the great days of the previous Hindu dynasties and to find inspiration in traditional Indian rather than Western culture. Consequently he became the leader of the radicals, seen as the more dynamic leader of the nationalist movement, and known by the British as a seditious troublemaker. His first major opposition came in Bombay in 1896 following an outbreak of plague when he thought British troops had overreacted by forcefully entering the sanctity of Hindu homes. In the ensuing trouble two British officers were shot and Tilak was accused of protecting the culprits; he was sentenced to eighteen months in prison. Tilak then supported the Hindu opposition to Curzon's partition of Bengal and in 1908 he was given a six-year jail sentence for sedition when he campaigned for two men who had thrown a bomb at the chief magistrate of Muzzarfarpur. He served his time in Mandalay, returning to India somewhat chastened in 1914, and supported the Morley-Minto Reforms and the British war effort. In his later life he despaired of converting Gandhi and Congress to his more extreme home rule views and founded the All India Home Rule League. An admirer of the Russian Revolution, Tilak was also responsible for giving greater focus to traditional Hindu practices. He made the worship of Ganesh a major part of people's lives and was also an early exponent of swadeshi, supporting Indian-made goods and boycotting foreign imports, something Gandhi was later to develop so successfully.

The legacy of Gokhale and Tilak was to be played out in the respective factions in Congress throughout the 1930s and 1940s. However, they both also had a profound influence on the greatest of Congress leaders, and arguably the greatest Indian of modern times, Mohandas Karamchand Gandhi. It was Gandhi more than any other man who had brought Congress so close to its goal of independence and who, although less directly involved by 1947, still exercised enormous influence. Gandhi was one of those extraordinary men who come to change world history by force of intellect and character and one of the very few who sought no material or financial reward for doing so. Many people loathed him. To the more reactionary of the Raj and to right-wing British politicians he was wily and unscrupulous – Churchill called him a 'seditious fakir'[4] – and Wavell described him as 'intransigent, obstinate, uncompromising'[5] (although he also applied that view to Churchill and Jinnah). The far right of the nationalist movement hated him as they thought he compromised with Islam, and eventually they would kill him. He drove many of his Congress colleagues mad by his changing moods and priorities, reducing Nehru to tears on several occasions. Many Muslims loathed him because they felt he was a Hindu nationalist at heart who wanted to deny them Pakistan. Modern cynics delight in making fun of his undoubtedly slightly strange sexual practices, and hardly a year goes by without some new lurid revelation about his sex life. Yet to many hundreds of millions of Indians, and to a wider international diaspora, he was the *Mahatma*, the 'Great Soul'.

What is equally remarkable about Gandhi as a leader, apart from his absolute rejection of any material benefit, is that the nationalist creed he preached and its intellectual and spiritual underpinning were largely original. Deep down a Hindu, he hated many Hindu customs, and he was in fact really an adherent of his own religion. He interpreted his role, and by extension that of Congress, not just as getting rid of the Raj but also of replacing it with an Indian culture based on what he saw as the essential wholesomeness of its millions of poor villagers. There was an element of expediency about this, and it was a useful and clever way of attacking the Raj, but equally it was founded on genuine belief and it has remained deeply influential in modern India.

Like many of the main characters in the extraordinary story of 1947, Gandhi was from Gujarat, born in 1869 into a middle caste, a *modh bania*, family of officials in Kathiawad, a small Princely state on the western coast. He was educated at the single college in the state where only English was spoken during his last three years. His father was a devout Hindu, a member of the *Vaishnava* sect, devotees of the God Vishnu, but the family were equally influenced by the Jain tradition, which was particularly strong in Gujarat. He was married in his early teens to Kasturbai, a girl from the same caste group in Kathiawad, and who, together with ther son, would probably suffer the most from her husband's more eccentric beliefs. After the early death of his father Gandhi was sent aged nineteen to study law in London, something he accomplished with some success. He found less racism in London than he might have anticipated, and, like so many of his counterparts, left with a respect and affection for Britain but unable to comprehend why the British could not practise in India what they preached at home.

From 1891 until 1914, with a short break back in India in 1902, Gandhi practised law in South Africa, concentrating on fighting for a fairer deal for the large Indian settler population there. He was at this stage strongly supportive of the British, positioning himself as a defender of Queen Victoria's 1858 proclamation, which had promised impartiality regardless of race and creed throughout the Empire. In South Africa, Indians were regarded by the Boers as a sub-class, required to register under a 'pass' system, subject to discriminatory immigration acts and, from 1913, only having their marriages recognised if they had been conducted with Christian rites. Gandhi's line was clever. He portrayed Indians as the civilised, rational equals of the white citizens of the empire. He learnt to understand how to manipulate the media, starting his own paper, and the value of engaging directly with senior politicians. He also came to realise that even in South Africa the Indian community was divided along religious lines and just what a massive task bringing Hindus and Muslims together would be; in 1908 he was beaten senseless by a group of Muslims who thought he had betrayed them to the government.

He also developed his own very individual way of living that was to become his hallmark. In 1906 he announced to the long-suffering Kasturbai that he was becoming celibate and they should abandon their comfortable lawyers' lifestyle to live in a commune. His eldest son, Harilal, did not like that at all and took himself back to school in India, but for the last of the Gandhis' eight years in Africa they lived this very public life as Gandhi's spiritual pilgrimage progressed, embracing a lifestyle based on an idealised version of a rural Indian

village where people were supposed to live as an unselfish community, sharing what they had. Gandhi was much influenced by Tolstoy,
with whom he briefly corresponded, and particularly by his belief
that man should conduct daily manual labour before he has the right
to eat. He was also a follower of John Ruskin, who had argued that a
labourer with a spade served society as fully as a lawyer with a brief
and that riches were 'just a tool to secure power over men'.[6] Turning
from Western civilisation, which had meant so much to him in his
London days, he harked back to a simpler, older Indian civilisation
that probably never existed. He started wearing homespun cotton
and spent many hours at his spinning wheel; the spinning wheel
would become a totemic element of his life.

Life in Gandhi's ashrams, as the communities where he lived were
called, were not to everyone's taste. 'My heart sank when I first saw
the place', wrote Motilal Nehru's eldest daughter, Nan, sent there to
get over an elopement with a Muslim journalist. 'Everything was so
utterly drab and unpleasing to the eye. Rising at 4 am for prayers,
we went to the chores of the day, which consisted of cleaning and
sweeping our living quarters and washing our clothes in the river.' The
food was awful. 'Several vegetables grown in the garden were thrown
together into a steam cooker without salt, spice or butter and eaten
with home-ground chapattis or unpolished rice', which she thought
was specifically designed to 'kill one's desire for food.' The only enter-
tainment was listening to long readings from the *Bhagavad Gita* and
the Holy Qu'ran. When Gandhi discovered that a young couple had
been sleeping together, he sent for them and made the beautiful girl
cut all her hair off. He then went on a fast for several days as a way
of making his displeasure known. No wonder Nan was desperate to
escape back to the comforts of her father's house in Allahabad.[7]

Gandhi's religious beliefs also developed in these South African years.
Although the Hindu holy books and particularly the *Bhagavad Gita*
would remain important to him, he rejected some of Hinduism's basic
tenets and waged a lifelong struggle against the caste system, which he
described as an 'excrescence'. He studied other religions widely, reading
both the Bible and in 1907 began studying the Holy Qur'an. He took

much inspiration from Islam, and although many Muslims believed that he promoted Hindu/Muslim unity as a way of opposing Pakistan, it was, in fact, based on a deep affinity for what Islam taught. Essentially Gandhi came to believe that God is to be found in each one of us and he would quote the Sufi poet's lines 'At last I looked into my heart and found Him there, only there and nowhere else'.[8] He was also very attracted to the Jain concept of the many-sidedness of truth.

Alongside this profound change in lifestyle and strengthening belief in God, Gandhi developed a political creed that would provide the guiding principles that drove India's campaign for independence. He was essentially a socialist, albeit a religious one, but he led a movement very different from the more violent socialist models and one that emphasised the moral correctness of what they were fighting for. His creed was based on the concept of swadeshi, or belonging to one's own country and people. This meant that home rule, Swaraj, was both natural and correct. Yet he believed that it was both ineffective and morally wrong to use violence to achieve it, particularly against a British Raj that spent over a quarter of India's revenue on its armed forces and police. Instead the campaign for Swaraj should be non-violent, practising ahimsa, and emphasise the hypocrisy and illogicality of British rule, pointing out that Indians were merely asking for the very freedoms that Britain was so fond of telling the world it extolled. Coupled with his absolute rejection of material reward, this made Gandhi a most effective campaigner, arguably the greatest in the modern world. He was not just the *Mahatma*, the great soul, but also *Bapu*, or father. He was also an attractive and witty character with wide and diverse interests. When criticised for going to see George V in Buckingham Palace wearing only a dhoti and a loincloth he replied that he couldn't see what all the fuss was about as 'The King was wearing enough for both of us',[9] and he amazed Lord Irwin's ADCs while waiting once to see the viceroy by going through the form of the Derby field in intricate detail.

Working alongside Gandhi, his heir and to some extent his disciple, was Jawaharlal Nehru. The Nehru family were Kashmiri Brahmins with a history of government service. Jawaharlal's grandfather had been chief of police in Delhi during the Mutiny. Moving to Allahabad, the family continued their prosperous life under the Raj with Jawaharlal's father, Motilal, pursuing a highly successful career as a lawyer. Motilal was typical of Gokhale's followers, an enthusiast for British culture and someone who believed that self-government would come through working with the Raj rather than opposing it. He sent the young Jawaharlal to Harrow and Cambridge before he, like Gandhi, qualified as a barrister in London.

In 1914 Gandhi returned to India. He was still pro the Empire at that stage, and supported the British war effort. However, he gradually came to associate the alleviation of India's real problems, her poverty and disease, her ignorance and the unequal division of power, directly with Swaraj. In 1916 he took up the case of indentured labourers and in 1917 campaigned for workers on the Bihar indigo plantations against their landlords; the government appointed a commission of enquiry and many of Gandhi's recommendations were adopted. Back in Gujarat he next took up the case of the *patidars*, small farmers with considerable influence in their local communities who were being asked to pay unreasonable rates of land tax. The government this time refused to back down and Gandhi started his first of what would be many satyagraha campaigns, which effectively were civil disobedience. This was followed by a campaign to persuade the mill owners of Ahmedabad, the large industrial mill town, the Manchester of India, to restore the plague bonuses they had been paying to their workers to stop them returning to their villages when plague had struck in the city. As the threat of plague receded, the mill owners had cut these payments, which made up three-quarters of workers' daily pay.

These campaigns brought him into contact with the leaders of both Congress and Tilak's Home Rule League. Through his campaign in Bihar he got to know Rajendra Prasad, later president of Congress and the first President of India, and Vallabhbhai Patel, his main lieutenant in Gujarat, who played such a major part in the events of 1947. Patel was yet another Gujarati lawyer trained in London and who practised in Ahmedabad. He was to become the 'tough, determined party boss, attractive in his own way but ruth-less and a communalist'[10] according to Wavell, while Mountbatten much enjoyed his company and found he had a 'considerable sense of humour'.[11] Gandhi also got to know the Nehru family, Motilal being a considerable force in Congress in the United Provinces.

Gandhi was also acquiring a considerable public profile as some-one who saw India's problems move from the perspective of the peasant and the villager rather than the landowner or the lawyer, the classes from which Congress largely drew its support. He came to be seen as the natural leader of the independence movement. However, Gokhale remained influential and by the time he died in 1915 his policy of working with the British to achieve peaceful self-government within the Empire was still accepted by the major nationalist leaders. India was not only supportive of the British war effort but the Montagu declaration followed after the war by the Montagu-Chelmsford Reforms seemed to promise an early realisa-tion of what Gokhale had preached. The greatest opportunity for a peaceful transition came in 1918, but it was a historic moment that a muddled, bitter, post-war Raj would quickly squander.

The lack of any real progress towards self-government after the reforms, the Rowlatt Acts and finally the Amritsar Massacre, and the British reaction to it, would convince Gandhi, Jawaharlal Nehru and Congress that Gokhale's approach was now flawed. At the 1920 Congress meeting at Nagpur, Gandhi persuaded the party that their goal must change to become complete independence rather than self-government within the British Empire; this was the same meeting at which Jinnah, still convinced of the benefits of working with the British, left. The next three decades of Gandhi's life would be dedi-cated to Swaraj. Although Tilak died in 1920 it was to be his legacy, not Gokhale's, which now guided the independence movement and although Gandhi's insistence on non-violence would prevail, more or less, it was Tilak's more extreme form of nationalism that would define the Congress agenda. Together with the Nehrus and Patel, Gandhi determined to achieve Swaraj through active opposition to the Raj, not through violence but by civil disobedience. It would be, he wrote, 'the greatest battle of my life'.[12] A Congress Party that had habitually started its early meetings by singing 'God Save the King' now sang a very different tune.

The next fifteen years, from the Nagpur Congress to the 1935 Government of India Act, were marked by the gradual establishment through satyagraha, or 'fighting with peace', of the moral case for independence, and by the reaction of successive British governments that failed to appreciate the strength of opposition the Raj faced. Britain continued to offer too little too late. Some in Congress were initially sceptical of satyagraha, including Motilal Nehru and men like C. R. Das, the Congress leader in Bengal, who disliked Gandhi's support for social change and his opposition to Western education. Das and many of the Congress old school did not want to threaten what they saw as hard-won reforms, such as the Legislative Councils, nor break Congress' support from the middle classes. Satyagraha also got off to a bad start. There was rioting in Bombay during the visit by the Prince of Wales and in 1921 twenty-two policemen were massacred in the United Provinces, something which affected Gandhi deeply. In 1922 he was jailed for six years and started the first of what would turn out to be frequent periods in Yeravada jail near Bombay, which would almost become many of the senior Congress' leaders second home in the 1920s and during the Second World War. Overall Gandhi would spend nearly seven years in jail – he was arrested thirteen times – before his final release in 1944.

Out of jail in 1924 Gandhi gradually honed the weapons of sat-yagraha, and a pattern emerged of a civil disobedience campaign, a period in jail, followed by his release and then talks with the British government. His most effective campaigns were those that caught the public's imagination rather than causing any great material problem for the Raj. The Salt March was perhaps his most successful. The government held a monopoly on the production of salt, an essential substance for everybody in India's climate, and also taxed its sale. It wasn't an onerous tax, but it formed a significant part of indi-rect revenue and, as with the land tax, fell hardest on the poorest.

Opposition to it fulfilled all Gandhi's requirements. Salt was a native product, taxed by a foreign government, which was denying the basics of life to India's poor and should be resisted. The salt tax, like the Raj who collected it, was morally indefensible. In March 1930 Gandhi announced that he would walk from Ahmedabad to the sea at Dandi to gather free sea salt in protest. With a group of followers he covered 240 miles in nearly a month arriving on the beach where he duly proceeded to do so. The march had no effect on the salt tax but it did act as the catalyst for mass civil disobedience, and attracted huge international publicity. Nearly 60,000 people were arrested across India. Gandhi was, predictably, arrested again and returned to Yeravada. Another campaign that was highly successful emotionally, although again it had little practical effect, was the 1930 campaign to boycott English cloth. Spinning, and the production of native cloth, was portrayed as wholesome and good, with Gandhi himself still spending a period of every day at his spinning wheel. Indians should buy and wear their own produce rather than support the Lancashire mills and hence British imperialism. It was a simple and obvious message that neatly summarised Gandhi's creed.

At the same time as he was pursuing satyagraha Gandhi was reforming Congress. Visionary and publicist as he undoubtedly was, he also had a good head for business and was helped by strong-minded organisers like Patel. Congress was becoming a mass movement and needed structure. Congress District Committees were formed, each with about 1 million people, all paying a small subscription, and not unlike the British administrative districts. However, above district level Congress ignored the Raj's provinces, organising itself instead around twenty of its own 'provinces' based on linguistic areas. The provincial committees sent delegates to the roughly 400-strong All India Congress Committee. Once a year the full Congress would meet in different towns across the subcontinent, a 'vast and remarkable gathering in an atmosphere that was part gipsy camp, part bank-holiday fair'.[13] At these sessions the president was chosen along with a fifteen-strong Congress Working Committee, the CWC, which directed policy. Alongside Patel, Nehru and Prasad on the CWC were men who would also play a major role in 1947, people like Chakravarti Rajagopalachari, the intellectual from the south, and the mild-mannered and charming Muslim Maulana Azad. Azad's presence pointed to Congress' claim to represent all Indians although in practice Muslim membership never rose above 15 per cent.

While Gandhi was reorganising, fasting and tramping the villages from his ashram on the banks of the Sabarmati river near Ahmedabad, Jawaharlal Nehru was pursuing a rather different course. Although a devotee of the older man, and from an early stage seen as his natural successor, Nehru was subject to a different set of influences. He had gone through a sort of double Damascene moment after Amritsar, hardening in his attitude to full independence but also, from his privileged background, now seeing 'a new picture of India' which 'seemed to rise up before me naked, skinny, crushed and utterly miserable'.[14] Yet while he was in sympathy with Gandhi's vision, which he would later draw on to some extent as India's first prime minister, he had a broader interest in international socialism.

The Nehrus were rich, and despite experimenting with rejecting his wealth for a brief period in 1924, Jawaharlal soon came round to his father's sensible advice that to be an effective campaigner you should be free of money worries. In 1926 he went back to Europe, taking his wife, Kamala, who had just lost a son and was also suffering from TB. While Kamala was treated in Switzerland, Nehru attended the Congress of Oppressed Nationalities in Brussels. Here he met Einstein and, among others, Ho Chi Minh. Importantly he developed links with the British Labour Party and in the spring of 1927 he visited Russia. He flirted with Marxism and, although he was never converted to it, he was certainly a socialist and saw in Russia a direct parallel to India not just as a nation that had thrown out its Tsarist government but one grappling with mass rural poverty. Returning to India in late 1927, when Congress was going through one of its periodic periods of gloom, he became president of the All India Trades Union Congress, which gave him a useful platform, and when the manifest unfairness of the Simon Commission revived Congress' fortunes, he was at the centre of the ensuing protest. In

1928 his father was asked by Congress to draw up a draft constitution for a new India. Motilal produced a successful draft but it
contained two controversial elements. First, it recommended India
should retain Dominion status within the British Empire, by now
an anathema to Jawaharlal and the socialists in Congress; and secondly, although it recommended abolishing separate electorates for
minorities per se, it allowed for distinct communal representation.

Nehru's problem, as a highly educated, well-travelled socialist,
was that he thought religion was irrelevant. To him India's problems were economic and social, with religion merely an excuse used
by various groups to further their own economic position. In 1931
he produced his 'Fundamental Rights and Economic and Social
Changes' paper, which Gandhi accepted; although not particularly
influential at the time, the ideas would later become core to Congress
policy. It focused heavily on issues such as state ownership and an
equitable tax structure. Gandhi also, although deeply religious, was
largely agnostic as to creed and believed that much of India was a
like-minded community of small farmers and peasants, meaning that
Congress was becoming dangerously ignorant of how deeply religion
actually mattered to the vast majority of people. In particular, it
meant that they failed to appreciate the depth of belief that Islam
engenders, the strong communalism of groups such as the Sikhs and
the strength of the Hindu Mahasabha.

There was a third, more radical faction in Congress, which took
particular exception to the 1928 constitution. This was led by Subhas
Chandra Bose, an upper-class Bengali Hindu, again educated at
Cambridge and who had passed into the Indian Civil Service, as that
august body started to accept more Indians, but refused to actually
serve in its ranks. Bose was virulently anti-British, believing that
'only on the soil of sacrifice and suffering can we raise our national
edifice'.[15] He opposed Gandhi's policy of non-violence and agitated
for more direct action. Building up a power base in Calcutta, where
he was mayor in 1930, he campaigned against Gandhi who did his
best to prevent him gaining influence. Like Nehru he travelled widely
in Europe, visited Ireland, learned about leading revolutions against

Britain from Michael Collins and the IRA and, like all Congress leaders, spent a fair proportion of the 1920s in jail.

The 1935 Government of India Act, the longest piece of parliamentary legislation on the British statute book, was seen by some in Congress as offering a way forward but by others, such as Nehru and Bose, as inadequate, with Nehru describing it as a 'new charter of slavery to strengthen the bonds of imperialist domination'.[16] They did, however, decide to work within it although they remained determined to 'combat it and seek the end of it'.[17] Congress agreed to contest the ensuing 1937 elections. Their subsequent success and the emergence of a strong 'Congress Centre', which gave direction to the various Congress provincial governments, offered India that brief period of stability she enjoyed before the start of the war. It also taught men like Nehru and Patel, intelligent students of how the Raj had managed to exercise total control across India with only the slenderest of resources, the importance of maintaining a tight central grip on power in Delhi. Looking back to the original 'Reserved Subjects' of the Montagu-Chelmsford Reforms, and later seeing how the Raj managed both the military and the economy during the coming war, they realised that a country as diverse as India, with its many different nationalities and languages, would only work when they were finally in government if they held the key levers of the administration – defence and security, foreign affairs, communications and finance. It was a lesson that was to make Congress very wary of federalisation to the extent that partition would come to be seen as preferable to power sharing.

Tensions in Congress remained, with Bose getting himself elected as president much to Gandhi's disapproval in 1938, and arriving to assume his position in a chariot pulled by fifty-one bulls, reinforcing his strong Hindu and nationalist credentials as well as his tendenecy to the dramatic, but it was the outbreak of war that imposed the more serious strain on party unity. Despite Linlithgow's arbitrary declaration of war, and the resignation of the Congress ministries, Gandhi and Nehru were initially supportive of the war aims, even more so once Hitler invaded Russia. Nehru saw it as a just war against fascism but wanted India to participate as a nation that had been promised independence rather than as part of the British Empire.

Bose on the other hand, and 'the extreme end of Congress believed they should do some sort of deal with the Japs'. They saw the war as an opportunity.[18] Although he was elected a second time as Congress president in 1939, Gandhi managed to secure the position for Nehru. Bose was anyway put under house arrest for encouraging civil disobedience in reaction to Linlithgow's declaration. In early 1941 he escaped and, travelling via Afghanistan and Russia, reached Berlin. Here he started the Indian Legion of prisoners of war captured by German troops in North Africa. Its members had to swear allegiance to both Hitler and Bose himself and it would later form part of the Waffen-SS. However, Bose correctly sensed richer pickings in Asia, and reasoned that by joining forces with the Japanese he could threaten British India. Transferring by submarine to Tokyo, in 1943 he founded the Indian National Army (INA). The INA was never effective as a military force, and Bose himself was killed in an air crash in 1945, but its legacy lived on not just in the very public trials, which demanded Wavell's attention in February 1947, but also in Bose's own radical followers in Congress.

The Japanese victories of 1942, the failure of the Cripps mission and Congress frustration at extracting any guarantee of post-war independence led, as we have seen, to the Quit India movement of August 1942 and the subsequent imprisonment of the Congress leadership. For nearly three years, Nehru and the key Congress leaders had been incarcerated, only being released in June 1945 as Allied victory seemed certain. Gandhi's imprisonment had ended a year earlier in May 1944 because Wavell was worried he would die after one of his periodic hunger strikes. Their conditions in prison were comfortable enough, with free association. It was one of the curious aspects of the British relationship with Congress that the Raj would try to make their confinement as civilised as possible; Gandhi himself was held in one of the Aga Khan's palaces near Poona. On their release he insisted on the long-suffering Vallabhbhai Patel accompanying him to a natural health clinic to have his spastic colon treated. Yet they had still been denied their freedom at a critical time when Jinnah was consolidating the position of the Muslim League. Confronted within two months of their release by the King's Speech, which at last promised a real opportunity of realising their goals, Congress needed quickly to re-establish the initiative.

By 1946, although it was as near the universal voice of the Hindu majority as it could be, V. P. Menon looked at Congress as three distinct factions.[19] First there was Gandhi, the spiritual inspiration, and while now not involved in daily politics still hugely influential and capable of taking his own line as he had done over civil disobedience in 1921 and Quit India in 1942. Gandhi's view on partition was, however, uncompromising. He saw India as an indivisible unity where it did not matter whether people were Muslim, Christian or Hindu. It was a laudable but ultimately unrealistic position. Wavell, who could never see him as anything other than 'an inveterate enemy of the British' was relieved that in February he was conducting 'village meanderings in East Bengal, where he reminds me of a submarine re-charging its batteries on the surface well away from any hostile craft'.[20] Then there were the hard, pragmatic nationalists, epitomised by men like Patel. They wanted a rapid, complete transfer of power that preserved a strong centre. They understood the depth of communal rivalry and by February 1947 were beginning to realise that partition might just be acceptable if it let Congress govern. They were 'for working with HMG [His Majesty's Government] on the Cabinet Mission Plan' thought Wavell, as the best option currently on the table to achieve that.[21] They were also 'strongly influenced by the Capitalists' and Wavell thought that Patel lived 'in the pocket of one of them – G. D. Birla'.[22]

Thirdly, there was Nehru and the socialists, equally as determined to get on with self-government, but who continued to see India in economic and social terms. Religious creed was also unimportant to them but for different reasons to Gandhi. While Nehru was centre left, there was a more extreme 'left wing', led by 'Jai Prakash Narain and Sarat Chandra Bose, brother of the now deceased Subhas, who were 'anti any co-operation with the British at all'.[23] On the far

right of the nationalist movement were the more extreme Hindus
who would accept no compromise with the Muslims and who were
epitomised by the paramilitary Rashtriya Swayamsevak Sangh, or
the RSS. They would soon make their mark, but in the early months
of 1947 they were too disorganised and lacked influential support.

Despite these groupings, which were not formalised, the 'quix-
otic, emotional, socialistic' Nehru, as Wavell described him to
Mountbatten,[24] was the undisputed leader and although his relations with Patel were worsening, and would ultimately lead to a
very public break, that was in the future. Nehru also still regarded
Gandhi as his father figure, however much he may have been
exasperated by him, consulted him frequently and respected him
deeply. Gandhi in his turn promoted and protected Nehru, likewise
beginning to turn against Patel, becoming increasingly critical of
his interventions and 'firing off venomous letters' to him, despite
his paternal concern for his insides.[25] Nehru was also vice president
of the Executive Council in the Interim Government established
the previous September and Minister of Foreign Affairs; Patel, the
practical realist, held the Home Affairs portfolio, Rajendra Prasad,
who would evolve to be one of the key influences on the Congress
high command, was responsible for agriculture and Rajagopalachari
for education. A Sikh, Baldev Singh, whom Wavell thought 'rather
a light weight'[26] was defence minister while the highly respected
'very sensible, level-headed and quite imperturbable'[27] Liaquat Ali
Khan, the League's representative, was in charge of finance. Mighty
as these ministerial portfolios were, there were two central issues
that dominated all their thinking: how to make the British actually
hand over power and how to do so without partitioning India into
Hindu and Muslim blocs.

The answer to the first question was not long in coming. In an
increasingly fractious correspondence in the first three weeks of
February 1947, Wavell, Pethick-Lawrence and Attlee struggled to
agree on a way forward. It was clear to everyone that the League's
withdrawal from the Constituent Assembly had left that body dead;

Congress had followed up Jinnah's announcement by demanding that the League withdraw its members from the Interim Government.[28] Wavell now reverted to his earlier suggestion, which the Cabinet had considered carefully, of Britain simply stating that she would leave India on a given date whatever the state of internal politics. Wavell set out his argument in a minute to London on 3 February. 'Since HMG has refused to accept my proposal for a phased withdrawal', he started, rather peevishly, before going on to say that 'we no longer have any real power to control events' and that 'if we stay we may become involved in a situation like Palestine'. He said that the final departure date should be linked to the final withdrawal of British troops, harking back to the still-prevalent fear of mass violence against Europeans, the 80,000 still present, and that it should be in the last quarter of 1948.[29] Wavell had still not at this stage received Attlee's letter sacking him; on the very day he was writing this minute, his successor, Mountbatten, was already asking Attlee to put Cripps into the India Office and planning his own staff.[30]

Wavell's mood predictably did not improve when Attlee's letter finally arrived. 'You are causing me to be removed', he remonstrated to him, 'because of what you term a wide divergence of policy. The divergence, as far as I see it, is between my wanting a definite policy for the interim period and HMG's refusing to give me one'.[31] Yet Attlee was now working towards the very policy Wavell had been advocating. On 8 February he showed Mountbatten a draft with a withdrawal date of 30 June 1948, earlier than Wavell had suggested but still in line with his overall recommendation. Wavell saw the draft on 10 February and it was circulated around the provincial governors. Their reaction was not encouraging. Sir Frederick Burrows, the Governor of Bengal, said that 'announcement of a definite departure date could lead to widespread unrest and disorder'; Sir Evan Jenkins, the Governor of the Punjab, agreed.[32] Wavell now did something really very odd, even allowing for his poor relations with Whitehall. He wrote back to Attlee saying that he had changed his mind and that he did not think there should be an announcement of a firm date after all. It is hard not to sympathise with Attlee's reply, as angry as the stilted protocol of government correspondence allows, pointing out that it was Wavell who first encouraged the government to adopt such a policy 'yet we are now faced by the opinions of provincial governors that publication will be likely to cause grave disturbance if not civil war'.[33] 'Your views', added Pethick-Lawrence, the Secretary of State for India, 'have placed us in a most difficult position. The proposal to announce a definite date for the withdrawal of British authority was an essential feature of your original plan'.[34]

Attlee ignored Wavell. On 20 February he made a statement to the House of Commons announcing that Britain would leave India by a date not later than June 1948. He also announced that Mountbatten would take over from Wavell as viceroy.[35] The initial reaction in India was euphoric. 'The British Government has at last seen the light and taken a historic decision' triumphed the *Hindustan Times* although more soberly it went on to say that 'The Muslim League and Mr. Jinnah are now face to face with reality'. Predictably the League's paper, *Dawn*, took the opposing view saying, 'It is a rebuff to Congress ... HMG will now have to enter into agreements for Muslim majority areas with the Muslim League' and that 'Muslims welcome the declaration as it justifies their position that the Constituent Assembly was invalid'.[36,37] Nehru said that the announcement was a 'wise and courageous one'[38] and the Nawab of Bhopal, Chancellor of the Chamber of Princes, said that, 'The [Princely] States now have their chance of playing a vital role in helping to construct the new India' although he went on to say, more circumspectly, that the announcement should 'bring home to people ... the stark realities of the situation which faces them'.[39]

However upbeat the *Hindustan Times* and *Dawn* may have been, and however welcome the change in the attitude to the British, the situation across India by late February showed that it was Bhopal who was the most prescient. The announcement of 20 February was indeed historic and had answered the first of the two great issues that confronted Congress. The question now was how to answer the second and to do so within sixteen months. While the Raj, Congress and the League debated and argued, India slowly continued to burn.

Reviewing the returns from the provinces on 12 February, the staff at Viceroy's House noted that in the United Provinces, the 'UP', robbery had increased by 56 per cent in the last year, murder by 47 per cent and dacoity, that peculiarly Indian form of violent assault, up 60 per cent. Wavell wrote to London to tell them that of the British ICS officers who still ran fourteen of the nineteen key departments of the government, three had resigned and seven had applied for long leave.[40] Francis Tuker noted that in Bengal there had been a dramatic increase in the underground arms trade with both Hindu and Muslim communities frantically buying weapons. Revolvers in the port city of Chittagong were now selling for up to £50 and rifles £60.[41] Tuker was particularly irritated with the American forces who had been stationed in Bengal during the war and had been very careless in disposing of their surplus ammunition. Much of it would be used to kill in the coming months.

In Lahore the Sikh Aridaman Singh Dhillon recalled that he was now told not to play with Muslim children at school. Local politicians went round stirring up their respective communities. It was not hard. 'Distrust was already there. It had been there for centuries', Dhillon added. Som Amand, a Lahore Hindu, remembered: 'My mother's attitude – she didn't allow a Muslim to enter her kitchen'. Zahoor al Din, a Muslim wrestler, said that when he went to drink water the Hindus wouldn't let Muslims use their glasses; they 'considered us as more untouchable than the untouchables'.[42] Bir Bahadur Singh, a Sikh from near Rawalpindi, thought the way his community treated Muslims was shaming. He had been taught by a Muslim woman, and thought that

> when we needed them they were always there to help, yet when they came to our houses we treated them so badly ... If a Musalmaan was coming along the road, and we shook hands with him, and we had, say, a box of food or something in our other hand, that would then become soiled and we could not eat it; if we were holding a dog in one hand and food in the other, there's nothing wrong with that food ... how can it be that two people living in

the same village, and one treats the other with such respect and the other doesn't even give him the consideration due to a dog?

Bir Bahadur would pay horribly for those slights by his community.[43] Now the prospect of the British leaving and uncertainty as to what would happen to the Punjab was beginning to expose these deep-seated grudges. 'The Sikhs are greatly agitated over what is happening ... they cannot contemplate a Muslim League dominated Punjab', wrote Baldev Singh to Wavell on 6 February.[44] The British governor, Sir Evan Jenkins, agreed. 'It is', he thought, 'quite impossible for one community to rule the Punjab within its present boundaries'.[45]

Meanwhile the Wavells were preparing to leave India. Attlee's letter was not only a professional blow but its timing was also personally inconvenient. The Wavells' daughter was due to get married on 20 February and 800 guests had been invited to Viceroy's House. Wavell asked Attlee to delay the handover. 'You can hardly have failed to appreciate the inconvenience and expense which you are causing me and to the whole of my large personal staff ... I hope I shall be given until the second week in March to avoid the indignity as well as the inconvenience of a scuttle.'[46] The handover was eventually settled for safely after the wedding, on 23 March. Wavell and Mountbatten knew each other well and corresponded amicably enough, despite Wavell's hurt. Mountbatten wrote to him on 18 February saying he 'was absolutely staggered when [Attlee] told me that the Cabinet wanted me to succeed you', which was slightly tongue in cheek as Mountbatten had in fact known since December and had been negotiating details with Attlee ever since.[47] Wavell had already sent his congratulations and went straight into the important detail: 'Horses we will keep for you. Grandee is still here and I have one nice horse but they are getting difficult to come by. Do you want saddlery?'[48]

But the last weeks in Viceroy's House were not happy ones. Wavell told Auchinleck privately that 'he had been dismissed as if I were a cook'.[49] 'What a shabby way of treating a great man who gave the best years of his life to the service of the State', thought Shahid Hamid, Auchinleck's Muslim ADC who kept a diary throughout the year.[50] At the private dinner party he gave for his staff, Wavell typically summed up his feelings by quoting some lines of poetry:

> The banished monarch, now put out to grass
> with patient oxen and the humble ass,
> said, as he champed the unaccustomed food,
> 'It may be wholesome, but it is not good.'[51]

John Christie, one of his personal secretaries, was sad to see him go. Much as he liked him, he acknowledged that he 'was tired and could make no progress. He was liked and trusted by all; except for the murderous Calcutta riots in August 1946, he had managed, more or less, to keep the peace between Hindus and Moslems; he had maintained the political dialogue but he lacked the flair, the zest and perhaps the imagination to break the deadlock'.[52] Attlee reflecting on Wavell thought him a 'great man in many ways but a curious silent bird'[53] while Wavell's own valedictory was more straightforward. 'I have heartily disliked my enforced connection with politics', he told the king.[54]

3. MARCH

THE MUSLIMS DISAGREE

*'Never was there a nature whose qualities
provided so complete an antithesis of its inner
worth'*

(SAROJINI NAIDU on Jinnah)

On 3 March, Malik Sir Khizar Hyat Khan Tiwana, Premier of the Punjab and leader of its fragile coalition government, resigned. His had not been a strong administration. He was not a supporter of Jinnah, opposed the idea of a separate Muslim state and had been expelled from the League in 1944. He had ruled with those non-League Muslims who still agreed with him, with Congress and the Akali Sikhs.[1] Khizar's ministry had foundered badly at the end of January when they had tried to ban the paramilitary organisations of both the Hindu and Muslim communities, an order they had quickly rescinded. The League, who operated on the assumption that they had a God-given right to govern the Punjab,[2] had long been agitating for Khizar to go. He had, he told Sir Evan Jenkins, become increasingly gloomy about his ability to govern after he had heard Attlee's 20 February announcement and that the 'League must be brought up against reality without delay. They had no idea of the Hindu and Sikh feeling against them'.[3] His resignation marked the end of twenty-three years of coalition government in the Punjab and would come to be seen as a harbinger of the sad fate the province would soon suffer.

Yet it was what followed that would make the events of the coming August inevitable. The League reaction to Khizar's fall was 'jubilant and noisy'.[4] On 4 March Muslim gangs, egged on by the League paramilitaries, attacked Hindus and Sikhs in Lahore. There was serious rioting and six people were killed that first afternoon. By 5 March large parts of the city were in flames and the police considered the situation 'extremely grave'.[5] The next day the violence spread to Multan. Non-Muslim students staged a march shouting 'Quaid-i-Azam Murda-bad', which roughly translates as 'Death to Jinnah'; by the end of the march, 150 were dead.[6] In the following week the violence became widespread throughout the province and Sikhs retaliated against Muslims in Amritsar. As with so much of the inter-communal violence in India, the reasons were not just political or religious but also local and criminal.

One of the worst incidents occurred in Bir Bahadur Singh's village of Thoa Khalsa near Rawalpindi. It was a rich village with 'fifty to sixty large traders',[7] mostly Sikhs and Hindus who were also the larger landowners. They were thought to have been taking advantage of the current shortages of cloth and sugar to overcharge and operate a black market.[8] The village had an important Sikh temple, a gurdwara. The Muslims, who Bir Bahadur Singh thought so badly treated, lived in the smaller satellite settlements without shops and were mostly employed as farm workers or servants, although some families had a son in the army. Lieutenant General Frank Messervy, the army commander in the area, thought that these settlements contained a sizeable *goonda* element, who 'lived for violence and robbery'.[9] Encouraged by these *goondas*, a Muslim mob attacked the village for three days but were beaten off by the well-organised Sikhs. On the third day both sides decided they should try to reach some sort of truce but there appears to have been an altercation with the Muslims demanding that the Sikhs hand over some of their women. It may have been that news reached the Sikhs of another Muslim mob who had demanded the return of a Sikh woman they had kidnapped and forcibly converted in the North West Frontier Province but who had subsequently escaped back to her family. This was rightly considered outrageous and seems to have made the Sikh population across the Punjab fearful that the same thing would happen to their own wives and daughters.

Whatever the final provocation, the Sikh community preferred to kill their women themselves than risk having them defiled by Muslim men. Bir Bahadur Singh's father and uncle gathered their extended family in one house. There were about twenty-five girls. First, a man with disabled feet, who knew he couldn't run, asked to be killed to avoid forced conversion to Islam. He clutched Bir Bahadur Singh's father's feet. His head was taken off in one swing of Bir Bahadur Singh's father's kirpan, his curved Sikh sword. Next the old man lined up his daughters.

> He killed two and the third was my sister Maan Kaur ... my sister came and sat in front of my father ... but when my father swung the *kirpan* perhaps some doubt or fear came into his mind, or perhaps the *kirpan* got stuck in her *dupatta* [plait]. ... No one can say. It was such a frightening, such a fearful scene. Then my own sister, with her own hand she removed her plait and pulled it forward ... and my father with his own hands removed her *dupatta* aside and then he swung the *kirpan* and her head and neck rolled off and fell ... I crept downstairs, weeping and sobbing and all the while I could hear the regular swing and hit of the *kirpans*. ... twenty-five girls were killed.

One girl who was pregnant somehow was not killed and was later shot by her husband who then killed himself and his father.[10] Death was preferable to dishonour.

The Sikh vengeance in Amritsar, where they were in a clear majority, was swift. By the evening of 7 March the city 'was completely out of control. Many buildings were burning. Most of the population seemed to have produced arms. Masses of people are running away'.[11] By 17 March 'several important streets look as if they had a heavy raid with many shops and houses completely down and the roads heaped high with rubble. There was no electricity. The Muslims suffered worse'.[12] In retaliation in Lahore a gurdwara was set on fire killing all twenty Sikhs inside.[13] Sikh folklore has it that in one village near Rawalpindi one thousand women jumped into a well to avoid rape and forcible conversion, which, although an obvious exaggeration, gives some indication of the depth of fear in the rural areas. 'The disturbed area is full of crowds of villagers armed with *lathis* [heavy bamboo sticks with metal bound ends], spears, axes, agricultural implements and ... firearms. In several villages the Hindus have all been massacred', noted the Inspector General of Police.[14]

By the third week of March, when Jenkins had assumed control of the province under 'Section 93', the clause in the 1935 Act that allowed governors to reassert control in times of crisis, and the British and Indian armies had finally restored order, it is estimated that 5,000 people had been killed and 3,000 seriously injured. The Punjab Police, already demoralised and short of officers, and 90 per cent of whom were Muslim, had been found to be useless. The Hindu population lost what little faith they had in them, something that was soon to have a disastrous impact. The majority of the casualties were Sikhs and Hindus, and most of them in the Rawalpindi area; the killings quickly became known as 'The Rape of Rawalpindi'. Messervy, an old India hand with extensive service in the Punjab, 'would never have believed that agitation could have aroused the normally chivalrous and decent Punjabi Muslim peasant to such frenzied savagery'. He noted that ex-soldiers had played a significant part in its organisation.[15]

There were, apart from the unbridled savagery and obvious human suffering, two serious consequences. First, the Sikhs 'felt they had suffered more than the Muslims and that they had been caught unprepared. They were therefore likely to have their revenge', noted Jenkins.[16] Sensing what was coming, Sikh leaders would spend the spring arming and organising their community. Secondly, the Congress Working Committee, the CWC, publicly called for the partition of the Punjab, an anathema to Jinnah and the League for whom an undivided Punjab was an essential part of their plans for a Muslim entity in an independent India.

The violent animosity between the Muslims and the Hindus and Sikhs in India in 1947, which has translated into the friction and bad relations between Pakistan and India today, is all the more tragic because history does not suggest that it was inevitable. One of the most depressing things in researching this book is that it is virtually impossible to find one Indian commentator with anything good to say about Pakistan and vice versa; indeed that trait has been equally prominent in Indian–Pakistani relations since 1947. Yet for long periods of Indian history, both communities coexisted and cooperated.

About one quarter of India's population in March 1947 was Muslim. Islam had not come in the great Arab conquests of the seventh and eighth centuries, which had culminated in Persia, but much later. In 1192, Mahmud of Ghazni, a renowned Afghan warrior, had conquered the Punjab in a campaign still remembered for its ferocity but it wasn't until the fourteenth century that Islam spread south and, under the leadership of the Delhi Sultanate, reached most of India. Yet this was due as much to conversion as to conquest. India's Muslims were not an immigrant population but generally native Hindus, usually low caste, who preferred the freedom and spiritual promise that Islam offered. It was more attractive to be considered equal before God, and to live one's life with the promise of salvation and paradise, than under the rigidity of caste and the weariness of endless cycles of reincarnation. This was particularly true in Bengal, where a largely animistic peasantry resented Hindu domination and quickly succumbed to the teaching of the *pirs* and Islamic preachers. Vallabhbhai Patel's dismissive comment that all Indian Muslims were just converted Hindus was often true but it underplayed the sincerity of that conversion, and throughout India's independence struggle Congress can justifiably be accused of consistently underestimating both the depth of belief that Islam engenders and the attraction of its offer of equality before God.

This pattern of conversion also explains why the Muslim population was so widely and unevenly spread. Sometimes a few families had converted; in other cases a whole community would go over, sometimes for political reasons, as Muslim warlords extended their influence. By 1947 the far western provinces, Sind and the North West Frontier Province, were effectively Muslim. There were large Muslim populations in the United Provinces, in Bihar and Orissa, originally having part of Bengal, and in Bombay. Muslims formed the majority, as we have seen, in the Punjab and in Bengal proper.

The coming of the Mughal emperors in the sixteenth century did not bring about further mass conversion. Rather the Mughals were content to work with Hindu states and communities. Muslim warlords did take over large tracts of land but they tended to rely on Hindus for their administration, such as the Nehrus in Delhi. Consequently there was never really a Muslim middle class, well illustrated by Hyderabad ruled by a Muslim Nizam but with only a few Muslim families who governed an overwhelmingly Hindu population. What the Mughals did do was institute a Persian legal system, which the British initially kept until they gradually replaced it with their own complicated and foreign code. In 1835 English became the language of government and of the courts, with Muslims beginning to feel increasingly marginalised. In 1867 Muslims held 11.7 per cent of government jobs in Bengal; by 1887 that had shrunk to just 7 per cent. In 1871 they enjoyed 12 per cent of 'gazetted', in other words public, appointments but by 1881 that had been reduced to 8 per cent.[17]

The period of introspection that followed the Mutiny was interrupted by thinkers such as Sayid Ahmad Khan (1817–98) who thought that Islam should now come to terms with the West. He was influential at a time when there were many across the Islamic world who advocated the same thing, men like Mohammed Abduh in Egypt who argued that there was nothing in the Holy Qur'an or Hadiths that precluded Muslims taking advantage of Western progress in much the same way that the West had used Islamic scientific invention in the medieval world. Ahmad Khan cited a common Judaic/Christian heritage which, he argued, justified Indian Muslims working with the British. He founded the famous Aligarh College in 1875, the Mohammedan Anglo-Oriental College, which became the Oxford of Muslim India, producing generations of Western-leaning thinkers. Realising, as the nationalist movement took root, that an independent, democratic India would inevitably mean a Hindu majority government, he also saw a vested interest in Muslim cooperation with the Raj as some sort of guarantee of their interests. It was this influence that lead to the inclusion of a separate Muslim electorate in the 1909 Morley-Minto Reforms.

Again it was the British actions during the First World War that changed Muslim perception. Muslims were unhappy at the British fighting the Turks, whose sovereign was still the Caliph. They also, like Congress, thought that the 1909 reforms were the first stage of full independence once the war was over and saw that continued cooperation with the Raj may not necessarily work in their best interest. The All India Muslim League, founded at Dacca in 1906, came together with Congress at Lucknow in 1916 and produced the Lucknow Pact in which Congress accepted separate electorates. The harsh terms imposed by the Allies on Turkey after the war meant that many Muslims were comfortable in supporting Gandhi's call for non-cooperation but gradually, as Atatürk swept away the Caliphate and it became clear that Congress saw itself as representing all Indians, whatever their creed, some of the leaders of the League began to realise that they would have to fight on their own. Jinnah left Congress at the end of 1920 after its stormy meeting in Nagpur. Many others followed him after Motilal Nehru's 1928 draft constitution seemed to negate the key Muslim demand of separate electorates.

The late 1920s and early 1930s were something of a period of crisis for India's Muslims. There was clearly little future now in sticking with the Raj, although right up until 1947 there were many who identified closely with Britain and still saw the Attlee announcement of 20 February as a betrayal. Equally they felt betrayed by Congress, although some Muslim leaders were to stay with Congress throughout, such as the mild and approachable academic Maulana Azad, who would go on to serve as Congress president and to play a major role in the coming events. But, V. P. Menon thought, 'The Muslims with Congress were not a very impressive lot. Azad was not man of the crowds. He was retiring. A very good man – his heart absolutely in the right place – but not a strong leader'.[18]

How were they therefore to protect their future interests? In 1930 Sir Muhammad Iqbal suggested the concept of a separate Muslim homeland in the north-west. It was in part a spiritual inspiration, a movement that never caught on as Gandhi's did but at least served to give Muslims some sort of collective identity. It was also part practical. The homeland would be called PAKIstan; the 'P' came from the Punjab, the 'A' from Afghanistan, reflecting both the Pathan population of the North West Frontier Province and the lack of definite geographical limitation to Iqbal's idea, the 'K' was Kashmir, the Princely state with its majority Muslim population, and 'S' was for Sind; 'stan' was the Central Asian suffix denoting a country which referred to Baluchistan, the remote area west of the Indus delta which bordered Iran. It was an inspired choice as Pakistan meant 'land of the pure' in Urdu. Yet Pakistan remained just an idea. It was at this stage simply an expression for a Muslim entity within India; Pakistan and Hindustan were seen as two parts of the same whole and would go through many different variations before they became separate countries in August 1947. Even as late as March 1947 it was not at all clear what, if anything, Pakistan would look like.

The 1930s also produced a leader for the Muslim community in the form of Muhammad Ali Jinnah, the *Quaid-i-Azam* whose death the Hindu students in Lahore had so imprudently been demanding. Of all the great leaders of the independence movement, Jinnah is one of the hardest to fathom, partly because so little of his correspondence has been released. He is the one with the least sympathetic profile outside Pakistan, with none of Nehru's easy cosmopolitan charm nor Gandhi's ability to connect to the masses. Reserved, frequently aggressive in argument, and famously described by the Raj's officials as a man with a problem for every solution, Jinnah was also man of impressive conviction, penetrating intellect and who inspired

prophet-like devotion among his followers. Even Nehru, ever cour-
teous, said he was 'one of the most extraordinary men in history'
although he could not resist adding, inaccurately, that he was 'a
financially successful though mediocre lawyer'.[19] By 1947 he was as
undisputed a leader of Indian Muslims as Nehru was of Congress. In
Pakistan today he enjoys similar status to George Washington in the
United States, is known as *Baba-i-Qaum*, or 'Father of the Nation',
and his birthday, 25 December, which he shares with another notable
leader, is a public holiday.

Like Gandhi and Patel, Jinnah was a Gujarati and in fact his
early life was very similar to Gandhi's. Born into a middle-class
Ismaili Muslim family in Karachi, he spent his childhood in Bombay.
Married young like Gandhi, he was sent to England to work in a
shipping company. His young wife and his mother died while he
was in London, where he changed to study law. After qualifying by
the age of twenty, he returned to Bombay where he established a
successful practice. His period in London turned him, like Nehru,
into someone who liked and admired the British way of life but
equally someone who detested the British inability to practise
in India what they preached at home. London would remain his
second home throughout his life and he became a very English sort
of Muslim. Although he habitually wore his Jinnah cap, it usually
topped immaculate Savile Row suits, and he both drank and smoked.
Although nominally a Shia Muslim by virtue of his Ismaili birth,
Jinnah in fact defied narrow Islamic theological stereotyping, regarding himself just as a 'Muslim'. V. P. Menon wondered if he 'even
knew how to perform his prayers'.[20] Jinnah was never a religious
leader as such; to him India's Muslims were rather a political body.
He was, as such, a Muslim leader ahead of his time and one who
saw the tenets of Islam as no barrier to the community flourishing
in a modern state.

His interest in politics started in London, where he listened to
Naoroji, just elected as the first Indian to sit in Parliament. On
his return to India he initially opposed the idea of the Muslim
League and of separate electorates but that did not stop him taking

advantage of them to get elected to the Imperial Legislative Council in 1909. A supporter first of Gokhale, he, like Gandhi, turned to Tilak during the First World War, became a supporter of the Home Rule League, and eventually a firm supporter of the Muslim League. Initially he worked closely with Gandhi, although he saw Gandhi as more of a social reformer than a nationalist leader and questioned his support for the British war effort in the First World War. It was Jinnah who led the political opposition to the Rowlatt Acts while Gandhi's oratory fired the masses to protest. Up until 1925 it was perfectly possible that it would have been Jinnah who emerged as the political leader of the nationalist movement but he disagreed with Gandhi strongly on two points. First, he thought civil disobedience was flawed and that the way to ensure home rule quickly was through reasoned negotiation with the British. Secondly, he thought Gandhi was using India's Muslims cynically. He objected to the Khilafat Movement, through which Gandhi had harnessed Muslim anger at the way the British were treating the Ottoman emperor who was still the Caliph. This had, he correctly felt, been rendered pointless by Atatürk turning Turkey into a secular nation and who had no intention of restoring the Caliphate. Jinnah came to see the Khilafat Movement as a Congress ploy to marginalise the League. Strongly principled, and not one to compromise, Jinnah left Congress after a stormy session in Nagpur in 1920 when he was howled down for opposing satyagraha. His train was stoned at stations all the way home to Bombay. Gandhi emerges at his most vitriolic and scheming in opposing Jinnah. Later, once the Khilafat issue had, as Jinnah predicted, died out, Congress again opposed Jinnah's 1927 proposals, the Delhi Proposals, designed to find common ground between Congress and the League. It was another of those tragic missed opportunities that would ultimately lead to 1947.

In 1918, Jinnah married again, this time to Rattanbai Petit, always known as Ruttie, daughter of one of India's two great Parsi houses and twenty-four years his junior. Her family strongly opposed the marriage, but it produced a daughter and the family lived together in comfort on Malabar Hill in Bombay. His obsession with politics and Ruttie's bohemian nature meant that the marriage struggled. They separated in 1929 and soon after Ruttie died.

Much has been made of Jinnah's apparent aloofness to Ruttie but, despite her parents' disapproval – Jinnah never spoke to his father-in-law until the day she died – theirs was a genuine love match and Ruttie's death affected him deeply. Her death, coming soon after Congress' rejection of his Delhi Proposals, and later the depressing, empty years following the Simon Commission, marked a particularly low point in his life. He returned to London. From then on it was his sister, Fatima, who looked after him, particularly as he developed the early stages of the lung disease that would eventually kill him.

In London, living in Hampstead, Jinnah got to know Sir Muhammad Iqbal. He eventually became a keen disciple of Iqbal and participated in the first of the London Round Table conferences, but devoted the first half of the 1930s to his law practice. Shahid Hamid first met him in 1932 when he was an officer cadet at the British Royal Military College at Sandhurst. He had gone to London for the weekend with his brother-in-law and was sitting having a cup of tea in the Park Lane Hotel. Jinnah walked past their table and 'noticing a questioning look in our faces, he stopped' and joined the two young cadets in an easy and interested conversation. Hamid, a product of Aligarh University, and who would go on to be a general in Pakistan, became an instant admirer.[21]

Others who knew him well also give the lie to the stereotype of the humourless, dour Jinnah of legend. Sarojini Naidu, one of Gandhi's greatest admirers and later an important Congress politician, held an even greater admiration for Jinnah.

Never was there a nature whose outer qualities provided so complete an antithesis of its inner worth. Tall and stately, but thin to the point of emaciation, languid and luxurious of habit, Mohammed Ali Jinnah's attenuated form is the deceptive sheath of a spirit of exceptional vitality and endurance. Somewhat formal and fastidious, and a little aloof and imperious of manner, the calm hauteur of his accustomed reserve but masks, for those who

know him, a naïve and eager humanity, an intuition as quick and
tender as a woman's, a humour gay and winning as a child's. Pre-
eminently rational and practical, discreet and dispassionate in his
estimate and acceptance of life, the obvious sanity and serenity
of his worldly wisdom effectually disguise a shy and splendid
idealism which is the very essence of the man.[22]

In 1934 he was persuaded by Muslim leaders in India to return
as the Government of India Bill began to increase the possibilities of
independence. Re-established on Malabar Hill in Bombay, Jinnah
would devote the remaining fourteen years of his life to realising his
vision of Pakistan, although it would not quite work out the way he
originally envisaged.

Before the 1937 elections, Jinnah approached Congress to try once
more to work out some sort of power-sharing agreement. In the event
the League did not perform well and Gandhi and Nehru, flush with
their own success, and still refusing to accept the notion of a separate
Muslim entity within India, reneged. They could not see the need
for the League, judging that they had sufficient control both in the
provinces and in the central federal legislature. In fact they actively
went about appealing to Muslims, causing Jinnah to mount a counter campaign portraying Congress as an anti-Muslim party that he
accused of violent Hindu nationalism. It was, on reflection, 'one of
the gravest miscalculations by the Congress leadership in its long history',[23] and perhaps the last time when some sort of power-sharing
could have been worked out and an arrangement which would, given
their share of the vote, have been to Congress' advantage.

It was a rejection that had a profound affect on Jinnah. Once
again Congress had refused to work alongside him. He was now
determined to pursue the idea of Pakistan, whatever it might look
like, and to establish the League as the sole voice of India's Muslims.
He realised that part of Congress' success was their superior organisation and he set about creating a League structure that looked
almost identical to that which Gandhi had initiated in the 1920s.
Iqbal rightly pointed out that part of the reason the League had done

so badly in the elections was because the 'Muslim masses have so far, with good reason, taken no interest in it'.[24] The League must appeal to the poor just as Congress had done. A two anna[25] annual membership fee was introduced, half what Congress were currently charging, and a district structure was put in place.

Jinnah's task was always going to be more complicated because, insist as he might that the League spoke for all India's Muslims, it was very clear that it did not and the two Muslim majority provinces, the Punjab and Bengal, had manifestly not elected League administrations. In 1937 in Bengal the League had won only 39 seats but independent Muslims had won 42. In the Punjab there were 71 Muslim Unionist members while the League had just 1. Clearly he had his work cut out. Nehru, now more waspish, noted that 'his creed was enormously successful ... always to avoid taking any positive action which might split his followers; to refuse to hold meetings or to answer questions; never to make a progressive statement because it might lead to internal Muslim dissensions.'[26]

Jinnah was helped by the outbreak of war and a Raj that realised that Congress would prove an unreliable partner. After Linlithgow's rash declaration of war in 1939, the Raj increasingly turned to Jinnah as being a more sympathetic ally, and treated him as a community leader on a par with Gandhi. Linlithgow and Jinnah established a working understanding. On 18 October 1939, Linlithgow assured Muslims that: 'It was unthinkable that we should proceed to plan afresh, or to modify in any respect any important part of India's constitution without again taking counsel with those who have in the recent past been so closely associated on a like task with His Majesty's Government.'[27] Jinnah, Linlithgow later added, had given him 'valuable help by standing against Congress claims and I was duly grateful'.[28]

In March 1940, taking advantage of these more favourable winds, the League produced a statement of their position. The Lahore Resolution, drafted by the respected jurist and member of the Viceroy's Executive Council, Sir Muhammad Zafrullah Khan, demanded a united homeland for Muslims and the creation of an independent Muslim state. The press declared it as a triumph for

Jinnah although it was predictably repudiated by Congress. But whatever the media may have thought, the Lahore Resolution was not an accurate portrayal of Jinnah's position. Only a few months before, Jinnah had said that any future constitution must recognise that there were 'in India two nations who must share the governance of their common motherland'.[29] Why would the League, so determined to be the sole spokesman of India's nearly 100 million Muslims, opt for a homeland that would exclude a large proportion of them? Even if at this stage they thought it was realistic that the Punjab and Bengal may be included in this new state undivided, with strong Muslim guarantees of the rights of what would be minority Hindu and Sikh communities, they would still be excluding tens of millions of Muslims in Bombay, where they made up about 18 per cent of the population, and the huge Muslim communities across the United Provinces, Bihar and Oudh.

Jinnah's true position was surely best served by having the same 'strong centre', the power base in Delhi that enabled the Raj to function and which Nehru and Patel had quickly realised was key to governing any future independent nation. The only way that Jinnah could truly speak for all India's Muslims would be if he could have a secured role in that. The issue was how to persuade Congress, particularly after their brutal repudiation of his approaches in 1937. Was the Lahore Resolution therefore more of a bargaining counter, a statement that would serve to unify Muslims, make the League impossible to ignore and force Congress and the Raj to come to terms? Jinnah's behaviour in the latter half of March and April 1947 would suggest that perhaps it was. When Wavell debriefed the British Cabinet in Downing Street on 28 March, he said that 'although he [Jinnah] would continue to press for Pakistan in the widest sense, he no doubt recognized that there was no chance of securing this' but that he could reach a stage 'where it was impossible for him to go back on his public statements'. However, Wavell thought that 'there was still some hope that when faced with the practical difficulties of partition that both sides might achieve agreement on a federal scheme'.[30]

Jinnah was also very likely to have been influenced by the British government's 1939 White Paper on Palestine. What was happening in Palestine was watched closely from India, with many of the grumpier Raj types complaining that, for a tiny country with a fraction of India's population, it seemed to get much more attention. 'Palestine was "chicken-feed" when compared to India', thought Geoffrey Lamarque, an ICS officer, though it seemed though to 'be of enormous interest to the people of England'. Having the Palestine affair put before India was a 'shock'. Britain had 'her priorities in the wrong order'.[31] Although the White Paper was never in fact formally approved, it acted as a policy framework within which Westminster subsequently addressed the issue of a Jewish homeland – in other words, the issue of a religious minority living among a much larger Arab population. It actually said that it was not British policy that Palestine should become a Jewish state as that would have been 'against the will of the Arab population of the country'. It also rejected the Jewish call to partition Palestine. Crucially, however, it went on to say that the British government's objective was to establish, within ten years, an independent Palestine in which Arabs and Jews shared government 'in such a way as to ensure that the essential interests of each community are safe guarded'.[32] To Jinnah, struggling to establish exactly what it was the League wanted, it must have offered a very workable solution.

The League's subsequent success in the 1946 elections, winning 86 per cent of the vote in the Central Assembly and 79 per cent in the Provincial Assemblies, and the dispatch of the Cabinet Mission that May, seemed to vindicate Jinnah's approach. He interpreted the Cabinet Mission Plan, with its emphasis on a strong centre responsible for defence, foreign affairs and communications running a federation of provinces whose governments would represent their respective communities, as basically helpful. He had accepted the plan on 6 June 1946. His subsequent refusal to participate in the Constituent Assembly, which should have been able to turn this plan into a new constitution, was because he thought that Congress and to some extent Wavell had double-crossed him. Instead of the provinces being compulsorily grouped, which, Jinnah thought, was what the Cabinet Mission had intended and would mean that the League could speak for Sind, the North West Frontier Province, Bengal, and, he hoped, the Punjab and Assam; instead Congress were insisting on a looser, voluntary system which would have considerably weakened Jinnah's claim to command a key role in the central government. Although the League did subsequently join the Interim Government in October 1946, they came 'to fight rather than to co-operate'[33] and Jinnah's line was increasingly to push for a separate Pakistan, in other words for partition, in the hopes that the reality of this might bring Congress to compromise. In February 1947 he had said very publicly that the Muslim League would not yield an inch of ground in their demand for a separate Islamic State of Pakistan and he started to raise the issue of dividing the army, the very idea of which would shock both the British and Congress. He was making the issue of a Muslim entity, Pakistan in its widest sense, something that could not be ignored, but he was expecting the British and Congress to come up with the solution more along the lines of the Palestine model. It was, as Wavell had noted, a dangerous tactic. Whereas Gandhi saw it as a sacred duty to keep India united, some in Congress, the pragmatists like Patel, were for letting the League have their 'rural slum' on the grounds that it would soon prove untenable.

Felicity Wavell's wedding to Peter Longmore had been duly celebrated on 20 February. The number of guests was 1400. There were glorious wedding presents, 'heaps of gold and silver' from the many maharajahs and nawabs who came, and 'the reception was held in the Moghul Gardens', the gardens of Viceroy's House, 'which were already blooming in a riot of colour'.[34] Given that they were tended by 418 gardeners, this was perhaps as expected. It was the same day as Attlee announced Britain's departure and Mountbatten's appointment. Wavell made his farewell broadcast on 22 March. Its tone seemed to sum up all his paternalistic affection for the India he had known. He said:

I came close to knowledge of the common Indian people. I learnt enough of the language to speak with the villagers where I camped and shot with my *shikharis* in the hills of Kashmir. My first independent command on active service was a detachment of thirty three Indian soldiers, a *VCO [a Viceroy's Commissioned Officer – see glossary]*, eight Sikhs, eight Punjabi Mussulmans, eight Dogras and eight Pathans – all magnificent men.[35]

He spent his penultimate evening having dinner with his old friend Auchinleck; they played mess games with the military staff after dinner. But that world, the world of sahibs and memsahibs, of polo matches and clubs, of durbars and maharajahs, of the Raj in all its genteel fragility, was ending.

Mountbatten was sworn in as viceroy on 24 March. The Raj mustered all its impressive ceremonial for the last time. Mountbatten, a serving rear admiral, the substantive naval rank to which he had reverted at the end of the war, was 'in full regalia and Lady Mountbatten was dressed in ivory brocade and wore medals', noted Shahid Hamid who was present.[36] They moved slowly to their red and gold gilt thrones in the Durbar Hall to fanfares of trumpets and escorted by the Viceroy's Bodyguard, the Indian Household Cavalry, now reduced to one squadron half Sikh, half 'Punjabi Mussulman', dressed in long black jack boots, scarlet tunics and puggarees. They had been converted to a parachute squadron in the war, getting 'ready to jump on Rangoon if the atom bomb had not forestalled them', wrote Lieutenant Colonel Paddy Massey, their commanding officer, who had been busy training them up for this important moment.[37] As the Chief Justice of India, Sir Patrick Spens, administered the oath, another fanfare sounded and Mountbatten was duly installed as the twentieth and last governor general and viceroy. It was, he reflected, slightly ironic. He had proposed to Edwina twenty-five years earlier in that very palace, sitting out a dance while he was accompanying the Prince of Wales on his tour. Lady Reading, the vicereine of the day, disapproved of the engagement, saying she thought Mountbatten lacked prospects.[38]

It was then time for Mountbatten to address 'all the political leaders, ruling princes, civil and military officers' and all the many ranks of the Raj arrayed before him in Edwin Lutyens's great hall. 'I believe', he said, 'that every political leader in India feels as I do the urgency of the task before us'.[39]

Mountbatten's appointment had been generally well received. He was seen as young, being only forty-six, energetic and had a 'good war' in which he had been singled out by Churchill for his forward-leaning views and his interest in technical development. He was given responsibility in 1941 for the Combined Operations Staff, a planning team consisting of naval, army and air force officers who would lead in preparing for the invasion of Europe in 1944. Their first operation, the raid on Dieppe in August 1942, saw significant casualties and attracted considerable criticism so that Mountbatten's position came under threat. However, in August 1943, Churchill promoted him again, over the heads of many more senior officers, to be Supreme Commander of Allied Forces in South East Asia, an appointment that culminated in the defeat of Japan and the com-plexities of dealing with the emerging nationalist movements in Burma, Malaya and Indonesia. Mountbatten was not only a cousin of King George VI, which gave him considerable standing among many in India, particularly the princes, but he was also, somewhat unusually for someone of his background, sympathetic to the Labour government and enjoyed good relations with Attlee and several of the Cabinet, including Cripps. He was therefore in many ways an ideal choice – a progressive, capable member of the royal family but one who could be relied on to take a liberal view in India and, most importantly, not to embarrass the government.

History has though, recently, been unkind to him and he has taken much of the blame, probably too much, for many of the disasters of the coming nine months. This is partly because he tried, particularly in his latter years, to ascribe to himself more of a role than he in fact played. Had he let his record speak for itself, and fully acknowledged the contribution of others in London and India, then his reputation would probably not have suffered as it has. In 1975 he gave a series of interviews to two journalists, Larry Collins and Dominique Lapierre, which resulted in the publication of *Freedom at Midnight*, an exciting account of Indian independence but one that was considered more a hagiography. In these interviews Mountbatten claimed he had been given special plenipotentiary powers by Attlee but, if so, no record of them exists; Attlee's direction to Mountbatten was a very clear letter written on 18 March explicitly stating that decision-making remained with the Cabinet.[40] Mountbatten also told Collins and Lapierre that the only things Wavell handed over were his insignia as Grand Master of the Order of the Star of India and a plan called Operation Madhouse, being his emergency evacuation plan. While it is true that Wavell was still persisting with this idea, and John Christie was working on it at the time, this neglects to mention his detailed briefings about the Interim Government and his concern over the Mountbattens' domestic arrangements, both of which survive in the records. In a subsequent series of interviews with the authors, Mountbatten also downplayed the number of deaths caused by partition, which by that stage were fairly clearly established.[41]

Whatever tricks old age played on Mountbatten, there is no denying the extraordinary difficulty of the task facing him and it is of note that his reputation is stronger among Indians than among the British. Many Indians, although few Pakistanis, think that his decisions during the coming months were correct and that had he done things differently the casualty toll would have been even worse. He was not the originator of any startling new solutions but what he did do was use his considerable charm and charisma to deliver what Attlee wanted, which was a British exit. Mountbatten was the ringmaster, and a good one, but the masters of ceremonies remained in Congress, with a supporting caste in Downing Street. It is Attlee and Cripps who are as responsible for the consequences as are Nehru and Patel. Kushwant Singh thought Mountbatten had a certain amount of panache and, critically, common sense rather than any great ability.[42] He was, he thought, more of a functionary but that he was a good functionary and did an almost impossible job well.

Certainly in March 1947 most people in Delhi were very pleased to see him. His arrival promised a new impetus to a process that had become stale and fractious. John Christie, who was to continue as a private secretary, thought 'that of the Viceroy himself . . . one cannot write except in superlatives. He was brilliant, inspiring, courageous, tireless; he was also a great leader, the perfect commanding officer. He drove his staff hard but never harder than he drove himself'.[43] He had also brought with him from London some of his own staff, who were an impressive group. Hastings 'Pug' Ismay was his chief of staff, an Indian cavalry officer who had served as Churchill's chief military assistant during the war. He knew India well and was generally liked and trusted by both the ICS and the Indian leadership. 'He had an acute and tenacious mind, and the kind of genius which is a combination of inexorable common sense with the taking of infinite pains', recalled Christie.[44] Ismay had just retired after a hectic war and had been looking forward to life on his farm in the Cotswolds. Despite the fact that 'there had been an almost record snow-fall, followed by a prolonged frost' and that 'there was a grave shortage of coal, and electric power was drastically restricted; food and clothing rationing were still in force; and finally there had been a very rapid thaw, with much flooding', he found leaving England much more difficult than before. He went because Churchill had asked him to and because he had a deep respect for Mountbatten, whom he found 'had a commanding influence, a flair for improvisation, dynamic energy, and a remarkable readiness to accept responsibility'. Before he arrived in Delhi he 'had thought that a period of fifteen months was far too short a time in which to complete arrangements for the transfer of power' but he had not been there three weeks before he had concluded that 'far from being too short, it was too long'. He was particularly pleased on arriving at his allocated house on the viceregal estate to find pensioner Abdur Rahman, who had joined the 21st Cavalry as a recruit at the same time as Ismay and who had been his orderly for twenty-five years. Ismay had been paying him a small supplementary pension but just before he had left home he had been told by his bank manager that Abdur Rahman had stopped drawing it. He had assumed he was dead but Rahman had heard on the radio that Ismay was due to return to India and the next day had taken a train to Delhi so he was there when he arrived. He immediately resumed his old duties.[45]

George Abell, the ICS officer who had played cricket for England, remained as principal private secretary but was joined by Eric Miéville, ex-private secretary to the king and an experienced colonial administrator. Alan Campbell-Johnson, who had been Mountbatten's PR officer in South East Asia Command (SEAC), now returned to the same job. Critically, and he was to prove one of the new viceroy's most valued advisers, V. P. Menon, the reforms commissioner, stayed on as well. There were suspicions among the staff that he was too pro-Congress and becoming less objective. He was certainly close to Patel but within two months both Mountbatten and Abell would be very grateful to him. Mountbatten also brought his long-standing naval secretary, Ronald Brockman, and Vernon Erskine-Crum, 'a young soldier with a fine war record and an extraordinary talent for straightening out in the minutes the tangled skein of debate and decision'.[46] It is to Erskine-Crum's precise pen that we owe the exceptionally clear record of the next four months. His task was not always straightforward. Mountbatten tended to conduct meetings one to one without Erskine-Crum present and then give him a verbal résumé afterwards. This meant that the viceroy and his correspondent could leave with rather different opinions as to what they had agreed.

The effect of this new team was, Christie thought, electric. Immediately Mountbatten started meeting with the Indian leadership. On the same day he was inaugurated he sat down for the first time with Nehru. Mountbatten realised that he must get on with the volatile Nehru at a time when Nehru was becoming increasingly exasperated. Two things played on Mountbatten's mind. First, he had quickly come to realise that India was nearer to a complete breakdown of law and order than his masters in London appreciated. Ismay noted that 'communal bitterness had grown to incredible proportions since I was last in India'. A 'spirit of bitter animosity had been rampant throughout the country for several months ... and there was tension everywhere. There was no knowing when a new outbreak might start'.[47] The need for the Raj and Congress to be seen to progress a political solution was vital. Dr Prem Bhatia, a Delhi industrialist on the edges of the nationalist movement, said that even at his level the Mountbatten–Nehru relationship 'was invaluable'.[48] The recent massacres in the Punjab had reminded everyone what could happen if negotiations broke down. Attlee's announcement of 20 February had also, almost overnight, transformed the relationship between the Indians and the British, who were no longer seen as the public enemy, but that could change and throughout Mountbatten's early months there is frequent reference to the need to protect the remaining 80,000-odd Europeans. Memories of 1857 were long and, as it turned out, far too long.

Yet Mountbatten, more politically astute than Wavell, also knew that there was a strong direct link between Congress and the Labour government. This was in part a shared socialist vision but it was also based on Nehru's own personal standing and contacts. Wavell discovered when he got back to London that Cripps had been operating a direct briefing system behind his back, with Congress passing information via Krishna Menon, secretary of the Indian League in London and their unofficial 'ambassador'. Krishna Menon lived a life of many parts and strongly divided opinion. A committed socialist, a Labour councillor and at one time a Labour parliamentary candidate, his power base was his strong friendship with Nehru. He was known as 'Nehru's evil genius' and Eisenhower famously described him as a 'Menace'; later in his political career *Time* magazine would put him on its front cover surrounded by cobras with the caption 'Snake Charmer'.[49] Yet divisive as he undoubtedly was, Menon did have Cripps's ear. Mountbatten knew the importance of the Menon–Cripps relationship and he also knew how much influence Cripps exercised over Attlee on Indian affairs; it had been Attlee who had persuaded Churchill to send Cripps on his first mission in 1942. Mountbatten therefore knew that if Nehru did not like his approach he had a method of getting his views heard around the Cabinet table independent of what the viceroy advised. He had made a point of

befriending Cripps, whom he tried to persuade Attlee to put into the
India Office instead of the increasingly ineffective Pethick-Lawrence,
and had been to see Krishna Menon before he left London; he also
made a point of telling Attlee and Cripps he had done so.

Mountbatten therefore needed Nehru more than Nehru needed
Mountbatten, and the viceroy, ever a pragmatist, realised that
progress would be impossible without Congress' support. The 20
February announcement had effectively relegated Britain to the
role of facilitator. The story of the next five months would in reality be one of Congress deciding what it wanted to do and using
Mountbatten to execute it. The two men in fact went on to develop a
genuine friendship. By April Mountbatten was writing that, 'We have
made real friends with him' and that 'I feel his friendship is sincere
and will last'.[50] There were those, like Patel, who felt that Nehru used
Mountbatten too openly, describing him as 'a toy for Jawaharlal to
play with'.[51] There was also much speculation about the relationship between Nehru and Edwina Mountbatten. Whatever the truth
behind those rumours, the practical impact was damaging. Paddy
Massey was with the Mountbattens at Delhi airport one day as they
were departing on a visit. Nehru, who was accompanying them,
kissed Edwina in public. It was a perfectly normal greeting to the
cosmopolitan, Westernised Nehru but one which 'sent a frisson of
horror through the Mahommedan community', noted Massey, and
contributed, he thought, to the Muslims feeling that even at this early
stage 'Mountbatten was too pro Hindu'.[52]

The first meeting therefore predictably went well. Mountbatten
noted that 'Pandit Nehru struck me as most sincere' although he was
slightly surprised to be told that the 'greatest problem facing India at
the present time was economic'.[53] Nehru was also slightly distracted
as he had chosen that week to host an Asian Nations Conference on
the Purana Qila Ground, a site with ancient Indian connotations.
Delegates from thirty-one countries came. An enormous canopy was
erected under which 20,000 people sat to hear speeches about the
need for greater Asian cooperation, concluding with one by Gandhi.
It was a clear statement by Nehru that he was the leader in waiting.

No anti-British speeches were made but the League boycotted the event as they were not asked to co-host it and Liaquat Ali Khan held a Pakistan Day rally in Delhi instead.

Next Mountbatten saw Patel. He was equally charmed, although possibly a little taken back by Patel's uncompromising approach to the Muslim League, which he said must be got rid of, and his repeating that most Indian Muslims were just forcible converts from Hinduism.[54] Menon thought that Patel was becoming increasingly impatient. 'He felt that the sand was running out', he recalled and that: 'He was a man who appreciated power. He was a sick man also – he suffered from jail. He was tired. He wanted to get on with things. He was anxious to get into power'.[55]

On 31 March, Mountbatten met Gandhi. He was always going to make a point of getting on with Gandhi. It was part of the Labour approach. Wavell had been horrified at what obeisance Cripps and the Cabinet Mission had shown to the old man the year before when they had insisted on attending his prayer meetings but then Wavell was never prepared to see anything good in Gandhi. Mountbatten was also genuinely impressed with the old sage, but again he appreciated just how much influence he still wielded and that his support would be critical to any new initiative. In the event it was more of a social chat, Gandhi sizing up the viceroy who was thirty-two years his junior. They sat having tea in the Moghul Gardens, both making sure there was ample time for press photographs first.[56] Gandhi had been walking through Bihar, trying, as he had done with limited success in Bengal, to mend relations between Hindus and Muslims. His spiritual exhortations were meeting a similarly sceptical response. 'How transitory is life. Everyone has to die one day. It is difficult to comprehend the ways of God', he had told a group of grieving widows at Pipalwan, who might have been hoping for something more concrete.[57]

He had recently had another sharp exchange with Patel over the Congress Working Committee's announcement that the Punjab should be divided. Whereas Nehru had answered diplomatically, Patel had been more forthright ending sharply, 'You are, of course, entitled to say what you feel is right'.[58] Mountbatten would soon become aware that partition of any sort remained an anathema to Gandhi and, should it come to that, managing him would be challenging. Gandhi, however, quickly summed up Mountbatten, who sent a telegram back to London summarising their meeting and purring that 'it is his considered opinion as a student of history and world politics that never before, in any case of history he had read about in recent or past times, had so difficult or responsible task been imposed on any one man as that which now faced me. I thanked him sincerely for realising the position in which I was now placed'.[59]

Another group also made a beeline for Mountbatten in those early days and that was the princes. They had, so far, played only a limited part in the debate but now they sensed that with a fellow royal in Viceroy's House, and a man who several of them already knew, they had an opportunity to put their case. The Maharaja of Bikaner did so on the day of the inauguration. He said that the princes as a group were divided. The key Rajputs, the great rulers of the central Indian plains, men like Jaipur, Jodhpur and himself, were generally for Congress, who they saw as the one entity with the capability to govern and to prevent India descending into chaos.[60] Others though wanted to go their own way. Sir C. P. Ramaswami Aiyar, the dewan (chief minister) of the huge southern state of Travancore said that neither he nor his ruler had any intention of taking part in negotiations over a future constitution. If the British went then Travancore would become a Dominion like other ex-British colonies as, he pointed out, Travancore had a bigger population than Australia.[61] A third group, and the majority, however, saw Congress as a left-wing party which posed a direct threat to their interests. The Nawab of Bhopal, Hadji Sir Hamidullah Khan, the greatly respected Chancellor of the Chamber of Princes, and an old friend of Mountbatten, was their leader.

There was one more key relationship that Mountbatten needed to foster and that was with his commander-in-chief, Auchinleck. Relations with Auchinleck were never going to be easy. Auchinleck had been a close confidant and friend of Wavell, with whom he shared the common experience, some would say distinction, of being sacked by Churchill as commander-in-chief in the Middle East. To make matters worse, when Auchinleck was told that his consolation prize was to be commander-in-chief in India, he was also told that the job was losing operational responsibility for South East Asia, which would pass to the new SEAC, whose first supreme commander would be none other than Mountbatten. It had been a harsh blow, which effectively relegated Auchinleck to a supporting role. He subsequently christened Mountbatten 'Pretty Dickie' and his staff mocked what they saw as the ineffectiveness of SEAC. Now the two men must work together at a time when not only was internal unrest inevitable but when the Indian Army, which Auchinleck had devoted his whole life to, may have to be divided.

Auchinleck had joined the Punjabi Regiment in 1904 after a difficult childhood. His father, also a regular soldier, had died when he was eight and his mother had been left to bring up her young family in rented rooms on a meagre army widow's pension. He had won a Foundation Scholarship to Wellington College, which had enabled him to be privately educated, and from there went straight into the army. The Indian Army had been his life ever since. He took part in the North West Frontier skirmishes before the First World War and fought with his Punjabis in the muddled and bloody campaign in Mesopotamia, where he had seen his battalion reduced from 942 to 247 men in their attempts to relieve the besieged British force in Kut. Picked out for his successes commanding on the Frontier again in the 1930s, he was rapidly promoted at the beginning of the Second World War when senior British officers with recent operational experience were hard to find. He was sent to try to sort out the mess at Narvik during the Norway campaign in 1940 after which he was entrusted with the defence of southern England against possible German invasion. In 1941 Churchill sent him to replace Wavell as commander-in-chief in the Middle East.

His initial successes, clearing the Germans and Italians from Cyrenaica and taking Tobruk, were overshadowed by Rommel's subsequent counter-attack, when he threatened Egypt. Auchinleck was dismissed and replaced in August 1942. In 1943, as Wavell was appointed to succeed Linlithgow as viceroy, he took over as commander-in-chief in India. His personal life had not been happy either. In 1945 his wife, Jessie, left him in a very public separation for Air Chief Marshal Sir Richard Peirse, a man of sixty-two and a contemporary. It was not an easy humiliation to suffer in the stuffy world of the memsahibs. It was at least some consolation that he was near universally liked and respected throughout the Indian Army. Speaking Hindi, Punjabi and Pashtu fluently, he was never happier than when chatting to his soldiers and their families, people he saw as almost a separate constituency above the tawdriness of nationalist politics. It was his great strength but it would also prove his undoing.

Auchinleck's power was, in the words of V. P. Menon who saw it at first hand, 'immense'.[62] He was not only the arbiter of the Indian Army, which by 1947 still numbered over half a million men despite its post-war reductions, but also of the 50,000 British troops still in India. He was commander-in-chief of the Royal Indian Navy and Air Force and a key member on the Viceroy's Executive Council, and effectively Member for Defence, although Baldev Singh had been appointed defence minister, at Nehru's insistence, in the Interim Government in September 1946. This double-hatting, as both commander-in-chief and with responsibility for formulating defence policy, dated back to Curzon's bitter row with Kitchener forty years before, which had ultimately led to the vindication of Kitchener and Curzon's resignation as viceroy. But beyond that Auchinleck's power rested on the fact that, with an increasingly ineffective police, and the Raj had never managed to establish a police force with equivalent morale and expertise to its army, his military forces, both Indian and British, were the only effective instrument of power in the government's hands. It had been the army that had stopped the Great Calcutta Killings the previous August and it had been the army that had just managed to quell the unrest in the Punjab. The army also still had an extensive administrative and logistic element, with its own food supplies, farms, workshops and factories, a leftover from the war, which gave it self-sufficiency.

It should, perhaps, have been obvious that, in the uncertain times ahead, the army would need to play a central role and that Auchinleck would have to work closely with Mountbatten to ensure that it did. Later he was very polite about Mountbatten. Talking to David Dimbleby in 1974, he said that Mountbatten was 'very good indeed as Viceroy. A very difficult job and one had to support him'.[63] But V. P. Menon thought that Mountbatten was 'overwhelmed with the idea that the army and the services might not do as he said'[64] and Shahid Hamid, admittedly a possibly biased observer given his dislike of Mountbatten whom he thought too pro-Congress, wrote that after Mountbatten and Auchinleck met on 31 March, Auchinleck returned in a frightful temper. Mountbatten had wanted troops to be used more in support of the civil authorities. Auchinleck had tried to persuade him that that course was 'fraught with danger as they could become partisan. With communal feelings running high they should be used sparingly'.[65] He told Hamid that Mountbatten did not understand India or the Indian Army. Mountbatten for his part wrote that Auchinleck was in 'a frame of mind which made him more difficult to deal with than I can remember at any time since October 1943'.[66] It was not an auspicious beginning. In the months ahead Auchinleck would become increasingly focused on the army itself and its beloved regiments rather than on the job it was there to do. The consequences would be serious.

AN INTRACTABLE PROBLEM

*'It was Congress who insisted on partition. It was
Jinnah who was against it'*

(AYESHA JALAL)

By early April the 'boiling heat' of the Delhi summer had started.
Gone were those few cool months of the Indian winter when the
flowers are in bloom, the daytime temperature is bearable and
when 'a glimpse of paradise is vouchsafed to man and beast, to
sustain them during the purgatory of the months ahead', noted
John Christie. No matter how long one lived in India, the summers
never got any easier to bear. Spring is hardly noticed and then the
hot weather starts, when 'all living things move more slowly and
seek the shade. A hot wind rides in from the desert like an invading
army, its impact a physical assault. For weeks and months the sky is
hidden behind a lurid pall of dust, and night brings little or no relief
from the obsessive heat'.[1]

Normally the beginning of the hot weather would signal a move to
Simla, the 'hill station' 7,000 feet up in the foothills of the Himalayas
where the Raj escaped during the summer so that the business of
government could continue in relative comfort. Simla boasted a
complete set of houses and offices, Viceregal Lodge being a rather
weird cross between a Scottish shooting lodge and a Victorian sea-
side hotel completed for Lord Dufferin in 1888. Not all viceroys or

their vicereines liked it. 'The outside is hideous,' complained Lady Minto. 'It is quite bare without one creeper, and reminds me of a nouveau riche house on the 1000 islands.' She didn't like the interior much either. 'The furniture is very bad and the electric light fittings criminal. The Finance Minister had a fit of economy when the house was being built and reduced the hall by half, which quite spoils the proportions.'[2] Around this strange house, clustered on the hillside, were the residences of the commander-in-chief and the senior officials, more in keeping with a Kent resort than the mountains of Asia. Here the Raj's social season had taken place for the last sixty years: balls, dinners, picnics among the stunning scenery. A special narrow gauge railway ran up the mountain from Kalka in the plains through 107 tunnels and over 864 bridges to bring the enormous bureaucracy with all its documents, staff, sahibs and families for the annual pilgrimage.

This year there was to be no migration. The government would stay in Delhi and the critical debate on the future of India would take place in the relentless, sapping heat of a Delhi summer. By May the average temperature would be 40 degrees Celsius, dropping slightly in July when the air would gather the humidity of the coming monsoon. It was, many thought, the hottest spring for seventy-five years. Few buildings had air conditioning. Mountbatten's study did, which he kept at 21 degrees. When Gandhi visited, Lady Mountbatten would come in and turn it off, fearing that the frail old man would catch pneumonia given that the outside temperature was 43 degrees.

For hundreds of millions of Indians what was about to happen was remote and largely irrelevant. Even in the better-off villages, those lucky enough to be on fertile land, they lived in a morass of dust, or mud in the rainy season, and ordure, mostly in flat-roofed mud houses. The unreliability of the rainfall, and the almost total lack of agricultural development under the Raj, meant that, as the population gradually expanded, so land became more scarce; holdings of half an acre were considered rich and many villagers were in hock to their landlord or the moneylender. They would probably never have seen a British official and a visit by the District Officer to their village, should it happen, would be a major event.[3] Their priorities were growing enough food to survive, their concerns were their neighbours and their landlords, their politics almost entirely centred around their community and the implications of being governed by the British or by Congress opaque. Despite the extensive reorganisation of both Congress and the League, and their mass recruitment campaigns, they remained largely urban parties.

In southern India, which would be more or less untouched by the coming miseries, Delhi seemed even more remote. Geoffrey Lamarque, who was so annoyed at how much attention the Labour government was paying to Palestine, had been stationed in Madras. He felt that when the government in Delhi legislated, 'It would only have in mind the Indus and Ganges Valleys'. The Madras government and the central government were 'in a state of perpetual conflict, always having violent verbal arguments' as what Delhi ordained was 'not appropriate to south India because the conditions were so different'. The south had a way of life that, he felt, worked remarkably smoothly. There was very little communal tension in Madras with its overwhelming Hindu majority and a Brahmin led government. The British had been there for 300 years in 1947, far longer than in places like the parvenu Punjab, and Anglo-Indian relations were easy although there was still the usual Raj refusal to socialise regularly with the locals. English was spoken widely and well and often as a first language. The ICS tended to pay lip service to what they were told to do. When they were instructed to impose a sales tax, for which Delhi demanded income tax figures, Lamarque simply sat down with the telephone book, rang up a few traders, asked what their turnover was, and sent in figures that were decidedly advantageous. One young officer, sent to demand tax from a recalcitrant village, set out with his platoon but never found it; no one in the government had ever been there before. This was not the all-efficient British bureaucracy that legend associates with the Raj but it was a form of governance that fostered an easier coexistence. Madras would escape the horror to come because it was a Hindu province and the transfer of power would go remarkably smoothly.[4]

Even more removed from what was going on in Delhi were the many peoples who lived on India's fringes. Before he moved to join the viceroy's staff, John Christie had been the deputy commissioner, which meant he was also inspector of police, judge, district engineer, inspector of schools, public health officer and district agricultural officer in the Chittagong Hill Tracts, the strip about forty miles wide and one hundred and fifty miles long that ran parallel to the Bay of Bengal, twenty miles inland from the port of Chittagong. The country was low bamboo-covered hills interspersed with numerous rivers, which provided the only means of transport apart from elephants. Christie had two: Daisy, who was over fifty years old, and a young tusker called Lal Bahadur, who proved his worth in taming the wild elephants who roamed in herds. It was a tribal area, with three chiefs, rampant disease and one small Baptist mission hospital. The cropping pattern was to clear an area of jungle, cultivate it and then move on in a couple of years once the soil was exhausted. For Christie and his young family it was an idyllic period, but the affairs of Delhi and of wider government hardly impinged on a way of life that had not changed in a millennium.[5] Soon the future of Chittagong would come into all too sharp a focus.

Christopher Beaumont, who would also play a major part in the events of 1947, had earlier been posted as agent in another tribal area, over a thousand miles west of Chittagong, on the border of the Punjab and Baluchistan. Dera Ghazi Khan, where the temperature reached 46 degrees in the summer, was a land of Muslim tribes who lived in scattered villages across a landscape that was barren beyond the Indus valley. There was the usual tribal rivalry but 'no political movement, no political activity' and the 'local population had been completely disinterested in the war'.[6] Soon that would also change very much for the worse.

For many others serving on India's borders the political turmoil of Delhi and the violence in the Punjab and Bengal sounded more as a distant rumble than as something that would soon change their lives for ever. J. P. Cross was posted with his battalion of Gurkhas at Razmak in Waziristan 'in the isolation of the North West Frontier, still using heliograph and semaphore' to communicate 'and in its pre-war, esoteric ritual, much of what went on India reached us as rumour or not at all. Mail from home took six weeks and any newspapers sent out were as slow if not slower. One top priority signal, "Operation Immediate", took six weeks to reach us from Delhi. Certainly none of us had wirelesses, yet I do not remember that the lack of news worried us'. The local cinema was still showing the Allied crossing of the Rhine as headlines on its newsreel (two years after it happened), although Cross admitted that even they were a bit surprised not to hear about the plan to create 'a new state called Israel until six months after the event'. But in the spring of 1947 he noted 'hordes of Pathans', the tribesmen who lived on the Frontier, 'moved eastwards on camels and foot. Several weeks later they returned in one long convoy, shooting bullets in the air, laden with booty, having raided Kashmir'. He realised then that 'big trouble was brewing'.[7]

The few remaining ICS officers were still concerned about what would happen to them and their families and what financial provision the government would make for them. There had been the usual deafening silence from both Whitehall and Delhi when anyone mentioned money. The problem was that, when the issue was first discussed in 1946, the British government had insisted that the full financial liability for their compensation be born by the new Indian government. Patel, at his best in handling such matters, had strongly objected; first he thought that it was unfair for India to pay British pensions and, secondly, he did not want to allow the Indian members of the ICS the opportunity to retire. Wavell, true to his word, had been pursuing this issue vigorously and had advised Mountbatten to get it resolved before he arrived. Mountbatten duly took his advice and the Cabinet agreed generous terms for both British and Indian officers, which Britain would pay for. It was a good package, which increased Mountbatten's popularity and 'it was a great encouragement', noted Ismay, 'that the men who had borne the heat and burden of the day in India, and were about to lose their means of livelihood, were at least assured of monetary compensation on a not ungenerous scale'.[8] Congress, however, continued to resist the package being offered to Indian officers, arguing, with some justification, that just because the British were leaving it did not mean that the administration of India should necessarily stop with them.

Many also felt that what was going on in Delhi was not commanding sufficient attention in London. There is no doubting Attlee's personal commitment to India. He knew the country well. He had served alongside the Indian Army at Kut in 1916, been a member of the Simon Commission in 1928, an experience he found deeply frustrating, and played a major role on the Select Committee in Parliament that had developed the 1935 Act. He had in fact led the opposition to much of what had originally been proposed, arguing that it left too much power in the hands of the viceroy, allowed the princes too great a role and was 'premised on a mistrust of Indians'.[9] His position was that India should be a fully self-governing Dominion within a set timescale and that its constitution should enshrine the 'strong centre'. During the war, when Churchill reacted to any talk of furthering Indian independence with a growling fury, Attlee had taken the opposite view. He believed the war effort would have been better served by full Indian cooperation and he was strongly critical of Linlithgow whom he thought a 'crude imperialist'.[10] It was Attlee who persuaded Churchill to send Cripps out in early 1942, although when Cripps's mission failed, as, some would agree, Churchill had always intended it would, he did subsequently endorse imprisoning the Congress leadership until the end of the war.

By April 1947 though, Attlee's approach suffered from two disadvantages. First, India was but one of the several significant overseas issues he had to deal with. In January 1947 he had announced, to Conservative Party criticism, the withdrawal of large numbers of British troops from the Middle East although not from Palestine where 80,000 remained. On 14 February, Bevin, the Foreign Secretary, had announced that the issue of Palestine would be referred to the United Nations. The Cabinet were consumed with trying to stem Jewish emigration from Europe and were preparing for another summer of bloody violence between settlers and the native Arabs. Those like Geoffrey Lamarque were right to complain that Palestine seemed to be taking too much of the government's time but it was the question that dominated the international headlines.

Secondly, there is little in Attlee's correspondence to suggest that he really understood what Jinnah was seeking or that he had come to terms with what Pakistan should be. His advice on India in those months was one-sided. Pethick-Lawrence was ineffective as Secretary of State, waffling at great length about the more esoteric points of future bilateral arrangements. Indian politicians nicknamed him 'Pathetic-Lawrence'. He would soon be replaced but his successor, Lord Listowel, entered the debate too late to affect its outcome. The most influential voice on India in the Cabinet was Cripps, the veteran of two missions, strongly influenced by Nehru and Krishna Menon, and who saw things from the perspective of Congress. Attlee, Cripps and Nehru were from that generation of socialist politicians who saw problems in social and economic terms and underestimated the depth of Indian communal tension. After the Great Calcutta Killings Attlee had written to Wavell that he hoped that 'there is just a chance that these events may serve to bring some sense of reality into the minds of the contending politicians'; it was an almost naive view.[11] He was, as Nehru aptly described him, 'a well intentioned liberal' but one who failed on the specifics.[12]

Attlee trusted Mountbatten implicitly. He liked him personally, thought that he had 'a gift for getting on with all kinds of people' and the idea that he was related to the royal family appealed. He 'felt sure that the first Empress of India [Queen Victoria] would be glad to see a descendant complete the last part of a century's work'.[13] It would be Mountbatten he would rely on to advise him on what Jinnah wanted. That should have become apparent in the early days of April when Jinnah started a series of meetings at Viceroy's House.

Before his first meeting with Jinnah, Mountbatten sent back his first 'Personal Report' to Attlee; interestingly these reports were copied to Cripps, as well as to the king, the India Office, and the Secretary of State for Defence. Mountbatten wrote:

The scene here is one of unrelieved gloom. The country is in a most unsettled state. There are communal riots and troubles in the Punjab, the North West Frontier Province, Bihar, Calcutta, Bombay, UP and even here in Delhi. In the Punjab all parties are seriously preparing for civil war, and of these by far the most businesslike are the Sikhs. I am convinced that a fairly quick decision would appear to be the only way to convert the Indian minds from their present emotionalism to stark realism and to counter the disastrous spread of strife.[14]

The *Hindustan Times* had reported the previous day that there had been twenty-eight incidents in Calcutta alone. The police had fired fifty-six rounds. Five people had been killed and forty-two injured.[15]

That 'fairly quick decision' would depend on Jinnah. He came to Viceroy's House on 5 April for the first of what would be a series of five initial talks. They did not start well. First Jinnah had joked that the welcome photograph, in which he stood in between Mountbatten and Lady Mountbatten, was a 'rose between two thorns'. Actually he didn't mean that, and had assumed that Lady Mountbatten would be in the middle, but it was symptomatic of what would be an awkward relationship that he still trotted out his prepared lines. Mountbatten had wanted to spend the first session getting to know the *Quaid*, much as he had Gandhi and Nehru, but he found Jinnah in a 'most frigid, haughty and disdainful frame of mind' and wanting immediately to lay down exactly what was acceptable to the League. 'For half an hour he made monosyllabic replies to my attempts at conversation', Mountbatten recorded, and his chief message was that 'on the Muslim side there was only one man to deal with, namely himself', the familiar Jinnah refrain which he now protested too frequently. Sadly there is, as yet, no public record of what Jinnah thought of Mountbatten.[16]

At the second meeting, which took place on 7 April, Jinnah laid out his agenda more clearly. The Constituent Assembly was dead and the spirit of trust that had fluttered briefly and hopefully in the middle of 1946 'was destroyed'. The only thing to do now was to hand over

India province by province and 'let the provinces themselves choose how they formed into groups', in other words reiterating the League's position that a simple majority of Muslims in Bengal, the Punjab, Sind, the North West Frontier Province and possibly Assam would ensure he could balance central power with Congress. He then went on to say two things which perhaps portrayed his real position more clearly. He first castigated Mountbatten over Attlee's declaration that the British would leave by June 1948, come what may. 'Is it your intention', he asked him, 'to turn this country over to chaos and bloodshed and civil war?' Secondly, he emphasised that the League would insist on the armed forces being divided, something he made Liaquat Ali Khan follow up in writing that evening.[17]

At their third meeting, on 8 April, he went on to say that any idea of partitioning the Punjab and Bengal was 'a bluff on the part of Congress to try and frighten him off Pakistan'. He did not, he insisted, want a 'moth-eaten Pakistan', in other words just Sind, the North West Frontier Province, and the western half of the Punjab, with a remote East Bengal and part of Assam in the east.[18] When he was debriefing his staff after these meetings, Mountbatten told them 'he did not believe that Mr. Jinnah had thought of the most elementary mechanics whereby Pakistan was to be run'.[19] This was not surprising; Jinnah was not then intending it to be a separate nation outside a federal structure. The appeal for the British to stay longer, the insistence on the division of the army, which he and Liaquat both thought would be unacceptable, and even if it was accepted would take several years, re-emphasised that Jinnah was, as Wavell had pointed out, using the idea of partition as a threat to get what he wanted. But Jinnah did not actually say what he wanted, Mountbatten did not grasp it and the two men had not managed to establish a constructive working relationship. On 11 April, Mountbatten told his staff that Jinnah 'was a psychopathic case. He was impossible to argue with. Until he had met Mr. Jinnah he had not thought it possible that a man with such a complete lack of sense of responsibility could hold the power which he did'.[20] It was, on every count, a profound misjudgement.

Maybe Jinnah realised that he had failed to impress his position on Mountbatten. After his fifth meeting with the viceroy, on 11 April, he went to see Eric Miéville, who found him 'positively jokey!'. Jinnah related, 'How much he had enjoyed lunch at Buckingham Palace' the previous December. He had found 'The King pro-Pakistan, The Queen even more pro-Pakistan' and 'Queen Mary was 100% pro-Pakistan'. Miéville, with true civil service reserve, regretted that their Majesties had expressed an opinion on political matters![21]

More significantly, Jinnah sent Liaquat back to see Mountbatten. He knew Liaquat was liked and respected by the Raj officials, although they had been annoyed by his recent budget; this had increased capital taxation, stealing some of Nehru's socialist thunder and also placing him in a difficult position with industrialists like Birla, on whom Congress depended for funding. Liaquat now made four clear points. First, he emphasised that establishing an independent Pakistan would be very difficult; secondly, he insisted that the British government's responsibilities would last beyond June 1948; thirdly, he said that the division of the army was non-negotiable and finally, making a strong play for continuing British support, he said that Pakistan would need British officers in both the Civil Service and the Army for some time to come.[22]

With these initial discussions complete, Mountbatten and his team in Viceroy's House had a deadline but no plan. They would now draw up the options and map out an approximate timetable. First they would sketch out the possibilities, they would then discuss them with the provincial governors, after which the viceroy would call the political leaders together to get their reaction. Ismay would then take the draft plan back to London to get Cabinet and parliamentary endorsement before it was announced.

The result of the viceroy's staff meeting on 11 April was one of those classic instructions which senior British officials so nonchalantly issue to their subordinates, a trait the British Army has long and cynically referred to as 'Big Hand, Small Map'. That afternoon Hastings Ismay sent V. P. Menon a note which read: 'Could you possibly have a go at a plan for the Transfer of Power – preferably by tomorrow afternoon?' What would become known as 'Plan Balkan' was the result. It was, in effect, a derivation of the Cabinet Mission Plan but envisaged the partition of the Punjab, Bengal and Assam; a separate plebiscite in the North West Frontier Province, and that the provinces would work out their own respective constitutions leaving the central government with the three 'union' subjects of defence, foreign affairs and communications.[23] Menon, now no stranger to drafting papers on the future of his homeland, set to work and on 15 April Mountbatten duly called in the provincial governors to discuss his product.

The eleven men who answered his call represented a formidable body of intellect and experience. Many Indians saw their attitude as patriarchal, even arrogant. 'There was a tendency on the part of politicians in India to regard all British members of the Civil Service as bigoted, scheming bureaucrats, and the Indian members as mere stooges of their British colleagues', thought Ismay, whereas the reality was that both the new administrations would soon be dependent on 'this handful of highly-trained, loyal and upright men'. But by any measure they were an impressive group. Sir Archie Nye, Governor of Madras, was a distinguished general who had been Field Marshal Alanbrooke's deputy as Chief of the Imperial General Staff during the war. Commissioned from the ranks due to his impressive record as a sergeant in the First World War, he was as highly rated by Nehru as he was by the British Army. The Scottish industrialist Sir John Colville, Governor of Bombay, was an ex-member of the Westminster Cabinet and had served as both financial secretary to the Treasury and Secretary of State for Scotland. A third, Sir Frederick Burrows of Bengal, although too unwell to attend in person, and represented by his secretary, John Tyson, was an ex-general secretary of the National Union of Railwaymen, who delighted in telling his rather grander Raj contemporaries that while they were 'Huntin' and shootin'', he had been 'Shuntin' and hootin''. He rated his proudest achievement as having been Regimental Sergeant Major of the Grenadier Guards in the First World War.

The remaining eight were all ICS men. One, Sir Chandulal Trivedi, Governor of Orissa, was an Indian; the remaining seven were all British, men who had spent their careers in India, who spoke the languages and knew the people, and had a genuine love for the country. Portraying such men simply as arch imperialists, bent only on furthering British interest, is simplistic and ignores the complexities and apparent contradictions of the Raj. That relations remained so good between Indians and British during the terrible months ahead, and why relations today are so much better than they might be, is precisely because men like Sir Francis Wylie of the United Provinces, Sir Hugh Dow in Bihar, Sir Frederick Bourne in the Central Provinces and Sir Andrew Clow in Assam were all people who had dedicated their lives to India, while Trivedi was soon to be given one of the most demanding roles in the new nation. And as they gathered in Viceroy's House on that hot April morning they felt challenged and, understandably, confused. Not only was the world to which they had given their careers about to end but they were not at all sure how.[24]

Mountbatten opened the conference in the way that meetings of senior British officials have always started, and still do, with a pep talk. He said that the Labour government's instructions to him were 'to regard himself less as the last British Viceroy than as the head of the new Indian state'.[25] He regretted recent comments by one senior ICS officer who had said, when he heard the announcement of 20 February, 'That bloody fool Attlee must be mad', and another who had reportedly said on being told half his town was on fire: 'We are leaving anyway. What do we care.' It was important that everyone appreciated the urgency of what they were doing. After an embarrassed shuffling, people became more positive when the generous terms of the ICS retirement package were explained.

The main business of the conference was more sanguine. The first day was spent surveying the state of the country province by province. Madras remained quiet. Bombay was unsettled but manageable, although Colville complained that he now had just twenty-two ICS officers left to manage his province of approximately 30 million people. The United Provinces were also unsettled. Meerut district was on the edge, only kept quiet by constant patrolling by a Special Armed Constabulary maintained by Premier Pandit Pant's administration and commanded by the most effective brigadier, Mahomed Akbar Khan, a soldier who had risen from the ranks of Probyn's Horse and who would soon play an even more prominent role. The week before there had been serious rioting in Agra, where the police had gone on strike. The week after the conference Cawnpore would also erupt. The Central Provinces were containable, while spasmodic violence continued in Bihar where the police were now ineffective. Orissa remained relatively quiet although, as General Sir Francis Tuker noted to his evident disgust, 'large numbers of students turned communist for want of other political diversions'.[26]

More time was spent discussing the provinces that would be more directly affected by the transfer of power, Bengal and the Punjab but also Assam, Sind and the North West Frontier, and where the governors were subject to particular pressure. Tyson summed up the position in Bengal as seen by Sir Frederick Burrows and the few remaining Raj officials. Effectively there were only two communities in Bengal, 33 million Muslims and 25 million Hindus. Among the Hindus were 9 million of the 'scheduled' castes, in other words the lowest castes previously called Untouchables, the people who Jinnah thought would support the League rather than their higher-caste Congress brethren, although Burrows's advice was that only about a quarter of them might do so. Partition of the province would be easier than in the Punjab as districts tended to be discretely Muslim or Hindu rather than mixed, with the bulk of the Muslims living in the east; of the population of a putative East Bengal, 26 million of a total of 38 million would be Muslim, while in what might become West Bengal 14 million of a population of 22 million were Hindu with only 8 million Muslims.[27] The Hindus, who had so vigorously opposed Curzon's partition in 1905, now strongly preferred partition, with West Bengal becoming part of 'Hindustan', to the possibility of becoming a minority in a Muslim-dominated state or, as the premier, Huseyn Suhrawardy, wanted, for a united Bengal to

become an independent country where they would again find themselves in the minority.

The problem, as Burrows saw it, was that East Bengal on its
own would be unsustainable. In a remarkably prescient analysis,
he queried how any country could function when one part would
be a thousand miles from its parent state and he could not see how
it would survive economically. West Bengal could work, assuming
it included Calcutta, whose population was 70 per cent Hindu and
where Hindus owned 90 per cent of the investment. It would have
all the coalmines, minerals, factories and all but two of the all-
important jute mills. Neither would East Bengal be able to feed itself;
it had a food deficit of 225,000 tons a year, without which people
would starve as had recently been so horrifically proved. It would
'stagnate to such an extent and become so poor that it would end up
as a rural slum', and 'he shuddered to think of its condition in seven
years' time'.[28] In the meantime he was concerned about the growth
of communism, something to which, as an ex-senior member of the
British Trade Unions movement, he was particularly sensitive. Could
communists be declared illegal? he wondered. Nye said that they
dealt with them in Madras by imprisoning them for other crimes.
In fact, although they would later become increasingly influential in
Bengal and eventually form the government, communism did not
play that significant a role in the coming events. Suhrawardy thought
them insignificant although 'he sometimes wished they had gone in
for violence as it would have been easier to deal with them'.[29]

Suhrawardy's concept of an independent Bengal had found very
little support among his Muslim supporters. He said Jinnah never
listened to him anyway and unless he got all his points over in the
first two minutes, the *Quaid*'s attention had wandered. Suhrawardy
emerges, as he twists and turns his way throughout this story, from
being Minister of Supply during the famine to Premier of Bengal
after the 1946 elections, as someone who could let his imagination
overtake him. He told Sir Terence Shone, soon to be British High
Commissioner to India, that he was worried about Indian aggression
to a Muslim Bengal. 'After all Mr. Nehru, on a big black horse, might

lead a Hindu army against Muslim Bengal'. When Shone pointed out that Nehru hardly seemed to be cast for such a role, Suhrawardy said that 'as an alternative Mr. Nehru might try to induce the Nepalese to move against a Muslim Bengal'. He then went on to muse as to where in the world 'One could go nowadays to settle down in peace? Ireland? Or perhaps the Balearic Islands? He believed hall porters at hotels in New York did very well'.[30] In fact, fate had other plans for him. On 26 April he saw Mountbatten, argued his case strongly and said that the army should be split three ways between Hindustan, Pakistan and Bengal. But Congress were never going to entertain such a plan and neither was Whitehall.

Having had the rather depressing discussion on Bengal, which had revealed all the pitfalls of partition but led to no other practical solution, the conference discussed Assam. It was the province north and east of Bengal, a beautiful wild country of forests and tea plantations, home to indigenous tribes and scene of some of the fiercest fighting in the recent war as General Bill Slim's 14th Army had turned the Japanese invasion of India at Imphal and Kohima. Assam had originally been part of Bengal but was made a separate province in 1911 when Bengal was reunited after the Curzon debacle. Hindus were, narrowly, in the majority, numbering 4.21 million out of a population of just over 10 million and the 1946 election had returned Gopinath Bardoloi leading a Congress administration. There were 3.44 million Muslims and 2.41 million from the 'tribes' but most Muslims, about 2 million, lived in the Sylhet district in the most southerly part of Assam and bordered solidly Muslim areas of Bengal. Sir Andrew Clow, who liked plain speech, said the 'whole of the rest of Assam would be very pleased if Sylhet left as it was a deficit district and a liability'.[31] Although no supporter of partition, believing that a separate East Bengal could cut Assam off from India, he favoured a separate solution for Sylhet. This was duly noted.

The conference then turned its attention to the western areas. The violence in the Punjab and the Rape of Rawalpindi dominated. Sir Evan Jenkins, now governing under Section 93 and dismissive of repeated League approaches demanding they be invited to form a new government, described what had happened. He said that in part of the Jhelum district there had been 'an absolute butchery of non-Muslims. In many villages they were herded into houses and burnt alive. Many Sikhs had their hair and beards cut off and there were cases of forcible circumcision. Many Sikh women who escaped slaughter were abducted'.[32] There was little more he could add; all those present realised that partition of the province was almost unavoidable, however hard Jinnah protested. Jenkins did, however, make two key points, neither of which were given the attention they subsequently would prove to have deserved. Accepting that partition was looking more or less inevitable, he emphasised that it could only be imposed by force and that 'a large number of troops would be required'. He had previously estimated this at four divisions, or roughly 100,000 soldiers. Secondly, he said he 'thought the Muslims' demand for Pakistan was potentially much less dangerous than the possible subsequent pressure which might come from non-Muslim parties to ensure that they got it'. Even as he spoke Congress were debating how to do exactly that.

There was a short discussion about Sind. Mountbatten had been fielding complaints from Nehru that Sir Francis Mudie was 'being too pro Muslim' and unfair to Congress. This was not altogether surprising, given that Sind was an overwhelmingly Muslim province. Originally part of Bombay, it had become separate only in 1936 with its capital at Karachi. Yet in the 1945–6 elections Congress had entertained hopes that, even if they couldn't win an outright majority in the Karachi Assembly, they could at least prevent the League from forming a ministry by allying with Muslim independents. They had given eighteen Muslim candidates financial backing. The League's position was anyway weak, with a strong breakaway faction led by G. M. Syed, and with widespread electoral corruption; a vote was said to cost the minimum of 1 rupee. In the event the League had won enough seats, 27 out of 60, so that Mudie could legitimately invite their leader, Ghulam Hussain, to form the administration. However, Congress polled a significant vote and came in as the second party, so that Patel accused Mudie of prejudice in not including them.[33] Mudie, fresh from being the Home Member in the Delhi government, had been robust with him as he now was with Mountbatten. He told the viceroy that Congress didn't like him because he had imprisoned their leaders in the United Provinces when he was posted there in 1942; Nehru's complaint was symptomatic of a Congress that was finding its cry that it spoke for all Indians regardless of religion to be coming under severe pressure in the Muslim majority areas.[34] Nowhere would that be more evident than in the North West Frontier Province, and much of the rest of the conference was taken up with discussing the difficult situation there, one described by its governor, Sir Olaf Caroe, as 'being liable to drop to bits at any minute'.[35]

Ismay thought Caroe looked 'terribly tired and strained' that day and it was hardly surprising.[36] Congress vitriol for Mudie was nothing compared to what would be heaped on poor Caroe. Worthy, experienced, intellectually astute, Caroe suffered from not being his predecessor, the legendary Sir George Cunningham, who had captained the Scottish rugby team, governed the Frontier from Peshawar for nearly ten years and of whom the warlike frontier tribes were reputed to walk in fear. 'Everyone regarded him with deep affection and respect', said Norval Mitchell, who had worked closely with him 'and his presence was thought to be the equivalent of two divisions on the Frontier'. Mitchell was Caroe's chief secretary in Peshawar, the North West Frontier capital, that April and clearly also rated him as a man 'with an extraordinary degree of fortitude and distinction', although he leaves much unsaid.[37] However, N. Mukherji, an Indian ICS officer who also worked under Caroe at the time, and who came from a strongly nationalist family, had the fullest praise for him, saying he did an 'exceptional' job.[38]

The North West Frontier was as politically complicated as it was physically wild. Its population of 3 million was predominantly Muslim, although it had two significant Hindu areas, Charsadda, immediately north of Peshawar, and the Banu district to the southwest. The province bordered the tribal agencies, responsible for a further 3 million people, the Mahsuds, Wazirs, Daurs, Afridis,

Shinwaris, Salmanis and Kullaghoris, mostly Pathans, almost totally Muslim and to whom Islam was fundamental to every aspect of their lives. Peshawar itself, only forty miles from the Afghan border, 'was still a bastion of Kiplingesque behaviour. It was neatly divided into two separate cities. The cantonment', the British area, was 'entirely surrounded by barbed wire' and 'was as spick-and-span as any English country village. There were bungalows with well-tended lawns, one of the most luxuriously appointed clubs in the whole of India, and every week the Peshawar Vale Hunt met to chase, not foxes, but jackals, complete with mottled English squires in red coats and horse faced ladies', wrote Edward Behr, then a young officer in the Garwhal Regiment who had just been made Intelligence Officer to the Peshawar garrison.[39] He goes on:

> Across the railroad tracks lay Peshawar City, so different from the cantonment it was difficult to believe the two towns were in the same country. Peshawar City then was still an exotic medieval walled city, with eleven massive gates abutting a huge fort. Inside was a maze of shops, markets, tiny workshops, and the narrow streets jammed with Pathans, mostly armed with home made Lee-Enfield rifles.

The Pathans, 'the toughest, hardiest people in the world', mostly lived in the border areas by marginal subsistence farming, adhered to their own strict code, the *pashtunwallah*, and fought each other for generation after generation over obscure family feuds whose initial cause had long been forgotten. They had never fully accepted British rule, and the Frontier was run on the basis that neither side would interfere in the affairs of the other providing nothing happened to upset the status quo. Occasionally, when it did, the Raj would mount military expeditions, for which they kept specific forces in Frontier garrisons.

The Frontier had been fairly quiet during the Second World War, Pathan appetite for fighting having been partially sated by the uprising led by the Faqir of Ipi, which had tied up a sizeable number of British troops. Neither had the Pathans paid much attention to the subsequent developments in Indian politics, so that in both 1936 and 1945 they had elected a Congress government; there was strong Congress support in both Charsadda and Banu. This was led by the remarkable Khan brothers. The first, Abdul Ghaffar Khan, a dedicated Congress supporter, was known as the 'Frontier Gandhi' as he copied Gandhi's campaign for self-sufficiency. Unlike Gandhi he had raised an irregular force, the Khudai Khitmagars or Red Shirts, who gave him considerable influence. They lived in a camp in Charsadda, where they 'drilled, spun cloth and held indoctrination courses', and had played a major role in the nationalist campaigns of the 1930s. Behr got to know them well and thought that 'although they may have been Gandhian in spirit' they were 'not averse to violence to make their presence felt'.[40]

The Congress government had resigned in 1939, as did all provincial Congress governments, being replaced by a short period of direct rule. Between 1943 and March 1945 there had been a fairly ineffective and corrupt League administration, but in January 1946 Congress won the election once more, with 30 out of the 50 seats, again helped by the Red Shirts. This victory surprised many; it was ascribed partly to the fact that Congress had strong historic Muslim support from its leadership of the Khilafat Movement, the campaign to restore the Ottoman Caliphate in the 1920s, but it was more likely because the majority of Pathans simply did not appreciate the significance of the political process. Conditions on the North West Frontier were unique, and they were reluctant to come under the sway of any centralist party.

Abdul Ghaffar Khan's brother, Dr Khan Sahib, was the Congress premier. He had been a distinguished army doctor and was very well liked and respected throughout the Frontier; he was a close friend of Cunningham and regularly played bridge with him. Mitchell had 'a deep affection' for him and thought that he was 'determined to do what he thought best for the Frontier' while Caroe described him as 'the most impressive Indian I have ever met'.[41] The problem was that what Dr Khan Sahib and Congress thought best, and what they thought the 1946 election result had given them a mandate for, was that in the event of partition the province should be part of India. Caroe, realising that the League had not impressed the tribes, and knowing that they would never accept being assigned to a Hindu-dominated government, argued strongly that there must be a plebiscite on the specific issue of whether a majority wished to join Pakistan. He had considerable previous experience on the Frontier, and he had also asked Mitchell, who had spent much of his career there, to write a paper summarising the case for each jurisdiction. Mitchell concluded that unless there was a plebiscite there would be civil war and that the electorate was likely to vote overwhelmingly to be part of whatever Pakistan might be.

Nehru and Patel realised that if they could wrestle the Frontier for Congress, and India, Jinnah's 'moth-eaten' Pakistan would look so moth-eaten that it would consist of just Sind and West Punjab, along with the 'rural slum' of East Bengal, which might mean it would never happen or at least collapse soon after it came into existence. Again Nehru misunderstood the depth of communal feeling. He did not know the Frontier, and logically assumed that as Dr Khan Sahib had won the election, that there was a popular mandate for Congress. He had, however, visited the province the previous year. Caroe had tried to stop him, pointing out that his visit would simply draw attention to the growing divide, and arguing that he should bide his time until he had a specific message for the tribesmen. Nehru ignored him. His visit was a predictable disaster. A *jirga* of Afridi leaders refused to meet him. In Waziristan the locals said plainly that they did not like him or Congress. Nehru told them they were 'pitiful pensioners', referring to the allowances the Raj paid them to behave, while they retorted that they regarded Hindus as their serfs. At Landi Kotal, at the foot of the Khyber Pass into Afghanistan, the army had to open fire to extricate Nehru from a hostile crowd and in Malakand his car was fired on. Back in Peshawar with Caroe, with a badly bruised ear and chin, and an even more bruised ego, Nehru accused the Raj and their political agents among the tribes of organising the protests. He never forgave Caroe.

On 18 April, as the conference neared its end in Delhi, Mountbatten gathered Caroe, Dr Khan Sahib and Nehru together.[42] He had previously sought the advice of Colonel de la Fargue, who had been chief secretary before Mitchell and a man who emerges rather badly from this affair. De la Fargue told the viceroy that although 'Caroe had a great knowledge of the Frontier, he was biased against his Congress government and had lost the confidence of fair minded people' and that 'his continuance in office was in fact a menace to British prestige'.[43] Mountbatten sensibly treated such direct advice with caution. However, he found his meeting with Dr Khan Sahib and Caroe unsatisfactory. Dr Khan Sahib complained that Caroe interfered with his decisions while Caroe argued that he had to maintain law and order. Dr Khan Sahib said that if things were left to him there would be 'no rioting, no processions, no murder' but Caroe retorted that Dr Khan Sahib's policy was to 'let everyone who was likely to vote for him have a gun'. Unsurprisingly the viceroy determined to visit the Frontier to assess the situation for himself.[44]

On 27 April Mountbatten arrived in Peshawar. Lady Mountbatten, who played an important and sometimes understated part in so much of this story, accompanied him. Mitchell 'had no words to describe the degree of anxiety and suspense that preceded' their arrival. 'It was as if clouds covered the sky from horizon to horizon waiting for the simultaneous flash of lightning and crash of thunder.' Once news of the visit got out, a massive crowd of Pathans started to converge on Peshawar, making it plain that they insisted on seeing the viceroy and impressing on him their determination not to be assigned to India should partition happen. Estimates of their numbers vary, but it was somewhere between 50,000 and 100,000, most of whom were armed. They declared they would march on Government House and occupy it if the viceroy refused to see them, and the previous night the General Commanding had his house raked by gunfire. It was a delicate moment. Mountbatten knew Nehru's depth of feeling on the issue of the frontier, and the critical importance of not upsetting Congress. Yet he also knew that if he ignored the Pathan demonstration he risked an incident that might rival the slaughter of Amritsar. On his arrival he drove to consult with Dr Khan Sahib who agreed that the Red Shirts would be kept in the background and that Mountbatten should be seen by the crowd. He and Lady

Mountbatten duly drove with Caroe to a railway bridge from where the three of them were clearly visible. It was a masterstroke, the sort of gesture at which Mountbatten excelled. The temperature was 38 degrees, the mood one of 'fanaticism, anger and communal hatred' and it would have taken little for it to turn into a full-scale riot. But the Mountbattens' appearance, with the governor, equally unruffled, calmed them. In fact the crowd became 'in excellent spirits and greeted his appearance with shouts and flag waving'.[45] Much was made of the fact that the viceroy was wearing a uniform of dark green, the holy colour of Islam, but Mitchell, who was present for most of the visit, said this was a later misinterpretation as the Islamic green was a totally different shade. Mountbatten could not resist his customary self-congratulation at the success of his appearance. He reported to London that he distinctly heard shouts of 'Mountbatten Ki jai', or 'Long Live Mountbatten' and that 'I felt it was most awkward that they could look on me as some sort of saviour'.[46]

The important result of the visit was that Mountbatten agreed with Caroe that there had to be a second election in the province. Nehru, predictably, disagreed and disagreed furiously. Mountbatten wrote to Nehru in surprisingly direct terms on 30 April. He said Dr Khan Sahib was being unfair to Caroe and that the tribes were very clear they did not want to be part of a Hindu-dominated country. They now wanted Dr Khan Sahib's government out and had said they would prefer to be part of Afghanistan rather than India, although it was fortunate for them that the latter contention was never actually put to the test. The logical Nehru must have appreciated the reasoning, but the political, public Nehru was outraged. It was the first and only time Mountbatten would stand up to him on a matter of substance. Among the many milestones of 1947 it was this decision that would shape how Congress now proceeded. In the event of partition, a Congress-dominated assembly in the North West Frontier Province would inevitably, if the decision was left to them, vote that the province should join India. What would Pakistan then be other than Sind, and parts of the Punjab and Bengal? But a plebiscite would almost certainly give Jinnah control of the North

West Frontier Province and meant that he would have the makings of a viable political bloc, whatever shape Pakistan finally took.

The subsequent question was then whether Dr Khan Sahib's government should remain in office until the plebiscite had taken place or should it be removed and leave Caroe to govern under Section 93 as Jenkins was doing in the Punjab? Outside Peshawar there was continuing violence. The south of the province was 'as bad as the Punjab, with only the River Indus separating two vast areas of looting, burning, massacre and rape'.[47] Shri Mehr Chand Khanna, Dr Khan Sahib's finance minister, told the *Hindustan Times* that League agitation had led to 400 Hindu and Sikh deaths, with 150 injured and 300 forcibly converted, with 50 places of worship and 1,600 houses destroyed.[48] Even Dera Ghazi Khan, which Christopher Beaumont had found so settled, was in chaos. Caroe had asked Auchinleck for more troops to help contain the violence but the commander-in-chief had replied that he was being alarmist and the army was too busy. He was generally being unhelpful, telling Mountbatten on 14 April when consulted before the governors' conference that dividing the armed forces would take at least a year and require a large new staff. He said, correctly, that Congress would wreck Plan Balkan, the plan for the transfer of power V.P.Menon was even then furiously drafting, and that the declaration of Pakistan would cause 'any amount of trouble'.[49]

Caroe and Mitchell both strongly advised Mountbatten to leave Dr Khan Sahib's administration in place, advice that was ultimately accepted. This meant that there was at least some form of representative government on the Frontier, but the Khan brothers were now seething. They would look for new political opportunities when it became apparent that Nehru had accepted the inevitability of a new vote.

The conference wound up on 16 April having reached two conclusions that were rapidly becoming obvious. First, that a quick decision was vital if the country was not to disintegrate. They estimated that there were now twelve private armies operating, which numbered more than 400,000, from the 7,000 in Abdul Ghaffar Khan's Red Shirts to the 100,000-odd in the Hindu Mahasabha, the nationalist movement that proclaimed that India should be a country for the

Hindus. Master Tara Singh and Kartar Singh had already raised 50 lakhs of rupees (a lakh is 100,000) for the Sikh militias in the Punjab. They were circulating a pamphlet which urged Sikhs that 'in your veins is yet the blood of your beloved *Guru* Gobind Singhji! Do your duty; we have to fight this tyrannical Pakistan'.[50] Secondly they realised that it was probably impossible to preserve India as a united country. That was something Plan Balkan acknowledged.

Throughout the last two weeks of April, V. P. Menon drafted and redrafted 'a new version almost daily'[51] as Plan Balkan slowly took shape. Yet in reality the initiative had already passed to Congress and their attitude was, as Jenkins had so accurately predicted, hardening all the time. The impressive Chakravarti Rajagopalachari, then Minister for Industry and Supply in the Interim Government, told Mountbatten that he should remember that in India 'most leaders took a long time to obtain sufficient influence to become leaders and once this happened they were usually embittered old men who had become obstinate and not open to reason'.[52] However unkind that may have been, the events of the past weeks had only strengthened Congress' resolve that partition of some sort was a price worth paying for getting on with self-government. They knew what Jinnah wanted but they were not prepared to let him have it. The experience of Interim Government, from its painful inception the previous year, had shown them that they could not share power with the League and they knew they could not govern India without that strong central power base which had been core to their policy for so long. Patel told Mountbatten decidedly on 1 May that Congress would never consider parity in central government.[53] The decision to hold the Frontier plebiscite, which they knew they must lose, had been the final straw.

The Interim Government was simply not working, with Congress and League ministers concentrating on fighting each other rather than attempting to govern. Ismay was dismayed to find himself at a dinner party with a Congress minister on his right and a League minister on his left. 'Throughout the meal both of these cultured men, who normally had impeccable manners, spoke to me unceasingly and in loud voices about the iniquities of the opposing community.'[54] Jinnah remained uncompromising. A unified India was, he argued, an artificial creation; it had never really been one even under the early Hindu and later Muslim emperors. Partition of Bengal remained a 'red herring' and the Sikhs, 'in many ways an admirable people' but who 'unfortunately lacked leadership of a high order and while they were successful in small ways of business, seldom produced outstanding men in law, science or politics' would be much better off under Muslim government.[55] The leaders of Congress were 'so dishonest, so crooked and so obsessed with the idea of smashing the Muslim League that there are no lengths to which they will not go to do so'.[56]

One such length was for Congress to report to the Constituent Assembly on 28 April its definitions of the three crucial policy areas that the centre would control actually were. These were so extensive that they would leave the provincial governments virtually powerless and responsible for doing little more than running local services. Defence was now to include not only the armed forces but also all defence industry and special powers, reminiscent of Section 93, by which the central government could take charge of provinces in an emergency. Foreign affairs included all overseas trade, immigration and all overseas financial transactions. Lastly communications was interpreted as including all airways, telephones, shipping, broadcasting ports, much of the railway network and waterways. Beyond that the report recommended a series of financial measures that meant the centre would be self-financing rather than dependent, as the League wanted, on contributions from the provinces. The key taxes were to be retained by the central government, as were all the key financial and commercial instruments to regulate banking and insurance. There wasn't much left for a provincial government to do.[57] If they could not have parity in central government, then the League would be left virtually powerless, effectively running a series of provincial administrations that would be little better than county councils. If they wanted effective power they would have to accept an independent Pakistan, truncated or moth-eaten.

It was in this last week of April that Congress 'explicitly denied Jinnah's ultimate hopes; this was the decisive reversal, not Mountbatten's froth and fury', nor the endless carefully worked drafts flowing from V. P. Menon's pen. 'The price of keeping the Muslim provinces inside the union had to be a weak federal centre incapable of controlling any of its provincial arms.'[58] This was unacceptable to the Congress High Command. Congress had decided that Pakistan should therefore be an independent state and that British India should be partitioned. It was a state which they thought would not last, and one with which some key functions could be shared, such as defence, but one that needed to be established so that they could govern. 'It was Congress that insisted on partition.' It was Jinnah who was against it.[59]

5. MAY

PLAN AND COUNTER PLAN

*'The proposals would only encourage chaos
and disorder. The transfer of power would be
obstructed by a mass of complications and by the
weakness of the central government and its organs'*

(JAWAHARLAL NEHRU)

By the beginning of May the heat in Delhi was oppressive, almost unbearable. Nehru was 'overworking to the point of a breakdown'[1] and becoming very difficult. Krishna Menon, out in Delhi specifically, so he told the viceroy, 'in the hope of being of use to him personally as a friend',[2] asked Mountbatten to take him away on holiday. In a very public speech in Gwalior, Nehru had said that the Princely states must either join the Constituent Assembly or be considered 'as hostile'.[3] It was not helpful, nor what Nehru meant as he subsequently clarified. Mountbatten himself was tired. He had been working seventeen-hour days since he arrived and also had to continue the round of normal viceregal entertaining and ceremonial. Viceroy's House was constantly busy with dinners and receptions, and he was amused to hear one Raj old-stager complain of Lutyens's great palace that 'it makes me absolutely sick to see this house full of dirty Indians'.[4] Mountbatten estimated that during their viceroyalty he and Edwina Mountbatten had 15,000 people to dinner and 12,000 to lunch,[5] although this does seem like an awful lot.

The heat and the uncertainty were affecting Calcutta as badly. Congress leader M. N. Saha complained to Rajendra Prasad on 4 May that there was 'no law and order, people are being murdered in broad daylight'. One Muslim organisation, he maintained, was paying 25 rupees for every Hindu killed and 15 rupees for every one injured. In the border areas outside the city Hindus had to abandon their homes. Several prominent men had been murdered. Dr Abani Nath Sarkar, son of the highly respected historian and ex-vice chancellor of Calcutta University, Sir Jadunath Sarkar, was stabbed by an assassin on the footpath near the church at Dhurmatollah Esplanade at 6.00 p.m. in full daylight and many people watching. Sir Jadunath felt the shock so much that 'he has aged considerably and his life has been shortened'.[6]

The Hindi Rashtra Seva Dal, not the most militant of the militias, 'since all they taught in most places was squad drill, P.T., the control of crowds and the preservation of order', was recruiting vigorously.[7] It is amazing anyone joined up, since the initial syllabus demanded recruits master twenty-four different drill movements, including 'Dressing at Intervals', but sign up they did so that by May the Bombay branch had 56,868 members.[8] Arms continued to flow into Calcutta, many taken from the American dump at Kanchrapara before the army had cleared it. There was continuing violence on the railways and riots at Dacca University where Muslim students demonstrated at the rustication of one of them for allegedly pushing a Hindu girl. On 15 May, they demonstrated again, this time rather less seriously, walking out of their exams as they said the questions were too hard.

More serious unrest was developing in Gurgaon, in south-east Punjab, and only twenty miles from Delhi. Today it is very close to the new Indira Gandhi airport. The minority Muslim Meo tribe was being harassed by the Hindu Jats, who greatly outnumbered them. It was clear that, however the Punjab was divided, the Meos, living so far from the main Muslim areas, could not hope to be in Pakistan. They were seen as fair game by the Jats and arson, looting and killing has been going on over a wide area. Trouble had been developing since February when a false report that a Hindu boy had been stabbed by a Muslim led to riots in the major Gurgaon town of Rewari but came to a head in April when a Hindu mob burned the Meo village of Khori Kalan. Normally the villagers ran away when the mob approached but this time they were surprised and had no time to run. Twenty-six were burned to death, including women and children. In retaliation the Meos burned seven Hindu villages.[9]

Then 'Jat mobs numbering up to 30,000 now began to besiege Muslim villages, destroy the houses and then kill the inhabitants'.[10] It sounded very similar to the Rape of Rawalpindi two months previously, only this time it was the Muslims who were the victims. Even in Delhi the violence was rising; twenty-two people had been killed on the streets in April with sixty-seven injured.[11]

In Viceroy's House a team had been put together under Ismay, consisting of George Abell and Eric Miéville, to turn V. P. Menon's initial draft into a fully worked up plan. Ismay left to take this to London to get Cabinet agreement on 2 May. The plan had been formed as a result of the many meetings with Indian political leaders, the governors' conference and the pressure that was growing daily to move the process forward before India imploded. Ismay sent it to Mountbatten on 25 April with a covering note that warned that British authority was 'in the process of liquidation. If we stick to the last date and the last hour, we shall probably find the country in turmoil and a measure of responsibility for this state of affairs will be attributed to HMG'.[12]

What was properly known as 'A Plan for the Demission of Power',[13] V. P. Menon's Plan Balkan was so called because it was seen to divide India into a series of loosely correlated states, and accepted some degree of partition but in a way that still allowed considerable leeway for the provinces to choose. Each province would elect their own Constituent Assembly, which would appoint an Executive Council. His Majesty's Government would hand power over to these councils who could then choose to join the existing Constituent Assembly in Delhi, in other words to be part of Hindustan, as India was then still referred to, or to join a new Constituent Assembly for Pakistan. There would be a joint council with equal numbers of representatives from Hindustan and Pakistan, presided over by a governor general and which would decide on the three 'reserved subjects' of defence, foreign affairs and communications. The armed forces, which the plan accepted had to be divided, would answer to the commander-in-chief and the governor general via their respective Executive Councils thus preserving operational coherence. The idea behind this was optimistic. The plan envisaged that it would take both Hindustan and Pakistan four to five years to frame their respective constitutions during which time it was felt that 'so many matters would require joint agreements that they may ultimately come round to the view that an impassable barrier cannot be created between the two Indias and that after all a unified constitution is better for all concerned'. It was to prove a vain hope but it was very much the spirit in which Ismay and Abell would portray it.

The plan was based on Madras, Bombay, United Provinces, Bihar, Orissa and the Central Provinces and Berar all choosing to be part of Hindustan. In Bengal and the Punjab the existing assemblies would be asked to sit in two factional parts. In Assam 'territorial constituencies', including Sylhet, would be invited to sit separately. It was confirmed that there would be a plebiscite in the North West Frontier Province. The Sind, the new assembly in the North West Frontier Province and the split assemblies in Bengal, the Punjab and Assam would then be invited to elect representatives on an agreed quota and vote on whether their provinces should be divided. Thereafter, dependent on the results, representatives of the provinces or subsequent half provinces would be asked to decide which Constituent Assembly they wished to join or act on their own. The Princely states would also be free to join whichever Constituent Assembly they chose.

It was, on the surface, a masterpiece of Indian Civil Service drafting. The issue was then how far it should be cleared with the Indian political leaders before Ismay took it to Attlee. The intention had been to do so but Mountbatten, always conscious of maintaining support in London, thought that the Westminster Cabinet should see it first. In the end it was agreed to show it just to Nehru and Jinnah. Miéville took it round to them while Mountbatten was away in Peshawar. Whereas Jinnah 'protested strongly against the partition of the provinces and demanded the immediate dissolution of the [existing] Constituent Assembly',[14] Nehru appeared to be content with it apart from the provision for fresh elections in the North West Frontier. Whether he was just tired, with too much on his mind, or whether the fact that it was Miéville who briefed him rather than Mountbatten himself, Nehru evidently did not take in, or chose not to take in, the importance of what he was being told. In fact on 1 May he wrote to Mountbatten asking why he had not seen the draft Ismay was taking to London, emphasising again that Congress would accept partition although he did not go as far as saying that they were now actually planning on it.[15] No one seems to have reacted to that letter, evidence again of an overworked staff with too much to do. What Ismay was even then about to brief in Whitehall would be irrelevant without Congress support. The realisation that they now controlled merely the process, while Congress made policy, had not yet dawned on the Raj.

On 1 May, Mountbatten told Attlee, referring to the violence that would inevitably accompany partition, that his staff were discussing the troop deployments necessary to 'nip such trouble immediately in the bud'.[16] Yet the military staff in Delhi, and Auchinleck himself, appeared to be more concerned with the appalling prospect of dividing their beloved Indian army between Hindustan and Pakistan. On 3 May, Auchinleck appointed Major General Irwin, the Deputy Chief of the Indian General Staff, to head a committee charged with doing so. Armies exist to do the bidding of their governments and of the taxpayers who pay for them; they should not adopt a persona of their own, thinking that they are in some way separate from or above the political system that sustains them. Yet this is exactly what the

Indian Army had done for decades and which now, when it would be needed more than ever to maintain law and order, it allowed to become all-consuming.

To be fair to it, the Indian Army was a particularly complicated and sensitively adjusted body, which had previously partly achieved its mission, historically preventing unrest within India, through its communal, or 'class', organisation. Until 1939 it had remained, despite its distinguished performance in the First World War, a child of the Mutiny, and as the body the Raj looked to for protection against riot and revolution and any chance of the terrible events of 1857 being repeated. It measured its operational effectiveness partly by how it maintained law and order on the Frontier, where it was organised into specific task forces for the purpose, and partly by its ability to fulfil its communal recruiting quotas. The measures taken after the Mutiny were still largely in place in 1939. The army favoured recruiting from what it thought as the 'martial races'. Consequently just over half its soldiers, 55 per cent, came from the Punjab, being about 20 per cent Sikh and 35 per cent Punjabi Muslims. Of the remaining 45 per cent, 10 cent were Dogras from Jammu and Kashmir, about 8 per cent Hindu Jats, 7 per cent Pathans from the Frontier, 6 per cent Hindu Rajputs, with 4 per cent Mahrattas from Bombay and 3 per cent from Madras.[17] There were very few Bengalis, who were believed, incorrectly, to be militarily unreliable. D. K. Palit, a Bengali who would end up as a major general, 'was surprised I got into the Army. Bengalis were always seen as anti-Brit'.[18] Taken together, the Punjab and the Frontier, which represented just 7.5 per cent of India's population, accounted for around 60 per cent of her army. This was seen as manifestly unfair by those outside the favoured provinces, given that the army provided good salaries, pensions and grants of land to veterans.

The system of recruiting specific 'classes' to companies and squadrons also persisted, so that a regiment might have one company of Punjabi Muslims, one of Sikhs and one of Hindus. Frequently whole sub-units would come from a particular caste or tribal group. Recruiting, usually in the hands of retired soldiers in a locality, would favour particular families and villages. This was popular with the regiments as they had a trusted source of manpower and one that was fairly effortless to find but it was also both unfair and inflexible when mass recruitment was required. This had been the case in 1914 and again in 1939. Officers remained predominantly British although 'Indianisation' was slowly increasing. In 1923 two cavalry regiments and six infantry battalions had been selected as guinea pigs to have Indian officers. In 1932 an Indian military academy was established at Dehra Dun. Lastly British troops continued to be 'brigaded' with Indian regiments, a system that lasted until the outbreak of war.

By the end of the 1930s not only was the 'martial races' policy being questioned but the governments in both London and Delhi were wondering whether the Indian Army was really producing value for money, consuming, as it did, approximately 26 per cent of the Indian national income. Why was such a large army still required to maintain law and order and to police a frontier that seemed to have stabilised at a routine level of violence? In 1938 the government in London asked Admiral Sir Ernie Chatfield to assemble a committee of experts to report on the defence of India. The resulting Chatfield Report recommended an urgent review of that 'Forward' policy, whereby military effort was concentrated on the Frontier and said that instead India should focus on strategic threats from the east and on the security of her sea lanes.[19]

The Chatfield recommendations, prescient as they were to soon prove, were almost immediately overtaken by events. Between 1939 and 1945 the army increased from 120,000 to nearly 2 million men, with 15,700 Indian officers, and the old class recruiting system was found to be inadequate.[20] Many new recruits now came from what had been thought of as 'non-martial' classes, with full regiments being raised from Madras, Bihar, Assam and from caste groups previously thought unmilitary. By proving itself conclusively as a fighting force in Burma the army showed that the previous structure was an anachronism. Nevertheless, bizarrely, as early as 1943 Churchill was asking for confirmation that the 'martial class' composition was not being diminished too far, requiring Auchinleck to reply that the 'Teeth Arms', the fighting arms of the armoured corps and infantry, were still predominantly 'pure'.[21] What made this intervention even stranger was that the Royal Indian Navy and Royal Indian Air Force operated a system where all 'classes' and creeds were inextricably mixed.

In 1945, with the Japanese defeated, the issue the army had to resolve was how it should structure itself for the future. It obviously had to reduce in size and by 1947 it was down to 561,000,[22] but how should it now recruit and for what roles should it be trained? Auchinleck appointed a committee under Lieutenant General Sir Henry Willcox, until recently commander-in-chief of Central Command, to examine this. There was criticism that the committee was not headed by an Indian but it was an interesting group, which included both Brigadier Enoch Powell, later to become a well-known British politician, and Brigadier K. M. Cariappa, who would become India's first post-independence commander-in-chief. They recommended, strongly, reinstating the old 'class'-based system, arguing that even by 1945 there was an obvious risk in bringing new and untried classes such as Bengalis into the army.[23] By mid-1947 much of the army was therefore reorganised along its old class lines, despite the fact that very few of its pre-war officers, who had been its principal advocates, remained in regimental posts.

Many thought the old army had gone with the war. Veterans like Evan Charlton remembered the pre-war army as a family affair. Recruiting tours in the Punjab were almost a triumphal procession. As the regimental party approached they would be met by a band and escorted to the centre of the village where there would be a white cloth on a table and a bottle of whisky. The officers and non-commissioned officers would talk about old times while the young recruits, the sons and cousins, were produced and marched off to join the Colours, giving their families status and income. It was not, Charlton thought, 'so much an army – more a way of life'. The soldiers certainly engendered a unique and special loyalty to each other, the regimental spirit which meant so much. 'The loyalty and bravery of the Indian Army was quite unique', Charlton thought, 'they were prepared to die on a battlefield fighting for something in which they had no vested interest themselves'.[24]

The army was certainly seen as glamorous and exciting, the stuff of the tales of Indian life that captured the imagination of schoolboys at home. The comedian Spike Milligan was brought up in military camps as his father was an artillery officer. The picture of the colourful parades and ceremonial stayed with him all his life.

> O God the picture! The elephant batteries came on six in a line, with their leather harness all polished up and the regimental banner was hung on the forehead of the lead one – the one in the middle. The *mahouts* wore a striped turban, and they used to come on with a drum beat, and they got those elephants to put their trunks up all together as they went past the stand of course to a storm of applause. And of course band music was always playing – as one faded into the distance a fresh one came on so there was an endless conveyor belt of music and colour and all this dust rising up from the *maidan*. It looked like a dream picture – something through a strained gauze curtain – marvelous. It was only after the war when they tried to mechanise these regiments one realised it had all been a dream. It was something that would never, never come again.[25]

But what was the post-war army there for? Throughout all the reviews that had taken place, from the 1938 'Modernisation' Committee,[26] to Chatfield and to the 1945 restructuring, the role that was consistently prioritised remained internal security. The 1938 report looked at the requirements for 'the maintenance of law and order in the event of widespread disaffection', recommending a force of a minimum of fifteen British battalions and twenty-five Indian battalions or equivalent be held as a reserve. Chatfield went further. It examined how India could fight an external war while simultaneously dealing with 'widespread civil unrest'. It identified the most likely areas for trouble as being the Frontier, the Punjab and

Calcutta. It recommended increasing the forces to be held against these contingencies to twenty-one British battalions but reduced the Indian requirement to fourteen; the report's authors, which included Auchinleck, discussed these numbers in detail with the relevant provincial governors. Critically they recommended that the British forces should now be grouped separately in mobile brigades.[27]

For British soldiers stationed in India life was less glamorous. Before the war, their role, unless they were lucky enough to be sent to the Frontier, was simply to be there and they became very bored. There was no privacy, no social life, living in barrack rooms, being restricted to the barracks, with its canteen and cookhouse, no contact with women, not much training and just endless drill, kit cleaning and parades. The scheduled castes did their menial jobs for them in exchange for a few annas and most remembered spending hours and hours asleep on their beds trying to escape the dreadful heat. They still carried their rifles into church with them on Sundays just in case there was another mutiny. Many could never get over the poverty that surrounded them. Denis Lambert, a cavalry officer serving in Hyderabad in 1935, would always remember the locals being allowed as a privilege to take home the rats they found in the stables to feed their families, and that the children would go through the horse dung with their teeth to pick out the undigested ears of grain.[28]

In 1945 many of the regiments that had fought in Burma with the 14th Army stayed on in India; the battalions of the Royal Norfolk Regiment, the Yorks and Lancs and the East Lancashire Regiment who restored order to Calcutta in August 1946 had all been in Burma the previous year. Although the longest-serving soldiers had already been sent back home under the scheme known as 'Operation Python', many soldiers who had been posted to their units more recently were still serving and keen to now be demobilised. Although post-war life for the soldiers in India was marginally better than it had been before 1939, it was still boring, hot and unattractive. It did not help much when, on 12 May, with consummate timing, the War Office decreed that canteen concessions and free airmail for British troops were being withdrawn.[29]

In 1946 the Army headquarters held an exercise called 'Embrace' to ascertain exactly how the military might deal with widespread civil unrest; it looked specifically at moving units quickly to trouble spots in the event of 'open insurrection' and a breakdown of law and order. Much of this was still geared to the protection of Europeans. Then in August 1946 Tuker's Eastern Command had intervened to stop the Great Calcutta Killings. They had used a mixture of British and Indian troops for this. Much of the security work was carried out by the British infantry, but they worked alongside Indian battalions such as the Rajputs, in other words soldiers from another part of India. They had also used the Gurkhas, the Nepalese battalions which formed such a major part of the Indian Army; by 1947 there were 32,440 of them serving in twenty-seven battalions. Six of these were deployed overseas but twenty-one battalions were available for public order duties in India.[30] Although mostly Hindus, the Gurkhas were considered non-partisan.

Early in 1947 Auchinleck's staff assembled the lessons the military had learned from the previous year and published a comprehensive all India 'Internal Security Instructions'. These took the 1938 and Chatfield recommendations, the results of Embrace and Tuker's reports and turned them into an overall plan. This specified a series of strongpoints linked by mobile patrols, minimising the former but maximising mobility so that troops could cover as much country as possible. Special plans were made for the security of the railways. Detailed proposals were included for the Punjab. The old Rawalpindi, Lahore and Meerut districts were to be closed down and a new headquarters established in Lahore responsible for the Northern Command area. Brigades were to be stationed in Rawalpindi, Lahore, Ambala and Ferozepore. A similar plan was made for Calcutta. Armoured trains were to be kept, not to be regarded 'as moving forts but as a means of moving quickly and safely from point to another'. There followed detailed instructions for how to ensure protection of vulnerable trains and the troops required to do so. The lines considered most at risk, and for which protection was carefully thought out, were the main Frontier routes from Delhi via Ambala, Julundur, Lahore and Rawalpindi to Peshawar and from Delhi to Landi Khana. The mobile British brigade groups, of which there were six totalling 30,000 men, together with 33,500 of the Royal Indian Air Force, of whom 11,273 were British, were considered vital to these operations.[31]

Despite all this work, the strong warnings coming from Sir Evan Jenkins in the Punjab that in the event of partition a force of at least four divisions would be needed, Caroe's call for extra troops for the Frontier and the experience of Sir Frederick Burrows and Sir Francis Tuker of using British and Indian troops together successfully in Bengal, Auchinleck now seemed fixated by the impossibility of dividing an army that was already organised to some extent on communal grounds and whose raison d'être was precisely the job the governors were demanding it should do. No wonder Mountbatten became frustrated. The anachronistic view that British troops were only there to protect Europeans remained prevalent among some of the senior staff, a continuing hangover from the Mutiny. This would soon have very serious consequences.

Much as the military authorities played down the effect of the Indian National Army, the relative ease with which it had managed to recruit soldiers from among Indians taken prisoner by the Japanese and from the Indian civilian population in Burma had been unsettling. Militarily the INA never posed any serious threat. Allied intelligence staff rated the effectiveness of an INA brigade, about 5,000 men, at the same as a Japanese company, about 70 men. Neither did the Japanese take them seriously, some commanders regarding them as little more than a nuisance. Captain Shah Nawaz Khan was an officer in the 1/14th Punjab Regiment who went over to the INA when he found himself in a Japanese prisoner-of-war camp. He was captivated by Bose and ended up as a senior INA commander. He kept a diary during his service. He was 'very disappointed at the type of work our soldiers have to do and their treatment by the Japanese'. He complained to his Japanese superior that his men were being treated as little more than labourers. On 4 July 1944, four Garhwalis died of starvation as they had not received any rations. Khan complained to Major Hikari Kikon but he did not seem to have taken the least notice. By 15 July, the men were beginning 'to die like flies, with some committing suicide' but the Japanese gave no help. In fact their answer to the shortage of rations was that 'our sick men at Terraun should commit suicide'.[32] All the time Bose was proclaiming that 'our long awaited march to Delhi has begun and with grim determination we shall continue that march until the tricolor national flag that is flying over the Arakan mountains is hoisted over Viceregal Lodge and until we hold our victory parade at the ancient red fort of Delhi'.[33]

When the Japanese tried to mount a clandestine mission to infiltrate some INA men back into India to stir up unrest, it was a fiasco. In April 1943 nineteen men were put on trial in Madras who had been landed in rubber boats from a Japanese submarine. They had been trained in the Japanese espionage school at Penang. All nineteen said they had been bribed to undertake the mission and had no intention of doing any spying once they had landed; they just wanted to get home. All had been working as civilians in Burma before the war rather than being prisoners of war. They had landed at night at Tanur on the Malabar Coast beside a Muslim village but as it was during Ramadan the whole village was awake and eating. Their cover story, that they were on a pleasure trip from Travancore and had landed to fix a leak in their boat, was predictably unconvincing and they were quickly arrested.[34]

The attitude of many INA soldiers was well summed up by a message from Supreme INA Headquarters in Rangoon in late 1944. 'One thing is certain, that we can expect little help from the Nippon authorities. The feeling of impotence and frustration for not being able to do anything to lessen the suffering of our comrades is terrible.'[35] But even if the INA was 'not a success in material terms, it strained the administrative resources of the Raj and contributed to its declining prestige'.[36] While its existence had no impact on the army's morale, D. K. Palit thought most soldiers had never even heard of it, its existence was uncomfortable politically.[37] Of the 60,000 Indian soldiers captured by the Japanese, approximately 20,000 had joined the INA, which was a discomfiting number. Even though Indian Army recruiting had been very successful in the early years of the war, it was difficult to sustain through into 1944 and 1945, by which time the Punjab alone had provided 700,000 men and the thriving wartime economy was providing more attractive alternative careers. By May 1944 one regiment was complaining that 'recruiting for the army is well nigh impossible when ordinary labour is so much more profitable'. Desertion became a serious issue. Even in 1943 it was running at about three thousand per month.[38]

The INA also had a deeper political impact. For the Congress leadership, who had seen their Quit India campaign of 1942 fail to gain real traction, the fact that so many of the men they had hoped would be campaigning for freedom had instead joined the British forces was galling. Gandhi was very direct about it. He told Wavell that he had 'fallen into the common error of describing the Indian forces as having been recruited by "voluntary enlistment"' when he believed that 'a person who takes to soldiering as a profession will enlist himself wherever he gets his market wage'. He was unhappy at the number of volunteers coming forward, and objected to the idea that they might in future fire on other Indians on British orders. 'Were those who carried out the Jallianwalla Bagh massacre volunteers', he asked, referring to Amritsar.[39]

Nehru was also much affected and his dislike and distrust of the military grew as he languished in jail while his countrymen fought for the very regime he was trying to overthrow. He did not like the idea of soldiering per se and never really understood the army; later as prime minister he would keep the military distant from power. 'The soldier drops his humanity and kills inoffensive and harmless persons who have done him no ill',[40] he wrote and he did not like the idea of the Indian Army being used to maintain internal order. He favoured expanding the police or creating a special Peace Preservation Corps instead, neither of which were practical ideas in 1947.[41] This was soon to have serious repercussions. Congress took its lead from Nehru. There was no single person in its high command who made any attempt to understand the armed forces or why they were such an essential part of India's fabric. To them the military remained a force of oppression, inextricably linked to the Raj. Patel

'Direct Action Day' in Calcutta, August 1946. Three days of rioting between rival Hindu and Muslim mobs left 5,000 people dead and 10,000 injured in what became known as The Great Calcutta Killing. The savagery appalled even soldiers hardened from fighting the Japanese in Burma.

The Bengal famine of 1942–44 caused the deaths of up to 3 million people, approximately six times the total of all other British Empire losses in the Second World War. One, against stiff competition, of the most disgraceful events of Empire, it showed not only that the Raj's administration had collapsed but that it had lost its remaining moral authority to govern. Here (above) starvation victims lie dying on Calcutta's streets, while (below) their emaciated bodies are burned.

The passing of the Rowlatt Acts of 1919 caused serious unrest to break out in the Punjab, already suffering from heavy recruitment during the 1914–18 war, increased taxation and epidemics. On 13 April, martial law was imposed. The same day Brigadier General Dyer (above left), the local British commander, ordered troops to open fire on a protesting crowd in the confined area of the Jallianwala Bagh; 379 were killed and over 1,000 wounded. Indians were made to crawl along a street in which a European woman had allegedly been molested (above right) and public flogging was instituted (below). Called 'a monstrous event' by Churchill, the Jallianwala Bagh massacre caused a major change in Indian attitudes to the Raj.

Mahatma Gandhi (above) as he is usually remembered, wearing homespun, carrying his staff and tramping rural India with his disciples. Although more marginal to the daily working of Congress by 1947, he was still hugely influential. When he visited Mountbatten (below), Edwina Mountbatten had to turn down the air conditioning in the viceroy's study so that the old man did not get pneumonia.

Auchinleck, Jinnah and Fatima Jinnah in 1947. The signs of the disease that would soon kill the Quaid are evident.

BLITZKRIEG.

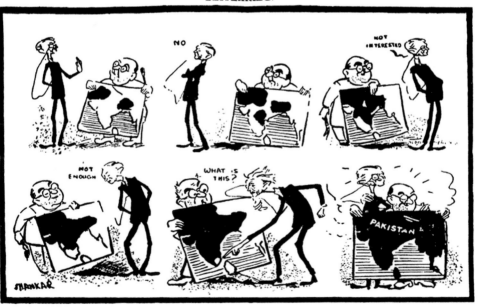

The popular Hindu view of Jinnah's ambitions for Pakistan. The cartoonist was more accurate than he realised. Jinnah wanted a federal arrangement, which would have included all India's Muslims rather than the 'moth-eaten' Pakistan he ultimately had to accept.

Dramatis Personae

V. P. Menon, who rose from lowly beginnings to become the architect of independence and of much of modern India.

Wavell in his study. A sincere and honourable man who had run out of energy and ideas by 1947, he represented an India that had all but disappeared.

Hamidullah, Nawab of Bhopal and Chancellor of the Chamber of Princes, who felt the British had betrayed the hereditary rulers.

Vallabhbhai Patel, the hard man of Congress, whose attitude to Pakistan was uncompromising.

A rose between two thorns, as Jinnah unfortunately remarked to the Mountbattens as this photograph was taken. He had thought that Edwina Mountbatten would be in the centre.

Sir Evan Jenkins, Governor of the Punjab, and one of the ablest servan of India. Had his warnings been heeded then much of the slaughter i the Punjab could have been avoided

Jawaharlal Nehru, visiting a refugee camp with Gandhi (above) and with Sir Stafford Cripps (below). Gandhi remained very influential on the Congress leader throughout 1947, while Nehru maintained direct links with Attlee's government in London via Cripps.

Soldiers

Auchinleck was popular and respected throughout the British Indian Army and was at his happiest chatting to its soldiers and their families. His devastation at having to break up the great institution he led would lead to serious strategic misjudgement.

State troops. The Maharajah of Rampur's forces stage a parade for Auchinleck. Armed with old-style muskets in 1947, as the maharajah had preferred to spend his budget on education, they played little part in events. Other state forces became actively partisan.

Subhas Chandra Bose struts past a female squad of INA in his jackboots. Early recruits had to swear an oath of loyalty to him based on that of the Waffen SS. Ineffective militarily, the INA were nevertheless a significant political force.

had begun to grasp that once in power Congress would have to deal with military issues, hence his intervention in the naval mutiny, but his thinking seems not to have extended to embracing the army's role in maintaining internal order.

Nehru was, however, although cautious in public, an early if equivocal supporter of Bose, despite their political differences, and of the INA. In 1945 he became a key part of the defence of the INA soldiers put on trial for treason in Delhi, defending Shah Nawaz Khan among others. The trials themselves were turned by Congress, supported by the League, into a propaganda coup. How, Nehru argued, could soldiers who had been fighting for India be guilty of treason? The first three, including Shah Nawaz Khan, a captain in the Indian Army although promoted to major general in the INA, were convicted of treason and sentenced to death but the ensuing public outcry meant the sentences were commuted to cashiering, or being thrown out of the army without any benefits. By 1947 twelve INA remained in jail, all of whom had been convicted of war crimes rather than treason; one had been sentenced for having an Indian soldier publicly flogged to death. However, Nehru supported by Liaquat, maintained his campaign to have even this remaining hand-ful released and was deaf to a plea from Attlee, who implored him not to undermine the morale of the army. The matter was still not resolved by April 1947, with a motion in the Assembly demanding their release, something Auchinleck and the army staunchly resisted.

The League was generally more supportive of the military. Muslims made up about 38 per cent of the Indian Army. However, it suited Jinnah and Liaquat to exaggerate this figure, reinforcing the link between the Muslims and the British and strengthening their argument that dividing the army would be very difficult; at one point Jinnah had claimed that the army was 65 to 70 per cent Muslim.[42] He had supported the 1945 Willcox proposals, which gave Muslims a greater share of jobs, and Liaquat wrote to Mountbatten on 7 April 1947 protesting, strongly, that the army was reducing Muslim numbers prior to partition.[43] The idea of a loyal Muslim element in the army being betrayed by the British leaving was quite widespread. Ismay reported that an old friend of his, a senior officer, greeted him when he arrived in Delhi in March with the words: '"We soldiers have trusted you for forty years, and now you are going to betray us". With that, he walked out of my room – and out of my life'.[44]

What really upset Auchinleck though was that 20,000 men of the British Indian Army should have changed sides in the first place, however brutal conditions were in the Japanese camps. He was now faced not only with doubts about the loyalty of the organisation that had been his home and his life since his late teens, but also the prospect of dividing and effectively finishing it off. Personally he had still not got over his divorce and the events of the next three months would see him having to work with politicians who disliked and distrusted everything he and his long career stood for. At a time when both the Indian Army and the British troops in India should have been fundamental to the planning and policing of what countless experienced people had warned would be a period of unparalleled violence, they instead marginalised themselves. Shahid Hamid claimed that Mountbatten constantly kept Auchinleck out of the loop, that he wasn't invited to the governors' conference and that 'at no stage did he consult the Auk when he was preparing the Plan. He seems to have no confidence in the Commander-in-Chief and is doing his level best to keep him in the dark'.[45] Even allowing for Hamid's strong prejudice against Mountbatten, relations were clearly uneasy. As the bloody and violent days of May ground on, there appeared to be an increasing reluctance from the key players to use the one force that might be able to enable the transfer of power to happen with minimal bloodshed.

Ismay arrived in London on 5 May and went almost immediately to brief the India and Burma Committee of the Cabinet. This group, chaired by Attlee and dominated by him and Cripps, also consisted of A. V. Alexander (defence secretary), Listowel (the new secretary for India) and Addison (Dominion Affairs and leader of the House of Lords). Although the full Cabinet would meet to discuss the plan, it was this small committee, together with Ismay and Mountbatten, they would be guided by.

Ismay started by emphasising that the communal feeling in India 'was far more bitter than he had expected and had become an obsession with both Hindus and Muslims'. He acknowledged that 'no one in India thought the plan was perfect. Yet nearly everyone agreed that it was the only solution that had any chance of being accepted by all political parties. It was not', he insisted, 'a gamble'. Critically, Ismay briefed, both Nehru and Jinnah were happy with it. It is one of the oddities of the British system that the government will send its best people overseas, tell them that they will be guided entirely by their recommendations but then proceed to try to outguess them on the detail of critical policies with very little understanding of the context. Both Attlee and Cripps thought they knew India well and they now proceeded to make seven amendments to a plan the staff in Viceroy's House had prepared in meticulous detail after hours of painstaking work. In fact the changes they asked for did not, as Ismay appreciated, change any of the fundamentals but they did give the impression that a meddling and out-of-touch British government was interfering in the nearest approximation to a plan for the smooth transfer of power as had yet been achieved.[46]

The next five days saw an endless stream of telegrams between Whitehall and Delhi as the Cabinet Committee's amendments were factored in. There wasn't now much secrecy about the plan itself. The *Hindustan Times* had somehow got hold of a copy and published it on its front page on 3 May. Mountbatten was justifiably furious. An investigation in Viceroy's House concluded that the culprit was either Nehru, Baldev Singh or Patel, most likely Patel who had probably acquired it from V. P. Menon. The accompanying leader read: 'For the first time since Lord Mountbatten assumed the Viceroyalty the feeling that he may not be playing fair has come among some Congress and Sikh leaders', and went on to get to the heart of what Congress was upset about. 'The Congress Working Committee made the Frontier question a test case. It has been made clear to the Viceroy that any proposals to dismiss the Frontier ministry and hold fresh elections will make Congress change its entire attitude towards the British government'.[47] Just when the British finally thought they had an agreed plan, Congress seemed determined not to give in to a plebiscite on the Frontier. They would now play Whitehall for two long weeks.

Meanwhile Mountbatten had taken Krishna Menon's advice and invited Nehru to stay with him at Viceregal Lodge in Simla, a welcome escape from the now terrible heat of Delhi. They arrived on the same day as Ismay arrived in London, and Krishna Menon came too. Opening the house had required 333 staff to be moved up from Delhi. While he was there Nehru was invited to attend several of Mountbatten's key staff meetings. It seems as if that week Congress, furious at the prospect of losing the Frontier, had decided to try one final onslaught on the Raj. Maybe, now they were so close to a solution, they could just persuade the British to leave immediately, handing over power to the Interim Government, in other words Congress, and leaving them to sort out Pakistan. Nehru put this forward to the viceroy's staff on 8 May. He said power should be 'demitted' to the Interim Government by the end of June 1947, in other words a year earlier than planned. The Interim Government would answer to the Constituent Assembly. The issue of Pakistan would be shelved and it would be left to the provinces to form groups, as originally envisaged in the Cabinet Mission Plan. Miéville, duly shocked, said the League would never accept this. Even Mountbatten's customary sangfroid momentarily lapsed.[48] Gandhi joined in the attack. Writing in his spidery handwriting to the viceroy while on a train to Patna he reiterated his personal opposition to partition in any form.[49] Patel led the international attack. On 9 May he told Associated Press that the British policy of 'remaining neutral, but holding power is a way of propagating civil war'. Power should be passed immediately to the Central [Interim] Government 'as it now stands'.[50]

It was, on the face of it, a fairly extraordinary last-minute attempt to undo the months of negotiation but the issue of the Frontier plebiscite went deep. Congress knew that without fresh elections, or a referendum, there was a chance that Dr Khan Sahib's ministry could swing the assembly behind Hindustan – behind India. Without the Frontier, Jinnah's Pakistan would be unsustainable. He could have it, as they had already decided, but it would not be long before they could re-assimilate the Sind and western Punjab back into a united India. And Nehru had not yet finished.

By 10 May, after five days of frantic exchanges, the Cabinet were ready to accept the plan. Draft announcements were prepared for both Whitehall and Delhi and a parliamentary timetable was worked out. The Cabinet's amendments had been included, and it had been decided, taking the advice of the governors, that the form the Frontier plebiscite should take would be a referendum rather than fresh elections to the Assembly. It was a compromise that still would not satisfy Congress, while in Punjab and Bengal it would be up to the assemblies to decide, both Jenkins and Burrows advising that holding referenda would be impractical. By the evening of 10 May Mountbatten had the final draft. He decided, on a hunch, to give a copy to Nehru that evening, unofficially and on a friendly basis, prior to it being formally briefed to India's political leaders. Mountbatten would later explain to Attlee that his experience in South East Asia Command (SEAC) 'had taught me that if I have a "hunch" it is best to follow it'.[51] Attlee may have read that reflection with a wry smile. Certainly the staff told Mountbatten it was a bad idea.

Mountbatten honestly described what happened next as a 'bombshell'.[52] He remembered Nehru, who had been through the plan with Krishna Menon, as being 'white with rage'.[53] Nehru himself admitted that he reacted to the proposals

very strongly. Indeed they produced a devastating effect upon me. The relatively simple proposals that we had previously discussed now appeared in the garb that HMG had provided for them, in an entirely new context which gave them an ominous meaning. The whole approach was completely different from what ours had been and the picture of India that emerged frightened me. HMG seems to function in an ivory tower of their own isolated from the realities of India.[54]

Genuine as Nehru's reaction undoubtedly was, and he could certainly flair up, it does seem a bit strange that he should profess to have been so shocked by a plan the substance of which he had certainly seen and which, even if he hadn't taken it all in, had already been on the front page of the newspapers. V. P. Menon talked to Patel, rather than Nehru, and it may have been that Patel was not passing enough information over. It may also have been in part contrived, commensurate with the scheme to see if Congress, still fuming over the Frontier, couldn't force a quick British exit. It was certainly partly because Nehru objected strongly to British civil servants sitting thousands of miles away fiddling with his country's future. It was arrogant of them to try. 'It is not possible for the British to devise an acceptable solution for India', he told Mountbatten's staff the next day.[55] But most of all it was because, as he said, the plan as presented did not stress the centrality of a unified India. It was written in such a way that it delivered

> not so much a union of India, from which states could later vote to secede but a 'large number of successor states'. People would think India was Balkanised. The proposals would only encourage chaos and disorder. The transfer of power would be obstructed by violence, by a mass of complications and by the weakness of the central government and its organs.

The provinces had too much freedom to choose; the idea that any, specifically Bengal, might choose independence was unacceptable. Pakistan must be seen to be secessionist, not a country on equal terms.[56]

Most proconsuls would have been cast down by such a strong and emotional rebuttal of the plan they had based their entire policy on, on which the prime minister and Cabinet were agreed and which even then was being prepared for referral to Parliament and briefing to the public, but that was not Mountbatten's style. Those who can find little good to say about his viceroyalty might reflect on his performance over the next fortnight. Telling his staff, correctly, that it was just as well he had consulted Nehru, he set V. P. Menon, who now becomes routinely referred to in official correspondence by the honorific 'Rao Bahadur', to redrafting, something on which he regularly consulted Vallabhbhai Patel. Meanwhile poor Ismay, alone and unbriefed in London, wondered what on earth was happening. 'Ministers here feel very much in the dark and I am unable to enlighten their darkness as I have been left out of touch with important developments that have taken place since I left', he complained with uncharacteristic frankness on 14 May.[57] Attlee too was becoming agitated. He liked Nehru, saw him as a fellow socialist, and was stung by his very direct criticism of his government. Mountbatten had sent Nehru's letter, in which he had rationalised and set out in full his reservations about the plan, back to London. 'I can't understand what Nehru means when he says that things that emerge from London are so peculiar', Attlee wrote and told Mountbatten that he should return to London to explain himself or the Cabinet would dispatch a further Cabinet Mission.[58]

Between 11 and 17 May, Rao Bahadur V. P. Menon, that extraordinarily able man who had worked his way up from manual labourer to the highest ranks of the Indian government, crafted the future of South Asia. Nehru's outburst had at least made the British realise what had been evident to many since the February announcement, that it was Congress who held the initiative; they were merely the ringmaster. Menon conferred with Patel and Nehru. The fundamentals of the plan remained but it would now be presented very differently. Gone was the idea that provinces like Bengal might choose independence; Suhrawardy had a last attempt to press his case on 16 May, telling Mountbatten that he and Sarat Chandra Bose thought the new country should be called 'The Socialist Republic of Bengal'. He was disappointed when it was pointed out that this might not be very well received, not least by Patel; he then compromised on the 'Free State of Bengal', which might have sounded slightly better but by that stage any idea of West Bengal and Calcutta not being an integral part of the new India had vanished.[59]

The plan that Mountbatten would now take back to London

presented the current Congress dominated Constituent Assembly as the successor state to the Raj, the new India, with the new, Pakistani, Constituent Assembly as a 'group of dissentient elements', those Congress were so sure would soon see sense and return to the fold. Provinces and the Princely states now had just two choices. They must join one or other of these two bodies, effectively becoming part of Hindustan, which Congress insisted on being called India, or Pakistan. Nehru and Patel discussed the plan fully with Mountbatten on 17 May with Rao Bahadur V. P. Menon present. Nehru, who wrote and spoke English with such clarity and emotion, confirmed what Congress had already decided some time ago, that they would 'accept proposals which involve a partition of India with great regret and in considerable agony of spirit' as 'we earnestly desire a peaceful settlement of our problems and the least compulsion of any group or area'.[60]

Later the same day Mountbatten met Jinnah and Liaquat. After rehearsing the same familiar arguments – their opposition to partitioning the Punjab and Bengal, their ability to accommodate for the Sikhs in an undivided Punjab, that the British could not leave so soon and that it would take at least four years to divide the army – Jinnah was left with very little choice. The Pakistan he had so long demanded was now being offered to him. It may, as he continued to describe it, be 'moth-eaten', it may exclude a huge number of India's Muslims, it may consist of two unconnected halves one thousand miles apart and it was certainly not the sharing of power in a federal India he had craved, but once Congress had denied that to him he was left with no alternative but to accept. In both meetings the date for the transfer of power comes up again; Mountbatten says it must now be by 1 October 1947 at the latest. There is no record of any disagreement.[61]

On 18 May Mountbatten returned to London. Nehru sent Krishna Menon back at the same time. The Cabinet were briefed, again, on 19 May with Mountbatten present. They agreed the plan, this time resisting the temptation to fiddle with it. They then agreed a parliamentary timetable and Attlee dispatched Mountbatten to find Churchill, as leader of the Conservative Party and therefore the Opposition, to see if he would support it. Mountbatten found Churchill, predictably, in bed. Grudgingly, and Mountbatten was of course his protégé, the man who had for so long resisted Indian independence, fought the 1935 Act, opposed Congress, reviled Gandhi and who saw the British Empire victorious in the recent war rather than being in decline, agreed.[62]

In India an intelligence report from Lahore provided a detailed breakdown of Sikh plans for their offensive against the Muslims in the Punjab, revealing that it was being funded by big business and the Maharajah of Patiala. The staff in Delhi commented it was 'ungraded', and therefore unreliable. On 22 May Jinnah told Reuters that the two parts of Pakistan must be joined by a land corridor across Northern India; Krishna Menon told Mountbatten that Congress just wanted to be rid of Jinnah. In London it was announced that the Indian political leaders were invited to a conference in Viceroy's House on 2 June.

6. JUNE

AN ACT FOR THE
INDEPENDENCE OF INDIA

*'It has been impossible to agree on any plan that
would preserve the unity of India'*

(MOUNTBATTEN)

Liaquat Ali Khan, himself an important Punjabi landowner,
returned from a fact-finding visit to Gurgaon late on 31 May. He
had been appalled at what he had seen. The violence was not, he told
Mountbatten, 'a spontaneous flare-up of communal feelings but a
planned, pre-meditated and well organised attack with the object of
completely suppressing the Muslim community of Meos numbering
about one million'.[1] What made matters worse was that the state
troops of Alwar and Bharatpur, two neighbouring Hindu Princely
states, had crossed the border into the Punjab and were helping the
Hindu lynch mobs. 'What is actually taking place is a large scale
invasion of the Muslim villages by thousands of armed and disci-
plined men',[2] Liaquat continued. The army had, as Auchinleck had
agreed, deployed a brigade but it was composed almost entirely of
Hindu troops. The regiments were behaving in a 'shameless and
atrocious manner'; one battalion had made four Muslims lie on their
backs and then driven heavy army lorries over them.[3] Unsurprisingly
the army reacted strongly to such accusations. Auchinleck pointed
out that of the brigade troops, one battalion were Gurkhas, who

were considered non-partisan, and although two others were entirely Hindu battalions from Madras and Kumaon, both the 3/15th Punjabis and the 6th Rajputana Rifles had Muslim companies. Liaquat replied, accurately, that both those Muslim companies had, for some reason, been left behind when the brigade deployed. Both Mountbatten and Auchinleck subsequently apologised[4] but not without Auchinleck complaining again to Ismay that he could not reorganise the army and at the same time maintain law and order.[5]

By 1 June about sixty Meo villages had been burned and over one hundred people killed, although the Meos continued to react with equal violence and 'did considerable execution' as Jenkins reported when he visited. The army was, slowly, beginning to get a grip on the situation and to stem the flow of armed men across the River Jumna, which formed the boundary with the United Provinces. An army patrol of a *naik* (corporal) and six men in the vicinity of the Meo village of Kardipur were suspicious that the nearby Hindu villages seemed to be being evacuated, correctly seeing it as a warning of impending trouble. They entered Kardipur, which was soon surrounded by a Hindu mob of 4,000 who got rather a shock to find this small force opposing them. The *naik* warned the mob that if they entered the village he would open fire but they ignored him, attacking with shotguns and home-made bombs. The *naik*, as good as his word, held his fire until the mob were within a hundred yards of the Kardipur village outskirts and then opened up. The fight went on for over an hour until military reinforcements arrived and the Hindu Jats melted away, carrying numerous dead with them.[6]

Jenkins was already preoccupied with the continuing violence in Amritsar and Lahore, where the arson was out of control, and, with daytime temperatures now reaching 47 degrees, the police were 'finding it rough'.[7] Nehru, whose mother was from Lahore and who had spent part of his childhood there, complained later in the month after visiting a refugee camp at Hardwar, that over one hundred Hindu properties in Lahore were being burnt every day. 'At this rate', he wrote, 'the city of Lahore will be just a heap of ashes'.[8] He reckoned there were already 32,000 refugees in the camp with 200 new arrivals daily.

Sandtas Kirpalani, an ICS officer, had recently been posted to Lahore into what he regarded as his dream job: financial commissioner in charge of the Punjab Canal Colonies. Although a Hindu from Karachi, he knew the Punjab well and had previously been responsible for Lyallpur. The Canal Colonies were those tracts of fertile land created by the government irrigation schemes on the upper reaches of the Punjab rivers. Because the land was reclaimed it belonged to the government which could therefore allocate it; much of it was consequently settled by ex-soldiers.[9] One such was Sant Singh, a veteran of the beaches at Gallipoli; he had considered himself very fortunate but his luck was about to change.

Kirpalani's family were not with him so he moved temporarily into the palatial residence, near the government officers' residential estate, of his friend and successful Lahore lawyer, J. G. Sethi. He appointed a Muslim as his bearer, noting that the rest of the household staff were Muslims apart from Sethi's own bearer who was an old Hindu, Rattan, someone he had known for twenty years. Almost immediately Rattan took him to one side to say that it was 'highly unwise' to have a Muslim bearer and begged him to intervene with Sethi to get all the Muslim staff sacked. Kirpalani, who had been abroad for some time, and who had been used to Lahore when it was a cosmopolitan mix of creeds and races, was shocked and disturbed. Then the Muslim ruler of Kharipur, a state in Sind, offered Sethi 600,000 rupees for his house. Why they wondered, did Kharipur need a house in Lahore? Sethi put it down to 'the old boy carrying a torch for a dancing girl in Amritsar'. Kirpalani was not satisfied with that rather simple explanation and urged Sethi to sell but his friend laughed off his concerns. Later that week Kirpalani refused to release government fuel demanded by the Muslim League. His deputy, a keen League supporter, then 'flew into a towering rage, accused me of anti-Muslim bias and warned me that it was but a matter of a few short weeks before the League assumed the reins of power in the province and that I would get short shrift'. He soon realised that Lahore was now a city of 'stabbing, looting and arson' where 'an unspoken terror gripped the populace'. The Sikh's curved sword, the kirpan, had become a symbol of death. Muslim squads on bicycles would ride up behind them, yank the kirpan out of its sheath, stab the victim, and then vanish before any help could arrive.[10]

Mountbatten and Ismay arrived back in Delhi on 31 May. Ismay vowed never to undertake a long flight with him ever again. 'The idea of a reasonable degree of comfort never entered his head. Speed was all that mattered', he complained, as they landed at midnight.[11] But there was a need to hurry. The Indian political leadership had been called to a meeting in Viceroy's House on Monday 2 June to give their final endorsement to the modified plan the viceroy had brought back with him and which was now given to them. Ismay woke up that morning feeling distinctly nervous. He sent Mountbatten a short note. 'This is like D-Day 1944', he wrote, 'and not less exciting: and I just wanted to send you this line of good cheer and good luck'.[12] Both Congress and the League were coming forward with amendments and reservations that could still wreck things and no one was sure how Gandhi would react. The meeting could end with agreement and a definite plan for the transfer of power, for the independence of India and the creation of Pakistan, or it could dissolve into argument and failure, much as had happened three weeks before at Simla.

At 10.00 a.m. they assembled in the viceroy's study, purposefully gathered around a small round table to create an atmosphere of fraternity. Nehru and Patel represented Congress, along with Congress president, Kripalani, whom Nehru had argued with Mountbatten should be included. Jinnah, Liaquat and Sardar Abdur Rab Nishtar, the Minister for Communications in the provisional government, represented the League while Baldev Singh represented the Sikhs. Ismay, Eric Miéville and that most articulate of soldiers, Vernon Erskine-Crum, who took the minutes that would create two nations, sat at the back. Interestingly, V. P. Menon, the architect of the plan, was not present.

Mountbatten was, once again, at his best.[13] He took the gathering through the history of the past five years, the Cabinet Mission Plan, to which the League would not assent, a point Jinnah immediately confirmed. He then emphasised that although he had arrived assuming that power should be handed over in accordance with Attlee's 20 February announcement, he now felt that June 1948 was far too late. Power, the British Cabinet believed, should be handed over as soon as possible. There was soon to be a major twist to this. He then came to partition. Congress objected to the partition of India but agreed that areas containing a Muslim majority should not 'be coerced into joining the existing Constituent Assembly', in other words to the partition of provinces; the League, on the other hand, demanded the partition of India but not of the provinces. Mountbatten explained that he had made it clear to his government 'the impossibility of fully accepting the principles of one side and not of the other'.

He then went to some lengths to explain that the question of India had become something of an issue between political parties in Westminster, with Churchill and the Conservatives still not fully supportive. The Indian leaders took this point in silence, realising that Churchill, to whom they ascribed the failure to achieve independence in 1935 and whom they regarded as no friend of India, was now all but irrelevant. Mountbatten then covered the need to look after the Sikh interest, something his government had concluded could only be achieved by partition of the Punjab and a carefully constructed Boundary Commission. Next he covered Calcutta and the question of Bengal. He went to surprising lengths to discuss whether there should be a referendum there, taking trouble to dismiss Jinnah's argument that the scheduled caste Hindus would support Muslim rule. Patel would have grimaced at this point; nothing would induce Congress to accept anything other than Calcutta remaining in India.

The viceroy then explained that power would be 'demitted on a Dominion status basis', in other words both India and Pakistan would become members of the British Commonwealth, an issue which had occupied much time in the past few months. It had, obviously, been pre-agreed, and offered a way of maintaining links and some sort of federated structure which would allow cooperation between the two new countries. Both countries would choose a governor general, at that stage envisaged as being the same person, and British officers could continue to serve in both the civilian administration and in the forces. It was on this basis that a bill was now being rushed through the Westminster Parliament, creating 'an all time world-wide legislative record'. The parliamentary session finished in late July and Attlee had given orders that it was to be passed by then, something that Churchill had assented to. Power should then be transferred as soon as possible thereafter, so not in June 1948 as everyone had thought, nor in January 1948, not even in the autumn of 1947 but in two and a half months' time, on 15 August.

The political leaders were all then asked to take copies of the plan and obtain the written agreement of their Working Committees that day in writing. Mountbatten said that he intended to broadcast the plan worldwide the next evening, 3 June, and Nehru, Jinnah and Baldev Singh should speak after him. Nehru and Patel agreed and Nehru undertook to do so. He said that 'there could never be full agreement of the plan from Congress, but, on balance, they accepted it'. Baldev Singh was reluctant to broadcast. He had nothing to say, he argued, and could not make up his mind to support the plan until he knew Congress and the League had agreed it. He was persuaded to change his mind and at least to make a call for violence to cease.

Jinnah demurred. He could not speak for the League Working Committee nor for the Muslim League Council which was due to meet later that week. It would be best to hear what they had to say rather than present them with a fait-accompli. He was also not sure whether he could respond to the viceroy in writing. He would, however, come to brief the viceroy verbally and he did, crucially, agree to broadcast the next day although he would not submit his speech beforehand despite much needling from Patel.

As the meeting broke up, Gandhi came in to see Mountbatten. It was the meeting both he and Ismay had been dreading but the old man declared that Mondays were his day of silence so he could not speak. Instead he handed Mountbatten a note, written on old envelopes with a stubby pencil. 'I am sorry I can't speak; when I took the decision about the Monday silence I did reserve two exceptions – about speaking to high functionaries on urgent matters or attending upon sick people'. There could hardly be a higher functionary than the viceroy, nor a matter more urgent than the future of India. 'But I know', Gandhi added tellingly, 'you do not want me to break my silence', although that did not stop him adding a postscript demanding once more that Mountbatten sack Caroe from the North West Frontier Province.[14]

The viceroy should not really have been surprised. The plan he had just briefed was, after all, Congress' plan, amended as Nehru and Patel wanted by V. P. Menon in those final days of May. All the British government had done was to put their stamp on it. Skilfully as Mountbatten and his team played its transmission, they were in fact just confirming what Congress had already decided, that what they thought would be temporary partition was the price worth paying for getting on with governing and for the preservation of a strong central government. Gandhi, for all his frequent spats with Nehru, was not going to upset that. The man who had not got what he wanted on 2 June was Jinnah who even now played for time.

He went back to see Mountbatten that evening as agreed. He immediately described the plan as 'scandalous'. He himself would reluctantly support it but he could not speak for the Muslim League Council. The best Mountbatten could squeeze out of him was a grudging acceptance that Attlee could go ahead with his planned announcement to the House of Commons the next day. But Jinnah could not really hide behind the League Council. It was he, as he had constantly reminded everyone, who was the 'sole spokesman'. In reality he had little choice but to accept this 'moth-eaten' Pakistan. 'He had no alternative', reflected V. P. Menon later, 'he had rejected so much so many times'.[15] 'Later that night', Ismay recorded, 'letters arrived from Kripalani, as Congress President, and Baldev Singh, accepting the plan',[16] although with some rather wild amendments. Jinnah could play for time no longer.

The next morning the same party reassembled in the viceroy's air-conditioned study overlooking the fabulous Moghul Gardens. Mountbatten opened by saying that all three parties had accepted the plan albeit with some proposed amendments which had no chance of being mutually acceptable so he saw no point in discussing them further. He therefore thought there was no reason that the plan could not now be made public. 'The Conference appeared to be quite happy to accept this somewhat naïve reasoning,' recorded Ismay and, critically, Jinnah remained silent. Mountbatten then distributed a thick thirty-page document entitled 'The Administrative Consequences of Partition'.[17] It had been drawn up by John Christie, Chaudhuri Mohammed Ali, who would later become Prime Minister of Pakistan, and H. M. Patel, both ICS officers. It explained the different parts of the Indian government and its bureaucracy that would need to be divided. It was a daunting list. Starting with the armed forces, it then covered government staff and their records, railways, post and telegraphs; broadcasting; civil aviation; meteorology; public works; tax; customs and excise; accounts and audit; scientific services; waterways; power; government buildings and installations; the Reserve Bank and currency holdings; jurisdiction and the courts; powers of domicile and diplomatic representation. It recommended a Partition Committee to undertake the management of this immense and complicated portfolio. Issuing this bulky dossier at this juncture was intended to concentrate minds on the reality of what partition actually meant. It certainly did so. The meeting broke up agreeing that the broadcasts would go ahead that evening.

It was a momentous evening for India. Mountbatten spoke first and well. 'For more than a hundred years, hundreds of millions of you have lived together, and this country had been administered as a single entity', he said, but

> it has been impossible to obtain agreement on any plan that would preserve the unity of India. But there can be no question of coercing any large areas in which one community has a majority to live against their will under a Government in which another community has a majority. The only alternative to coercion is partition. The whole plan may not be perfect but like all plans its success will depend on the spirit of goodwill in which it is carried out.[18]

After he had finished the full plan was read out in detail. It was the first time the whole country had heard definitively what Pakistan was to be, that there would be a plebiscite in the North West Frontier Province, that the assemblies in the Punjab and Bengal would decide on partition and then the future affiliation of their provinces, that the boundaries of the new countries would be decided by an independent Boundary Commission, that special arrangements would be made for Sylhet although not for Calcutta and that the armed forces would be divided. Nehru followed, speaking in English and Hindi. The proposals gave him no joy in his heart, he said, but he had no doubt that it was the correct course. 'It may be', he said, tellingly, 'that this way we reach that united India sooner than otherwise'.[19] He was followed by Jinnah who spoke in English. He was balanced, statesmanlike, paid tribute to Mountbatten's 'highest sense of fairness and impartiality' and seemed excited to be addressing 'the people through the medium of this powerful instrument'. It was the first time all but a handful of his 100 million followers had actually heard his voice. He prevaricated about the plan, saying its ultimate acceptance was a matter for the League Council, but went on to say that everyone should help ensure it was delivered in a peaceful and orderly manner. It wasn't quite full acceptance but it was taken to be so. His speech was well received. 'The Quaid's talk was masterly', noted Shahid Hamid approvingly, 'and in simple language which could be understood by the common man. He ended it with the words "*Pakistan Zindabad*". It was the first time this term was heard over the radio. It was good to hear'.[20] The speech was then translated into Urdu.

Baldev Singh spoke last and most prosaically. 'We have closed a dreary chapter', he said, 'and a new leaf is now turned. It would be untrue to say I am altogether happy. Seldom has a settlement like this been tarnished with so much fear and sorrow.' It did 'not please everybody in the Sikh community' but he urged its acceptance.[21]

The broadcasts on 3 June did not produce an immediate reaction. People wouldn't remember where they were that evening so much as they would later on 15 August. The plan was complicated and it took several days to understand exactly what it meant. Tuker produced an excellent two-page résumé for his soldiers, particularly concerned about the division of the army, but he over-optimistically ended it by saying that the leaders of both new states were bound to cooperate.[22] Many were elated that there was finally an agreement; others felt rather flat, as if acceptance of partition was a failure. Ratan Singh, a high-caste Hindu from Bikaner, wrote to the *Statesman* blaming his own kind. 'The Hindu must not eat food touched by the Muslims, nor allow them entry in their temples, not even as visitors. Such blind and discriminatory Hindu orthodoxy practiced for generations has ultimately led to this division. Unless Hindus learn to treat their Muslim brethren on an equal footing, socially and politically, this unfortunate division has come to stay.'[23] For Sandtas Kirpalani, in Lahore, his immediate thoughts were the horrors of partition. For others in positions of power it was the realisation that they had very little time. John Christie's magnum opus 'The Administrative Consequences of Partition' was but a brief summary of the enormous amount that now had to be done to create two nations out of one. Chaudhuri Mohammed Ali and H. M. Patel would run the Partition Committee and they started work that same day. On 4 June 'a calendar appeared on every official's desk with '70 days left to prepare for the Transfer of Power – and so on, in diminishing sequence', wrote Christie.[24]

The League Council finally met on 9 June in a secret session although not so secret that Patel hadn't been able to smuggle in a Congress spy who took full shorthand notes. The council said, predictably, that they could not agree to the partition of the Punjab and Bengal, but agreed that they must take the plan as a whole and gave Jinnah the authority 'to accept the fundamental principles of the plan as a compromise'. They would not, however, put their agreement in writing. Congress was furious. Why had Jinnah gone to the full council? And why did they now say the plan was just a compromise? That meant Congress should refer the plan to the full All-India Congress Committee. Patel demanded Jinnah should now give full acceptance in writing himself. Jinnah refused. Mountbatten then attempted a compromise, suggesting Jinnah write to him saying that he was authorised to accept the plan as a compromise settlement subject to the

All-India Congress Committee doing the same thing. Jinnah refused to sign any such letter until after the All-India Congress had actually decided. Mountbatten then decided to take responsibility himself, writing to Kripalani that Jinnah had given him a verbal undertaking. Next Gandhi seemed to be wavering. He went to see Mountbatten, who talked him round. Gandhi had always advocated leaving the choice to the Indian people, which was what the plan now did as far as it was practically possible. It allowed for the British to go and go quickly, exactly as the Mahatma had always urged. Dominion status retained the bonds of friendship. Gandhi was won over. When the All-India Congress Committee met on 14 June he also supported the plan. Peace in the country was, he argued, essential. He deplored partition but even he now realised that, however unpalatable, it was the best solution on offer. Nehru had prepared him well.[25]

The choice of 15 August as the date for Indian independence and the creation of Pakistan remains something of a dilemma. There is very little correspondence about it in official files. Mountbatten said later that he had decided on it off the top of his head as he was briefing the political leaders on 2 to 3 June and he mentioned it publicly on 4 June. He had chosen the 15 August as it was VJ Day, the day the Allies in South-East Asia declared victory over Japan in 1945. What is clear is that during the discussion with the Cabinet in late May there had been general agreement to Mountbatten's insistence that the handover be as soon as possible and that, from the Whitehall perspective, meant as soon as they could clear a bill through Parliament. Given the complexity of the bill, and even with Churchill's agreement not to oppose it, passage through both houses would still take until the end of July. Early to mid August was therefore the earliest possible date in legislative terms, which would seem to be why the date was chosen. It didn't turn out to be an inspired choice. Astrologers declared it an inauspicious day and the final programme had to be changed to accommodate their very powerful reservations.

But what it had done was create an extraordinarily short, and many would argue far too short, period in which to complete the mass of work necessary not only to decommission the Raj but to hand over its functions not to one government but two. Mountbatten will continue to be heavily criticised for trying to rush things, particularly by the British Raj officials and army officers, and by Pakistan, although not by many Indians. Paddy Massey spoke for many of his kind when he wrote, 'Mr. Attlee and Lord Mountbatten were not interested in a consensus – all they wanted was out, partly because of Socialist ideology and partly from American pressure. The Indian leaders did not realise this. Mountbatten only had the interests of Mr. Attlee at heart. Hence partition and a blood bath. Both were avoidable'.[26]

Others would say that Mountbatten just wanted to hand over as quickly as possible so he could return to his naval career but that is an unfair accusation, not least because he stayed on in India for nearly another year as governor general. More relevantly, it wasn't actually Mountbatten's decision, although again, in later life, he would perhaps ascribe greater powers to himself than he actually exercised. The decision had already been taken by Attlee and the Cabinet in late May, undoubtedly discussed in that informal but powerful clique of Attlee, Cripps, Krishna Menon and Nehru, which is why Congress did not demur when it was floated as a possibility in that first week of June. They wanted to govern as quickly as possible. Many fair-minded Indians, closer to the fear, the violence and the inter-communal hatred than the few remaining Raj officials, agreed that the sooner the better; if the British had tried to hold on any longer, with the shadow of what had only ever been a wafer-thin administration, civil war would have been inevitable. 'I have no time for people who blame Mountbatten', said the journalist and diplomat Prem Bhatia, whose family were to lose everything in Lahore. 'He was only carrying out orders and he thought the longer he waited the worse it would become and he may very well have been right.'[27] A. K. Damodaran, the Congress activist, intellectual and again a future Indian diplomat, thought the

Brits all feel Mountbatten rushed it – but many Indians felt that more people would have been killed if they had tried to stagger on for another year. Despite the Calcutta killings, the cosy Delhi elite had an overromantic view of the Punjab. They never expected

what happened. We took a very purist Hindu logical view of partition. In retrospect we were being too clever by half.[28]

But behind all this runs the hand of Nehru and of Patel. They
wanted to get on with governing. They wanted the British out and
they wanted them to go as quickly as possible. Nehru, with Gandhi's
strong support, had recently tried to get Mountbatten to consider
handing over in June. He never questioned 15 August; Congress was
impatient for power. Had the date not been Nehru's decision then
there would undoubtedly have been a major protest. There was none.
Mountbatten had little choice. He was merely once again putting
into practice what Congress wanted.

The major issues for resolution, initially run by the Partition
Committee of Christie, Chaudhuri Mohammed Ali and H. M. Patel,
were taken up from 12 June by a more senior Partition Council,
chaired by the viceroy and with Patel, Prasad, Liaquat and Nishtar
as full-time members; Nehru and Jinnah joined it on 27 June.[29] A
key issue was, assuming that the Punjab and Bengal did actually vote
for partition, how would the boundaries of the partitioned provinces
be decided? Whereas in Bengal the inter-communal divisions were
reasonably clear, with the respective communities living in areas
that were readily divisible, in the Punjab Hindus, Sikhs and Muslims
were intermixed, especially in the areas around Lahore, Jullundur,
Ferozepore and Amritsar. The matter was further complicated by
the important Sikh holy places in western Punjab, and the difficulty
of dividing the irrigation systems so that headwaters were not split
from the rivers they spawned. The plan involved establishing two
Boundary Commissions, one for the Punjab and one for Bengal,
which would also adjudicate on Assam and Sylhet. These were to
consist of an independent chairman with two Congress and two
League members each.

The idea was that each party would nominate men of 'high judi-
cial standing'. Congress responded quickly, putting forward Mr
Justice Mehr Chand Mahajan and Mr Justice Teja Singh, a Sikh, for
the Punjab and Mr Justices C. C. Biswas and Bijan Kumar Mukherji

for Bengal. It took the League longer to decide. In fact throughout these critical middle weeks of June the League comes over as an organisation reeling from the shock of now having to face up to the reality of just what creating a new country involved. It wasn't until two weeks later, and after some prompting, that they came forward with Mr Justices Din Mohammed and Mohammed Munir for the Punjab and Abu Saleh Mohammed Akram and S. A. Rahman for Bengal. They were unlucky men, charged with perhaps the most unenviable task in the history of India, deciding which side of the new boundaries their countrymen would live. Communities and families would inevitably have to be divided from their land, from each other and either move or become part of a nation that they felt they did not belong to. Unsurprisingly these eight judges ended up adjudicating along communal lines and much of the final decision-making rested with the Boundary Commission chairman, for both the Punjab and Bengal, Sir Cyril Radcliffe. Attlee had originally asked for a High Court judge to be chairman but, in a reply which showed a depressingly narrow appreciation of national priorities, Jowitt, the Lord Chancellor, said they were all far too busy.[30] Instead he recommended Radcliffe, a distinguished barrister who, Jowitt thought, might be prepared to do the job. He was coming to the end of a brilliant career, although, typically for the legal profession, the Lord Chancellor's initial concern was what fee he might earn, telling Listowel that he commanded over £60,000 per annum at the Bar. Radcliffe knew nothing of India, and was apolitical, but these were both arguably advantages as they meant that he would arrive with no preconceptions. Much to his credit, he agreed to take on this poisoned chalice and actually did so for a very modest fee. The final composition of the commissions was not, however, publicly announced until 30 June and Radcliffe did not arrive in the stifling heat of Delhi, where he was to work, until 8 July. That gave him approximately a month to draw lines on a map that would decide the fate of millions.

The votes in the Bengal Assembly on 20 June and in the Punjab on 23 June went as expected. Having divided into communal blocs as specified under the plan, the Hindu-dominated West Bengal bloc voted by 58 votes to 21 for partition; the Hindus, who had so vociferously and violently opposed Curzon's partition plan in 1905 were now determined that they, and Calcutta, would remain part of India. The East Bengal Assembly members predictably voted 106 to 35 that the province should not be divided. Having been outvoted on that, they then voted 107 to 34 that East Bengal should join Pakistan and by 105 to 34 that Sylhet should be amalgamated with the new state. In the Punjab, amid tight security, with the 'approaches blocked by barbed wire barriers and the vicinity under heavy police guard' and 'with large sections of Lahore and scores of villages throughout the province fire blackened ruins',[31] the 168 members of the Legislative Assembly cast their votes. The East Punjab members rejected a motion put by the League's leader, the Khan of Mamdot, that they should remain a united province, voting by 50 to 22 for partition and to join India. The West Punjab members predictably rejected partition but, accepting that it was now inevitable, a majority of 91 decided to join Pakistan.[32]

The next major issue to resolve was how to divide the armed forces. On 12 June an Armed Forces Committee was established as part of the Partition Council, both Nehru and Liaquat insisting that the process should be under tight political control and that Auchinleck should be accountable to them. The principles were straightforward and had in fact already been thought through and summarised in an Indian Office paper on 27 May.[33] It was agreed that troops should be moved so that by 15 August the maximum number 'would be located in the state to which they belonged, that is in either of the two Pakistan states or in the rest of India'.[34] Muslim units would be transferred to Pakistan, Hindu and Sikh units would remain in India. The Willcox Committee, however flawed its concept, had at least made that division relatively easy. In the navy, air force and the army's supply services, where classes and creeds were all mixed, individual soldiers could choose; no Muslim would be forced to serve Pakistan nor any Hindu forced to serve India. The new Pakistan Army was to be based around Headquarters Northern

Command in Rawalpindi, which would move to Karachi while the Indian Army would be based on Central Command in Meerut, which would move to Delhi, with subordinate headquarters initially at Poona, near Bombay, and at Ranchi in Bihar.

The Royal Indian Navy ships would be divided, thirty-two to India and sixteen to Pakistan. Royal Indian Air Force aircraft were to be divided on a squadron basis. In the army the division was roughly two thirds to India and one third to Pakistan, so India received twelve armoured regiments against Pakistan's six, and seventy-five infantry battalions against thirty-five for Pakistan. This roughly reflected the army's communal make up of 70 per cent Hindu and Sikh versus 30 per cent Muslim, despite Jinnah's attempts to argue that the Muslim percentage was higher.[35]

Simple as all this might seem, it did not of course reflect the emotional issue of dividing regiments which had served together for decades, including through the recent war, and who rightly prided themselves on their communal harmony. 'At regimental level, as throughout the army, there was a sad, indeed a grim feeling of frustration and doubt, anxieties both general and personal for the immediate future extended to all ranks, including the British officers', wrote Captain Pocock of the 19th Lancers.[36] Sixteen British officers had already been posted out, most found places in regiments in the British Army, and they had been replaced by 'young and inexperienced officers both Hindu and Muslim'. The 19th Lancers were stationed in Peshawar and were to become part of the new Pakistan Army. Now not only would those new Hindu officers have to leave but so would their Sikh and Jat squadrons. The Sikhs were to go to Skinner's Horse and the Hindu Jats to the Central India Horse, both to become Indian regiments. The Muslim squadrons from the Poona Horse and the Central India Horse would move to Peshawar to become the 19th Lancers. Their journeys were to prove almost as dangerous as fighting the Japanese in Burma. The tensions had already caused the British officers to send all the regimental silver back to England, an unpopular and tactless decision. It was not finally returned to Pakistan until 1950.

'There was very little Muslim/Hindu antipathy in the army', recalled D. K. Dalit of the Baluch Regiment, the officer who had assisted with famine relief in Bengal, 'but we were very sad at losing each other. But those who felt we could have one army were unrealistic and people buckled to and reconstructed. Quite a few Hindus opted to stay with their regiments in Pakistan but most eventually came back to India. In my battalion, the sixth, we had three Muslim companies – one of Pathans and two of Punjabi Muslims, and one company of Brahmins' who went back to India. Dalit himself was posted to command an Indian Gurkha battalion. He took it over from a British commanding officer, David Armor, but the rest of the British officers still in post were resentful of him and behaved badly. Again they were packing up all their silver, as if the regimental tradition would end with the Raj, and Dalit had to appeal to the honorary colonel to have it returned. He then asked all British officers to leave immediately.[37]

K. P. Candeth, the Indian artillery officer, thought that although initially nearly every officer was against dividing the army, having grown up together in their regiments and with deep unit loyalty, they began to realise during 1946, given the violence and as the political atmosphere became toxic, that 'one class' armies were inevitable. His regiment was stationed in the West Punjab and was made up of Punjabi Brahmins and Punjabi Muslims. The Brahmins started to lose family in the March killings and resentment grew against his Muslim soldiers. The Muslims left in July so that by 15 August, when the regiment was stationed back in India, it was an almost entirely Brahmin unit. They would soon be heavily involved in trying to police their homeland.

The reorganisation also meant that just when the army should have been at its busiest maintaining order it would be consumed with reorganising itself. It was, however, always made clear, and agreed by the leaders at their 3 June meeting and again at the Partition Council on 16 June, that the needs of internal security should take precedence.[38] Auchinleck was told to 'impress upon the Provincial Governments on behalf of the Partition Council the need to reduce to the absolute minimum the number of troops they required'. He did so constantly and too eagerly, his heart never really being in using his beloved army to do what was arguably its primary role.

The British also had the very clear notion, which does not appear to have been fully taken in by either Nehru or Liaquat, who tended to lead for Jinnah on military matters, that both the new armies would remain under a central Supreme Commander, initially Auchinleck, with a 'Central Administrative Machinery'. This would answer to a Joint Defence Council to be chaired by the governor general. This was partly because of the realisation that they would need to deploy troops on a joint basis during the coming months, partly to sweep up the endless administrative issues that division entailed but also because there was a feeling the two new nations would be able to work together in some sort of federated way on matters that involved the armed forces. Looking back it may seem naive; at the time it was a worthy objective and shows just how far the coming holocaust would cause relations to break down.

It was also seen as a natural extension of the Dominion status, which was consuming so much political time. If both states were members of the Commonwealth, and acknowledged the King's role as its head, even if his style of address had to be changed so there was no mention of him being an 'emperor', a word India justifiably hated, then it would be possible for British officers to stay on and help the new armies find their feet. There were very few senior Indian officers, with only one major general, the forthright and charismatic K. M. Cariappa, who spoke no Hindi so only communicated with his soldiers in English, and still dressed formally for dinner every night even when dining alone. Only 5 per cent of the brigadiers and 10 per cent of the colonels were Indian. At the beginning of June there were still 8,200 British officers serving in the Indian Army, 630 in the air force and 240 in the navy.[39]

Liaquat had persistently said that Pakistan would like British officers to stay on, a request which had formed part of the League's negotiating tactics. Nehru was more circumspect. His dislike of the army was still occasionally boiling over. During his visit to the

Punjab on 22 June he had 'lost control of himself and demanded the sacking of every officer from the Governor downwards' and Patel made the by now rather stale comment that the 'Brits had no difficulty in maintaining law and order when putting down Congress and the Freedom Movement'.[40] Auchinleck commented acidly that he didn't think many officers would want to stay on in India given speeches like that and 'the mistrustful attitude frequently adopted towards them'.[41]

Field Marshal Montgomery, then Chief of the Imperial General Staff and Britain's most senior soldier, now decided to intervene in this already complicated debate. He had no business being in India, which was acknowledged as very much the commander-in-chief's domain, added to which Auchinleck heartily loathed him for the tactless way he had taken over from him command of 8th Army in North Africa. He now took it upon himself to visit Delhi and interview Nehru, who was remarkably gracious in the circumstances. Montgomery had two questions. The first was how India would react should the British retain Gurkha regiments in the British Army as opposed to the Indian Army. This may have seemed a strange thing to ask, given that the Gurkhas were recruited from Nepal, an independent country, but they would be dependent on India for transport and support. Nehru disliked the Gurkhas even more than most soldiers. He told Montgomery that they were unpopular troops as they had been used for 'imperial purposes. A year ago they had come into conflict with the Indonesians and caused much resentment'. Retaining them in the British Army could appear as a 'continuation of the old imperialist method of holding down colonial territories'. He strongly opposed using such soldiers 'against people struggling for freedom'. He was also suspicious that the British might continue recruiting in Pakistan. Ultimately he did agree, partly because the Indians wanted to retain Gurkhas in their own army, and an allocation was agreed of six regiments staying with the Indian Army and four to the British, although so many individual Gurkhas wanted to stay in India that the Indian Army subsequently soon had to create extra regiments.[42]

Among the Gurkhas themselves there was considerable anger at how the selection of regiments was handled. J. P. Cross was sure his 1st King George V's Own Gurkha Rifles would go to the British Army being the most senior regiment. 'Bitter indeed was our disappointment at not being chosen', he recorded, 'we could not understand how and why we had been omitted from the list'. It appeared that the decision was, typically, largely financial, it being cheaper to take those regiments with a battalion outside India into the British Army. 'We knew', he continued, 'that it could not have been on merit. We officers were left without positive directions so could give none. Pressure of events obscured the heartbreak. Nor was there any properly planned handover to Indian officers. They never came till after the bitter end and the end was bitter'.[43]

Montgomery's second question was put to both Nehru and Jinnah. When did they want British troops to leave? The consensus was by February 1948 although Jinnah again requested that British soldiers should stay on to serve with the new Pakistan Army.[44] Auchinleck was, predictably, furious, pointing out that it was up to him to make arrangements for the future of British troops in India.[45] But Montgomery's question touched on a wider issue, which was what were British troops to do in the meantime? There was still, even by June, the feeling that they were primarily in India to protect Europeans but there were a lot of them, over 30,000, they were well equipped, mobile and had already been most effective in internal security duties as they were seen as impartial by most people, if not by Nehru. There was considerable correspondence between Whitehall and Delhi on the subject, which came to the conclusion that they should not be used for internal security duties after 15 August unless requested to do so by the new governments. In the meantime they sweated, bored in their barrack blocks, relishing the chance to get out and put down the odd riot.

There were the inevitable disagreements in the Armed Forces Committee, many of which were sorted out by Sir Chandulal Trivedi, the governor of Orissa, who Mountbatten drafted in as a troubleshooter after having one of his 'brainwaves'. Trivedi was a good choice. A life-long friend of Liaquat, he was also trusted by both Nehru and Patel and had been secretary of the Defence Department during the war. After eight days negotiating he got the committee's final report agreed by all sides so that when it came to the Partition Council on 30 June it 'went off more smoothly than any meeting' Mountbatten had seen.[46]

There is no doubt that the reorganisation of the army was a considerable administrative achievement. However, armies are well used to moving and regrouping, and much of it stayed put. Throughout June and July Auchinleck would argue that he could not guarantee that the army would 'retain its cohesion or remain a reliable instrument for use to aid the civil power in the event of widespread disturbances during this period of reconstitution'[47] yet he still had his British soldiers and the Gurkhas, both unaffected by communal issues, and numbering nearly 65,000, and, at least in India the Dogras and Garhwalis, single-class regiments. Southern Command, in Madras, for example, had thirty deployable British battalion-sized units, seven Gurkha and thirty-nine Indian, many of whom were single class.

In Westminster Attlee was doing his best to get the Indian Independence Bill through Parliament. The Labour majority and Conservative acquiescence made its passage a foregone conclusion, but the drafting was complex and even now Churchill tried to have one last dig at it. He objected to it being called an 'independence' bill. His agreement had been based on the acceptance of Dominion status and he wrote to Attlee on 1 July suggesting that the bill would be better styled as the 'Self Government Bill' with both India and Pakistan becoming 'two self-governing dominions'.[48] The parliamentary authorities then said it was unthinkable in protocol terms to give Nehru and Jinnah advance copies of the bill, and it took Mountbatten to intervene directly with Attlee to ensure they were. The princes, fearful as to what the future might hold under Congress, were also lobbying in London and using all their Conservative Party contacts.[49] Dominion status had also raised the delicate and esoteric issue of what to do with the monarch's crown as Emperor of India. It had been purchased for the 1911 Durbar at a cost of £60,000, paid for by India. It couldn't exactly be divided so the decision was that it should stay in London.[50]

Nehru was finding the British as difficult as ever during those June weeks, and despite both he and Mountbatten working hard at their relationship there were the inevitable flare-ups. He would frequently lose control in meetings. Mountbatten thought Nehru was not sleeping and that he was 'under very great strain'.[51] The Frontier issue still rankled badly with Congress. Khan Abdul Ghaffar Khan and the North West Frontier Province Congress party were openly urging people 'who believed in a free Pathan state' not to vote in the coming referendum. Mountbatten remonstrated with Nehru for saying in a press interview that Congress would probably boycott the referendum anyway,[52] although he did finally give in to his and Gandhi's demands that he sack Caroe. He wrote to Caroe on 6 June, a nice letter suggesting that, as all British governors would have to retire on 15 August anyway, perhaps he could go on leave until then? It would really help, he explained, to strengthen his hand with Congress.[53] Caroe accepted his fate 'with deep sorrow' but with good grace and went on holiday to Kashmir. Nehru was delighted. 'The part Sir Olaf played as Deputy Commissioner in Peshawar in 1930 when there was large-scale shooting and killing of peaceful demonstrators still evokes bitter memories', he noted,[54] although the League predictably immediately objected. Caroe's successor was Lieutenant General Sir Robert Lockhart, who had been running Southern Command. His immediate concern was preparing for the referendum, planned for 6 to 17 July with a Congress ministry still in power who were violently opposed to it happening at all. The solution was to draft in a team of British army officers who knew the Frontier and get them to run it instead.

Nehru and Mountbatten did, however, agree on the important issue of who should be the governor general. Another advantage Dominion status offered was that it meant there could be a governor general, a very different role to the pre-independence viceroy, who was also a colonial governor general, and more similar to the governors general in Canada and Australia. The role carried no real political power, and would be largely ceremonial, but could, it was hoped, act as an arbiter between the two new states until the full process of partition had been completed if so required. In June 1947, and particularly given the joint command structure envisaged for the armed forces, it seemed sensible that one person should combine this role for both India and Pakistan, thus keeping them in some sort of federated structure, however loose. Constitutionally it again made it easier for British officers to stay on with both the new administrations. Nehru had invited Mountbatten to be the first Governor General of India and it was assumed that Jinnah would extend the same invitation from Pakistan.

By 23 June no answer had been received from Jinnah. He had already been making approaches to secure British officers as both provincial governors and as chiefs of the new armed services but remained silent on the issue of the governor general. Mountbatten was uneasy and prompted him for a definite reply.[55] He had accepted the Indian offer on the understanding that he would also be asked by Pakistan and therefore able to carry out a useful function but on 2 July, Jinnah told him that he was going to be governor general himself. It was, in a history of fractious meetings between the two men, the worst so far. Mountbatten asked Jinnah if he realised what this might cost him, given that there would be no one person arbitrating the continued division of assets. Jinnah replied that, 'It may well cost me several crores of rupees in assets' to which Mountbatten replied acidly, 'It may well cost you the whole of your assets and the future of Pakistan'. Mountbatten then got up and left the room.[56]

It is difficult to understand Jinnah's logic until one appreciates something that he alone knew at that stage. He was dying. His tuberculosis, not improved by his chain-smoking and drinking, was slowly killing him. He could not possibly have let this be known publicly. The whole idea of Pakistan was embodied in his person. However small-minded his decision seemed at the time, and it produced a furious reaction in Delhi and London, he undoubtedly felt he was not well enough to take on the enormous responsibility of being premier of a new country, split as it was by a thousand miles. He probably also thought that establishing Liaquat in that role while he was still alive and able to support him would give Pakistan a stable start. Mountbatten's detractors say that Mountbatten's reaction was caused by wounded pride but again that is not entirely fair. The logic in having one combined governor general was inescapable and would soon be proven in the bloodiest of circumstances. There was nothing for Mountbatten to gain personally although he was now faced with the issue of whether he should refuse the Indian offer, based, as it was, on the envisaged combination of role. After much soul-searching, consultation, and a masterly paper crafted by Vernon Erskine-Crum setting out the advantages and disadvantages of him accepting, the unanimous advice of King, prime minister and Cabinet was that he should still accept. He duly did so.[57]

CUIUS REGIO

*'How can we, the Rulers of Independent States,
throw in our lot with a political party whose
resolution is that India should become a republic?'*

(NAWAB OF BHOPAL)

Lieutenant Colonel Mohindar Singh Chopra was one of the handful
of Indian officers who, in 1927, had been educated at Sandhurst
alongside his very good friend Mohammed Ayub Khan, who would
go on to be both prime minister and president of Pakistan. Singh
Chopra had a distinguished record of service, had fought in the
Frontier campaigns of the 1930s with what was nicknamed the
PIFFER Group, one of those forces the British were so good at assembling for irregular warfare, and raised a battalion of Frontier Force
Rifles deep behind Japanese lines in Burma during the war. In early
1947 he was ordered to leave his comfortable post at Ambala, 120
miles north of Delhi on the Grand Trunk Road, and move, with his
family, to Shillong, the capital of Assam, to assume command of the
1st Battalion of the Assam Regiment. His young daughter remembered the excitement of the journey, the three-hour crossing of the
mighty Brahmaputra river, moving from the heat of the plains to the
'Assam Hills with their evergreen forests, full of flora seldom seen
in the north', and the charm of Shillong 'an extremely picturesque
and English-looking town'.[1]

No sooner had Mohindar Singh Chopra taken over his battalion than they were moved to Sylhet to support the referendum; although the East Bengal Assembly members had voted overwhelmingly for Sylhet to join their side of the soon to be partitioned province, part of the 3 June provisions was that there should be a referendum in Sylhet to confirm that this was what the people wanted. It was scheduled for 6 and 7 July and there was already considerable agitation by both Congress and, even more so, by the League, as they campaigned. Being an area with a large Muslim majority, the League had the upper hand and Singh felt that 'Congress supporters definitely have the wind up'. Singh assumed command of a force of nearly two thousand men, partly infantry of his own Assam Regiment and partly transport troops, with a sizeable amphibious element, given that the easiest way to travel around the area was by water. The League, raw from their experience in Gurgaon, demanded that at least half Singh's force be Muslim. Singh retorted, with some pleasure, that 75 per cent were either Christian or Animist.

There were 239 polling stations and Singh had his soldiers conduct regular patrols around them accompanied by the local police. Carrying weapons had been banned on 3 July and in the event the referendum went off smoothly, although not without Congress accusations of foul play. The result was, predictably, a massive vote in favour of joining East Bengal. Apart from Singh's frustration, when he had requested wellingtons for his soldiers operating in the soaking ground, at finding the army had then sent 13,000 left-footed ones, the whole process was judged a success. The planning and cooperation between the governor, Sir Akbar Hydari, who had taken over from Clow only the month before, his staff, the administration in Sylhet, the police and the army had been good. The first planning meeting had only been held on 20 June but two weeks later they had been able to hold a successful referendum across a huge area with difficult terrain and amid inter-communal friction. It was an experience Singh would remember wistfully when he found himself six weeks later in the Punjab.[2]

*

On 17 June, Jinnah had announced that the capital of Pakistan would be Karachi, the port on the Indian Ocean that was also the capital of Sind. The capital of East Pakistan would be Dacca, but Jinnah was finding it difficult to recruit a British governor. He first tried Lord Killearn, who refused; next he asked Sir Archibald Rowlands, who did not reply. He then asked Mountbatten to approach Sir Frederick Bourne, who accepted and was currently searching for a house suitable to his new status. Several of the League's influential supporters were annoyed about Karachi. Apart from Liaquat himself, men like Sir Muhammad Zafrullah Khan, a big League donor, and Malik Ghulam Mohammad, an important and aspiring League supporter, were Punjabis and there had been a assumption, given that Lahore was already the capital of the Punjab, that Rawalpindi would be chosen. There was a certain regional snobbery that made Punjabis look down on the Sindhis and not many relished leaving the Punjab's dry and relatively agreeable climate for the unhealthy humidity of Karachi.

Almost all the best property in Karachi belonged to Hindus or Parsis and was not easily available. Santdas Kirpalani went down to stay with his brother who had an important steel-importing business there and who lived in great splendour in the seafront area of Clifton. Having seen what was happening in Lahore he begged him to move but his brother, a close friend of the Premier of Sind, Sir Ghulam Hussain Hidayatullah, told him he was scaremongering and Sir Ghulam, 'a massive hulk of a man', had promised to protect him. Within weeks Kirpalani's brother had lost both his steel stocks and his house, which was requisitioned for a fraction of its value, a mere 300,000 rupees, something even the well-intentioned Sir Ghulam could not stop. Kirpalani's sister also lived in Karachi. Her house was requisitioned too. A truck was sent to remove her furniture. Her sixteen-year-old son tried to remonstrate and blocked its passage. He was run over and killed. Kirpalani's sister somehow blamed him for the boy's death and would not speak to him.

Liaquat had, not unreasonably, asked in the Partition Council that one of the six government printing presses be moved to Karachi so that Pakistan could start the business of government. In one of the petty rows that was to so damage relations over the next few months, Patel 'flared up and said all the presses were fully occupied with Government of India work and none could be spared'. When asked to reconsider this somewhat unhelpful answer he shouted, 'No one asked Pakistan to secede'. Mountbatten, who was present at this exchange, thought that, 'It was a shocking spirit in which to start partition'.[3]

Nehru was in as tense a mood as Patel but what was concerning them both was not the detail of dividing printing presses but the more substantial issue of what would happen to the Princely states, those mini kingdoms that occupied half the landmass of India and where lived a quarter of her population. The 3 June plan had been remarkably vague as to their future. It simply said that 'paramountcy', the relationship that ensured their allegiance to the British crown, the 'Paramount Power', would lapse on independence and that the states should enter into a federal arrangement with the successor governments. But not all the princes saw things that way.

There was, as with so much in British India, little logic to the pattern of the Princely states. Some, such as the great Rajput states like Jaipur, Jodhpur and Udaipur, were immensely old. The rulers of Udaipur were of such ancient and respected lineage that they claimed descent from the sun; the first portrait in the long line of portraits in the maharajah's dining room was a cheerful portrait of a radiant sun shining in all its glory. Most, however, originated from the break-up of the Moghul empire when its satraps had simply assumed ruling powers in the territories they were responsible for. The Nizams of Hyderabad, who ruled their vast central Indian territory of 82,000 square miles and 16 million subjects, had been the Moghul viceroys of the Deccan. The East India Company, whose interest was purely commercial and whose early governors found the business of government tiresome, allied themselves with successive states according to where they perceived the most profitable arrangements to be. Initially they made treaties with Hyderabad and Oudh as they fought the French. Later they fought Mysore and the Maratha chiefs as they needed to establish commercial dominance in central and southern

India. The favourite possession of Tippu Sultan, the ruler of Mysore, who was defeated and killed by Wellington (later of Waterloo fame) in 1799, was a mechanical model which showed a tiger devouring a British East India Company red-coated soldier.

Most princes were happy to make arrangements with the company. They were left to rule more or less in peace and found the Company's condition that they should accept British military protection not inconvenient. However, and as with so much in the decades leading up to the Mutiny, an increasingly moralistic Company began to question why they were protecting regimes that were largely feudal and in many cases medieval in their practices. One of the sparks that finally ignited the resentment that caused the Mutiny was Dalhousie's annexation of Oudh on the grounds of mismanagement, something he was clearly warned by old India hands would be highly unpopular. This was appreciated in the post-Mutiny settlement and Queen Victoria's 1858 declaration stated very clearly that 'We shall respect the rights, dignity and honour of the native princes as our own'.[4] The crown would continue to exercise 'paramountcy' and posted Residents to the princes' courts but they were in practice little more than observers who were happy to be well provided with tigers and ducks to shoot and who were advised that 'often not the least valuable part of their work was that which they left undone'.[5] They put little, if any, pressure on the princes to introduce representative government and in turn, as the agitation against the Raj grew, the princes began to realise that their interests were best served by the continuing British presence. They also appreciated the British emphasis on display and pageantry in government, important in India, and the assistance they received with their state forces, something they amply repaid in their wartime service. It was, however, a curious position for the nation that boasted to be the mother of all democracies to preserve and protect autocracy over half its Indian empire.

In the post-First World War reforms a Chamber of Princes was introduced into the Central Assembly, a sort of House of Lords but consisting of people who still wielded considerable power. Congress were more circumspect towards them as a group than may have been supposed for a republican party. Although Indian politicians saw the hypocrisy in concentrating their campaign just on the British provinces, the princes were at least Indians. India had long been comfortable with the tradition of personal rule and family dynasties; it would in fact continue long after independence with Nehru's own family. Gandhi himself had grown up in a small Princely state and his family had been employed by the ruler. Yet there was an assumption by both Congress and the majority of princes themselves that when independence came they would be swept up into the new democracy. At the 1932 Round Table Conference they suggested that they join the new India on a federal basis, something eagerly seized on at the time and which, although it would later prove an anathema to Nehru, was used by the more pro-independence lobby in Westminster to encourage the conservative opposition. A federation of Princely states and self-governing provinces would not, they argued, be so much of a threat to British interests. The 1935 Act progressed very much on this basis.

In 1938 Gandhi did turn on them, partly because the princes' bloc vote in the Assembly was preventing Congress from controlling the Lower Chamber. He told them that they had better 'cultivate friendly relations with the organisation which bids fair in the future, not very distant, to replace the Paramount Power'.[6] Congress agitated in Jaipur, leading a civil disobedience campaign there and Gandhi started one of his many fasts to promote political reform in Rajkot. Yet it didn't last very long. By 1939 Gandhi had called off all Congress campaigns in the states and even apologised to the Maharajah of Jaipur. He was worried that the campaigns could have caused communal violence, especially in Hyderabad and Kashmir and, again, appreciated that Congress' first priority was to get rid of the Raj. The princes could wait.

By June 1947 there were 108 major states in India, whose rulers, autocrats over 60 million people, were automatically entitled to sit in the Chamber of Princes. Next came 127 middling states, who were represented by twelve elected members. The remaining 325 states were really just large private landholdings and were not considered as political entities. The chancellor of the Chamber of Princes, the Nawab of Bhopal until he resigned in disgust in June, was a powerful man in government circles and was assisted by a political department, the focus for the Residents, and run by the uncompromising royalist Sir Conrad Corfield, someone for whom Nehru reserved particular scorn.

The princes were not only powerful but many were also spectacularly rich, wealth being a useful by-product of autocracy. The Nizam was reputed to be the richest, and the meanest, man in the world. Given, as he would say, that he did not have to impress anyone, he would habitually dress in threadbare clothes, wearing old 'light brown socks lying loosely around his ankles, caramel coloured slippers and a brown fez perched on the top of his head'.[7] But he was unusual and it is the images of the princely courts with their elephants, fabulous jewels, harems, tiger hunts and swaggering ceremonial that has done so much to create the impression many people have of India under the Raj. Their enormous wealth, their Rolls-Royces, their glamorous lives in London or the South of France and their exotic shoots, which did little to help India's tiger population, have created a stereotype that is not altogether unfair. Stories of excess abounded. The Maharajah of Junagadh, who was excessively fond of dogs, spent £22,000 on the wedding of two of his favourites. The sinister Maharajah of Alwar, father of the man who was deploying his soldiers to assist the Hindu mobs in Gurgaon, eventually went so far that he was deposed. He had kept a fleet of Rolls-Royces to dispose of his household rubbish and set fire to his polo pony after a match in which it had displeased him. The Raj was accused of being party to this excess, having removed the princes' real power, reducing them to a mere ceremonial role; certainly the rules that governed definition of status and protocol were Byzantine.

One of the more curious rituals the Raj used to delineate this relationship was through gun-salutes, literally the number of guns fired in greeting when the prince appeared, the greater the number of guns the higher the compliment. There were 117 princes entitled to be saluted. Five, the most important – Hyderabad, Baroda, Mysore, Jammu and Kashmir and Gwalior were twenty-one-gun men; in addition they were referred to as 'Highness', with the Nizam of Hyderabad so important that he was called 'Exalted Highness'. Next were five entitled to nineteen guns, Bhopal, Indore, Udaipur, Kohapur and Travancore, who were also called 'Highness'. After these top ten were 107 allowed lesser salutes, mostly nine or eleven guns but the vast majority of princes, the remaining 450 or so, were 'no gun men', and rather resented it. The viceroy's correspondence over the years is punctuated with requests from princes to be allowed more guns.

In fact many of the major states were remarkably well governed and, although not exactly long on democracy, they had efficient and conscientious administrations. Baroda, Travancore and Cochin all had far superior primary education systems to anything found in British India and many like Jodhpur, had much better systems for famine relief. Most British Residents had also started to take their duties more seriously. Penderel Moon, a long-serving and distin- guished ICS officer, found himself by April 1947 as finance minister in Bahawalpur, a state 'about the size of Denmark lying between the Punjab and Sind'.[8] It was one of the few states with both a Muslim ruler and a majority Muslim population, about 83 per cent of its 2 million people, but with sizeable minorities of Hindus and Sikhs. It was largely desert but saved from total barrenness by the Sutlej, Panjnad and Indus rivers, which formed its north-western boundary. This water allowed the cultivation of a narrow strip, about five to thirty-five miles wide, which followed its course. Moon had been sent there to help the young nawab who had, through no fault of his own, found himself inheriting a massive debt to the Government of India for the Sutlej irrigation project. This had started in 1922 and over ten years had substituted four weirs for the old inundation canal system that had worked perfectly well for centuries. It was a classic example of the Raj's inability to manage large-scale capital projects, similar to the dam that caused Norval Mitchell so much grief. The new weirs did not work, more land could not be brought into irri- gation and the state incurred a debt of 14 crore rupees (140 million rupees). The nawab couldn't pay and found himself surrounded by a circle of British advisers to ensure he wasn't being profligate. Inevitably other services in the state suffered but Moon found it generally well administered and the nawab, despite long absences in England, surprisingly popular. 'If the army accounts were never audited and if there were leakages from various minor departments, the mass of people were no wiser and felt no worse ... nor did the people at large think ill of a ruler for wishing to spend more of the state revenues on himself than a civil servant would approve'.[9] The nawab's very fine Rolls-Royce, subsequently used by Jinnah, is still in the foyer of the Marriott Hotel in Islamabad. Within three months of Moon's arrival the state debt would be the least of his problems.

Many states also had their own armies. A few of these were completely independent, and their role was part internal security and part ceremonial, although in 1947 internal security was interpreted widely as with the Maharajah of Alwar's state troops in Gurgaon. Most, however, were part of the Indian States Forces Scheme, whereby the princes agreed to their forces being under the commander-in-chief in exchange for arms, equipment, staff assistance and training. Many of these had fought with great bravery in the recent war, and their rulers, not quite so many of whom led from the front as they had done in the First World War, were nevertheless generous supporters of the war effort. The Nizam of Hyderabad financed two Spitfire squadrons, in return for which he was presented with a captured Messerschmitt. The Maharajah of Nawanagar, the famous Jam Sahib, ran a camp for Polish refugee children. The great Sikh ruler, the Maharajah of Patiala actually deployed to North Africa with his forces and the Maharajah of Bundi won an MC fighting in Burma.

The problem in July 1947 was that Nehru and Patel had automatically assumed that paramountcy for the vast majority of states would transfer to the new Indian government and a few to Pakistan. Not all the princes shared that view. They had met in January and agreed that 'all the rights surrendered by the States to the paramount Power will return to the States'.[10] Some, like Hyderabad and Travancore, argued that they had made separate treaties with the British, which they did not agree transferred automatically, and said they were considering independence. Others would accept the 1932 federal solution but thought this implied retaining complete control of their own affairs with only a loose arrangement with Delhi, something Nehru would certainly not accept. For others, like Kashmir, with a divided population, the question was which of the new countries to join. The policy was that it was an issue for each ruler to decide. For most the decision was obvious. 'There are', as Mountbatten told them, 'certain geographical compulsions which cannot be evaded. Out of something like 565 States, the vast majority are irretrievably linked geographically with the Dominion of India'.[11]

The 3 June announcement was also remarkably vague as to what had been agreed about the states; very little had. It simply stated that paramountcy would lapse and that the states should either enter into a federal arrangement with one or other of the successor governments or enter into 'other particular political arrangements'.[12] Even Attlee had gone on the record as saying that paramountcy was not transferable.[13] Nehru had seen this problem coming, hence his Gwalior speech on 19 April, which had caused such concern, and which showed that, although he had not meant literally what he said, Congress' attitude was hardening. Jinnah was, at this stage, less concerned; it was fairly clear that states like Qalat and Bahawalpur would come to Pakistan and he and Liaquat would take a more relaxed view of negotiations than Nehru.

Mountbatten, who said that 'the full realisation of the problem only dawned on me gradually', first discussed the states with the Indian political leadership on 13 June. The Nawab of Bhopal had already resigned as chancellor after the 3 June announcement, saying that the British had let the princes down badly. He realised that Nehru's strong centre would make it almost impossible for a federated system to work and that the old Cabinet Mission Plan, which had semi-accepted that arrangement, was now dead. At the 13 June meeting, Sir Conrad Corfield unwisely expounded to Nehru his theory that each state should negotiate separately with the new

Indian government and in slow time, exactly, in fact, as Pakistan was to do, and that each state should consider having its own 'Dominion status'. Nehru, already tired, overworked and fractious, promptly exploded. He told Corfield he was opposed to India and should be immediately put on trial for 'misfeasance' – throughout all these countless meetings it is noticeable that Nehru's knowledge and use of English was far above his British counterparts.[14] What Corfield was suggesting was anyway totally impractical. If India became independent on 15 August without the states as part of the new country then it would lose half its landmass and a quarter of its population. This simply did not fit with Nehru's model of a centralised state. It was impossible to negotiate terms with all of them in the next two months. A common policy of accession had to be found and Corfield was not the man to do it. Nehru also suspected him of burning the records of his department. Corfield replied, with remarkable honesty, that he had only destroyed those that dealt with the personal misdemeanours of past rulers. He was sent packing back to England and Nehru established a new States Department, which, luckily, he agreed could come under Patel rather than directly under him. Even more fortunately V. P. Menon would become its secretary. Mountbatten, well placed as a cousin of the king to negotiate with princely families, would now spend much of July persuading, with Patel cajoling, the more reluctant princes.

It was, once again, Menon who managed to find a formula that would prove acceptable to the vast majority. Rather than ask the princes to give up all their power, it would, he argued, be enough for them to agree to accede only in the three key policy areas of defence, foreign affairs and communications. They could keep their land, titles and privy purses. Nehru and Patel both agreed, albeit reluctantly; the left wing of Congress remained sceptical. Patel anyway thought that the population of the states would rise up and overthrow their rulers after independence, an attitude that showed a surprisingly shallow understanding of rural India. On 5 July this revised policy was published and with it four pillars of agreement that were just about achievable in the time available. First, there would be a common Instrument of Accession; secondly, a central negotiating structure was established via the States Department; thirdly, there was a common 'Standstill' agreement, which guaranteed all other existing arrangements between the crown and the state would remain unaltered until new negotiations had taken place, and, finally, there was a mechanism for amending the draft Independence Bill. Congress refused to negotiate with the British Residents or their agents, and with only a sparse coverage of Congress or League representatives available, effectively the states had to come to Delhi to sign away their rights. Once again Menon, trusted as deeply by Patel as he was by Mountbatten, had prevented potential disaster.

Even this compromise was not acceptable to all. Mountbatten and Patel worried most about twenty-one-gun Hyderabad and nineteen-gun Travancore. They thought that if they could 'get them in ... nearly all other states will accede. If they refuse there are quite a number of other states, such as Mysore, Bhopal and Dholpur, who may stand out'.[15] Bhopal summed up the feelings of many of his fellow princes when he wrote to Mountbatten saying

how can we, the Rulers of Independent States, throw in our lot with a political party whose resolution is that India should become a republic? You cannot, my dear Dickie, mix oil with water. In any country in the world the two democratic barriers against the rising tide of Communism are the vested interest, which in India are the *jagirdars* and *zamindars*, and the money owners, which in India are the big industrialists. The Congress are at present busily engaged in liquidating the *zamindars* and *jagirdars*. The future intention of Congress is to mete out similar treatment to the Princes.

Many of the princes, he concluded, regarded Gandhi and Nehru 'as an enemy'.[16]

Travancore, in particular, did not like the idea of being part of a Congress-dominated, left-leaning administration. The state, actually a kingdom, occupied the extreme south-western part of the Indian peninsula. It had been ruled since 1729 by the Varma kings, although effective power was exercised by their prime minister, or dewan, Sir C. P. Ramaswami Aiyar. It had been him who had been to see Mountbatten when he first arrived to voice his concerns, pointing out that his population was larger than Australia's. Now, as the future became clearer, Aiyar declared on 14 July that Travancore would become independent. This was worrying. Travancore had a strong economy, its own ports, large foreign currency reserves and well-trained armed forces. It also enjoyed a strong ethnic and national identity. The stated reason was that they 'could not be forced to join a dominion whose leaders have at this critical juncture in world history established diplomatic relations with the Soviet Republic'. There had been ongoing opposition to Congress for some years and there had also been considerable communist agitation. Aiyar particularly disliked Gandhi. He went to see Mountbatten again in July and presented him with a series of files that purported to show that Gandhi was a 'dangerous sex maniac who couldn't keep his hands off young girls'.[17]

Mountbatten and Patel applied their carrot and stick tactics. Mountbatten told the dewan that he could not abandon India in her hour of need; history would judge him harshly. Patel pointed out that the Congress supporter and millionaire Sir Seth Dalmia had given the local Congress party five lakhs of rupees to stir up an internal uprising against the Travancore government after 15 August. Aiyar promised to ask his maharajah to reconsider. Shortly after his return he was attacked with a billhook and nearly killed but on 30 July the maharajah did telegraph his agreement to accede.[18]

Others, like the young Maharajah of Indore, a 'young, erratic and bad-mannered man', thought themselves above the whole process.[19] Indore was an important and populous Maratha state in central India, a nineteen-gun salute state, and its accession mattered. Yeshwant Rao Holkar of Indore did not like the British. He had been educated at a British public school, Charterhouse, where he was horribly bullied. His astrologers had also warned him that Guru, the only protective planet in his horoscope, had 'suddenly become weak and evil' and that its 'evil influence will become dangerous from January 1947', so he was not well disposed to cooperate.[20] He consequently refused either to answer any correspondence or to come to Delhi, despite a very senior deputation of his fellow Maratha princes, led by the Gaekwar of Baroda, a most important man, trying to persuade him. Indore simply left the princes in his drawing room. He finally did answer a summons to Viceroy's House where he was interviewed by Mountbatten. He mumbled some excuses in answer to his dressing down and then left without agreeing to anything. The States Department were consequently rather surprised to receive his signed Instrument of Accession in an old envelope in the ordinary post soon afterwards.

Hyderabad was altogether more difficult. Its population was 85 per cent Hindu but, for centuries, its 15 per cent Muslim minority had governed. It was, in most respects, already an independent country. It had its own currency and its own Parliament and the Nizam had decided that he would accede neither to India nor Pakistan but become an independent dominion, issuing a *firman* to that effect on 3 June. Although the Raj thought the Nizam was 'an incalculable creature, and may not be wholly susceptible to reasoned arguments',[21] his decision was not so much a protest, like Travancore, but more a reasoned assessment of the options he faced. His 2 million Muslims were vociferous and their extreme wing, the *Ittehad-ul-Muslimeen*, active. Accession to India would effectively render this class who had run the state and the army powerless. 'The problem of Hyderabad', wrote C. G. Herbert, the Resident, 'is a microcosm of the problem of the whole of India – a mixed Hindu and Muslim population with the Hindus primarily in the countryside and currently too busy in the fields to worry over much' but, he warned, if the Nizam did join India the Muslims would be infuriated and serious violence would break out.[22] Even the Parliament was weighted in the Muslims' favour and Jinnah had been active in trying to persuade the Nizam to join Pakistan, something which, under Jinnah's original plan for Pakistan, might have worked. Now, post the decision on partition, it was impossible. Nehru and Patel could never accept such an important state in the centre of India, surrounded entirely by Indian states, doing anything of the sort.

The Nizam had the good sense to enlist the services of a political adviser in the form of Sir Walter Monckton, who was reputedly paid £1,000 per day. Monckton, the lawyer who had guided Edward VIII through his marriage, was a clever choice. He had been in Churchill's last government as solicitor general and was influential among those politicians at Westminster who were not only opposed to Congress and sceptical of Mountbatten, but also naturally sympathetic to the princes. Monckton argued that Hyderabad had been a loyal ally of Britain for hundreds of years. The Nizam had governed well, if more in the interests of the Muslim minority, but there had been little bloodshed and there had never been a famine, something that could not be said for the British provinces.[23]

The Nizam's proposal was to allow the new Indian government to control his foreign policy, defence and communications but without actually acceding. This was still unacceptable to Patel. Negotiations continued throughout July and August but by the end of the month there was still no solution. Monckton told Churchill, Salisbury, Eden and Butler, in other words the leaders of the Westminster opposition, that Congress were spending a fortune trying to undermine the Nizam. Mountbatten was too feeble with Congress, simply doing everything they said and that 'the present exhibition of power politics seems an exact replica of those in which Hitler and Mussolini indulged', something he knew would stir a roar from Churchill. We must, he concluded, 'see to it whether this shameful betrayal of our friends cannot be prevented'.[24]

Smaller states in a similar position to Hyderabad, with a Muslim ruler and powerful elite but a majority Hindu population, and who did accede to India, did prove the Nizam's point. Rampur, a smaller state in the United Provinces, but still with a fifteen-gun salute, agreed to accede to India and was immediately subject to severe rioting. Muslims set fire to the state buildings and the police stations and murdered policemen. The nawab's forces lost control, not helped by the fact that they carried antiquated firearms as, the Nawab pointed out, he had preferred to spend his revenue on education. He was petitioned to join Pakistan, being told that it was his chief minister, Zaidi, the 'chief usher of darkness' who was responsible for bowing to Congress and alienating his subjects from him. Again the possibility of Rampur joining Pakistan had evaporated with the 3 June announcement; under Jinnah's original concept it might well have been able to have done so.[25]

Jinnah also tried to persuade Maharajah Hanwant Singh of Jodhpur to join Pakistan. He ruled a large and ancient state that would abut Pakistan but he was a Hindu as were the majority of his subjects. He had only just succeeded and was very young, his father, Umaid Singh, having died unexpectedly of a ruptured appendix only days after the 3 June announcement. Umaid Singh was a hard act to follow, one of those competent and visionary rulers whom the Indian dynasties habitually produced. In 1946 he had opened the Jawai dam in Godwar, a project which ensured Jodhpur a plentiful supply of clean drinking water. Famine had long been a concern in the desert kingdom and Umaid Singh was remembered in local folklore 'on his flying horses, soaring through the sky, over a Marwar (Jodhpur) he made green'.[26]

Jinnah had a series of meetings with young Hanwant Singh during which he offered the 'use of Karachi as a free port, free import of arms, jurisdiction over the Sind railway and a large amount of grain for famine relief'.[27] There was considerable alarm in the States Department that Jodhpur might actually be swayed, and that this might start a chain reaction with the other Rajput states that adjoined Pakistan like Udaipur and Jaisalmer. They had good cause. Jodhpur had historically ruled the district of Amarkot in the eastern part of Sind, its territory stretching as far as Hyderabad (a separate Hyderabad to the Nizam's dominion) on the River Indus. They had lost control of it after Napier's occupation of Sind in 1843 with the British paying them what they thought was a miserly rent of 10,000 rupees per annum by way of compensation. This had not been increased for eighty years. They had been lobbying for many years to have this historical wrong redressed. In 1916 Sir Pratap Singh had made a formal application only to have it firmly rebuffed, an insult that was keenly felt. Jinnah's offer now gave Jodhpur an opportunity. Twenty-two per cent of Jodhpur was Muslim and communal relations were very good, held together by a ruling family that had governed in the interest of the whole community since the fifteenth century. Hanwant Singh saw the issue more as how he could best protect Jodhpur and its way of life rather than as a decision between two new nations. 'The magic potion' that was Britain 'had finally worn off' for Jodhpur. 'The traders from across the sea were once again mere traders and for the first time in three hundred and forty-eight years Britain's interests no longer lay in India', says the history of the House of Marwar, the ruling Jodhpur dynasty. Hanwant Singh must now make the best deal he could with their successors.

A week away from the deadline, the maharajah, still uncommitted, was again summoned to Delhi to be given a lecture by V. P. Menon and taken off to see Mountbatten who was just getting out of his bath. Mountbatten told him that 'he had been a friend of his father's for twenty-six years and knew that he would have wanted to be with India'.[28] He warned the young maharajah that if he succumbed to Jinnah's offers then he would be leaving his state vulnerable to terrible future inter-communal violence. Hanwant Singh did not see it that way but did manage to secure significant concessions from Menon should he accede to India, effectively ensuring similar terms as those that Jinnah had offered. He returned from Delhi still undecided. It was probably his mother, a devout Hindu from an old Jaisalmer family, who finally persuaded him. Her brother, close to Patel, applied pressure and ultimately Jodhpur agreed to accede to India. Udaipur and Jaisalmer followed suit. When he returned to Delhi to sign, Hanwant Singh, a keen member of the Magic Circle, took a large pen that, once the top was unscrewed, became a small pistol. He had made it himself in his workshops and was rather proud of it. He was alone with V. P. Menon in the room, duly signed, and then, unscrewing the pen top, told Menon that if he tried to retract on the promises he had made he would 'shoot him like a dog'. The terrified Menon dived under the table on which the Instrument of

Accession sat, shouting to Mountbatten to rescue him. The viceroy dashed into the room and promptly confiscated the pen.[29]

Jinnah's attitude to those states that would definitely join Pakistan, like Bahawalpur, was more relaxed. He was in no hurry to have Instruments of Accession signed by 15 August and was content to take his time negotiating. The one that would cause him most trouble was Qalat, where a mighty khan ruled over a state the size of the British Isles and which constituted a large part of Baluchistan. The khan, like the Nizam, believed his state should become an independent country and, also like the Nizam, he employed Walter Monckton to argue his case, although it is unlikely he paid him quite so generously. He was happy to have a treaty with Pakistan and for Karachi to run his defence, foreign affairs and communications but would not actually accede; again Monckton's tactics were replicated. Why, the khan argued, should he accede if Afghanistan did not? Nothing had been resolved by August and the argument would drag on for many months to come until Jinnah finally felt he had to act.[30] The last Pakistan state, Hunza, did not in fact accede until 1973.

On 25 July the major princes were asked, en masse, to Delhi to be addressed by the viceroy in the Chamber of Princes and then to lunch at Viceroy's House. Some, like Indore and Bhopal, refused, Bhopal saying that they were being 'invited like the oysters to attend the tea-party with the Walrus and the Carpenter', but most accepted. It was a splendid occasion with everyone wearing their best uniforms, state robes and jewels, the last time such an event would take place under the Raj. Mountbatten, looking almost as splendid as his audience in his white naval uniform with decorations, and using the moral authority of his links to the British royal family, laid out the terms of accession again. He had, he said, 'wrung from the future government of India the best terms to which they will agree', which was undoubtedly true. 'Immediate accession on the three subjects of defence, external affairs and communications will not prejudice the position of the states', he continued, urging the princes to accede and to do so quickly.[31] Gandhi thought the viceroy spoke to them 'in very gentle terms. I liked his speech' but added, with the typical

Gandhi touch of sardonic humour, 'it was not a brief one'. Gandhi
was becoming agitated that the emphasis was continually on the
princes themselves but, he argued at his prayer meetings, 'the ruler
is nothing. The people are everything. The ruler will be dead one of
these days but the people will remain'.[32] But for the time being the
focus was very much on the rulers. Mountbatten's approach worked
well. Twenty-two more princes acceded after lunch.

'In the end', thought Penderel Moon, 'the princes were bullied'[33]
but it is hard to see how it could have been otherwise. Bhopal may
have been correct to say that, 'The British seem to have abdicated
power and what is worse they have handed it over to the enemies
of all their friends', something he looked on as 'one of the greatest,
if not the greatest tragedies that has ever befallen mankind. The
States, the Moslems, and the entire mass of people who relied on
British justice and their sense of fair play, suddenly find themselves
totally hopeless, unorganized and unsupported',[34] but in reality there
was no alternative. Hyderabad would soon discover the cost of not
acceding.

In fact many of the princes saw independence as an opportunity.
The more charismatic had not relished living under British control,
however much they had appreciated some of the benefits and comforts that the Raj afforded. A new India, and a new Pakistan, could
offer them opportunities to re-establish the ascendancy of their
families, which the British had suppressed for so long. On 9 August
some of the greatest rulers, the Maharajah Scindia of Gwalior, the
Raja of Faridkot, the Maharajah of Bharatpur, the Maharajah of
Panna, the Raja of Bhagat and the Maharajah of Alwar, sent out a
circular to the 'Princes and Leading Men of India' to join them at
a conference in Delhi. It was, they said, time for the Princely Order
to take advantage of the golden opportunity that independence
offered to provide fresh leadership to the Indian people. It would
take time, and there would be more clashes with Congress under
Nehru's descendants, but for those princes who took advantage of
the political and commercial opportunities, there was certainly life
in the new India.[35]

One prince who would not, however, find the new India, or the new Pakistan, offered him any opportunities was the Maharajah of Jammu and Kashmir. There were really three parts to his beautiful north-western state of 4 million people. Ladakh, to the east in the lower Himalaya, is a barren, mountainous area with its main town, Leh, at 11,500 feet. Its population, such as it was, was mainly Buddhist. It is still known as 'Little Tibet'. Jammu, to the south-west, was really an extension of the Punjab. Its eponymous main town, Jammu, at 1,000 feet, was the winter capital, known as the city of temples and an important centre of Hindu pilgrimage. Then there was the fabled Vale of Kashmir itself, the green valley fringed with snow-capped mountains that pushed north into the Himalaya and whose lakeland city, Srinagar, with its colonies of houseboats, was the government's summer capital. Its ruler was the Hindu prince Maharajah Hari Singh, whose Dogra family, Gandhi would maintain, had 'bought' the state from the British for 75 lakhs of rupees under the Treaty of Amritsar in 1846.[36] Logical as it may have seemed to the British, and advantageous to the maharajah, it imposed Hindu rule on a state that was 77 per cent Muslim and, in the Vale of Kashmir itself, 92 per cent Muslim.

Kashmir occupied a special place in the Indian psyche, and no more so than with Nehru whose family were long established Kashmiri Brahmins. Patel thought that 'Kashmir meant more to him than anything else' in India.[37] It was, Nehru wrote, 'a very poor state with an oppressive land system' and there was historic tension between the people and the maharajah's government, which was generally thought corrupt and inefficient. During the 1930s this opposition had structured around the Kashmir National Conference, led by the charismatic Aligarh graduate Sheikh Abdullah. He represented everything Nehru sought: he was a Muslim Congress supporter, who opposed the League, in a key Muslim majority state, reinforcing Congress' claim to speak for all Indians. He was also a social reformer campaigning for fairer land tenure and for democratic representation. Predictably he was put in prison while, according to Nehru, the maharajah's premier, Pandit Kak, tried to stir up inter-communal violence. Kak, who 'hated Nehru with a bitter hatred',[38] was a sycophant who had been in office since 1945. He was now trying to persuade his indecisive ruler to opt for Pakistan, an option he thought would allow him to retain greater power than he would have under a socialist Congress government. 'The normal and obvious course', Nehru countered, 'appears to be for Kashmir to join the Constituent Assembly of India' but 'the Maharajah is timid and is in a fix'.[39]

Nehru and Gandhi both now decided they should go to Kashmir to put pressure on Kak to release Abdullah. Kak, nervous of the effect on the population of an impassioned Nehru, protested to Delhi and Mountbatten consequently asked them not to. Instead he went himself on 18 June, intent on persuading the maharajah to hold a referendum, as was happening in the neighbouring North West Frontier Province. It was an inconclusive visit, and the maharajah feigned illness so he did not have to see him; Nehru said that was his usual trick and normally it was a tummy ache. Gandhi did in fact visit in late July, and was remarkably restrained. Nehru agreed not to go at all but by the end of July there was still no indication of what the maharajah was intending.

There was some concern in London that the princes, those old friends of Britain, were being virtually forced to accede. This was partly as a result of Monckton's lobbying, partly because of individual princes using their political contacts and also because the older hands in the India Office felt the viceroy was actually exceeding his brief. The prime minister had stated clearly in Parliament that the princes would not be under any pressure to accede and yet here was the viceroy doing exactly that. There was a wonderfully archaic exchange of minutes between India Office officials over Qalat. Mr Rumbold wrote to Mr Croft saying that the viceroy had misunderstood the constitutional position of Qalat and had got the issue 'quite wrong'. Mr Croft replied that he was in doubt but that His Excellency 'went astray' but that he was 'not too sure what there is to be gained by pointing it out'.[40] Eventually Listowel was persuaded to write. He asked Mountbatten to explain why the states had to have decided by 15 August and pointed out that it was contrary to the government's public line.

One of Mountbatten's strong points was how he played Whitehall. British governments are traditionally less trusting of the lieutenants they send to represent them abroad than other nations, such as the United States. How much to refer back to London has always been a delicate balance. The immediate focus in Westminster has long been on Parliament and the media, rather than achieving what is in the best interests locally. Usually Mountbatten was clever about this. He had worked out where power lay, with Attlee, Cripps and those who briefed them like Krishna Menon, and he spent long hours preparing his briefings for them – his personal reports are extraordinarily full for a man as busy as he was – but he did not consider Listowel as occupying a place in his pantheon. 'I am afraid you have completely misunderstood my purpose and what I am trying to achieve', he replied on 4 August. 'I am trying my very best to create an integrated India. If I am allowed to play my own hand without interference I have no doubt that I will succeed', which may have been fairly arrogant but many who have been in a similar position would strongly agree with him.[41]

There were, besides, many other pressing issues for the Partition Council to decide. What should happen to the Andaman Islands, that unhealthy archipelago in the Bay of Bengal that the Raj had primarily used as a prison. The British chiefs of staff wanted to keep them as a military base and suggested they be appropriated. Mountbatten's staff, mindful of Patel's reaction should the British start seizing parts of Indian territory, tactfully advised they be leased or some sort of 'joint control' be worked out.[42] Then there was the much more complicated issue of the Chittagong Hill Tracts, that strip of tribal territory south-east of the Ganges Delta, on the east side of the Bay of Bengal, where John Christie had spent so many happy days. Patel was warning of extreme trouble if they did not come to India but if they did they would be completely cut off by East Bengal. Their fate would occupy much of Radcliffe's time.

Effectively, Congress had decided to boycott the Frontier referendum, which was conducted over a prolonged period in mid-July by specially drafted army officers on the correct assumption that Dr Khan Sahib's ministry would not have run it fairly. The Congress logic was that if the turnout was subsequently low then the vote would have no legitimacy and they could argue to overturn it. Their tactic nearly worked, but not quite; turnout was just over 50 per cent and the vote overwhelmingly for joining Pakistan. The absent Caroe had been vindicated and Jinnah was cheered that Sir George Cunningham had agreed to return as its first Pakistani governor of the North West Frontier Province. Ninety-five Muslim ICS officers also now agreed to serve Pakistan, several of whom would go on to occupy high office, as did one Indian Christian, Cornelius, who would end up as chief justice. Fifty British ICS also said they would stay on with Pakistan rather than India.

In the Punjab, Sikh agitation was growing. Giyani Kartar Singh, President of the Shiromani Akali Dal, the Sikh political party headed by Master Tara Singh, said publicly on 29 July that the Sikhs would not accept any Boundary Commission award that they considered unjust, despite what Baldev Singh was saying in the Partition Council. Giyani said that Baldev Singh had no authority to give any such undertaking. 'The Sikhs', overall, thought Jenkins, 'are very puzzled and unhappy and do not quite know what to do'. Jenkins had told Giyani he should negotiate with Jinnah; there was nothing to stop Sikhs retaining their land and enjoying freedom of worship in Pakistan. Groups of Sikhs had in fact been in negotiation but Giyani said 'he had seen a good deal of Mr. Jinnah and had no confidence in him'. There was, Jenkins continued, increasing rural violence with heavy Muslim casualties in the Hoshiarpur and Jullundur areas. Partition work seemed to be going very slowly and he could not see how a major muddle could be avoided on 15 August.[43]

Jenkins's repeated warnings were beginning to have some effect. On 17 July Auchinleck briefed the Partition Council that the army was assembling a Punjab Boundary Force, the PBF, to assist the police in keeping order. It would be an Indian Army force, based on 4th Indian Division and commanded by the energetic and respected Major General Pete Rees, an officer with an excellent operational record, who would have senior Indian and Pakistani advisers attached to his headquarters. No similar plans were made for Bengal as the view was that there would not be serious trouble in Bengal with the possible exception of Calcutta.[44] The PBF was to be about 20,000 troops, five infantry brigades, so about one and a half divisions. Jenkins who, like most senior ICS officials had a good working knowledge of the military, had consistently recommended a force four times that size given the area over which they would have to operate, the density and pattern of the population and the fact that his Punjab police were now virtually useless. Warnings of the problems the army's class structure had caused in Gurgaon were ignored. Of Rees's seventeen infantry battalions, two were Gurkhas but the remainder all 'class-based' Indian units. Nearly all the battalions were locally based and two were actually from the Punjab regiment so made up exclusively of local men.[45]

Auchinleck's heart does not seem to have been in the PBF from the very start. Strongly opposed to the Indian Army being used for internal order purposes, and preoccupied with its division and reorganisation, the PBF was an unwelcome distraction. The Army Intelligence Summaries published in July and August dealt at length with matters in Palestine and the wider world but on the Punjab were restricted to commenting that, 'In spite of the announcement regarding the division of the Indian Armed Forces, the integrity and impartiality of Indian troops has remained unchanged' and that 'There has been no report of Hindu-Sikh-Muslim friction in any unit'.[46] Minds seem to have been completely shut to the possibility of using British troops, despite the fact that Tuker had deployed them in Bengal almost continually since the previous August and with clear effect. On 29 July Sir Arthur Smith, the chief of the Indian General Staff, so the professional head of the Indian Army, while Auchinleck was commander-in-chief of all Indian armed forces including the Royal Indian Navy and Royal Indian Air Force, published an order, the content of which was 'NOT to be divulged to Indians'. It said that British troops could not be employed in communal disturbances to protect Indian lives but they could if it was necessary to protect British ones'.[47] He was following a direct instruction from the Labour government in London, reinforced by a note Listowel sent to Mountbatten on 18 July.[48] As the PBF assembled, the 30,000 mobile and rapidly deployable British troops, and the available Gurkha battalions in India, a total force of over 65,000 with no 'class' bias, were simply excluded. The PBF was set up to fail from its inception.

Nehru did not exactly help in this debate. Smith had been to see him on 13 July to brief him as to how the new government might choose to exercise its control of the military. Nehru did not appear to grasp that it would soon be his responsibility, Smith reported. They then covered the possibility of disturbances in the Punjab post 15 August. Smith explained how the Joint Command structure would work, with Rees reporting to Auchinleck. Rees would need the authority to designate an area suffering violence as a 'Disturbed Area' and be authorised to apply military measures within it. Nehru responded vaguely. He was more annoyed with Auchinleck's attempt to retain control of military finances, insisting that the financial adviser must work to him while Nehru demanded he work to the Finance Department. Auchinleck, Nehru complained, seemed to think he was 'free to carry out administration in accordance with his own ideas'. He was also beginning to think that the commander-in-chief was biased towards Pakistan. Auchinleck was certainly concerned that the new Pakistan Army's thirty-five infantry battalions would be well under strength. Then there was a major row about splitting the air force. There were eight fighter squadrons and two transport squadrons. The initial recommendation was to split them 80 per cent to India and 20 per cent to Pakistan but Jinnah was now claiming he needed 70 per cent because of the requirement to control the Frontier. Auchinleck supported him. Nehru infuriated Jinnah by saying that he did not want aircraft used on the tribes he described as 'our people'.[49] As the Punjab staggered towards its awful fate, Nehru seemed unable to realise that the army he had so long despised was now all that could save his own countrymen from disaster.

In Bengal the violence throughout July was spasmodic. Huseyn

Suhrawardy, who would become Premier of East Bengal, was at loggerheads with Prafulla Chandra Ghosh, Premier-designate of West Bengal, Indian Bengal. Suhrawardy had continued to act as premier for the whole province, despite the Assembly vote for partition, but was now preoccupied with the division of assets. He came to Delhi on 30 July, intent on engaging viceregal support in the number of typewriters each state would have. He was particularly exercised about Calcutta Ice Plant. It had eight diesel engines but would run just as well on electricity so East Bengal was claiming all eight engines. Mountbatten by now concluded he 'was rather a gas-bag, bogged down with trivialities and not thinking about the bigger issues'.[50]

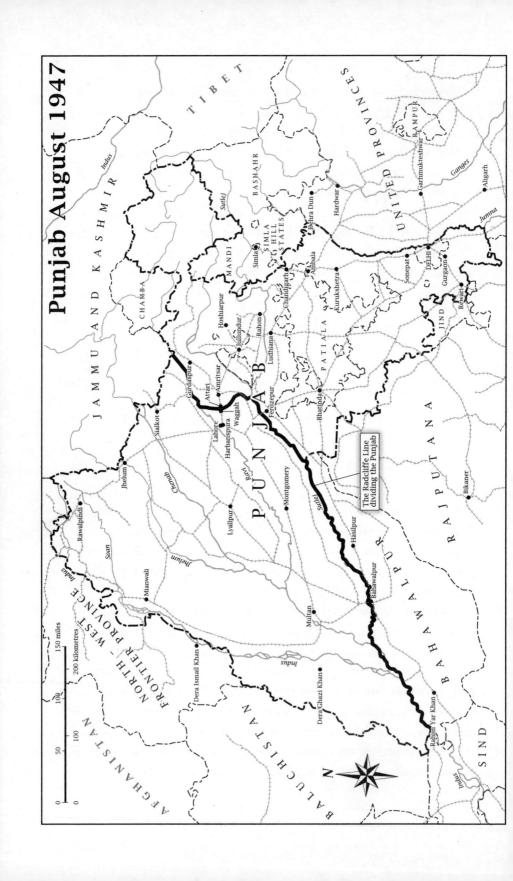

Punjab August 1947

TIBET

JAMMU AND KASHMIR

Indus

CHAMBA

Sutlej

MANDI

BASHAHR

SIMLA HILL STATES

Simla

UNITED PROVINCES

RAMPUR

Garhmukteshwar

Ganges

Hardwar

Dehra Dun

Aligarh

Jumna

Hoshiarpur

Jullundur

Rahon

Ludhiana

Chandigarh

Ambala

Kurukshetra

Sonepat

DELHI

Gurgaon

Rewari

JIND

Gurdaspur

Attari

Amritsar

Waggah

Ferozepur

PATIALA

Bhatinda

Sialkot

Lahore

Harbanspura

Ravi

Chenab

Jhelum

Rawalpindi

Soan

Indus

Mianwali

Jhelum

Lyallpur

Montgomery

Sutlej

Hasilpur

Bahawalpur

BAHAWALPUR

RAJPUTANA

Bikaner

The Radcliffe Line dividing the Punjab

PUNJAB

NORTH-WEST FRONTIER PROVINCE

AFGHANISTAN

Dera Ismail Khan

BALUCHISTAN

Dera Ghazi Khan

Indus

Multan

Rahim Yar Khan

SIND

Indus

150 miles

200 kilometres

100

50

100

0

0

N

THE NOBLEST ACT OF
THE BRITISH NATION?

*'At the stroke of the midnight hour, while the
world sleeps, India will awake to life and freedom'*

(JAWAHARLAL NEHRU)

'Our people have gone mad'

(LIAQUAT ALI)

The monsoon should have arrived by the end of July, that deluge of rain 'when nature is washed green and breathes again' and when 'for a few days, cool air and the smell of damp earth are blessings beyond price', but it didn't. The terrible, humid, cloying, all-enveloping heat just continued as if it would never end.[1]

There was nowhere to escape it. One of those it affected most was Cyril Radcliffe, a man who had never been east of Gibraltar, and who was now ensconced in a bungalow on the viceroy's estate. He had two weeks to finalise drawing the partition lines on the maps of Bengal and the Punjab. Christopher Beaumont had been appointed as his secretary and minder. He had applied for a position in Palestine and thought that he had left India for good when he was asked to take the job on. He arranged to meet Radcliffe in the Air Terminal beside London's Victoria Station. He was worried as to how he would recognise him. The BOAC lady suggested that he should wear a badge with his name on it but Beaumont, an old-fashioned man, was appalled at the vulgarity of the idea as he was by her subsequent suggestion that he should make an announcement 'over a thing called a Tannoy'. In the end he simply approached the most intelligent-looking man in the room.[2] At first he found Radcliffe 'a rather arrogant man, very self important, almost pompous, unemotional. I never heard him laugh very much'.[3] 'Meeting him', thought Mountbatten's press secretary, Alan Campbell-Johnson, 'was a cold experience'.

However, they agreed that he had both a formidable mind and that he was totally incorruptible. Beaumont later 'formed an affection for him' although he never knew whether this was reciprocated. When they arrived in Delhi they spent two nights staying with the Mountbattens in Viceroy's House. 'There were just four of us at meals. Mountbatten and Radcliffe did not get on well. They could not have been more different.' Mountbatten 'had few literary tastes'. Radcliffe, a Fellow of All Souls, 'was of outstanding intelligence and very quietly civilised. Lady Mountbatten, to her credit, adroitly kept the conversations on an even keel.' They then moved into their house on the Viceregal estate. There was no air conditioning. The first task Beaumont was given was to scour the bazaars for wine, preferably white; he managed to find some cases of Alsatian which seemed to cheer Radcliffe up as he started work.[4] Radcliffe and Beaumont had an assistant secretary, Rao Sahib V. D. Ayer, a Hindu in the ICS.

Beaumont found the two panels of judges assigned to sit on the respective Boundary Commissions were 'not much help as they always divided along communal lines'. There had been open sessions in court but again the arguments presented went almost entirely based on whether the person advancing them was Hindu or Muslim. There was little objectivity. 'Drawing the line was always going to be impossible to make acceptable and partition of the Punjab was always going to be acrimonious', Beaumont continued, 'it was a tremendously difficult job as the villages were all mixed up, especially the areas around Lyallpur, Ferozepore and

Ludhiana'. The problem was made so much worse because 'there was not enough time. It was rushed through. Much more thought should have gone into it, more advice taken' but there was no time. Beaumont had always been 'hugely impressed' by Nehru, for whom he had worked in the Foreign Ministry. 'He was very able, very easy to work with', but he was also emotional and 'he got the Punjab wrong – he didn't really understand the Punjab. He didn't believe the slaughter would occur and he persuaded Mountbatten it wouldn't happen – so Mountbatten disregarded men like Jenkins' who really knew what was going on'.[5]

A rumour seemed to spread that Radcliffe was treated like a hermit while he was working on the partition lines but that was not true. Beaumont recalled that he travelled to Simla, Lahore and to Calcutta, where he stayed with Sir Fred Burrows in Government House. He hoped he might see the ghost of Warren Hastings, which allegedly stalked the corridors looking for a file which might have helped him at his trial. In Delhi Radcliffe had frequent visitors – Walter Monckton, Auchinleck and the Lord Chief Justice, Sir Patrick Spens. However, Beaumont was never separated from him, part of his remit being to prevent unwarranted interference in his decision making.

Jenkins briefed Mountbatten and the political leadership in Delhi again on the situation in the Punjab on 4 August. Casualties in July, he estimated, had been 4,632 killed and 2,573 seriously injured, with three times as many in the rural areas as in the towns. His figures were, he admitted, almost certainly inaccurate as his administration was breaking down and the true figures were probably far higher. By the last week of July, 20,256 houses in Lahore had been destroyed. He justified the measures he was taking to keep the peace, given that he was exercising direct rule under Section 93 after the collapse of the provincial government in March, against the strong criticism coming from the League. Very soon such scruples would be irrelevant.[6] On 5 August, what was left of the Punjab Police Criminal Investigation Department reported that a major instigator of the Punjab disturbances was Pritam Singh, an ex-Indian National Army man who had been one of those trained by the Japanese at their Penang spy school and landed in India by submarine. Master Tara Singh was also, the CID believed, heavily implicated in the violence. He was 'completely one track on the subject of taking revenge on the Muslims' and there was a Sikh plot to kill Jinnah in Karachi on 15 August. 'The Sikh leaders', the report concluded, 'had lost control of their people'.[7]

On 6 August, Jenkins invited his staff to a farewell drinks party at Government House in Lahore. Santdas Kirpalani went along, intending to catch a flight to Delhi the next morning as he and the other remaining Hindu ICS officers took their leave. It was clear to them all that Lahore would go to Pakistan and anyway Kirpalani wanted to be near the centre of power in the new India. He left at 6.00 a.m. on 7 August to ensure he reached the aerodrome, six miles outside Lahore, on time, and duly arrived at 6.50 a.m. only to see his aeroplane already taking off. He later discovered someone had sold his seat for cash. Then he remembered that his colleague N. M. Buch had said at Jenkins's party that he was driving to Delhi that day. Kirpalani had been surprised. Driving had become dangerous but Buch said he had a special reason to do so. Kirpalani just caught him at Faletti's Hotel on The Mall as he was setting off and climbed in with him. A mile outside Lahore, Buch slowed down and asked Kirpalani if he was armed. He confirmed he was. Buch asked him to load his .38 while he loaded his own .45. Kirpalani asked what was happening. Buch explained that his Muslim bearer, an old friend of many years' service, had to get out to find his family in Jullundur and bring them back to Pakistan. If he went the normal way, by train, he was sure he would be butchered by Sikh gangs. Kirpalani turned round to see a pile of old blankets and rugs on the back seat under which the old man was hidden. Buch was a Gujarati, a 'Hindu of Hindus' and here he was risking his life for his old servant. Leaving Lahore a Muslim gang tried to stop them. Buch accelerated and they escaped, being showered with stones as they sped past. But thirty miles east they came across the first Sikh roadblock. There were a lot of them, they were armed and in an 'angry and bellicose mood'. They had no option but to stop. Then someone in the crowd recognised Kirpalani. 'Clear the road', he shouted, 'let them go. The Hindu officer we know'. They were lucky. A British engineer had tried to take his Muslim bearer out on a train a few days later and they would both be cut to pieces.

Forty miles on, past Amritsar, they ran into an Indian Army road-block. The soldiers explained they had been called out because of rioting in Hoshiarpur, twenty miles from Jullundur. Fateh Khan, a Muslim judge, was sitting down to breakfast with his family when a Sikh gang had thrown a bomb into their house, killing them all. The soldiers advised them to get to Delhi as soon as possible and that the Grand Trunk Road, past Ludhiana, was dangerous. Muslim gangs from Panipat were out of control. Two miles beyond the roadblock they dropped the old bearer off. 'I shall never forget the mute tears of gratitude on the face of that forlorn bearded old man as he turned to walk "home",' Kirpalani added.[8]

That same day, 7 August, Major General Pete Rees, the com-mander of the Punjab Boundary Force, flew over the area between Amritsar and Lahore in a light Auster reconnaissance aircraft. He had in his hand a report that had just come in that 'a band of one hundred and fifty Sikhs armed with firearms and swords had raided a Mohammedan village during the night and butchered eleven men, two women, one boy and three baby girls. Eight more were badly wounded and all the hay and bullock carts had been burned, the clothing and silver ornaments looted'. His task, he wrote, was not an 'enviable one and I can't please everyone. I am bombarded with demands to take over control, to show ruthlessness and to string up the malefactors from the lamp posts'. He was confident of his sepoys who were in 'good fettle' but it 'was a trying time for all. The temperature even in the shade averaged 100 degrees (38 degrees Celsius) and the 'night minimum' was 80–90 degrees (27–32 degrees Celsius). 'This is especially trying to Mohammmedans keeping the annual month's fast of Ramazan which this year is 19 July to 16 August' but, he guessed, 'our task is only a month or two after 15 August'. The Indian Army had, he thought, 'been a shining example of moderation, unity and solidarity' at a time when the mutual bitterness and hatred in the Punjab was growing so rapidly. His troops would not be reassigned to their respective new national armies until after their task was complete and they were to work directly to Auchinleck as supreme commander under the authority of the Partition Council as agreed in June.[9] But his force was totally inadequate for its task even given the limited role envisaged for it in that first week of August. His 20,000-odd men were to police an area of 37,500 square miles in the central Punjab, the twelve districts that had been identified as disputed by Radcliffe. It was an area about the size of Ireland, and with a population of 14.5 million, divided, like the rest of the province, in the proportion of 55 per cent Muslim, 25 per cent Hindu and 20 per cent Sikh.[10] He deployed his brigades, each under strength at about 4,000 men, with one covering Amritsar and Gurdaspur; a second in Jullundur and Hoshiarpur, a third in Lyallpur and Sialkot, the fourth in Ferozepore and the fifth, alongside his own headquarters, in Lahore. He had very little mobility and just one under-strength cavalry regiment.

There was, thought Penderel Moon, 'remarkable faith in the projected Boundary Force'. He did not share it. He thought the Sikhs were bound to attack the Muslims as soon as they had the opportunity. Either they would wait until the PBF was withdrawn or, if it was ineffective, they would simply ignore it. A Sikh major on his way to join it, and with whom he shared a railway compartment, agreed. He thought that a large proportion of the troops would be 'infected by the communal virus' and that anyway it lacked the mobility it needed to cover its vast area of responsibility. Moon and he thought that a force of 50,000, which was the figure he had heard the PBF was intended to be, would be pushed to do the job even if they were all mobile and totally reliable. They agreed that it would take at least the four divisions Jenkins had been persistently recommending. 'By the time I got back to Bahawalpur', Moon concluded, 'I had written off the Boundary Force completely'. Moon was equally pessimistic about the level of violence to come. He had been corresponding with Major Short, an ex-Sikh officer brought out from England, specifically at

Baldev Singh's request, to help the Sikhs with their negotiations. Short had asked Moon whether he would lobby for Radcliffe's line to be drawn sufficiently far west to allow the colony lands around Lahore to be included in India. Moon realised that this would mean that Lahore itself would be denied to Pakistan, something that would cause a terrible Muslim reaction. Just because the Sikhs, as a community, had done so much to develop the colony lands did not justify departing from the principle that 'contiguous Muslim-majority areas' should go to Pakistan. It was, he felt, inevitable that Radcliffe's line would run somewhere between Lahore and Amritsar.[11]

Sir Evan Jenkins had not given up. The last dispatch from this most clear-thinking and well-informed governor was on 13 August. He pointed out once more that the PBF was responsible for 17,932 villages. It was imperative Rees's force was reinforced by at least another two divisions, effectively doubling it. 'The lesson', he continued, 'is that once the inter-locked communities begin to fight over the countryside, the only remaining remedy is to employ a very large number of troops'. The police were now almost totally ineffective. A new Hindu police superintendent had arrived in Amritsar. His first act was to disarm all his Muslim officers. This not only created a sense of panic but led to a third of the police deserting. Amritsar itself now needed a lot more troops to replace them, two full-strength brigades instead of the single under-strength one Rees could spare. The Sikhs, Jenkins emphasised, were not only determined to have their revenge for the Rawalpindi massacres but to 'assert themselves on the boundary question'. They were behaving with 'extreme brutality. Parties of unescorted Muslim refugees were being routinely butchered. A harmless party of Pathan labourers moving west along the Grand Trunk Road near Amritsar had been set upon and thirty Pathans killed'. The Muslims would then avenge those attacks; already Muslim gangs had held up two trains in Rawalpindi and massacred the Sikh refugees trying to get to Amritsar. The army needed to take over railway security, a task that repeated exercises and studies had recommended as essential in the event of widespread internal disorder.[12]

Major General Hawthorn, the Deputy Chief of the Indian General Staff, so a very senior officer whose opinion should have carried weight, visited the Punjab on 11 August and recommended that air patrols were also essential. He estimated the killing at a daily average of one hundred people. Auchinleck did not receive his report well. He pencilled in the margin: 'There are very few aircraft for the job required of them. It is quite impossible to provide air "standing patrols"'.[13] Yet there were aircraft, a lot of them, with pilots who, after Nehru's and Patel's spat over how the squadrons would be divided, were available to fly them. The operational machinery was also there to deploy them, precisely why the Joint Defence staff had been established. There were then those 30,000 British troops, who could supposedly only be used to protect European lives, now sweltering bored in their barracks, alongside their 35,000 Gurkha colleagues. But there was no willingness by Auchinleck, obsessed with the reorganisation of the army or, as he saw it, its demise, to use them nor any pressure on him to do so. Nehru did not understand the military, Jinnah's attention was now on Karachi and Dacca, and Mountbatten was wary of crossing a military who he always worried would not listen to him. He was, V. P. Menon thought, 'overwhelmed with the idea that the army and the services might not take his advice'.[14] Rees's inadequate PBF was left to face the coming holocaust unaided.

However much Tara Singh may have protested to the contrary, and genuine as were the efforts of Baldev Singh and possibly those of other senior Sikh leaders, they were unable to prevent the more populist Sikh leaders from rousing their followers, organising and arming them. Helped by a considerable number of ex-army NCOs, and benefiting from the acquisition of weapons and money that had been going on since March, the Sikhs of the East Punjab were now a formidable force. They organised themselves, in a way which the Punjabi Muslims never seemed able to match, in a series of gangs known locally as *jathas*, led by *jathedars* who were often older men and respected community leaders.

Seven hundred miles away, Calcutta remained, to Tuker's surprise, relatively calm. The city was full of arms and ammunition and there had been flare-ups during July. The worst had been at the Bata shoe factory. Members of a Hindu Union had gone on strike and rumours started to circulate that they were looting the houses of the Muslims who were still working. In the ensuing violence over one hundred people were killed. On 30 July eighteen people were killed in a series of separate incidents but there was no widespread breakdown as there had been the previous year. This was partly due to Sir Khawaja Nazimuddin, who was from a well-known Dacca family, having obtained the premiership of East Bengal and established a good working relationship with Dr Prafula Ghosh's fledgling government of West Bengal. Ghosh was part of what was known in Bengal as the Khadi Group, Congress followers who were devotees of Gandhi, as were his ministers; the British unkindly referred to them as the 'government by love party' but Ghosh was doing his utmost to calm the Hindu population. The relative peace was also due to it being known that the hated Punjabi Muslim police, who had done so much to inflame the situation under Suhrawardy, would all be gone by 6 August as would 7,000 Muslim refugees from Bihar.

Then, on 13 August, Gandhi arrived and took up residence in a crumbling house in Balliaghata. His reception was hostile, an unwelcome novelty for him, and a Hindu crowd, indignant at his help for Muslims, showered his car with stones and bottles. He was soon visited by a joint Sikh/Hindu delegation who demanded to know why he was in Calcutta when he should be helping quell the violence in the Punjab. They threatened him with his own tactics, saying they would squat around his house until he left. Gandhi remained unperturbed. He started a series of daily prayer meetings, at which the attendance gradually swelled, and he also persuaded Suhrawardy to come and stay with him. Hindu wags wondered how the corpulent Suhrawardy would cope with Gandhi's simple fare. Gandhi was to stay on in Calcutta, missing the independence celebrations in Delhi, his presence helping, at least initially, to prevent the city from repeating the slaughter of the previous year.

Yet perhaps the main reason Calcutta remained calm was that

Tuker flooded the city with troops. In the first two weeks of August, five British and two Gurkha battalions were permanently patrolling alongside six Indian battalions, Rajputs, Madrassis and Punjabis, one advantage at least of the long-standing policy of not recruiting Bengalis.

Outside Calcutta, the rest of Bengal was also quiet. The main issue in East Bengal was once again food shortages, and Tuker found he had no problem in allocating aircraft to drop supplies. Bihar was now calmer, and the killings had stopped. Orissa was also calm and in the United Provinces Pandit Pant, that effective, forgiving man, had arrested the more extreme Hindu Mahasabha and Rashtriya Swayamsevak Sangh (RSS) leadership as a precaution. The Mahasabha promptly invoked habeas corpus; Pant ignored them.

Nevertheless Tuker felt the days drag by 'with feet of lead'. He half longed for 15 August when he could hand over responsibility yet also dreaded what might happen when British troops were withdrawn from the streets. Calcutta Muslims, by now aware that their city would almost certainly remain in India, had 'a sullen depression of spirits', not helped by the Mahasabha's and RSS's propaganda telling Hindus that as soon as it was created Pakistan's aim would be the conquest of 'Hindustan and the forced conversion of Hindus to Islam'. They condemned Congress, whose leaders, they said, had betrayed them, and called for a united Hindu uprising. Hindus living in East Bengal had generally begun to leave and move west, although in Chittagong joint 'Peace Committees' had been formed from both communities who were rounding up the Muslim *goondas* who were threatening them.[15]

Radcliffe's report was ready by 12 August. He had, he would always maintain, completed it without interference or bias. Later he would be accused of changing his allocation of the important Punjab city of Ferozepore and the district of Zira immediately to its east. Both had a small majority Muslim population and logically, under Radcliffe's guidelines, should have gone to Pakistan. Ferozepore was an important city which controlled the water supply to Bikaner state, immediately to its south in Rajputana, and was a major arsenal. It also had an important bridge over the River Sutlej. Jenkins had been particularly concerned about its future, predicting it could be a serious flashpoint should it go to Pakistan, and wanted to know whether he should deploy troops there. He had also been concerned about Gurdaspur, north-east of Amritsar and which controlled the land route to Kashmir. Radcliffe had, Beaumont said, sent Mountbatten a note with a draft map explaining what he was recommending so that he could give Jenkins early warning. This had, allegedly, been shown to the chairman of the Central Waterways Committee, Lala Adjudhia, who promptly told Patel. The evening before the report was due to be submitted, V. P. Menon appeared at Radcliffe's bungalow and said the viceroy wanted to talk to him in private. Beaumont said he was not available so Menon went away but the next day Radcliffe was summoned to lunch with just Mountbatten and Ismay. When he came back he allegedly changed the line so that Ferozepore and Zira went to India. The allegation is that the Maharajah of Bikaner, an important ally in the princely camp, put pressure on Mountbatten alongside Nehru, threatening to accede to Pakistan if Ferozepore went. In 1948 the Pakistan government claimed to have found Radcliffe's original map and complained to the United Nations but by that stage Radcliffe had shredded all his papers. Opinion was originally split as to whether this incident actually happened. The accession of Bikaner to Pakistan seemed incredible to many. Maharajah Gagul Singh, son of the great Sir Ganga Singh, who had been the only non-white member of the Imperial War Cabinet in the First World War and one of India's most progressive autocrats, had been one of the first to declare for India. However, in February 1992 Beaumont published his own account, drawing on his papers that he had deposited in All Souls, making it clear that Radcliffe had changed his allocation.[16] The pressure may have come direct from Bikaner, an old friend of Mountbatten's, but it was likely to have been reinforced by Nehru; Beaumont thought that his assistant secretary, Ayer, had been secretly briefing Nehru via V. P. Menon throughout the process and that it was him who was to blame rather than Lala Adjudhia. Nehru also seemed to know that the Chittagong Hill Tracts were destined for Pakistan well ahead of any official announcement. Nehru was equally known to be concerned about Gurdaspur because of its link to his beloved Kashmir, a remarkably prescient concern as events were soon to prove, but Beaumont did not think that Radcliffe had changed that city from Pakistan to India despite subsequent accusations.[17]

What Mountbatten definitely influenced was the timing of the Boundary Commission announcement, which he wanted delayed until after the independence celebrations on 15 August. He justified this by saying that although 'there was considerable advantage in immediate publication so that the new boundaries could take effect from 15th August', it had also 'been obvious all along that the later we postponed publication, the less would the inevitable odium react upon the British'.[18] Given that his job was to serve Attlee, there was some sense in that rather selfish view but many felt the uncertainty made the situation in the Punjab even worse. Auchinleck, never allowing an opportunity to criticise Mountbatten to pass, complained that it 'was having a most disturbing and harmful effect' but Mountbatten had his way and delayed briefing the political leaders until 16 August with the public announcement the next day.

There was also a genuine wish to make much of the significance of 15 August and the birth of two nations. 'Nothing', John Christie thought, should mar 'the rejoicing and triumph of those two days in the capital cities. There was', he continued, inaccurately, 'a lull in the communal ferocity'.[19] The 15th of August would be one of the most terrible days in the bloody history of Amritsar but in Karachi and Delhi the emphasis was now on the celebration of nationhood. Hindu astrologers had declared that 15 August was an inauspicious day to transfer power in India. The compromise was that instead it would be transferred at midnight on 14 August, with Pakistan's independence celebrations taking place earlier that day in Karachi.

Jinnah left Delhi for Karachi on 7 August. The Mountbattens flew to join him on the evening of 13 August for the start of the celebrations. Shahid Hamid accompanied Auchinleck. They went first to Lahore to confer with Jenkins and Rees. As they flew low over the East Punjab they saw large areas burning, obviously, Hamid noted 'Muslim areas' and column after column of refugees heading for Pakistan. 'Smoke covered the countryside. It presented a grim picture.' Rees pressed Auchinleck for more troops and more mobility. The soldiers he did have were already committed to villages but they needed to conduct more mobile patrolling. The railway staff were too afraid to leave their houses. There were no police to guard the trains anyway and it was yet another task that fell to the army.[20]

Mountbatten was rather pleased to be told that the crowd that lined the route as he drove into Karachi was 'noticeably larger than that which had lined the route for Jinnah's arrival' and, he could not resist adding, 'I found this hard to believe but it was confirmed from one or two other sources'. That evening there was a state banquet for fifty people in what had been the Governor of Sind's house, which was now Jinnah's official residence. The banquet was attended by some of the leading citizens of Pakistan, which, Mountbatten thought, 'included some very queer looking "jungly" men', the tribal leaders from the Frontier. Hamid felt the atmosphere was tense. Jinnah made a short speech and toasted His Majesty the King, the only time, Hamid thought, that he had ever done so to date. Mountbatten spoke at length and justified why the date for the transfer of power had been brought forward. After the banquet there was a reception in the garden for over a thousand people. Jinnah looked 'frail, tired and pre-occupied'. He told Hamid that he wanted to go to bed but Mountbatten wouldn't leave. Hamid was deputed to whisper to the viceroy that it was time to go.[21]

The creation of Pakistan, so different from how Jinnah had at first envisaged it, took place at a short ceremony in the Assembly hall in Karachi the next morning. Present in the circles of seats facing the stage were representatives of the wide cross-section of peoples who now made up this country of two halves, their capitals 1,000 miles apart. Alongside the tribesmen, the Pathans, Afridis, Wazirs and Mahsuds sat Punjabis and men from Baluchistan, and beside them the Bengalis from a province Jinnah had yet to visit. John Christie had written Mountbatten's speech. He had felt it was a bit predictable at the time. 'The birth of Pakistan is an event in history', it read, somewhat obviously. 'History seems sometimes to move with the infinite slowness of a glacier, and sometimes to rush forward in a torrent', Mountbatten intoned, although Christie had originally written 'spate'. 'We who are making history today are caught and carried on in the swift current of events. There is no time to look back. There is only time to look forward.' Mountbatten paid tribute to Jinnah and the two men seemed to be as near friendship as they were ever to achieve.[22]

After the ceremony Jinnah, his sister and the Mountbattens drove in open cars to the airport. This was more of a trial than it appeared as the CID, or what was left of it, which was effectively a young detective called Savage who should have returned to England, had confirmed that there was a serious threat of a bomb attack on the procession by Sikh extremists and the RSS. As the open cars crawled past the hundreds of thousands of cheering Pakistanis, Jinnah expected at any moment that both he and his dream would end in shattered fragments. When they did finally arrive safely at the airport, 'even the austere Jinnah himself showed some emotion'. He turned to Mountbatten and, putting his hand on the viceroy's knee, said, 'Thank God I have brought you out alive'. Fatima Jinnah then kissed Pamela Mountbatten on both cheeks with 'tears in her eyes'.[23]

Some of those who were present felt the atmosphere that day was muted. It was 'marked by a surprising lack of popular enthusiasm' and a 'general air of apathy', thought the correspondent of The Times, despite the celebrations coinciding with the feast of Eid and the end of the Ramadan fast. He did, however, say that Pakistan had emerged as the leading state of the Muslim world. 'From today Karachi takes rank as a new centre of Muslim cohesion and a rallying point for Muslim thought and aspiration.'[24] Others felt the day had been jubilant. 'All along the route there was great enthusiasm and wild cheering', Hamid recalled. 'It was a sight for sore eyes and difficult to describe. A dream was coming true and a state was being born. The name of the Quaid-e-Azam was on everyone's lips as well as their thanks to the Almighty.'[25]

In Dacca the celebrations were generally considered more lively. There was a distinct lack of the new nation's flags, the dark green with the Islamic crescent picked out in white, Mountbatten having failed to persuade either Jinnah or Nehru to include a small Union Jack in the corner, but people were in a more festive mood. Overall, the fact that the celebrations took place at all, that the ceremony was dignified and that the crowd control worked was a triumph for Jinnah and Liaquat who only a month before had been arguing over the number of typewriters their new nation should be allocated. Now they had to build a nation.

Early in the evening of 14 August, back in Delhi, Nehru's ministers, the men and women who would form India's first government, were blessed in Dr Rajendra Prasad's garden. A Brahmin holy man intoned scriptures while they were anointed with holy water and the red vermilion dot, the Hindu 'third eye', was placed on their foreheads. Later that evening, as the clock approached midnight, they started to gather in the Constituent Assembly. Hundreds of thousands would join them outside. Kushwant Singh, who had been practising law in Lahore, had driven down the Grand Trunk Road to be there. He described it as the most 'eerie' drive he had ever had. The road was deserted. He did not see a soul, no traffic, no bullock carts and no people apart from jeeps full of armed Sikhs whom he assumed had been butchering Muslims. The atmosphere in Delhi was extraordinary. The crowd was enormous. People were yelling and there was a great feeling of enthusiasm and euphoria. Everyone was shouting Gandhi's name; he was credited with bringing India to freedom, even though he was now hundreds of miles away in Calcutta.[26] The celebrations were wild, even though half the population of Delhi was living on the pavements or in refugee camps. There was a huge upsurge of goodwill towards 'the Brits' with 'stiff colonels lifted shoulder high and carried around the city'. Somehow everything the British had done in the past had been forgiven.[27]

The mood in the Constituent Assembly was, the *Daily Telegraph* thought, subdued. The members seemed nervous and silent.[28] Nehru spoke just before midnight. His speeches were never extemporaneous but rather the result of long hours of crafting and rehearsal. This, perhaps the most important speech of his life, was no exception and, with his understanding of the power of the English language and his soft, clear articulation, it has deservedly passed into history. 'Long years ago we made a tryst with destiny', he started, his voice broadcast to the vast crowds surrounding the Assembly building, 'and now that time comes when we shall redeem our pledge, not wholly or in full measure, but very substantially. At the stroke of the midnight hour, when the world sleeps, India will awake to life and freedom.' It was, Kushwant Singh thought, immaculately crafted and very well worded. Nehru made no mention of the unfolding tragedy but Kushwant Singh, who would lose everything he owned in Lahore, felt that did not matter. He felt somehow he would get back to it all. The two things, the celebration of independence and the realisation of the enormous tragedy it represented, seemed just to go side by side. As Nehru finished speaking, and as the clock struck midnight, a Congress trumpeter blew a conch shell in the Assembly gallery, unkindly described as a 'toneless shriek' but a nice juxtaposition to the pomp of the Raj's trumpeters.[29] The Assembly members then sang 'Hindustan Hamara', 'India is Ours', written by Mohammed Iqbal. 'Then Delhi became a babel of noise and rejoicing', the *Daily Telegraph* continued. 'Trumpets blared, motor horns roared, fireworks, temple bells, guns, conch shells all added to the din.'[30]

The next day, 15 August itself, started with Mountbatten, no longer viceroy, being sworn in as governor general. Scores of servants toured what was now Government House, changing everything from the coat of arms over the Durbar Hall to the bands on the cigars. Later that day he processed with Nehru and the now governor general's bodyguard to the raising of India's national flag at the Red Fort. There had been some nervousness about the bodyguard. Paddy Massey, who commanded it, had been to see Ismay to say that his men of both classes, Sikhs and Punjabi Muslims, were receiving 'news of horrible happenings in their homes and of murders of their kith and kin. He thought there was a real danger of their wreaking vengeance on each other'. Massey paraded his men and told them they represented two hundred years of unblemished tradition. The Muslim squadron would be sent to Pakistan to form Jinnah's Governor General's Bodyguard as soon as transport could be arranged. Surely the two factions could live at peace and continue to do their duty for the few days that remained? Both squadrons did eventually agree; they would perform their duties but no longer speak to each other.[31]

In the event the crowds were so thick they had to give up all hope of performing the ceremony. The flag was raised and the salute fired with the bodyguard, Mountbatten, Nehru and the Polish wife of a British officer, who was lost in the crowd, marooned in their carriage amid a vast throng of cheering people. 'This was done amid scenes of the most frantic rejoicing and as the flag broke on a brilliant rainbow appeared in the sky which was taken by the whole crowd as a good omen', Mountbatten wrote. 'There were lots of shouts of "Jai Hind" and "Mahatma Gandhi Ki Jai"', he continued to Listowel, 'but there were also lots of shouts of "Mountbatten Ki Jai" and more than one of "Pandit Mountbatten Ki Jai"', a tendency to self-congratulation, which was unnecessary given the significance of his achievement and something that would later so damage his reputation.[32]

Inder Malhotra had walked the ten miles into Delhi from the village where his father was stationmaster to be there. There were no trains. A Muslim village nearby had been attacked and most of the people killed. Some had fled into Delhi where they now joined the crowds of other refugees. Eleven had pleaded with his parents for protection. His father had hidden them and managed to signal a Pakistan special train that wasn't meant to stop until Lahore to pick them up. Despite this Inder was determined to celebrate. He found a spot near the Assembly on the evening of 14 August. A family next to them kept asking what the excitement was. A young girl said, 'Today is Mr. Nehru's coronation'. Inder, a convinced socialist who had tried to get himself jailed as a Young Congress member, screamed at her. He remembered the strange mixture of fear and anger on the one hand and enormous goodwill on the other. He felt that Nehru saying, in his 'gentle tones', that India was an entity where everyone was equal and a democratic, secular country, was his 'noblest legacy' and very brave considering the growing strength of strong Hindu nationalism.

Elsewhere in India there were very different emotions. In Lucknow, where the Union Jack had flown continuously from the Residency to commemorate the many British who had been slaughtered there in 1857, a noisy crowd arrived wanting to tear it down and replace it with the new Indian flag. Pandit Pant, despite his long years of incarceration by the British, intervened, refusing to allow them to desecrate a memorial to British dead. Instead the Union flag was lowered for the last time, the flagstaff cut down and the access steps up to it cemented up. 'We shall not', Tuker wrote, 'forget Pandit Pant'. In Calcutta the celebrations mostly went off peacefully. Rajagopalachari, Nehru's nomination as Governor of West Bengal, was not a particularly popular choice among Bengalis. As he arrived for his handover from Sir Frederick Burrows he was met by a mob chanting 'Go back, Rajagopalachari' but the ceremony went ahead as planned until near the end when a mob invaded Government House and stole all the silver. That apart, the mood in the city was 'of great jubilation and fraternization amongst all classes'. Would that it could last.[33]

The mood among those British who were left was mixed. Sir Alfred Watson, writing in the *Daily Telegraph*, spoke for the more unashamedly imperialist. 'The Indians have contended', he wrote, 'that left to itself India would have provided itself with all the apparatus of a modern state. The only answer to that can be that no Asian country, with the exception of Japan, has done so. The chapter closes upon a great chapter of British and Indian history, upon the most fruitful experiment the world has seen in the government of an alien people.' And, he added, untruthfully, 'Remarkable has been the material advance. There are those who hold that Britain's greatest gifts to India have been the system of British law, impartially administered and open to all, and the English language.'[34]

The Times paid a slightly barbed tribute to the British who had run India for both the Company and the Crown, saying that their presence "was marked not by any glittering display of intellectual gifts but by a certain refreshing diffusion of a wholesome air. In his image as nowadays presented by Indians, the British official in India was like the British climate, more than trying at times but very healthy to live with".[35]

In the Indian Army 2,590 British soldiers had said they would stay on. The figure had fluctuated wildly over the previous months but that was the 'official' number on 15 August. The Indian press continued to attack them, with headlines like 'Subtle move to retain Britishers in Indian Army'. In fact most would serve in Pakistan, where Jinnah offered a genuine welcome and where they would serve under a British commander-in-chief, General Sir Frank Messervy, and a team of British governors like Bourne in East Bengal and Cunningham on the North West Frontier. J. P. Cross and the officers of 1st Battalion 1st King George V's Own Gurkha Rifles dined together on 14 August. At the end of dinner the mess president stood and said quietly, 'Mr. Vice (the traditional army invitation to the vice president to propose a toast), the King Emperor'; 'Mr. Vice, at the other end of the table, stood up, gripped his glass, lifted it for the loyal toast and said, "Gentlemen, for the last time the King Emperor." We all rose and lifting our glasses in our right hands, intoned the solemn refrain to the litany of lament; "For the last time the King Emperor."' It was a ritual that would be repeated many times across the subcontinent. The next morning, Independence Day, they held a church service with the other five battalions in Razmak. Four of these were destined for Pakistan; only the Gurkhas and a battalion of the Rajputana Rifles would move to India. As the minister prayed for peace between the two new dominions, the Pathans started sniping them from a nearby hill. The Rajputana Rifles, dressed in their dhotis, responded by firing mortar bombs in reply.[36]

The 19th Lancers, stationed in Peshawar, held their final parade on 15 August and hauled down the Union Jack for the last time. The Muslim squadrons were staying put but they now had to get their

Sikh and Jat squadrons safely into India. 'The local population had shown little antipathy to Hindus but towards the Sikhs their hatred was murderous', originating, so the regiment thought, in the days of Sikh rule a century before. The commanding officer had therefore decided to keep the Sikh squadron out of the public eye until he could get them away. He kept them in barracks, making them responsible for the security of the camp and its perimeter. One morning, as a truckload of Punjabi Muslim infantry went past the gate, a young Sikh on guard duty loosed off a shot which hit their lorry. Nobody ever discovered what had made him do it and it was probably an accident, what the army calls an 'ND', or 'negligent discharge', but the effect was catastrophic. The Punjabis thought they were being attacked by the Sikhs, rushed to their own lines, aroused the rest of their company and mounted a full-scale assault on 19th Lancers' lines. A hysterical officer rang Edward Behr, still Intelligence Officer of the brigade. He rushed to find Brigadier Morris, his brigade commander, who was having breakfast on his lawn having just finished an early morning game of tennis. Together they drove straight into the 19th Lancers' barracks, Morris still wearing his tennis whites but with his red-rimmed general staff officer's hat rammed on his head so he was recognised. He told Behr to drive straight onto the parade ground in between the two opposing groups. This was a brave thing to do. Both sides were lying in fire positions taking potshots at each other and the Punjabis had brought up a machine gun, which was firing bursts into the Sikh barrack blocks. Behr stopped the jeep in the middle of the parade ground. The firing slackened. Morris told Behr to go over to the Punjabis and make them stand up while he addressed the Sikhs. 'Now then, what's all this nonsense!' Behr heard him shout. 'Get up! All of you!' The Sikhs sheepishly obeyed.

Luckily the only casualty of the morning was the Sikh who had fired the first shot. 'A young man, he lay on a stretcher waiting for an ambulance, and a fellow lancer was trying to keep the flies away from his appalling wound. From chest to crutch his stomach was like a model used in medical school for anatomy lessons.' He died soon afterwards.[37] The 19th Lancers' solution was ultimately for the two

Muslim squadrons to escort their Indian comrades to the border but they had to endure several more anxious weeks until that was possible. They didn't tell anyone, least of all the police, and conducted the operation in such secrecy that the Sikhs and Jats were well beyond the Indus river before anyone realised they had gone. It was the sort of incident that would soon be repeated many times.[38]

The week before, the senior Indian officers had invited their Pakistani counterparts to a party at the Delhi Gymkhana Club. K. M. Cariappa, the senior Indian, made a speech in which he said 'au-revoir' rather than 'good-bye' deliberately. 'I associate the honest and sincere wishes of every one of us here that we shall meet each other frequently as the best of friends in the same spirit of good comradeship that we have had the good fortune to enjoy all these years.' Brigadier Aga Mohammed Raza, the senior Pakistani present, replied in the same spirit. They then all sang 'Auld Lang Syne' and Cariappa presented Raza with a silver trophy of two Indian soldiers, one Hindu, the other Muslim, with their rifles pointing at a common enemy. The mood, although jolly on the surface, was, some felt, forced and 'the atmosphere charged with uncertainty'. Nehru attended but looked very 'off colour', as he usually did at military gatherings.[39]

For most, despite forgivable feelings of nostalgia, Independence passed quietly. Rumours circulated that the members of the Peshawar Club had shot all the Peshawar Vale hounds they had kept to hunt jackal rather than leave them for their Pakistani successors. It was precisely that, just a rumour, and the hounds and the club were both successfully handed over. The Peshawar Club is still there to this day with its library full of useful books from the Raj years such as *Big Game, Boers and Boches: A Sportsman's Notebook* by Lieutenant Colonel Prescott-Westcar and copies of *Thacker's Directory to the British India and Native States*. Much of what had given the Raj its distinctive flavour would remain, perhaps even more so in Pakistan than in India.

By 15 August the majority of the ruling princes had agreed to accede, even Bhopal, although he kept Patel waiting until the last minute, asking for a ten-day extension; eventually he signed the papers providing Mountbatten kept them in his safe until he agreed to their release. Just three held out. The first, Junagadh, had, some thought, possibly been too busy marrying off one of his dogs and simply omitted to file his papers; they would be very wrong. Although his was a relatively small state, the issue of its accession would soon cause a serious problem as would that of the other two major states, Hyderabad and Kashmir. The Nizam of Hyderabad had held a dinner on 14 August to celebrate Independence but it had been a miserable affair and not just because of his legendary meanness. Still dressed in his customary torn and faded trousers, the Nizam proposed a final toast to the King Emperor. John Peyton, an English guest, thought how sad it was to see two hundred years of history 'ending in one brief, pathetic gesture'.[40] Kashmir remained silent.

On 16 August, after the euphoria had abated, the Boundary Commission findings were briefed to the political leadership. Radcliffe submitted three separate reports and maps. The first dealt with the Punjab, the second Bengal and the third Sylhet and Assam. He said the Punjab had been very difficult, especially the area between the rivers Beas and Sutlej (see map on page 208) on the one hand and the River Ravi on the other. He had cut the key irrigation canals off from their headwaters, for example, the Dipalpur Canal was cut off from its Ferozepore headworks and the same applied to the Upper Bari Doab Canal. These decisions were, he argued, unavoidable but he thought it 'only right to express the hope that, where the drawing of a boundary line cannot avoid disrupting such unitary services as canal irrigation, railways and electric power transmission, a solution may be found by agreement between the two states for some joint control of what has hitherto been a valuable common service'. That was very much the original spirit of partition.[41]

In Bengal he had looked at splitting Calcutta but decided it was impossible. He had, however, awarded the Chittagong Hill Tracts to East Pakistan. This was a logical decision as Chittagong was completely cut off from India by East Pakistan but it caused an eruption from Nehru and Patel. Congress had given assurances to the local leadership that the area would come to India. The population was, Nehru swore, '97% Buddhist and Hindu'. Patel accused Radcliffe of looking after the interests of the chiefs and not their tribesmen. 'There was not the least doubt that the people themselves would prefer to form part of India' and 'Radcliffe had no business to touch them'. Liaquat, who represented Pakistan at the briefing, would not consider any changes. The commission's awards, taken as a whole, had, he said, been so unfavourable to Pakistan that he could not consider even minor modifications. It was wholly unreasonable that Darjeeling, the Bengal hill station and tea-growing region, and Jalpaiguri, the town below it on the plains, had not come to Pakistan. There was then a general disagreement about the Punjab but the Radcliffe awards remained unaltered. The two new states now knew where their boundaries ran, except in Kashmir, but what would the effect be on the ground as the awards were made public?[42]

Radcliffe left India on 18 August. Beaumont went with him. Radcliffe seemed bitter that he had been forced to rush such a critical job and that he would carry the blame for displacing so many millions. 'Nobody in India will love me for my award', he wrote to his stepson. 'There will be about eighty million people with a grievance who will be looking for me. I do not want them to find me. I've worked and travelled and sweated – I have sweated the whole time'. He never returned to India.[43]

Later, Christopher Beaumont went to see him in his Chambers in London and challenged him directly as to whether Mountbatten had asked him to change the allocation of Ferozepore and Zira from Pakistan to India. Beaumont pointed out that during those long, hot six weeks it had been the only occasion they had been separated. 'I was', Beaumont later wrote, 'a most unwelcome visitor. Radcliffe said he was very busy and shuffled me off. There was no discussion about the boundary.'[44]

The holocaust in the Punjab that followed Independence would see over 1 million killed and at least 10 million lose their homes. It was one of the worst disasters caused by man since the Second World War. It resulted, together with the conflict in Kashmir, in the two new dominions, far from cooperating as Mountbatten and Radcliffe hoped, or reuniting as Nehru and Gandhi had dreamt, ending up fighting two major wars and as antagonistic nuclear powers. It was, among stiff competition, one of the twentieth century's greatest tragedies.

Once the new border was known, the north–south line between Amritsar and Lahore that divided the Punjab in two, Sikhs and Hindus from across Pakistan, but mostly from the new state of West Punjab, left the homes many had occupied for centuries and tried to reach India. This was despite Jinnah's consistent message that they were welcome to stay and would have their rights protected. There were approximately 5 million of them, cut off from India by a stroke of Radcliffe's pencil. Muslim gangs, the *goondas*, attacked them as they fled, raping, murdering and looting, and forcibly converting those they spared. Where communities were slow to leave, their villages were attacked and they were forced out by those hungry for their land and property. In the East Punjab the pattern was reversed. Over 6 million Muslims fled west, driven out by Sikh *jathas*, often amid scenes of sickening, medieval violence and gratuitous cruelty. It was, as Liaquat Ali said, as if 'our people have gone mad'.

The endemic violence that had been continuing for a year, since the Great Calcutta Killings of August 1946, and which had periodically flared into spasms such as in Rawalpindi in March, now became widespread, frenzied and on a scale India had never previously witnessed. It 'amounted to determined and almost universal conflict throughout the twelve [border] districts,' Rees wrote. 'Large gangs, often 600 strong and more' operated 'and once open fighting started in a locality the number would soon swell to a few thousand'.[45] What made the killing even more abhorrent was the systematic raping, mutilation and then murder of captured women, something that both Sikhs and Muslims practised to bestial excess.

Independence Day itself was particularly bad. In Lahore a Muslim mob set fire to a Sikh gurdwara, burning its twenty-two guards and worshippers alive. A large picket of Muslim military police nearby did not intervene. In Amritsar that afternoon Sikhs paraded naked Muslim women, who were then publicly raped before being set fire to in the street. Some older Sikhs did intervene to rescue a few who survived, and gave them sanctuary in the Golden Temple. Up until the middle of August the worst of the violence was in the cities, or at least it was there it was most visible. Arson was so widespread that the fire brigade became irrelevant; on 15 August there were thirty major fires in Amritsar alone and twenty-one in Ferozepore. Jullundur was particularly badly affected. It was a predominantly Muslim city with a population of 120,000 living in its narrow lanes of whom only a few thousand were Sikhs. On 17 August thousands more Sikhs poured in from outlying villages and started a street-by-street massacre. Robert Bristow commanded the 11th Brigade who were stationed nearby. Entering the city he found the Sikh gangs at work. 'Armed with *kirpans*,' which Sikhs were, by law, permitted to carry, they were 'using long poles with burning rags at the top. They were setting alight to Muslim houses, of which the occupants had to choose between dying in the flames or being cut down in the street'. He found his Sikh soldiers firing high on purpose and not attempting to interfere. 'They were not unfriendly but conveyed by their demeanour that the Raj had ended and the conflict should be left to them to settle in their own way.'[46]

Abdul Haq was a seven-year-old boy when the attacks came. His mother and two sisters had already left for Pakistan but he and his father had stayed to look after the family's smallholding just outside Jullundur. Now, with Jullundur in flames, they tried to escape but as they fled his father collapsed and died in the road, leaving Abdul alone. He found his cousin who got him onto a train for Pakistan. It was absolutely packed with people escaping the fighting so Abdul sat on the roof. He remembered it crossing a river that was more blood than water. He was lucky. The train was ambushed by a *jatha* and everyone inside was hacked to death. Those on the roof managed to escape. Eventually he got across the border and was reunited with his mother but the shock had been too much for her and she died two days after he arrived. He and his sisters, aged twelve and two, were left alone. The poor but secure life they had enjoyed in a mixed Sikh/ Muslim world had collapsed completely within a week.[47]

The success of the Jullundur attacks encouraged the *jathas* to go on to attack Hoshiarpur and Ludhiana, where the atrocities were repeated. Appalled by what he had seen in Amritsar on 15 August, Rees called a meeting of the Sikh community leaders. He opened by saying that the 'situation could not be worse'. The police, now disarmed by their new Hindu officers, had lost what little effectiveness they had. There were only about two hundred Sikh and Hindu police left on duty and they were 'panicky, firing off wildly all night'. They would also not intervene to help Muslims and in fact often assisted the Sikh mobs. Rees gave Tara Singh, the leader of the Sikh political party, a message from Muslim leaders in Lahore offering a 'reciprocal laying off'. Tara Singh promised there would be no untoward incidents in rural areas and said he would try to stop the violence in Amritsar itself. The problem though was that the Muslim papers like the *Nawaiwaqt* were taunting Sikhs with headlines saying they were too cowardly to attack mosques. They then discussed starting an escort system to take Muslim refugees to the border. The PBF had twenty-eight lorries available. They would collect Muslim refugees and transport them with a Muslim escort. Tara Singh said the Sikhs would try to help with the safe collection of Muslims but they would not trust working with a Muslim escort. Was there no British escort available? That evening Rees sat down and tried to work out which tasks his 'class' troops could perform and which could be performed by any. Bristow's experience in Jullundur and the reports of Muslim soldiers' inactivity in Lahore were causing him to reassess his view that his soldiers were unaffected by communalism.[48]

There were some genuine attempts by the Sikh leadership to persuade their followers to reduce the violence in Amritsar and over the next few days it did slacken off slightly; Rees noticed that by 21 August there were even a few shops open. This was partly because by this time most of the Muslims had left and partly due to there being little Muslim property left to burn. It was also because the

PBF had been able to gather scattered groups who had managed to barricade themselves in protected strongholds called *kuchabandi*. However, it was also because the terror now moved out of the cities into the countryside, into those 17,000-odd hamlets and villages that the PBF could not possibly protect. Neither was there an effective police intelligence system to warn of attacks so that troops could be concentrated. This had evaporated as the officers who had run it had left. With the army's intelligence still, bizarrely, concentrating on Palestine and the Soviet Union, and the lack of aircraft, the PBF was operating blind while its movements were constantly reported back to the *jathas* by the locals. Consequently if troops managed to prevent raids it was often just coincidence.

Bristow described the technique of a Sikh attack when he witnessed the aftermath of a *jatha* raiding the Muslim village of Rahon, near the River Sutlej, from the air. Several thousand Sikhs were milling around the village loading loot onto bullock carts. The only survivors appeared to be about one hundred people standing in a straight line 'as if on a parade'. On closer inspection they turned out to be all young women and girls being 'inspected by a group of grey-haired *jathedars* in what looked like a distribution ceremony'. Several corpses lay around, cut down while they tried to run but most people had been slaughtered in their houses with the Sikh kirpans, presumably in front of the girls now being sized up. Bristow was being flown by a young Sikh officer. 'I am ashamed of my people,' he said. Their aircraft, being a reconnaissance plane, was not armed but Bristow had his pistol and they had a signalling pistol. They flew in low, circling the *jatha*, Bristow firing his pistol and the pilot letting off Very cartridges. The Sikhs promptly scattered. It showed, Bristow noted, how effective some ground-attack aircraft would have been. 'Surely', he added, 'the fiendish mass killing justified such a course?'[49]

Landing back at their headquarters Bristow immediately dispatched a patrol but it arrived to find only dead bodies. The Sikhs had melted away and protested violently at house searches in their villages, which they said violated the privacy of their women. The fate of the abducted Muslim women was, on the other hand, 'ghastly.

Most were murdered when the Sikhs had no further use for them'. Clifford Williams, an officer in Bristow's brigade, was driving along the Grand Trunk Road when he came across the naked, mutilated bodies of forty women of whom just one was still alive. Their breasts had been sliced off and 'the stomachs of the pregnant women slit open with their unborn babies beside them. While I gazed at this gruesome sight, a woman without breasts painfully sat up, saw me and sank back to die, and as she did so she pulled over a piece of clothing to hide her nakedness'.[50]

Such atrocities were not confined to the Sikhs. In the West Punjab Muslim gangs carried out acts of equal horror on fleeing Hindus and Sikhs. What the Sikhs did have was superior organisation and weaponry. The *jathas* had recognised leaders, who were often mounted, good communications and worked around a core with modern weapons, which would be reinforced by local villagers for specific operations. The PBF encountered *jathas* of five or six thousand when there was a raid on a train, for example. The Muslims generally failed to match this in East Punjab. There were exceptions, such as in Qadian, to the east of Amritsar, where the community organised itself to protect the holy Ahmediya shrine. Here they used proper signalling equipment and even two light aircraft from the local flying club until Rees grounded them. The Muslim gangs also had modern weapons but they suffered from not having the Sikh privilege of carrying the kirpan, most of which were more like large cutlasses than the intended ceremonial dagger.

The tactics both sides used were a mixture of attacks on villages, which would then be looted and burned, and ambushes either on trains or on columns of refugees. The crops were high, it being pre-harvest, and concealment was easy. The attackers would remain hidden until the last minute, then pour in a preliminary volley. The refugee column would break and scatter and then be pursued with swords and every sort of handheld weapon from farm implements to home-made hand-grenades. While there was some element of looting in village and train attacks, most attacks on refugee columns were motivated by killing for its own sake.

Moon, accompanied by the Nawab of Bahawalpur's dewan, Mushtaq Ahmad Gurmani, drove into Hasilpur, now firmly in Pakistan, a 'colony' town, inhabited by people who had been granted reclaimed land, on the edge of the desert watered by the Fordwah Canal. 'It was a growing and flourishing little market town with a bright future', Moon recalled. It had a sizeable population of Hindu merchants and, being a colony town, a largish government office and police station. But as they drove in they found it deserted apart from an old man who told them that all the Hindus had gone away. When asked where, he pointed in the direction of 'old Hasilpur', about two miles north. As they entered it they saw what looked like a couple of men lying on the ground. 'They're corpses', Gurmani exclaimed, and as they came into the centre of the village what they at first took to be heaps of manure turned out to be pile upon pile of bodies. 'Men, women and children were all jumbled up together, their arms and legs akimbo in all sorts of attitudes and postures'. Moon was reminded of pictures he had seen as a child of Napoleonic battle-fields. Near the top of the village, in a large two-storeyed building, they found the few survivors,

a throng of women and children whose sobbing and whimpering swelled to a deafening crescendo of mingled grief and resentment as soon as they caught sight of us. It was hard to endure. In an open space outside there lay two or three wounded men under an ill-contrived awning of tattered sacking. One of them, almost stark naked, was literally covered in blood and an old woman was pathetically fanning his face trying to keep the flies off him.

They counted three hundred and fifty corpses.[51]
Many of the atrocities in West Punjab carried a particular pathos. Niranjan Singh, a Sikh tea merchant in Montgomery Bazaar, had served tea to his friend, a Muslim leather worker, for many years. The week after Independence the man came running into his shop one morning shrieking 'Kill him! Kill him!' A gang of Muslim thugs rushed in. One cut Singh's leg with his sword; others killed

his ninety-year-old father and only son. The last thing Singh could recall was his eighteen-year-old daughter being carried off on the shoulders of 'a man to whom he'd been serving tea for fifteen years'.[52]

One of the most hateful aspects of the Muslim atrocities in West Punjab was forcible conversion. It was common practice for some *goondas* to offer captured Sikhs and Hindus their lives if they would become Muslims and many accepted. Moon came across a crowd of Hindus paraded by their Muslim captors on the side of the road near Khairpur. They staged a demonstration for him and Gurmani, one of them 'holding up a stick with a little green flag, gazing up at it and shouting'. He 'grinned ingratiatingly and, pointing up to the miserable bit of green cloth, said, "This is our flag. We now have Pakistan and Muslim Raj".' Then they noticed the man was wearing earrings. 'He's nothing but a Hindu shop-keeper', exclaimed their accompanying policeman. Closer inspection revealed that they were all Hindus. The four accompanying Muslims were arrested and an escort left in the Hindu's nearby village. The *thanedar* here, the community Hindu leader, explained that they had been given the choice of conversion or death when a mob had attacked the day before. Others were more resilient. A Hindu village near Lyallpur was marched en masse to a pond, made to wash and were then sat in a mosque to hear Koranic verses. They were then told that they had 'the choice of becoming Muslims and living happily or being killed'. Most accepted new Muslim names and converted. They were made to eat meat. One man, a Brahmin, went back to his hut on the pretext of collecting his family. As soon as he entered the house he took out a knife and killed his wife and children before committing suicide.[53]

There was the very occasional happy ending when humanity and decency overcame sectarian hatred. Sant Singh, a First World War Sikh veteran, had been given a plot of colony land between the Ravi and Sutlej rivers as part of his army resettlement. His life's work had been clearing it and building the house where he had raised his family. One of his Muslim workers warned him that his settlement would be attacked and it duly was. Singh and five others rounded up the village women and loaded them onto a truck but no sooner had they left than it ran out of petrol. A Muslim neighbour saw them and ran off. They feared the worse, thinking any minute a *goonda* would appear, slaughter them and carry off their wives and daughters. They took the decision to shoot their womenfolk rather than risk the fate that would inevitably await them. They lined them up alongside the track and blindfolded them. Each loaded their weapons. Singh quoted the Sikh scriptures as he prepared to kill his wife and daughters. Just as they were on the point of firing they saw headlights and heard shouting. They paused. It turned out to be an army patrol. They were Muslim soldiers but 'The officer was a good man, a major. He said he would save us'.[54]

Of all the terrible images of the Punjab that August, it is those pictures of trains, either overcrowded with desperate refugees or, more often, as ghost trains full of dead bodies, that have remained most vivid. Protecting trains had long been part of internal security requirements. There was a well-known railway protection scheme, which had regularly been rehearsed on exercises. This had been activated in late July with the early Muslim attacks on trains carrying Sikhs east. However, its problem was that it relied on the *Tikka Para* system, whereby each village was responsible for the smooth running of the railway through their area. It also relied on train crews not being terrorised and on adequate police being available; by 15 August none of these conditions could be met and protection devolved, as with everything else, to the military. With train attacks becoming increasingly common, and with the railway staff frequently colluding with the attackers by passing on details of routes and timing, train protection became a major task. Various techniques were tried from 'pilot trains', where a goods train or coal train would precede a passenger train in an attempt to spring any ambushes prematurely, attaching flat railcars with sandbags and machine guns front and rear and patrolling the lines with the limited aircraft available. Nothing worked very well and the train massacres that continued throughout August and September were among the most bloody and horrific.

John Moores, an officer in the 9th Gurkhas, was in charge of escorting a Muslim refugee train into Pakistan that had to go through Amritsar. It wasn't, he recalled, a proper train but just a lot of coal wagons. 'We loaded up these wretched refugees. It was very distressing. The journey from Ambala to Amritsar was usually 4–5 hours. In this case it took four days. There was no water.' They had their own water for his troops but 'they had a job to do'. As they came into Amritsar station they found it had been taken over by hundreds of armed Sikhs, not just on the platforms but across the tracks.

> They were like sardines. They all had weapons of some sort. Some were fairly modern rifles – some spears, swords. They were shoulder to shoulder, shoving, pushing. You realised you were just going into hell. They would have gone for us before the refugees. We had to look tough and let them know we meant business. We got our grenades out and primed them. Doing that made the crowds pull back. We must have been in the station for four hours . . .

But they managed to hold off an attack and take the train safely on. Later he met a refugee train from Pakistan at Ambala. It was a trainload of

> five to six hundred people, most of whom had been slaughtered. Most were elderly people, children, young women and they had been hacked and murdered – shot – I can remember seeing a young woman who had been hacked. Her head was open. We could see her brains but there was nothing we could do. We didn't have any surgical facilities. This extraordinary cruelty was something we really didn't know anything about.[55]

Quite apart from the failure to make anything like adequate security arrangements, neither had there been any planning to deal with what now became a flood of refugees, most of whom had lost everything and who were now destitute. Naffese Chohan, the thirteen-year-old girl who lived north-east of Amritsar and whose cousin had knocked on their door in despair having fled the Calcutta killings the previous year, and who had warned that the same thing would happen in the Punjab, was one of those who now fled. They were a well-off family with a field buffalo and a Hindu worker who looked after the farm. Things had started to go wrong in the spring, after the Rawalpindi killings. Their Hindu worker had started to refuse to come to work. Hindu shopkeepers would not sell them sugar or salt. Then, as Independence was being celebrated in Delhi, her grandparents were murdered. Her parents knew they had to get out quickly. They paid 300 rupees each for places on a truck. 'We didn't pick up our things', she recalled, 'We just wanted to survive'. After a terrifying journey, dodging Sikh roadblocks, they got across the border. They were directed to Lahore station, among a teeming mass of destitute people. The terror and the awful realisation that as a family they may be alive but had lost everything made Naffese and her sister break down. 'We just screamed and screamed and cried "We want to go home, we want to go home."' But 'home' was now the platforms of Lahore station where they would spend seven days living off scraps.[56]

Her family was but one of millions who now needed help but, with a total breakdown in government, the only people who could provide help on that scale quickly were, once again, the PBF. They had to escort the refugee columns and also run the makeshift camps as best they could, both for collecting outgoing refugees and as somewhere for the incoming columns to be held. Lieutenant Colonel K. P. Candeth, now serving with his new Indian regiment in Jullundur, remembers an 'unending stream of people moving both ways. Long convoys and columns on the roads and the trains all packed to the brim'. His problem was to ensure that the columns didn't meet as this inevitably led to violence, although, pathetically, by the last week of August the refugees were so exhausted and so numbed that they would pass each other in sullen silence. A more serious problem was when a train came in from West Punjab and they opened the doors to find only dead and dying. This enraged local people who would set out to attack the slow-moving columns of East Punjabi

Muslims heading west. Apart from trying to protect those leaving, his men also had to direct those arriving to concentration areas, many of which then became 'camps' by default but there were very few supplies. The Punjab was desperately short of petrol, the normal distribution system having broken down. There was no fuel resupply to Lahore from Karachi after 10 August. The Burmah-Shell oil company had 80,000 gallons in reserve, but with high military usage and the demands of the camps demanding 11,000 gallons per day, this was quickly exhausted and had to be rationed.

The general misery of the Punjab was made even worse by the monsoon. Having obstinately refused to break until mid-August, it now did so with unusual violence. Torrential bursts of rain, usually lasting several minutes, quickly turned the ground into a muddy morass and the many Punjab rivers into torrents. In between the showers, the heat and humidity remained terrible so that even the slightest movement left people perspiring and dehydrated. There was little clean drinking water to be had. Punjabis were used to reasonably pure and germ-free canal water but the same could not be said 'of the puddles and pools on the wayside, generally covered with a layer of green scum. The horrible thought of a mass outbreak of cholera rose like a grim and terrifying spectre'.[57]

The refugee problem started to become critical from 18 August. That week there would be 1.5 million already in the makeshift camps around Lahore, tying down the troops guarding them and presenting an ever-increasing humanitarian problem. In East Punjab there were roughly the same number. Nehru visited one of the camps on 22 August. 'I vividly recall the refugees wanted to kill him', Ashoka Gupta, a disciple of Gandhi's remembered.

> The man who grew up as the darling of the people was going to be killed by the same people. I had been a pro Nehru fellow. But that evening I did not feel because I thought the leaders of our country are truly responsible for all this havoc. I thought he was only harvesting what he had sown. So for the first time I felt no reverence towards him.[58]

Later Nehru attended a conference in Jullundur with Trivedi, the new Governor of East Punjab and Mumtaz Daultana, the new Pakistani Premier of West Punjab. They concluded that each government should be responsible for their own refugees but that the policy should be to encourage people to stay where they were. The camps should be centralised into a few big ones, which would be easier to protect. But sensible as these decisions undoubtedly were there was no practical hope of persuading people to stay put when to do so would probably mean that they would be murdered and who was to protect the refugees in the larger camps?

At the end of that first terrible week Pete Rees laid out the problems the PBF faced in his notebook. His first, urgent requirement was for more troops. The 'paramount problem is to produce bodies. If the Sikhs get more determined, the army will have to rely on bigger detachments' and so cover fewer villages. In East Punjab the refugee problem was 'assuming gigantic proportions'. All his existing PBF units were tied down. He desperately needed another two brigades, so about 10,000 men, for the south-east, Hoshiarpur and Jullundur, alone. His men were exhausted and had 'been going flat out for over three weeks' in the mud and stifling, humid heat. Liaison with the fledgling East Punjab was weak; he needed a deputy commander, was desperate for transport, for an intelligence staff to give him some notification of the movements of the *jathas* and *goondas*, needed a separate headquarters to plan for refugees, a press team to deal with the horde of international journalists all desperate to get front-page stories, and was frantic for more aircraft.[59]

Above all he was beginning to understand the reality, so hard for a professional British Indian Army officer like him to face, that 'class'-based units were not trustworthy. What Bristow had witnessed in Jullundur was becoming a widespread problem. Some troops, like the Nawab of Bahawalpur's state forces, were actively working with the mobs but now even his own battalions were siding according to communal affiliation. This was happening on both sides of the border. Liaquat had complained of Hindu units in the East Punjab attacking Muslims and there had been three occasions when the

Dogras and Baluchs had actually attacked each other.[60] What Rees now wanted, and wanted urgently, was Gurkhas and, although he couldn't say it given Attlee's policy that they should not be used to save Indian lives, those six well-equipped, mobile British brigades, one of whose regiments Mountbatten had travelled to Bombay to bid farewell to after the Independence celebrations on 15 August.

Nehru, conferring with Rees's senior Indian adviser, Brigadier Thimayya, 'an ancient patriot with high ambitions for India',[61] was coming to the same conclusion. Mixed troops were 'generally speaking not successful' and he had a 'grave disquiet that raids had been led by men in uniform'.[62] But Nehru's deduction, encouraged by Thimayya, was different. If the PBF was not working because of its 'class' units then, rather than bring in non-class formations – interestingly there was no problem at all with Indian battalions like the Mahars, generally made up of low-caste Hindus and who treated the Muslims with respect – the solution was to end the PBF and Indianise the force, with Pakistan doing the same thing in West Punjab. Nehru had never liked the Joint Defence Council anyway, and he was growing to dislike Auchinleck even more. Auchinleck himself remained solidly opposed to the PBF. 'The sooner I can break it up the better from my point of view', he told the Joint Defence Council on 30 August.[63] But without it, and with Indian troops now supporting Hindus and Sikhs in opposition to the new national Pakistan forces supporting the Muslims, liaison and joint working would go, and with that would go so many of the aspirations for a cooperative relationship between the new nations. It was a sad prelude to the coming catastrophe in October.

But Rees, denied support from Auchinleck, and with no civil government structures to support him, realised that 'the possibility of even attempting to maintain the present PBF as a neutral force for very much longer is dismissed as impossible. Two alternatives suggest themselves. Both dominions to be responsible with their own forces right up to their own frontiers for a strictly limited period with some kind of neutral HC [High Command] or a "Neutral Ship"', but he never developed that alternative further.[64]

On 29 August the full Joint Defence Council met in Lahore. They decided that from midnight on 1 September the PBF would disband. Its units would then join their respective armies. The Lahore area, in Pakistan, would be the responsibility of General Gane, one of the many British officers retained by Jinnah, while the East Punjab area, in India, would come initially under Rees but later under Thimayya. Separate Military Evacuation Organisations would be set up either side of the border to handle refugees and it was planned that each country would station some of their own troops across each other's border to escort refugees.

Far from calming people, once news of these changes got out it led to panic. Communities now thought they risked being trapped in hostile territory. One of the blackest days so far was 31 August. 'From north, south, east and west came reports of attacks, arson and abduction.' There was a huge increase in Hindu and Sikh refugees from Montgomery Bazaar. There had also been very heavy casualties in the south-east where the Sikhs were carrying out the systematic extermination of villages along the River Sutlej belt. In one attack 400 Muslims were killed. Hundreds of corpses started floating down the flooded River Ravi and on the River Sutlej stranded groups were left clinging to mudbanks as the waters rose.[65] The events of August were to prove just the beginning. The Punjab's suffering would only deepen in September.

A HEAP OF ASHES

'How could any civilised government permit such a state of affairs?'

(JINNAH)

By some miracle, Calcutta had remained peaceful during those last two weeks of August. Unlike the Punjab, the Boundary award seemed to have calmed people, at least temporarily, and given them a 'new found feeling of security'.[1] Gandhi's presence and his public prayer meetings undoubtedly helped, the Mahatma having refused to give in to the extreme Hindu threats he faced when he had first arrived. Would it last? Outside Calcutta, across rural Bengal, millions of refugees were on the move; overall 3.6 million Hindus from East Bengal would move into West Bengal, into India. Far fewer, only 700,000, West Bengali Muslims would make the corresponding journey east. So far the migration had progressed without serious violence and in Assam all remained quiet.

On the night of 31 August, four Hindu youths paid 4 annas to go to the cinema in Calcutta. 'The film was bad, the projector faulty and the picture jumped and sidled on the screen.' They complained to the Muslim attendant who told them, unhelpfully, that was all they could expect for 4 annas. One of the youths, enraged, drew a knife and attempted to stab him. An onlooker grabbed the boy's arm to deflect the blow and in doing so the blade just nicked the boy's face. A crowd gathered, bandaged the boy up and took him off to see Gandhi to demand satisfaction. The Mahatma sensibly saw the incident for what it was and refused to address the now swelling ranks of militant Hindus gathering outside, supporters of the 'Mahasabha-ites and Mr. Sarat Chandra Bose's Forward Bloc'.[2] Instead he said he was tired and wanted to go to bed.

By 10.30 a.m. the next day, 1 September, Calcutta had dissolved into violence once again. Hindu and Muslim mobs started fighting with stones and sticks but by early afternoon shooting had started. A young Hindu RSS supporter got into the Muslim area near Harrison Road with a Sten gun and indiscriminately slaughtered Muslims in their homes. The Muslims retaliated, the police panicked, poking 'their rifles up in the air and shooting down the road without taking aim'. A Hindu threw a bomb in Balliaghata, killing Muslim women and children and the riot entered a new phase of savagery. Shops and homes were, as always, looted with their contents spilt all over the roads.

By early morning on 2 September there were over five hundred people dead. It seemed as if the Great Calcutta Killings of just over a year ago would be repeated and they probably would have been had three things not happened. First, at 5.00 a.m. that morning the heavens opened and by 7.00 a.m. the streets were under three feet of water. Secondly, Gandhi sent out courageous Hindu volunteers, posting them in Muslim areas to tell Hindu rioters that the old man would hold them personally responsible for any further attacks. He then announced he was fasting until he was guaranteed of peace. He sent out 'Peace Processions', which were initially attacked, and the leader of one badly stabbed, but the Mahatma's involvement undoubtedly calmed the Hindu mobs, much to the disappointment of their more extreme elements. Gandhi was once again, they grumbled, siding with the Muslims. However, many did obey his demand that they surrender their weapons. Gopal Mukherjee would not, despite a direct plea from some of Gandhi's disciples. 'With these arms I have saved the women of my area. I saved the people. Where was Gandhiji during The Great Calcutta Killing? Where was he then? I've used a nail to kill someone. I won't surrender even that nail.' He also thought that the weapons that were laid at Gandhi's feet were 'of no use to anyone – out of order pistols and that sort of thing'.[3]

Thirdly, Gurkha troops were brought back into the city from Murshidabad; the new West Bengal government imposed a fifty-nine-hour curfew and gave the soldiers permission to shoot curfew-breakers on sight. They were tough measures, short of martial law, which the military had wanted, but still showed a resolve that people noticed. Gradually calm returned. Gandhi fasted for three days and then relented, much to the relief of the authorities. He was old and frail and there was increasing concern that if he actually died on one of these fasts the resulting holocaust against the Muslims would have been terrible. On 6 September he felt well enough to leave for the Punjab. He took Suhrawardy with him. Gandhi 'travelled third class by train, Mr. Suhrawardy by air'.[4]

Yet any optimism about Bengal was quickly dissipated by the deteriorating position in the Punjab. The violence had now spread east and south from the area immediately affected by Radcliffe's line so that there was widespread killing even in Delhi and Simla. In the first week of September, Lieutenant Colonel Mohindar Singh Chopra was reassigned from Assam to the Punjab and gathered his family for the long return journey. Crossing the 'mighty Brahmaputra' was more frightening for his children this time, the ferry tossing through the monsoon floodwaters. Joining a train at Pandu, his daughter noticed 'a section of troops with sten-guns and grenades were in a bogey for our protection'. They frequently had to lie on the floor in case of shooting. As they approached Delhi there was

a kind of silence that comes out of abject fear. When the train steamed slowly into Delhi Station late at night, there was not a soul to be seen. The scene around was one of utter chaos, with piles of rotting vegetables and mounds of charred mail, letters and parcels scattered on the platform. We could hear occasional gun-fire in the distance.[5]

The city that had only two weeks previously been thronged with the huge crowds that celebrated Independence was now on the 'verge of collapse'.[6] It was flooded with Hindu refugees and its large Muslim population had gathered in camps awaiting some form of transport into Pakistan. On 3 September a Hindu mob had butchered Muslim refugees at the same station where Singh Chopra and his family were now arriving. The platforms were covered in the telltale rust-coloured stain of blood.

The lack of effective police meant that much of the violence took place in daylight and with the connivance of the authorities. Major Paddy Massey's wife was still going for her accustomed early morning ride from the bodyguard stables. One morning she returned complaining that as she had crossed the airport road she had 'come across thirteen corpses whose heads had been cut off and placed in a neat pile'. Massey duly told his Sikh risaldar-major, his senior Indian officer, to investigate. The man apologised, said it was a government-placed ambush site but that he would see what he could do to get it moved further up the road so that it did not upset Mrs Massey's routine.[7]

Nehru, shocked by what he had seen in the Punjab camps, furious and saddened by how the first weeks of the new India were being wrecked, would wade in himself when he saw incidents on the street. Santdas Kirpalani was staying with his brother-in-law in his flat overlooking Connaught Circus, the circular shopping centre in the middle of New Delhi, and was enjoying his early morning tea on 7 September when he saw a Hindu mob of young men armed with knives and sticks attack the well-known Muslim saddlery shop Abdul Ghani & Co; saddlers in India tended to be Muslim due to Hindu inhibition at working with leather.

An old, bearded Muslim dashed out, trying to make a run for it but one of the rascals plunged a long knife in his back. The old man collapsed in a pool of blood, wriggled for a minute and lay still. The marauders entered and looted the place. Meanwhile at the other end of the block, other hooligans were looting Muslim establishments and running away with sewing machines, bicycles, tables and chairs.

Ten minutes later a jeep turned up with an army driver and Kirpalani recognised Nehru in the back dressed in his habitual white *khadi sherwani* and cap. As they turned the corner, 'Nehru jumped from the running vehicle and lustily clouted a young hoodlum who had collected a saddle. The looters in Abdul Ghani's shop scattered with speed'. Nehru's sudden chance appearance had worked 'like a charm' but he could not be everywhere.[8]

That night, around 10 p.m., Delhi was disturbed by the roar of flames from the poor Muslim area of Paharganj. Hindu mobs had set fire to the houses, burning down an area about a mile long and half a mile wide. The refugees from the fire swarmed onto their Prayer Ground, where luckily a military escort prevented further slaughter. That week Delhi 'became like an armed camp'[9] with troops rushed in but the violence continued and movement remained dangerous especially at night. Faiz Bazaar, linking Old and New Delhi, became a particularly perilous spot as Muslim militias set up a machine gun in the upper storey of a printing press.

Ismay, still serving with Mountbatten, frequently saw Muslims 'being systematically hunted down and butchered. In some places the dead lay rotting in the streets. The hospitals were choked with wounded. Arson and looting were widespread. Food supplies were disrupted. The Moslem policemen had deserted or been disarmed; many of the Hindu police were afraid to do their duty'. Ismay's daughter, Sarah, had suffered a horrible experience trying to get back to Delhi from Simla with her fiancé, Wenty Beaumont. Beaumont's Muslim servant had asked to travel in their carriage for his own protection. All went well until they were twenty miles from Delhi when a bomb exploded on the platform of Sonepat Station. 'This was apparently the pre-concerted signal for a general attack on all Moslem passengers. Men, women and children were pulled out of the train by their Hindu fellow-travellers and butchered in the most brutal manner.' Beaumont hid his servant under the seat and piled suitcases on top of him but 'two well-dressed and seemingly well-educated Hindus presented themselves at the door of the carriage and demanded the right to search for a Moslem who was believed to be with them'. Beaumont and Sarah were both armed. Flourishing their revolvers they refused and the Hindus backed off. Their servant, silent and shaking, was the only Muslim on that train who made it to Delhi alive. The Hindu armed police, in an adjoining carriage, made no attempt to intervene.[10]

Major General John Dalison was not so lucky. He was travelling with his Muslim bearer in a train with no escort. Outside Delhi they were attacked by a well-organised gang of five hundred *Nihang* Sikhs dressed in dark-blue and yellow uniforms. They broke open the window of his compartment, dragged his bearer out and hacked him to pieces in front of him. Every other Muslim on the train was similarly butchered. Dalison was spared; the Sikh leader said he had orders not to harm the British 'this time'.[11] James Cameron, a British major, who was travelling across the Punjab with his family, had a similar experience but his train had a small escort. The train was duly attacked by a Sikh *jatha* in a local station. He and the escort managed to get his family and most of the Muslims into the station buildings. Some Muslims refused to leave their property on the train and were slaughtered. One of his soldiers shot a Sikh. 'He killed him at 200 yards – a very good shot', Cameron elaborated. 'This had a very good effect' and gave them a breathing space. They realised though that they were trapped, surrounded by angry Sikhs and in the middle of nowhere. They decided they would be safer on the roofs. Cameron divided the group up into sectors, each led by someone armed. His wife and daughter both took charge of sectors, armed with shotguns. All night the Sikhs harassed them but they managed to hold them off. 'At every moment I thought I would have to shoot my wife and daughter', Cameron continued, 'and all the Muslim wives and children would certainly have been slaughtered'. With dawn another train brought relief.[12]

Ismay received a further shock when an old friend of his, Ali Sher Khan, who had won a Distinguished Service Medal serving with his regiment in France during the First World War, and who had finished his career as a senior officer in his regiment, turned up in rags at his door. A Punjabi Muslim, his village had been attacked by Sikhs, his family massacred and he had only just managed to escape. His house had been burned and he had lost everything. A while later a senior Sikh officer of the same regiment found Ismay to tell him that his home in Pakistan had likewise been burned to the ground although thankfully he had managed to get his family out.[13]

Edward Behr was also finding that the violence between regiments in Peshawar was not finished. News of the fighting between the Punjabis and the 19th Lancers had spread. Pathans started to converge on the town, thinking that their fellow Muslims were in danger. There was a general and justifiable panic among the town's Hindu and Sikh community. As Behr drove around the army lines he was flagged down by a policeman who showed him the bodies of thirty-three Hindus in a government compound; the men had been shot. The women had had their breasts cut off. Next the Pathan mob attacked the hospital and started butchering the largely Hindu hospital staff. Behr gathered what troops he could find in the brigade headquarters and rushed over. As they arrived he saw bodies in the hospital yard. There was shooting and screaming everywhere and the only way they could get in safely was through the back. They made their way to the roof and emerged to look down on Pathans dragging out hospital orderlies and nurses and murdering them in the yard. He took the Bren gun from the man carrying it and shot three Pathans in succession. Two things then happened. The Pathans down below rushed for cover and started to return fire and the man who had been holding the Bren gun grabbed it off Behr, shouting at him in Pashtu; only then did Behr realise that the soldiers he had so hurriedly got together were themselves Pathans. He thought he was about to 'relive the 1857 Sepoy Mutiny and that he was going to kill me for shooting his fellow Pathans'. In fact the man had said, 'Let me have a go too!' and he and the rest of Behr's small group now actively engaged the murderers in the courtyard below. Eventually Behr managed to extricate himself and bring in an infantry company; the remaining

Pathans duly surrendered. That night another Pathan mob set fire to a large area of Sikh tenements. The army's engineers blew up houses in the immediate path of the fire, thus stopping it spreading.

The next evening Behr was called to the house of Qayum Khan, the newly appointed chief minister who had just taken over from Dr Khan Sahib. On his lawn were hundreds of Sikhs and Hindus, nearly all well-off Congress Party officials, judges, barristers and civil servants. They were people Qayum Khan had known all his life but, Behr noticed, 'he had not even offered them a glass of water'. He now demanded Behr take these people away.

Later that night, standing on a verandah, he saw a bearded Hindu suddenly come into view, running apparently for his life. 'Pursuing him, a short distance away, was a Pakistan Air Force enlisted man, on a big black bicycle, firing a Sten Gun at him over the handlebars.' Behr rushed at the cyclist and kicked the bicycle hard, knocking him over. His driver, who was with him, grabbed the Sten and removed the magazine. Eventually, after sorting out what quickly became a tangled mass of arms, legs, bicycle and gun, they extricated themselves and apprehended the PAF man. They couldn't make him understand that he had done anything wrong – '"but he was a Hindu", he kept saying'.[14]

The troops that had been rushed into Delhi on 6 September were British soldiers, a battalion of the Royal Scots Fusiliers. Congress said they were there to 'protect British lives'[15] although no British lives were threatened. Why could British soldiers be used in Delhi but not in the Punjab where the situation was worsening daily? The *Manchester Guardian* was asking the same question. 'If the Indian Regiments could not have been relied upon to take action against their co-religionists, there were Gurkhas, and as long as British troops are in the country who can deny that they should have been used? A sufficiency of troops with jeeps and tanks and aeroplanes could have prevented the atrocities.'[16] Now, with the demise of the PBF, it was too late.

Much more had gone with the PBF than just the limited policing ability it possessed. Without it there was no automatic cross-border liaison and refugee operations had to be coordinated through a small control cell in Lahore. More seriously for the long term, the mechanisms established in June, the Joint Defence Council and the Supreme Command, were seen as ineffective. The first joint operation staged between the two new dominions had failed. The implications of this for the future relations between India and Pakistan would take some time to sink in.

The first week of September in the Punjab was the most violent yet. The BBC journalist Wynford Vaughan-Thomas described:

> A long line of bullock carts stuck in the middle of the drenching rain. Each cart carried a desperate, rain soaked family. The carts staggered on. There was no hope left amongst them. As we go on the rain lifted and the sun beat down. The whole countryside sparkled but in each village we passed we could see the reason the refugees were on the move. We could see armed gangs chasing their victims across the fields. By the time we interfered it was too late. Another family had been wiped out.[17]

What was so difficult to understand about the Punjab killings was their ferocity and vindictiveness. 'Sikh savagery was appalling', Tuker wrote. 'Long after the victim was dead they would slash and slash away at the body, carving it up. They were just like dogs that had taken to killing sheep – just an insensate, devilish lust to wallow in the blood of helpless creatures.'[18] A group of unarmed British soldiers waiting for a train in Delhi on 8 September saw a Sikh soldier in uniform butchering Muslims. The last man he killed was a very old Muslim with no chance of protecting himself. He ran towards the soldiers for protection but being unarmed they could do nothing and the Sikh cut him to pieces a few yards from where they were sitting. They remonstrated with the Sikh, asking if he had gone mad. He replied in English 'smothered with bad language' that they had better mind their own business or they would be next.[19]

Certainly communal madness does seem to have seized some

Sikh communities. Aridaman Singh Dhillon recalled that his grandfather initially tried to protect his Muslim neighbours but received death threats and then news started to come through of Muslim atrocities against Sikhs in Pakistan. His mood changed. He remembered one man in his village saying how much he revelled in the killing. When a raid was proposed he joined in, getting ready immediately.

> We went off raising war-cries even leaving our food. We'd go off in high spirits. I ran after this fucking Muslim with my sword and killed him. My sword was a curved one. It used to look magnificent. It used to feel good. They had killed so many of our people. We used to shout war cries and then chop people's heads off. We would cheer each other up and shout 'Be Strong'! I was very successful. The old and young would talk about me. I've lost count of the number of people I've killed – there were so many. Whoever came in front of me lost his head. Why should I feel bad? They kept killing our people. They wouldn't stop. Half our people had been killed. They said it was a good thing to kill us.[20]

The massacre of Sikhs and Hindus in West Punjab, in what was now Pakistan, was progressing with equal savagery. At 9 p.m. on 15 September a bomb went off outside the principal mosque in Bahawalpur. This was a prearranged signal for a riot and for the killing of Hindus and a general looting of Hindu property. One mob torched the main bazaar, killing any Hindu they came across. A second mob, led by a 'lame man on a white horse', moved into the city from the outlying villages, again massacring all Hindus and Sikhs they saw. Penderel Moon tried to restore order with the nawab's troops. There were so many bodies that the municipal lorries could not clear them all off the street. One Hindu corpse, stripped completely naked, lay across the road down to the Hindu shrine of Gosain. It stayed there for days, a grisly landmark of the violence. 'There was', Moon reflected, 'a complete breakdown, or rather reversal of the ordinary moral values. To kill a Sikh became almost a duty; to kill a Hindu hardly a crime. To rob them was an innocent pleasure, carrying no moral stigma; to refrain was a mark not of virtue but a lack of enterprise.'[21]

Moon and Gurmani, the nawab's chief minister, had been trying to evacuate the Hindus and Sikhs. The main Bahawalpur to Lahore railway line was too dangerous to be used. The only way they could be moved was by gathering them in the city, commandeering what lorries they could find, and escorting them to the small local station at Baghdad al Jadid where a branch line ran east to Bhatinda. But already one train had been attacked even on this route and all the Hindus murdered. They needed a train escort but they were not sure they could trust the Bahawalpur state troops. The Hindu community leaders refused to leave without a Gurkha escort. Earlier the state troops had captured eight Sikhs who they said had been firing at them with revolvers. Moon instructed that they were to be held securely. Later that night, walking through the main bazaar, he came across the bodies of two women and three children lying in the road. They had tried to commit suicide by jumping off a nearby building. One of the children was still alive. It transpired that they were the families of two of the detained Sikhs. Moon became suspicious and went to find the prisoners but there was no trace. All eight had, he subsequently discovered, been murdered and their bodies dumped in the river. One of them, Amar Singh, was the cashier at the local branch of the Imperial Bank where the state treasury kept its deposits. He had the safe keys in his pocket; for days Bahawalpur was without money.

The next day Moon succeeded in getting nearly one thousand Hindus to Baghdad al Jadid. The train arrived but none of them would get on it, terrified of a journey that would surely mean their deaths. Finally persuaded, they made a mad rush for it. Then the Muslim railway staff complained that they were being sent off in too much comfort and more should be packed in despite the fact that the train was already jammed and 'men, women and children crowded round, shouting, yelling and weeping, pushing and jostling and banging one another with their luggage without distinction of age or sex'. Moon had made a plan with Professor Mehta, a respected community leader, that he would bravely travel not only into India but return to say how safe this route was. In the event the train did get through safely but Moon never saw Mehta again.

Villagers across the Punjab said that one of the worst things about those weeks was that they had no information. There were no telephones. Gurdeep Singh, who would later become a major in the Indian Army, was seventeen in 1947. He found the indecision terrible.[22] No one really knew what was going on, often until it was too late. In areas that had not yet been attacked it was difficult to know whether to leave or risk staying put. Some Hindus did decide to stay in Bahawalpur. Most were moved to a camp outside the city but a few remained under the protection of a shrine in the city centre. On 17 September, Moon heard shots coming from the precinct. Rushing over he found Bahawalpur state forces with their rifles trained on a terrified group of huddled Hindus who were being systematically robbed before their inevitable murder.

Much as in India, violence in Pakistan spread well beyond the immediate area that Radcliffe's pencil had divided. The splendidly named Maynard Hastings Pockson was at the Indian Army Staff College at Quetta, now well inside Pakistan. One day he noticed a black pall of smoke hanging over the bazaar. All the students were called in, given a revolver and twelve rounds of ammunition and told to patrol the city. A refugee train had come in from India and every man, woman and child on board had been found dead. The Quetta Muslims had subsequently turned on the Hindus. Pockson met a party of Pathans with axes on long poles, usually kept to cut branches for fodder. He asked them what they were doing. 'Just looking around', they said, unconvincingly. The massacre in the bazaar was terrible. Later Pockson was put in charge of a group clearing up the corpses. He told his men to separate Muslim from Hindu so that they could be accorded proper rites. His men looked perplexed. How could they tell? Pockson, surprised, said by seeing if the men were circumcised. His soldiers explained that every body they found had its private parts cut off.[23]

Alongside the violence, the murders and the terror, the authorities in both India and Pakistan were also beginning to confront the enormous refugee problem. There was to be a macabre balance in weighing this human misery. Some 6.5 million Muslims were to flee India for West Pakistan and 4.7 million Hindus and Sikhs to leave West Pakistan for India. Looking after them would present both new governments with a major problem for years to come but the immediate issue that September was to gather them together in what were loosely known as camps, to protect them, get them food and water, prevent the outbreak of disease and then resettle them. In many ways they were the lucky ones in that they had at least survived but the conditions they had to endure could have persuaded them otherwise.

The problem was that, with the demise of the PBF, there was no structure to manage the required organisation. On 3 September, Liaquat and Nehru toured the Punjab and then held a summit in Lahore. They agreed to make every effort to restore abducted women to their families, not to recognise forced conversions and to ensure the safety of respective places of worship in both East and West Punjab. Both governments would become custodians of all refugee property in an attempt to stop expropriation and looting. But the decision that had most immediate impact was confirmation that their respective armies would assume control of refugees and that some Indian troops could be stationed in Pakistan to escort Hindus and Sikhs east and vice versa for Pakistani troops to escort Muslims west. Yet all that was more easily agreed than actually done and the next weeks would be consumed with trying to put the policy into effect.

The Indian government formed an Emergency Committee, which Patel asked Mountbatten, at his best in managing crises, to head. It was in some ways a strange request for the new administration to ask the last representative of the colonial power and it shows how much Congress both trusted Mountbatten and feared the consequences if they did not fix a situation that could have crippled the new nation in its infancy. Sandtas Kirpalani was drafted in to be its secretary. He was slightly surprised to be summoned to a Cabinet meeting in what was now the governor general's house and even more surprised to find Mountbatten in the chair. Patel was beside him, his 'usual dourly grim' self. Sitting between Nehru and Baldev Singh was a new face, K. C. Neogy, whom Kirpalani recognised from the papers and who was, he was told, to be Minister of Refugees (soon changed to Relief and Rehabilitation). It was Kshitish Chandra Neogy who, as a member of the Bengal Assembly, had been so outspoken about the mismanagement of the 1942 Bengal famine. Kirpalani was to be his senior civil servant. It was an appointment that would expose him 'to human tragedy on a colossal scale' but he had 'admiration akin to hero-worship' for Nehru and it never entered his head to refuse. He would soon feel the same way about Neogy.

After the meeting Neogy and he walked across to their new offices in North Block, one of the two monolithic administrative buildings that flank the approach to the governor general's house. They were allocated six rooms without a stick of furniture. They found another room full of dusty desks and chairs awaiting division between India and Pakistan. They dragged out a table and two chairs. Kirpalani sat one end, Neogy at the other. Kirpalani stood up and said, 'Sir, I am reporting that the Ministry of Refugees is officially open for business'.[24]

In East Punjab the 4th Infantry Division of the Indian Army, under Brigadier Chimni, became the Military Evacuation Organisation that Rees had been demanding for the past weeks. Its job was to coordinate the movement of the remaining roughly three million Hindu and Sikh refugees in Pakistan; they estimated there were twenty big 'camps' or gatherings with over forty thousand each and then a further forty camps with five to ten thousand plus numerous small pockets spread over the countryside. They divided West Punjab into the 'Near West', being the area within 150 miles of the border and which they thought they could evacuate by foot and lorries while the 'Far West', lying beyond that, would have to be by train. They could deploy soldiers into Pakistan to achieve this but they had to work closely with the Pakistan Army who, although they had all been serving in the same regiments only weeks before, they were now beginning to distrust.

The length and condition of the foot columns from the 'Near West' were, Mohindar Singh Chopra, recalled,

incredible. Stretching for scores of miles, divided into scores of blocks with twenty to thirty thousand evacuees in each block. Every block was twenty to twenty five miles long, moving along the road with bullock carts, loaded to the brim with household goods, on which were perched children while the elders walked alongside. Sides of the roads had cattle, sheep, goats, donkeys and camels, their backs bent with heavy loads and raising a cloud of dust. Protecting this mass of the poor and wretched were a thin screen of troops. At ad hoc staging camps were positioned dumps of food consisting of gur, rice, atta and parched grain.[25]

A similar plan was put in place to improve the evacuation of Muslims from East Punjab. There was, however, a marked difference of approach. The Sikh discipline and genius for organisation meant that their columns were becoming 'carefully planned and executed with military precision. There was little or no interval between the bullock carts, in which the women and young children and goods and chattels were loaded, and all the men who were capable of bearing arms moved in front and on the flanks of the column'. Muslim columns were less well organised. They seemed 'unpremeditated'. Columns 'straggled hopelessly over fifty miles of road. From the air they looked like a pathetic stream of ants'.[26]

An attempt was made to improve the security of trains but train massacres would continue until November. The attackers' technique was either to tear up track to force the train to stop or to wait until it stopped in a station. The attacks were ferocious on both sides of the border. A train that left Lahore with Hindus and Sikhs on 21 September was ambushed by a Muslim mob at Harbanspura; 1500 people were massacred. A Dogra officer passing on the following train, which was moving men of his regiment from Rawalpindi to join the Indian Army, saw bodies all over the track. The smell in the area was dreadful. They arrived just over the border at Attari and

The critical meeting in the viceroy's study on 3 June. Nehru and Jinnah are either side of Mountbatten; Ismay sits behind. They used a small round table to increase the sense of intimacy.

Refugees begin to move. Between August and December 1947, approximately 6 million Muslims would leave India for Pakistan and 6 million non-Muslims would move the other way.

Contrasting princes. The Maharajah of Junagadh (left), a Muslim ruler of a predominantly Hindu state, was excessively fond of his dogs and would spend thousands of rupees on their weddings. By August 1947, he had still not decided whether to join India or Pakistan. Hanwant Singh (right), by contrast, the young Maharajah of Jodhpur, a state with advanced famine-relief measures, decided for India but took far-reaching measures to minimise inter-communal violence.

(Left) Huseyn Suhrawardy, last premier of British Bengal and later prime minister of Pakistan. He argued strongly for Bengal to become independent in 1947.

(Right) Sir Olaf Caroe, Governor of the North West Frontier Province. It was Caroe who courageously stood up for a plebiscite on the Frontier, which would see that province choose Pakistan. He was consequently loathed by Congress, who got him sacked. Nehru thought that, without the Frontier Province, Pakistan would not be a viable country.

The Boundary Commission at Simla the week before their decision was announced

adcliffe sits front and centre. On his left is Mehr Chand Mahajan, who would become
rime minister of Jammu and Kashmir the next month and be in office during the coming
risis. Christopher Beaumont is second from the right (as you look at the photograph),
1 the back row. On his left stands V. D. Ayer, whom Beaumont suspected of leaking the
ommission's secret findings to Congress.

Muslim Meo children horrifically injured during the violence in Gurgaon, near Delhi, which started in April and May 1947 and which should have served as a warning of what was to come elsewhere in the Punjab.

Refugees cram onto a train. Attacks on trains became a favoured tactic of both Muslim and Sikh mobs during August and September. Once a train had been halted, the mobs would systematically butcher everyone on it and loot their possessions. The Punjab Boundary Force did not have enough resources to protect them.

Birth and Freedom

nah (above) announces the birth of Pakistan in Karachi on 14 August, while
ountbatten looks distracted. From their very first meeting, the two men did not get on.
xt day in Delhi (below), Mountbatten tries to get through the crowds to raise the new
lian flag while Nehru perches on the cover of the landau. Theirs was a much closer
ationship.

Punjab, September 1947

September in the Punjab was an even worse month than August. The refugee crisis led to the proliferation of terrible camps (above) where food, water and information were scarcely available, a situation made worse by the torrential rains. But in many ways those who reached them were lucky; approaching 1 million (below) lay butchered across the countryside.

boy contemplates the future from the misery of a camp. Resettling the vast numbers
refugees, sorting out their property and starting to repair their psychological wounds
ould place enormous demands on both India and Pakistan for decades.

A dog chews a corpse in railway tracks. For many,
human life seemed to have lost any value.

Kashmir October to November 1947

Hari Singh, the ineffectual Maharajah of Jammu and Kashmir, whose indecision would lead to the crisis. He refused to accept that the British were leaving.

A Pathan is arrested by Indian troops. Many of the lashkar were most interested in loot.

Indian troops of 1st Sikhs take up fire positions along the road outside Baramulla. India's military intervention in Kashmir was as militarily risky as it was politically controversial.

were given a rousing welcome by the local Sikhs. The only topic of conversation was what had happened to the refugee train and they declared that not a single Muslim refugee train would be allowed through to Pakistan. Every one would be attacked and its occupants killed. A few miles further on towards Amritsar, at Khalsa, where there was a well-known Sikh college, the troop train was delayed. The line had been tampered with to create an ambush spot. This was where the Muslims were to be butchered.

The next day, 22 September, a Muslim refugee train was attacked there. Fortunately it had a small escort of sixteen soldiers who managed to hold off the *jatha* while the track was repaired. After the train had passed, its furious attackers did a more thorough job in destroying the line between the villages of Wagah and Attari. For the coming weeks refugees would have to make the actual crossing of the border on foot, meaning they were more vulnerable.

A second train was then attacked by a huge group of about eight thousand Sikhs. It again had a small escort, one British officer, one of those who was serving on with the Indian Army, and fourteen Hindu soldiers from the artillery. They held the attackers off until they ran out of ammunition. They tried to retreat into the substantial college buildings but were overpowered. The British officer and one of his havildars, a sergeant, were shot; the remaining soldiers were spared because they were Hindus. The butchery of the Muslims on the train then started. A Dogra company, sent out to help from Amritsar, four miles away, arrived too late although they did succeed in driving the mob away. The train was recovered to Amritsar. It had been carrying between 2,000 to 2,500 people. About one hundred were found still alive under the piles of their families' bodies. It was unusual for British officers to be killed but several did lose their lives.

The Dogra officer's troop train left Amritsar for Delhi at 3 p.m. on 23 September. The smell from the dead bodies on the platforms on the stations they passed was unbearable. Everywhere were groups of Sikhs with spears and swords and knives. The Dogras saw one large group converging on a stationary train that had been heading up to Amritsar; the train had no engine. Its driver, hearing of the impending attack, had decoupled the engine and gone on to Amritsar on his own. His Muslim passengers, stranded, must have known what would soon happen. They were all butchered.[27]

Time after time, as bloody day succeeded bloody day, where there were sufficient, adequately armed troops they succeeded in driving the attackers off, whether Muslim or the better-organised Sikhs. Major D. H. Donovan, a Gurkha officer, was preparing the route to evacuate a refugee column with two jeeps each carrying eight men armed with Bren guns. He had paused in a sunken track, observing the ground ahead through his binoculars, when he saw a cloud of dust slowly approaching. 'After a short while it became clear that the cloud was caused by a large Sikh cavalry *jatha* for I could see their spears and fluttering pennants as they jogged along. The sun was behind me and it was about four o'clock in the afternoon.'

He realised that the *jatha* was poised to attack the village he was about to evacuate. He sent one jeep forward about five hundred yards with orders to open fire when he did. He let the *jatha* approach to within eight hundred yards; he estimated there were about five hundred of them. 'All were mounted, carrying spears, *kirpans* and shields and the sight', he thought, 'might have been straight out of Arabian Nights.' He opened fire, his forward jeep following suit. 'Pandemonium set in among the Sikhs, who did not know which way to go. Then in absolute terror they turned and galloped off.' The next day Donovan was able to escort 50,000 refugees safely to their staging camp.

The evacuation operations were just beginning to get more organised when they met with a major disaster. The monsoon should have started to ease off by the middle of September but instead, on 24 September, twenty inches of rain fell in three days. The River Beas, which flows east of Amritsar and so now well inside India, widened from half a mile to ten. The River Bein, normally a narrow stream, overnight became half a mile wide and the railway bridge collapsed. There had been a major staging camp beside the Bein. Two thousand people were lost. When the waters subsided the army recovered over five hundred bodies and two hundred dead bullocks, vital for people's livelihoods. The local Sikh villagers turned out to help. Surprised, Bristow, commanding his brigade in the area, asked why. They said because 'the floods were an act of God which made a difference'. Three days later they were back to attacking the people, with a *jatha* killing thirty of the wretched survivors and abducting ten young girls.[28]

The conditions in the 'camps' remained terrible. Ismay visited one of the staging areas for Muslims in East Punjab. There was no order to it, just a chaotic jumble of 'men, women, children, bullocks, donkeys and carts. A handful of scoundrels in houses overlooking the site were amusing themselves by firing occasional shots into the midst of them. A Moslem woman was killed by a stray bullet shortly after my arrival and her husband and others rushed at me, screaming "Sahib! Help us!".' The next camp he saw was in an old fort. 'Thousands of Moslems were herded within its walls. There was no shelter, no doctor, no sanitary arrangements, no means of communication'. Five women gave birth in the short time he was there, their babies being delivered into filth. He was again mobbed by people desperate for help. Lack of knowing what was happening was as bad in the camps as it was in the villages. There was no means of communication so rumour spread quickly. He gave an impromptu speech, saying that the Indian government was doing its utmost to help and to transfer them to Pakistan as soon as possible. As he was speaking there was a sudden storm of heavy rain. An umbrella was passed through the crowd so he shouldn't get wet. He was too moved to complete his speech.[29] He wrote, sadly, to his wife that he felt after a lifetime in India the British were finishing 'with all our work destroyed and leaving behind anarchy and misery and measureless slaughter'.[30]

The refugees found the fear of the future and what would become of them as frightening as the deprivations of the camps themselves. Naffese Chohan, miserable on the platforms of Lahore station, crying bitterly for the life and security she and her family had so suddenly lost, recalled that their biggest problem was lack of money to buy food and clothes. They were there for a week without any proper food, living off scraps. They were moved away from Lahore in a column and temporarily housed in an abandoned farm. They were then transferred to a 'camp' but it was little better. Then, a relation, a sergeant in the Pakistan army, sent someone to search for them. After seven days he found them, starving and soaking. He gave them some money. They were able to eat again. But it would take a very long time for Naffese's life to return to anything like normal.[31]

South of the Punjab, in the Princely states of Rajasthan, along the new frontier that ran south from Ferozepore, bordering the state of Bahawalpur through the desert, there was a smaller migration taking place. About eight hundred thousand Hindus and Sikhs would leave Karachi and the Sind for the Rajput states or Bombay; rather fewer Muslims would migrate the other way. There was violence in Karachi, and appropriation of property, as the Kirpalani family had discovered so tragically, but on the whole this was a more benign migration with both communities showing consideration for each other's predicament. In fact the Princely states – Bikaner, Jodhpur, Jaipur, Udaipur and Jaisalmer – handled the issue considerably better than the British/Indian administration in the Punjab. Having finally decided to accede to India, Maharajah Hanwant Singh of Jodhpur declared that he had 'two eyes', one Hindu, the other Muslim. If any harm came to members of either community he would feel as if he had lost his sight. His kinsman Narinder Singh, considered very much the family intellectual, was just back from having finished his education at Sherborne School in England. The maharajah seized on him and sent him to manage the Jodhpur state railway terminus at Mirpur Khas, well inside Pakistan. Through his careful planning tens of thousands of Rajput Muslims passed safely into southern Sind while hundreds of thousands of Hindus moved into India. There is still an active Karachi-Jodhpur Friendship Society in Karachi today. Reception arrangements were also much better than in the Punjab, with the Rajput administrations, used to providing famine relief, making proper provision for refugees; there is still an area near the railway station in Jaipur known as Sindhi Camp.

Even in the Punjab there were 'a few notable cases of humanity and kindness shown to the other community', Rees noted in his report, 'but these were very exceptional'.[32] In the hamlet of Ajnala, near the village of Issapur, the Muslim farmers and traders started to agitate against their Sikh landlords when rumours started that the area was to go to Pakistan. Two of the leading Sikhs, Sardar Ujagar Singh, and his nephew, Sardar Sahib Raghbir Singh Randhawa, gathered the local Sikh community together and insisted on no retaliation. To ensure their good behaviour they collected the kirpans. There was consequently no slaughter. Years later grateful Muslims would visit the Sikh family to express their gratitude. Two of the confiscated kirpans are now in the Partition Museum in Amritsar.

There was also very little violence in other parts of India with large Muslim populations, which the recent disturbances in Rampur, Bihar, and the United Provinces had suggested was likely. Once again Pandit Pant had acted swiftly in the United Provinces. He had authorised sweeping powers for the police and local authorities and forbidden the carrying of weapons, including the Sikh kirpans. Working with an effective military commander, General 'Tiger' Curtis, they threatened to impose martial law if any community took to the streets. By September the United Provinces were more or less calm.

Even more was to be lost with the demise of the PBF than the lives and homes of the Punjab. As early as 27 August articles started to appear in the Indian press strongly critical of its British officers. The *Hindustan Times* said they did not 'rise to the occasion', something the newspaper ascribed to them having lost interest in their jobs now that India was independent. The article went on to accuse what was left of the British administration of distributing arms among the Muslims in West Punjab and allowing Muslim officers free access to weapons while denying similar freedom to Hindus in Lahore. Rees, the paper asserted, was 'not a happy choice' as the PBF's commander.[33] Auchinleck protested, saying that it was articles like that which made it so difficult to get any British officers to stay on. He may have been missing the point. There was a feeling among the

British officers that there was a deliberate campaign to marginalise them, driven partly by Congress but also partly by aspiring Indian officers who wanted to take over their jobs. Bristow, commanding the 11th Brigade in Jullundur, was surprised not to be consulted by Nehru when he visited. He met the local Sikh leadership, Hindu politicians and Brigadier K. S. Thimayya, Rees's senior Indian adviser. Bristow liked and respected Thimayya, but felt he had a different view of the situation. Thimayya was an 'ardent patriot with high ambitions for India' while Bristow saw himself as 'a neutral charged with saving the lives of over a million Muslims'. More significantly he thought that Thimayya had realised that, as communal fighting had started in Jammu, there was inevitably going to be conflict with Pakistan over Kashmir. Thimayya's advice to Nehru was to disband the PBF as quickly as possible, get on with finalising the division of the army and get rid of the remaining British officers. That way India would be able to protect her interests, which could involve fighting Pakistan. It was a far-sighted, if depressing, analysis, and one that called into question once more the relevance of the elaborate joint machinery that the Partition Council had put in place only three months before.[34]

In the days after the PBF was disbanded this nationalist feeling in the Indian military, and accompanying criticism of Auchinleck, was to grow. On the same day that Mountbatten was asked to head the Indian Emergency Committee on Refugees, articles started appearing in the press demanding that Auchinleck resign and that the Supreme Headquarters be wound up. Auchinleck was accused of being pro-Pakistan. He had certainly always liked and respected Jinnah, whom he continued to see regularly, but to say that he was biased towards Pakistan at the expense of India was unfair; at that early stage his loyalty remained to the army, whichever side it went to. He did, however, lobby for stronger action against the Sikhs by the Indian government. 'The present policy of half-measures and appeasement of the Sikhs on religious grounds is in my opinion worse than useless and is fraught with the gravest danger for the future', he wrote to Mountbatten on 13 September. 'I do not question the sincerity of the leaders', he continued, but 'I am sure that not one single Muslim in Delhi today believes in the smallest degree in the good faith or intentions of this Government'. He went on to say, trespassing more into the realm of rumour, that he believed the Sikhs intended to create a Sikh state, with its capital in Simla, in which there would be 'very few if any Muslims and possibly not many Hindus either'. The Sikh Maharajah of Faridkot had, he maintained, 'personally warned British ladies in Simla that it was time they got out as their turn might be coming soon. He told poor Miss Hotz to get rid of all her Muslim servants overnight from Wildflower Hall – which she managed to do though there were six corpses on the road outside her gate next morning'.[35]

The failure of the PBF was also used to demonstrate the ineffectiveness of the Supreme Headquarters and this was a more justified criticism. Jenkins's and then Rees's continued and urgent demands for troops and resources had been consistently ignored while large numbers of troops, equipment and aircraft remained idle. Properly resourced, the PBF could have been effective. It could never have eliminated all the violence in the Punjab but it could certainly have contained it enough to suck the poison from India and Pakistan's early bilateral relations. The British brigades, so near the Punjab at Meerut in the United Provinces, in Calcutta and Bangalore with their excellent rail links, in Deolali, near Bombay (the most unpleasant of Indian postings which British troops particularly hated for its heat and boredom and from which the term 'going Doolally' comes), in Karachi and actually in Jullundur in the middle of the Punjab itself, were never deployed. Their eighteen infantry battalions, five artillery regiments and three armoured regiments and well-found logistic support units were never used. The world would pay a heavy price for this failure.

Auchinleck's position was actually under attack from another, unexpected angle. Montgomery, Chief of the Imperial General Staff in London, was also agitating for his removal. He wrote to Mountbatten on 1 September that: 'It is my opinion that Auchinleck's usefulness in India is finished. He is sixty-three; he has spent all his

life in India under a previous regime; he is too old to re-adjust himself to new ideas which he dislikes in his heart. He is viewed with
suspicion by the senior officers of the Indian army.' He concluded,
displaying the sentiment that made him so heartily disliked by his
peers, 'I personally consider that if you want military matters to run
smoothly and efficiently you will have to remove Auchinleck'.[36] It
was a strong censure, even allowing for the two field marshals' long-
standing dislike of one another, which dated back to Montgomery
superseding Auchinleck as commander of the 8th Army in North
Africa before the battle of El Alamein.

But the final move against Auchinleck came from Nehru who
told Mountbatten to get rid of him. Congress' position was, much
as Thimayya had briefed, that having a supreme commander and a
supreme headquarters meant that it 'towered over their own Navy,
Army and Air Force commanders'. Criticism of this in the Indian
Cabinet had been extensive and persistent. But there was also strong
criticism of Auchinleck personally, that he regarded himself 'as a
champion of Pakistani interests'. The Cabinet had therefore decided
to abolish the Joint Defence Council and the Supreme Headquarters
and, as those British officers who had agreed to stay on serving in
the armed forces were now under contract to their new employers,
there was no requirement for them to have a command structure.
Remaining British troops in India would come under a separate command until they had all been repatriated. The Indian Navy, Army
and Air Force would continue to be commanded by British officers,
respectively Admiral John Hall, General Sir Robert Lockhart and
Air Marshal Sir Thomas Elmhirst, but they would report directly
to their Indian ministers.

Mountbatten set all this out to Auchinleck in a long letter on 26
September. He concluded by reminding Auchinleck that he had often
told him he 'would willingly and indeed gladly fade out of the picture
if I were at any time to tell you that this would help me personally
or the general situation in this country'. That time, Mountbatten
said, had now come and he enclosed a draft letter of resignation for
Auchinleck to send to him as chairman of the Joint Defence Council.

Mountbatten had already secured Attlee's agreement to Auchinleck's removal, but had also obtained for him the offer of a peerage. In the event Auchinleck would decline it, saying that he felt he could not be honoured for having finished his career by dismantling his beloved Indian Army.[37]

He had never liked Mountbatten. It would not be the first time in British military history that personality issues have worked to prevent the correct application of policy. Auchinleck would later say that Mountbatten had, 'made many false steps. Kashmir was a lasting disgrace and tragedy. He has a good deal to answer for. His knowledge of India and Indians was practically nil. Also he had some odd advisers'.[38] It was strong criticism and partly unfair. Auchinleck himself must shoulder some of the blame for what happened in the Punjab. He became obsessed with the Indian Army as an institution, believing it had a life and importance above its duty to the people it served. It is a mistake many armies have made. In this case it had tragic consequences. Active lobbying by Auchinleck would also have allowed the deployment of those capable and bored British, Gurkha and non-class-based units in August 1947; this was his remit as much as Mountbatten's. Instead of looking forward to a new India he could only think back to the old one, which had been his life. The flawed 1945 reconstitution of the army along 'class' lines, the subsequent reluctance to use it to suppress 'internal unrest', despite that being what it was there for, and an obsession dating back to the Mutiny that British troops were in India only to protect British lives were all major contributors to the tragedy of the Punjab.

The demise of the Joint Defence Council, its Supreme Headquarters and its Supreme Commander impacted, of course, as much on Pakistan as on India. It meant that the fledgling Pakistan Army was confronted with having to police West Punjab, and East Bengal, but without any proper command structure. It had the units that had been transferred, and many of them had been stationed in what was now Pakistan anyway, but it lacked the brigade, divisional and army hierarchy that are so necessary to ensure that soldiers operate under a coherent plan and, at a higher level, to the political direction required. What this effectively did was to make Jinnah and Liaquat very dependent on the existing British senior officers. As the Indian Army moved to reduce them, and to replace them with Indians, Pakistan was content to allow them to continue in command and would do so for a long time to come. General Sir Frank Messervy, a much-respected veteran of Hodson's Horse, became commander-in-chief, and would be succeeded by another British officer, the Gurkha Douglas Gracey. It wasn't until 1951 that Singh Chopra's old staff college friend Mohammed Ayub Khan became the first Pakistani to take over. About five hundred other British officers continued in post. Admiral James Jefford continued as chief of Pakistan's Naval Staff until 1953 and there would still be a British chief of the Pakistan Air Force until 1957, ten years after Independence. India would claim that the British were too supportive of Pakistan; this is one of the reasons why.

Towards the end of the month the Indian press were attacking the British freely. Britain was supplying tanks to Pakistan disguised as scrap iron; Britain planned to reconquer India through the back door of Hyderabad and Pakistan; the right-wing British press were calling for all British personnel to be pulled out of India at once but made no mention of doing the same thing in Pakistan; a British military clique were fomenting the violence in the Punjab to justify reimposition of the Raj. More far-fetched but as damaging were allegations that British officers were leading the slaughter.[39] Mountbatten had to get Nehru to intervene after a leading politician, Pandit Kunzru, made a public statement saying that the worst killings had been deliberately inspired and encouraged by a British officer.[40] Master Tara Singh went even further. He was reported in the *Amrita Bazar Patrika* on 6 September as saying that there were 'hundreds of cases' in which British officers had ordered innocent civilians to be gunned down. The peace efforts of the local Sikh leaders had been powerless against these government organised attacks.[41]

There were two more significant results of this failure of the Joint Defence structure. As Pakistan struggled to establish itself as a country, and to build from nothing the basic institutions a country needs, it found itself reliant on the military to deal with its most pressing national issue, the slaughter and migration in the Punjab. The army therefore assumed a central role in the new Pakistani state from its very inception, something that would, as Pakistan's democracy floundered, lead to them assuming a political role. Jinnah, rather like Nehru, had little time for the military before the creation of Pakistan. 'Jinnah was not really interested in the army: he had no idea on the subject and said to me, "I have no military experience: I leave that entirely to you and Liaquat"', recalled Messervy.[42] With the Punjab and the coming tragedy in Kashmir, the military in Pakistan would develop subject only to light political constraints.

Even more seriously, the demise of the tortuously negotiated joint structures and the sheer scale and horror of the refugee issue would mean that early relations between India and Pakistan at government level would start very badly. Up until the first week of September there was a shared revulsion and shame at what Punjabi Muslims were doing to Sikhs and Hindus and vice versa. The summit meetings between Nehru and Liaquat (Jinnah now staying in Karachi) were if not friendly at least focused on solving a common problem, but as September wore on, and the killing intensified, that cooperation began to break down. By 10 September Liaquat was publicly accusing India of reneging on the agreement he had made with Nehru in Lahore. The Punjab Muslim League were demanding the immediate fortification of the border and compulsory military training for every Pakistani youth; Begum Shah Nawaz demanded the same for Pakistani women. Nehru tried to mediate with Liaquat but in New York Sir Muhammad Zafrullah Khan, now Pakistan's foreign minister and much respected internationally, put out figures suggesting that ten times as many Muslims were being killed in India as Sikhs and Hindus in Pakistan. The Indian government responded that there were more refugees coming from Pakistan than the other way. 'People do not uproot themselves by the million from their homes except when impelled by intolerable suffering and unspeakable terror', they replied.[43]

On 26 September the *Hindustan Standard* reported Gandhi

as saying at his daily prayer meeting that if 'Pakistan persistently refused to see its proved error and continued to minimize it, the Indian Union Government would have to go to war against it'. Predictably they ran the headline 'Pakistan's attitude may lead to war'.[44] Other papers followed suit, making the Mahatma's speech headlines across Asia. There was undoubtedly a strong element of journalistic interpretation of what Gandhi had actually said, and he quickly tried to redress the damage, pointing out that he remained firmly against war and that he was as wedded to non-violence as ever, but his intervention only increased the tension. Churchill did not help matters with an 'I told you so' speech on 27 September. He said the

> fearful massacres which were occurring were no surprise to him; that we were of course only at the beginning of these horrors and butcheries perpetrated upon one another with the ferocity of cannibals by races gifted with capacities for the highest culture who had for generations dwelt side by side in general peace under the broad, tolerant and impartial rule of the British Crown.[45]

His remarks caused predictable fury among Congress.

Although he would soon return home, Ismay remained a trusted agent of both Mountbatten and Nehru during those difficult weeks. He now flew from Delhi to Karachi to see Jinnah in an attempt to preserve the small degree of cooperation that still remained. He found Jinnah waiting for him at the top of the stairs of Government House. 'He looked very dignified, very sad and he spoke as a man without hope', Ismay thought. They went into his study and the *Quaid* 'let himself go. How could anyone believe that the Government of India were doing their utmost to restore law and order and to protect minorities?' he demanded.

> On the contrary, the events of the past three weeks went to prove that they were determined to strangle Pakistan at birth. The blood-baths taking place in the Punjab and in Delhi were the result of plans which had been prepared in the greatest detail.

The whereabouts of all Moslems had been systematically reccon-
noitered; the gangs of miscreants had been assembled and armed;
their duties had been apportioned; and finally, at the appointed
time, they had been loosed on their mission of murder. The conditions in the refugee camps were shameful beyond belief. How
could any civilized Government permit such a state of affairs?

Jinnah went on in a similar vein for twenty minutes. Ismay did
his best to reassure him of the Indian government's best intentions.
He said he firmly believed in Nehru's personal commitment and told
the *Quaid* how he had seen him 'charge into a rioting Hindu mob
and slap the faces of the ring-leaders'. More tellingly, he pointed out
that 'the situation which had developed with such suddenness would
have shaken any government in the world, however long-established
and experienced'. The Indian government was neither and had been
overwhelmed. Nor, he could have fairly added, was Pakistan's. He
explained that a ministry had been set up to deal with refugees,
and that Mountbatten was now chairing the Emergency Cabinet
Committee.

Ismay spent eleven hours talking to Jinnah, either in his office
or in Government House, which the fastidious Jinnah and his
sister, Fatima, were trying to make resemble the luxurious home on
Malabar Hill in Bombay they had recently abandoned. Jinnah had
discovered that the Governor of Sind had taken the library with him;
he demanded that it be returned. He then found that the Governor
of the Punjab had taken the croquet set; an order was dispatched
that it should be sent back forthwith. Ismay felt he had achieved
something but the coming month would see relations between the
two new countries plunged into a new crisis.

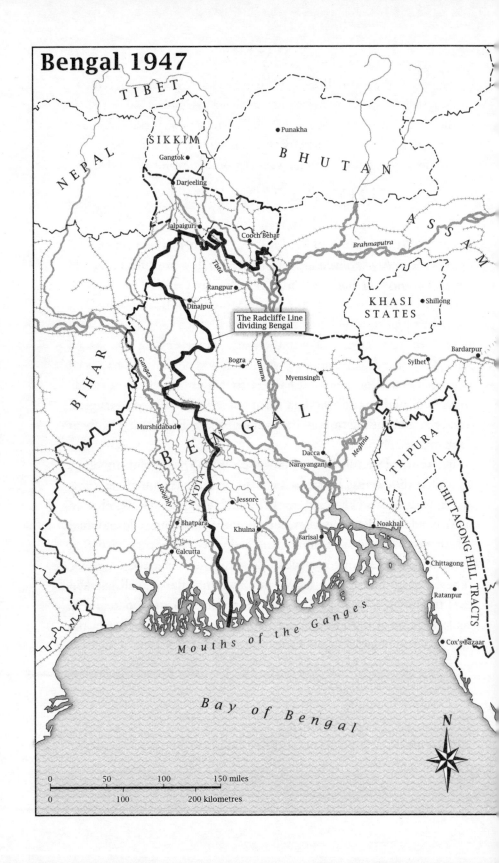

Bengal 1947

TIBET

SIKKIM

Punakha

Gangtok

BHUTAN

Darjeeling

NEPAL

Jalpaiguri

Cooch Behar

ASSAM

Brahmaputra

Tista

Rangpur

KHASI
STATES

Shillong

Dinajpur

The Radcliffe Line
dividing Bengal

Bardarpur

Bogra

Jamuna

Sylhet

BIHAR

Myemsingh

Ganges

BENGAL

Murshidabad

Dacca

Meghna

Narayanganj

TRIPURA

Hooghly

NADIA

Jessore

CHITTAGONG HILL TRACTS

Bhatpara

Khulna

Noakhali

Calcutta

Barisal

Chittagong

Ratanpur

Mouths of the Ganges

Cox's Bazaar

Bay of Bengal

N

| 0 | 50 | 100 | 150 miles |

| 0 | 100 | | 200 kilometres |

DIVIDED NATIONS

'Life here continues to be nightmarish; everything
seems to have gone away'

(JAWAHARLAL NEHRU)

Jinnah, as with many visionary men, found that he could think more clearly about the big things when the details of his personal life were well ordered. Now he and Liaquat had to concentrate on building a state, something they had not been expecting to do. They had not got what they wanted and now had to turn this 'moth-eaten' package into a nation. The framework of Pakistan had been laid down in the Indian Independence Act of July, which had in turn endorsed much of the 1935 Government of India Act. Pakistan would be governed by a cabinet under a prime minister; that was Liaquat. They were responsible to the Constituent Assembly. That assembly had two roles. It was to prepare a constitution and, secondly, to act as a parliament until that constitution was agreed. Pakistan was a Dominion, a member of the British Commonwealth, with a governor general appointed by the king but in effect selected by the Pakistan Cabinet; that was Jinnah.

Their first Cabinet contained a mix of the great names of the League, like Sir Muhammad Zafrullah Khan who became foreign minister, and professional administrators like Malik Ghulam Muhammad, the finance minister, who had risen through Aligarh

University and the ranks of the ICS. It was broadly based in that it contained two Bengalis, Fazlur Rahman and Jogendra Nath Mandal, and a member from the North West Frontier, Abdur Rab Nishtar, who had taken part in much of the negotiation that summer. They answered to an Assembly that was entirely dominated by the League but which would not play much of a role in the coming weeks.

The administration also retained its strong element of British personnel, thus achieving some continuity. Apart from the heads of the armed services and many subordinate officers, three of the four provincial governors remained British. Sir George Cunningham had agreed to return from St Andrews to the North West Frontier Province, Sir Francis Mudie moved from Karachi to Lahore to become Governor of West Punjab, and Sir Frederick Bourne was still trying to find somewhere to live that befitted his status as Governor of East Bengal. Jinnah had recruited Sir Archibald Rowlands, the last British finance minister in Delhi, to be the government's financial adviser and Sir Victor Turner, a brilliant statistician who had been born the son of a London butler, to be a Cabinet minister as financial secretary. For a man who in his early career had been so strongly anti the British official class, much as he always admired Britain as a nation, and who had castigated Gandhi so strongly for his support of the British in the First World War, Jinnah now clearly allowed his pragmatism to rule his inner feelings.

Even his closest advisers were surprised that he agreed to have dinner with a British regiment, the Royal Scots, just before they sailed for home. It was the usual grand regimental dinner, the Royal Scots being the oldest British infantry regiment apart from the Guards, with silver and bands much in evidence. At the end of dinner the commanding officer, according to regimental custom, toasted both the king and then the princess royal, their colonel in chief. Then, breaking with centuries of tradition, which is always a brave thing to do in a British infantry regiment, he stood up and said to Jinnah, 'Your Excellency, we consider ourselves good fighters; we consider you to be a good fighter also', and he proposed a toast to the *Quaid-i-Azam*. Jinnah was so overcome that he replied by proposing a toast to 'the British who have stayed in Pakistan to help us begin our work', concluding 'This I shall never forget'.[1]

His own personal staff also contained several British officials. His secretary was Colonel Bill Birnie.[2] Birnie was one of those men whose career and interests seemed to label him as a stereotypical British Indian Army officer. He was from the Guides Cavalry, the crack regiment raised to police the Frontier. In 1927, while big-game hunting, he had been surprised by the tiger he was stalking. The tiger, demonstrating both admirable restraint and sound judgement, merely bit him on the arm. It then picked up his rifle in its mouth and carried it off into the forest. In 1933 he had formed part of the team that made an attempt on Everest, surviving eight days below the summit at 25,700 feet. Yet, as with so many men of his type, he was also a brilliant linguist, a sensible diplomat and knew the Frontier as well as any man. He would serve Jinnah very well indeed.

Yet the essence of Pakistan in those early weeks was Jinnah himself. Much as he had been frustrated in his plans for the sort of Muslim state he wanted, and much as he would complain that he had ended up with a 'moth-eaten' Pakistan, from the people's point of view he was the embodiment of what they had achieved. Everywhere he went he would be met with cries of '*Quaid-i-Azam Zindabad*', and for a man to whom public speaking had never come easily, he now found himself able to command vast crowds just by appearing. Inevitably, in a Muslim country, he started to attract religious labels. '*Maulana Mohammed Ali Jinnah Zindabad!*' shouted one excited crowd in a small town where he had stopped. Jinnah waved to the crowd to be silent and wagged his finger at them. 'Stop calling me *Maulana*. I am not your religious leader. I am your political leader. Call me Mr. Jinnah or Mohammed Ali Jinnah. No more of that *Maulana*. Do you understand me?' The crestfallen crowd melted away, embarrassed and bemused.[3]

Establishing Pakistan as a state in which all religions were encouraged and where Islam was dominant but not intolerant was, paradoxically, Jinnah's key message in those early months. It was the central theme of all his major speeches. This was partly in answer to Congress' claims that he had created a communal problem where none had existed, partly because, as an Ismaili who personally took a very broad view of his religion, he was committed to a modern interpretation of the Prophet's teaching but also largely to do what he could to quieten the Muslim mobs in the Punjab. 'You may belong to any religion or caste or creed – that has nothing to do with the fundamental principle that we are all citizens and equal citizens of one State', he told the Constituent Assembly on 11 August.[4] He and Liaquat had chosen a flag that was three-quarters dark green, for Islam, but one quarter white, representing the minorities. 'It is not', Liaquat said, 'the flag of any one political party or community. The State of Pakistan will be a State where there are no special privileges, no special rights for any one particular community. It will be a State where every citizen will have equal privileges'.[5]

But what was this new state? It was a nation that was, whatever Jinnah and Liaquat may now be arguing, based on religion. It was a nation born in adversity, with an incoherent set of borders, opposed by its more powerful neighbour by whom it quickly felt threatened. It was a nation that felt that it had to rely on armed force to protect itself, a feeling that would become even more prevalent by the end of the month. It was, in many ways, very similar to Israel, another new state based on religion, which the British would create nine months later and whose development had so influenced Jinnah's thinking.

Pakistan consisted of a hotchpotch of constitutional parts: four provinces under their British governors each with their own Legislative Assembly; six Princely states, in varying degrees of acceptance or denial; Baluchistan, which was governed by an agent helped by locally appointed advisers; the North West Tribal Territories, which largely governed themselves according to local custom and who fiercely resented outside interference whether British or Pakistani; and the Chittagong Hill Tracts in East Bengal, which were again largely self-governing. These new territories answered to a new capital, Karachi, which many influential Pakistanis detested. The country had a population of just over eighty million people; over half – forty-six million – of these lived in East Bengal and a further twenty million in West Punjab. About 10 per cent of these were literate. Apart from a sizeable but reducing Hindu minority of about eleven million in East Bengal, and some Hindus in Sind, the vast majority were Muslim.

Inevitably therefore, because of this disparity and the speed of its birth, it would take time for the new country to function as a coherent nation. The existing provincial governments could continue their administration, albeit with very few people and not much money, but it would take a long time to establish a proper central government structure and to execute national policy. Apart from anything else, the preoccupation in Karachi was the Punjab and the refugee crisis. This was to have important implications before the month was out.

One of the problems associated with Jinnah having prevaricated so long as to what Pakistan was intended to be, and his inability to define it while the tortuous negotiations had dragged on, was that it left people free to interpret it in their own ways. For many, it was the inevitable result of the last few decades, something that had happened in a way they were not expecting but which they now accepted. They hated the idea of partition and bitterly regretted the killing, but tried to look beyond it. Alice Faiz had been working for W. H. Smith in London in the 1930s. She had joined the Communist Party in 1936 and got to know Krishna Menon. In London she moved in a circle with many Indian friends and became a passionate believer in Indian independence, using W. H. Smith's internal mail system to smuggle communist literature to Menon's contacts. In 1939 she went out to Amritsar to see her sister who was married to a Muslim teacher. She liked India so much that she stayed and in 1941 married herself. Her husband, Faiz Ahmad Faiz, was a writer and a journalist, later to become one of the most celebrated Urdu poets of his generation. Alice had been in Delhi in early 1947 and moved to Lahore before the worst of the violence started. Later she remembered the 'trainloads of dead' and the 'extraordinary, horrible feeling of massacres and fear' that still characterised Lahore that October. Her mood that month was very, very sad. Her parents, who had come to the subcontinent to be with their daughters, emigrated to South Africa, unable to live with such violence.

Yet neither she nor her husband ever regretted the creation of Pakistan. Strong early Congress supporters as they had been, and much as they hated the violence, which Faiz would articulate so movingly in poems like his famous 'Freedom's Door', they saw Pakistan as being the only way forward. She didn't think what happened in the Punjab was possible but it made her realise how deep the scars cut. But she and Faiz thought of Pakistan as the first step towards creating a fairer society, a step towards a goal of a democratic socialist state, which she saw as perfectly compatible with Islam.[6]

Others, like Saleem Siddiqi, saw Pakistan as some sort of indictment of the British failure. His father, an irrigation civil servant originally from the United Provinces, had to move Siddiqi and his nine siblings to Pakistan; they were lucky. Altogether sixty members of his extended family were killed in August and September. Siddiqi thought that the British had always denied Muslims power in India and that they favoured the Hindus, who enjoyed more wealth and who seemed to dominate the best jobs. The longing for Pakistan, which Jinnah had identified, went back a long way. For him the idea of Pakistan was equality of opportunity, a sort of re-establishment of Muslim identity, and especially the ability to get government jobs, which they felt had been so long denied them. Ironically Siddiqi ended up as mayor of the London Borough of Hackney, but his sentiments were echoed by many.[7]

For rulers like the Nawab of Bahawalpur, who returned to his capital on 2 October having spent the summer in Farnham, Surrey, the concern was that he had lost many loyal Hindu subjects who had lived happily under his autocracy for generations. Initially minded to compose a poem to thank Gurmani, his prime minister, and Penderel Moon for all their efforts at peacekeeping, he gradually came to blame them for, as he saw it, driving away loyal Bahawalpuris and replacing them with insolent Punjabi Muslims. He ordained that only refugees from Indian Princely states, who could be supposed to know how to behave, were to be allowed to settle. He would only accept families from Bikaner, Patiala, Alwar, Nabha and Bharatpur. Luckily many Bikaner refugees were crossing the border, given that Bahawalpur was the logical place for them to enter Pakistan geographically, but his preferences otherwise 'did not have much practical effect'. For the nawab, Pakistan should not be allowed to disturb the workings of his state.[8]

Then there were those, however much Jinnah and Liaquat tried to demonstrate otherwise, who did see Pakistan as an Islamic state, a feeling heightened by the horror of the Punjab. There was a group who came to see the new state as defined by Islam; its 1949 constitution would start with a dedication to God and specifies that 'Muslims shall be enabled to order their lives in the individual and collective spheres in accord with the teachings and requirements of Islam as set out in the Holy Qur'an and the Sunna'.[9] Containing militant Islam was to become one of Pakistan's greatest challenges. Many millions more, mostly outside the Punjab and Bengal, remained unaffected, probably aware that their nationality had changed but were not unduly concerned. For them, as for so many million Indians, the idea of nationhood was an intellectual luxury that seemed alien to their priorities of tilling, sowing and harvesting and worrying whether they would have enough food to keep their families alive for the coming year.

But one group who were directly and painfully affected were those who lived in Bengal. Radcliffe's line had left 11 million Hindus in East Bengal and 5 million Muslims in West Bengal. This latter group constituted a quarter of Bengal's total Muslim population and 15 per cent of the total Muslim population of the new India.[10] Both communities were as fearful of partition as their compatriots in the Punjab. The Great Calcutta Killings, the Noakhali gang murders and the riots of 1 September led many to think that the horrors of the Punjab would also be visited on them. It is one of the few positives of the story of 1947 that it never happened and although there were many small, localised outbreaks of violence and intimidation, there was none of the industrial scale savagery that happened a thousand miles west.

The reasons for this, and the story of Bengal's second partition, has been studied rather less than that of the Punjab, possibly because it would soon be overshadowed by the terrible wars of 1965 and 1971, and the famine that followed the flooding of the Brahmaputra river in 1974.[11] There are several factors that contributed, although none of these appear decisive. First, Gandhi's presence, and his ability to preach peace at his prayer meetings in Calcutta between 15 August and 1 September, and his fast after 1 September, showed the Mahatma's magic at its most powerful. Mountbatten described him in a speech as a 'one man boundary force who kept the peace while a 50,000 strong force was swamped by riots', referring, inaccurately and optimistically, to Rees's actually rather smaller PBF.[12] At the same time, Ghosh, the premier, displayed an uncompromising pragmatism and had effected a good working relationship with Tuker and the military. Although still resisting the imposition of martial law, which Tuker had seriously considered asking for on 1 September, the new West Bengal government's robust stance meant that Calcutta remained quiet throughout September. One of the unsolved questions of 1947 is why the military and civil administrations could work in harmony and effectively in Bengal when they seemed unable to in the Punjab. The fact that Calcutta did not erupt meant that the outlying rural areas remained calm as well; outside its few cities Bengal was largely a society of poor farming families.

Secondly, Radcliffe's line in Bengal was less contentious than in the Punjab and he had been receptive to advice on how it should be drawn. Although his panel of judges turned out to be of limited use, opining always according to party lines and lacking objectivity, Radcliffe had listened carefully to local opinion. The critical difference between Bengal and the Punjab was that in Bengal, Congress and nearly half of the population actually wanted partition to happen; without it Bengal's Hindus would always live under a Muslim majority government, hence the strong opposition to Huseyn Suhrawardy's calls for independence. Congress' chief tactical concern was also to ensure that Calcutta remained an undivided city. Consequently they offered a less partisan view outside the city than they might have done. Radcliffe also had a precedent for partition in Bengal – something he lacked in the Punjab – in Curzon's partition of 1905. His line would in fact be very similar. Congress had offered two 'cardinal principles' in Bengal. First, they asked that the two parts of Bengal should contain as much of the total Hindu and Muslim populations as possible. This may have seemed an obvious point but it allowed Radcliffe some leeway in deciding on where the final line should run. Secondly, Congress had asked that the ratio of Hindus to Muslims and vice versa should be roughly equal in both parts of the partitioned province. Radcliffe achieved this remarkably successfully, with East Bengal ending up 71 per cent Muslim and West Bengal only marginally less Hindu. There was therefore a basic feeling of equity.

Radcliffe also accepted more detailed proposals. He agreed to use the *thana*, effectively the area controlled by a local police station, and for which the most up-to-date census figures existed, as his 'unit' for partition. This meant that his line grouped communities more accurately than if he had relied on the larger *tahsils* as he had to in the Punjab. He also found that the geography of Bengal allowed him to allocate the river systems more coherently. Calcutta relied on the River Hooghly, which was not only its commercial artery but also, being part of the Ganges system, holy to Hindus. By allocating its headwaters of the Murshidabad and Nadia rivers to West Bengal, he preserved its integrity, even though this meant including the Muslim-majority Murshidabad district; in exchange East Bengal received the southern district of Khulna, despite it having a Hindu majority. There were areas of serious contention. The League were furious that the northern city of Jalpaiguri, the railway terminus before the hills and the entrepôt for the tea-growing region around Darjeeling, went to India. Similarly Congress complained vociferously about Chittagong going to Pakistan, and that despite having Darjeeling and Jalpaiguri in the north, together with the Princely state of Cooch Behar, they had no land link to West Bengal.

Thirdly, the movement of refugees was to be slower. Both Hindu and Muslim leaders spoke out strongly against any migration at all. The influential Sarat Chandra Bose, speaking at a press conference on 1 October, said any idea of a transfer of population was 'suicidal, ill-advised and wholly impractical' while Dr Syed Hossan, on behalf of the Muslim community, called the concept of a mass migration 'Monstrous'.[13] Only 700,000 Muslims would move from West to East Bengal that autumn; a similar number would migrate over the years ahead so that by the mid-1960s nearly one and a half million would have moved but it was a trickle compared with the huge flood from East Punjab. More Hindus would move to West Bengal: 1.1 million would move in the year following partition; 2.6 million had made the journey by 1951. Again, this was a more staged migration than that from West Punjab.[14] Many had already left the Noakhali and Tripura districts after the killings in 1946. They were also different people. The Hindu communities tended to be grouped either in the south, in Jessore, Khulna or in Dacca itself, or in the north, around Rangpur and Dinajpur. Many of these were quite well off, either landlords or successful traders, who managed migration more as a planned move by air or ship than in desperation. Of those 1.1 million who moved soon after partition, over half were 'rural gentry', or landowners. Relations with their Muslim tenants had not always been good. The villagers in Bardarpur, near Narayanganj just south of Dacca, resented the fact that the biggest landowners were the Hindu Biswanath family; the family did not improve things by insisting that all Muslims walking to the village bazaar take a long detour so they didn't have to see them cross in front of their house. They actually stayed put, although with far less power in the village, while others were forced out.[15] In Ratanpur, twenty miles south-east of Chittagong, thirty-nine houses belonging to the Hindu landlord Sitanath Das were burned. A correspondent who visited soon afterwards thought the place 'represents a ghastly scene, starving and panic stricken victims, some of whom have severe burn wounds' who surrounded him 'and narrated their awful story with tearful eyes'.[16]

Of the early refugees, 350,000 were urban craftsmen and businessmen, who found similar work in the west, although it would take time. A large part of the given Hindu population were also tribes people from Chittagong and the hill areas that bordered Burma. They were listed as Hindus for want of any other categorisation but had no intention of moving nor felt any pressure to do so.

Yet this was still a mass migration. Many Hindus who became refugees were very poor and they only moved, given the acute shortage of productive land in Bengal, because they felt they had to. Joya Chatterji analysed why refugees living in a village in Nadia, a southern district of West Bengal bordering East Bengal, had decided to leave. Eighty-two said they faced harassment from Muslims; forty-one cited fear of violence; sixteen had suffered actual violence. Twenty-three left 'because everyone else had' and because their community was disintegrating; many would cite poor Muslims now demanding to marry high-caste Hindu brides. For those in East Bengal, stories coming from West Bengal, where many had existing family ties, were not encouraging. Jobs and land were very difficult to find and most poor refugees would end up either in Calcutta, or in the swampy areas of the 24 Parganas and Nadia to the south.[17] Many would stay in the government-run camps for a very long time. Those who found jobs or livelihoods in Calcutta would swell its numbers so that it became the most densely packed city on earth.

Prafulla Kumar Chakreborty described a group of these unfortunates huddled miserably on Sealdah, one of Calcutta's stations. 'They had come away leaving behind all to live here with self-respect', he wrote, in a piece that was critical of the West Bengal government's lack of effort on their behalf. 'They could never guess what death in life awaited them in West Bengal. They got their first poisonous taste on Sealdah station.' Having been inoculated against cholera, 'they were herded into roped off areas on the platforms waiting transport to the camps. Five or six thousand people packed within this barely manageable space. Water comes from three taps. Women have two lavatories'.[18] Many had endured a difficult journey, and there were frequent complaints of belongings being looted by the Muslim National Guard, the vigilante body that operated on the fringes of the League. There was also a feeling that the poor had been abandoned to their fate by the richer Hindus who could afford to re-establish a similar life in the west. 'Their morale', wrote K. N. Dalal, for Associated Press, of the hundreds of thousands of poor, 'is completely broken with the evacuation of the middle class people'.[19]

The pattern among the Muslims who made the move east was not dissimilar. In the early stages government servants, their households, and well-to-do Muslim traders and businessmen went, mindful of the opportunities on offer. They were followed by people who came from areas where the violence had been worst in 1946, particularly from Calcutta and the cities. The Muslim population of Calcutta would fall from being roughly one third in 1947 to about a seventh by 1951. In Nadia town the proportion of Muslims fell by three quarters and in Jalpaiguri by 90 per cent. Others came from the rural districts of Nadia and the 24 Parganas, close to the border. However, the majority of the rural population stayed put. There was no mass migration from Murshidabad, for example, despite it being left in India. Yet there was a definite 'anti-Muslim' feeling in post-partition West Bengal, and an unjustified feeling that East Bengal had taken the most productive agricultural land. Muslims, used to commanding a majority, had to note Congress' dictat that the government would 'not tolerate the existence within its borders of disloyal elements'. Ashok Mitra, a local magistrate in Malda, wrote that there was a recurring tendency among Malda's Hindus to embark 'on a witch-hunt of Muslims' and said they ran a list of thirty thousand 'undesirable Muslim families'.[20] In the remote village of Patuabhanga the local Muslims were determined to state their case. On 25 October they sacrificed a cow, something inimical to Hindus for whom cows are sacred. The Hindus protested, saying such things should not now be allowed. The police intervened and six Muslims were shot.[21] Even Suhrawardy was heard to declare publicly that 'the mainspring of our policy [is that] we shall serve our country' and that 'we pledge support to the government of Pandit Jawaharlal Nehru – not merely lip support but true and loyal support'. It did not stop him later becoming Prime Minister of Pakistan.[22]

Lastly, many of the rural poor had other things on their mind. Although the terrible famine of 1942–44 was now under control, and there were some food stocks, there was still a threat of starvation that October, particularly in the very poor areas like Noakhali. 'Thousands of famished men, women and children, dressed in rags, were to be seen loitering in the streets of Chittagong day and night, begging for food and alms, a reminder of the pitiful scenes of 1943', wrote Tuker. 'Reports of deaths from starvation were constantly dribbling in from the villages. The general vitality of the people had deteriorated from want of proper nourishment'. Many cattle had been killed during the Monsoon floods and milk, a village staple, was now scarce.[23]

The new provincial government of East Bengal formed under the effective direction of Khwaja Nazimuddin. He selected two people to help him run the province: Nurul Amin, a quiet and well-liked barrister who had been the former Speaker of the united Bengal Assembly, and Hamil Chowdury. Their appointments were announced in *Dawn* on 15 August. They faced a difficult task. Many Pakistanis believed that East Bengal would not be able to survive, much as Burrows had predicted back in April. Famine was thought to be the inevitable consequence of an overpopulated area that now lacked commerce, communications and industry; partition had left it with just 12 per cent of Bengal's industrial capacity. Agricultural productivity was, despite the complaints of East Bengal having taken the best land, low and food production, insufficient to feed the growing population. The city of Chittagong, on the Bay of Bengal, was not developed as a port. The population density of East Bengal in 1947 was 700 per square mile compared to just 109 for Sind and the Punjab. Dacca was not a city like Calcutta. It was 'a city of bamboo and corrugated iron whereas Calcutta is proverbially a city of palaces', although some would argue that was being over-generous to Calcutta.[24] It was a thousand miles from its own capital in Karachi, its people shared few links to their compatriots in Sind or the Punjab, speaking a different language, and dressing and eating differently. Pakistan was oriented towards the Middle East; East Bengal was 'irrevocably part of Asia'.[25]

The lack of industry and the low agricultural productivity meant that the province's ability to raise revenue was limited. Nazimuddin faced a formidable bill for the provision of essential infrastructure and services and very limited means to pay for it. In 1947 provincial taxes would raise only just over 4 rupees per head, compared to 17 rupees for West Bengal; the comparable figures for the Western

Pakistani provinces were 18 rupees for Sind and nearly 8 rupees in the Punjab. One of the strangest British legacies was the 1793 Bengal land settlement, known as the 'Permanent Settlement'. This had been part of Cornwallis's reforms where he had tried to equate land tenure in India with the English system that he so admired. This well-meant piece of legislation capped the amount the Bengal government could collect in land tax from landowners but, by also creating a landlord class, it had left them free to extract higher rents from their tenants.

Enormous as the political and financial problems were, and however concerned the nation's new leaders may have been, partition was, at least to begin with, very popular among the majority of the now East Bengalis. The Hindus had bitterly opposed Curzon when he divided Bengal in 1905 but had strongly supported partition; the Muslims, once they realised that a unified Islamic state of Bengal was unachievable, now began to see the opportunities that partition offered. East Bengal was one of the most Muslim parts of India. There were more mosques in Dacca than in any other Indian city; it had proved fertile ground for Wahhabi preachers in the nineteenth century. Bengali Muslims were mostly converted low-caste Hindus whose popular history reminded them that they had held effective power until the arrival of the British and many had felt oppressed by their Hindu landlords. There was a discernible zeal for separation and the jobs they hoped it would now offer, a spirit that has translated into the modern nation of Bangladesh once the Province rejected its semi-colonial status as an adjunct of West Pakistan. The issue Nazimuddin faced was more one of making his remote province relevant to a Pakistani government grappling with similarly enormous problems. He was not helped when it was announced that the official language would be Urdu, almost unspoken in Bengal.

One strong unifying force for all Pakistanis, whether in Karachi or Dacca, was a growing antipathy to India. The Indians were seen as exploiting their vulnerabilities and abetting the murder of their fellow Muslims as they tried to flee. India that October was, however, in just as desperate a situation as Pakistan. 'Life here continues to be nightmarish', lamented Nehru, 'everything seems to have gone away'.[26] Santdas Kirpalani was finding establishing the Ministry of Refugees challenging. In early October his minister, Neogy, had met Liaquat in Lahore to see whether it would be possible to establish a Joint Refugee Committee but the talks ended without agreement. However, the military liaison through a joint Movement Control Office, also in Lahore, did seem to be working after a fashion and both Trivedi, the Indian Governor of the East Punjab, and Mudie, the British Pakistani Governor of West Punjab, thought things were improving. However much the senior politicians might hurl insults at each other, and however savage local communities were, in mid-October official level cooperation remained workable.

Like many officials in the new government in Delhi, Kirpalani was now exposed to just how thin the Raj's administration had become in its final years. With the exodus of British ICS officers, the migration of many Muslim officers to Pakistan, and the lack of recruitment of Indian officers in recent months, he, like many of his colleagues, found they simply did not have the basic machinery of government they had assumed existed. He could not even find a secretary for himself and his minister. His old friend, Sir Narasima Sarma, editor of a Calcutta paper, *Whip*, appeared in his office one day and said he had found the perfect person. He then put the CV of a twenty-five-year-old Punjabi girl on Kirpalani's desk. Kirpalani immediately retorted that it would be absolutely impossible. How could a girl stand up to the volume and nature of the work? Sarma persisted; Kirpalani was desperate. He finally gave in and Kamla Jaspal became his most efficient and hard-working assistant.

Their task, Kirpalani noted with fortitude, seemed to be never-ending. The finance ministry wanted an estimate of the overall number of refugees and how long it would take to rehabilitate them all. But by the middle of October

the end of the problem was nowhere in sight. In the third week of the month 570,000 Muslims moved east and 471,000 non-Muslims moved west.[27] It was abundantly clear that non-Muslims all over West Punjab, the North West Frontier Province, Baluchistan and Bahawalpur were in a state of panic, beleaguered as they were in groups big and small, under constant threat of attack.[28]

As the refugee organisation slowly got itself in order, and as the Military Evacuation Organisation began to bring some control to the refugee columns, so, horribly, the killing squads on both sides refined their techniques and tactics. Some of the very worst massacres would happen that month.

A train carrying over two thousand Hindus and Sikhs from Mianwali in north-west Punjab was deliberately misrouted. It was stopped twenty miles before it reached Lahore and a well-prepared group of Muslim *goondas* attacked and massacred everyone on it, including its small Gurkha escort. On 23 October, at Jassar near Sialkot, 1,500 'non-Muslims', having de-trained, were hacked to pieces as they were walking towards the border.

There were also massacres in Bahawalpur. One of Kirpalani's 'beleaguered pockets' was the Sikh population of Rahim Yar Khan. In September they had been subject to several attacks. Gurmani, the nawab's conscientious prime minister, had been investigating one report when he had come across a bullock cart standing on a bridge over a canal. There seemed to be some knobbly things sticking out of it. On closer investigation he discovered these were arms and legs and that the cart was full of corpses. Two men who were with it ran off; Gurmani's small escort from the Bahawalpur state forces fired at them but missed. They followed them into a village where they found 200 bodies lying in the open. Their crime had been to be Labana Sikhs who had been settled there by the nawab's family in the last century.

After that the remaining 2,000 to 3,000 Sikhs in the area were gathered together in two centres and demanded, with good reason, to be transported to India as soon as possible. The railway had, after Moon's earlier successful organisation of Hindu refugee trains, now got too dangerous to use so the problem was how to move them out safely. Gurmani decided the best method was to put people into a protected column and march them through the desert to the border with Jaisalmer, adjoining the south-eastern part of Bahawalpur and which seemed to offer the most direct route to Indian territory. It was a two-day trek but the route was well used and with camels and donkeys provided to carry water and the women and children, it should be perfectly possible. The only problem was that the escort would have to be from the Bahawalpur state forces who by this stage neither Gurmani nor Moon trusted. Gurmani's answer was to personally select a senior officer to command.

The column of about 2,000 Sikhs left Rahim Yar Khan on 26 September. Moon was relieved to receive a report a week later that they had all reached the border in safety and the Sikhs had expressed their deep gratitude to the Bahawalpur troops. Yet something did not quite ring true. He went to Rahim Yar Khan to investigate. Slowly the truth came out. Before they started the Sikhs had been told to surrender what weapons they had. They refused but had eventually been talked into doing so. On the first night Bahawalpur soldiers had begun to search the Sikhs and take their property. There was a fight and several Sikhs were shot dead. The commanding officer, no doubt aware that they were still close enough to Rahim Yar Khan for people to slip away and report what had happened, was conciliatory and promised it would not happen again. The next day the column marched on and by that evening it was well into the desert, far away from any help. The commanding officer then announced that all the refugees' belongings would be 'confiscated'. Unarmed, the Sikhs could do nothing but acquiesce as their animals and valuables were systematically stolen. The loot was loaded onto military lorries and driven away. On 30 September the column stopped just short of the Indian border, which they expected to cross the next day. In the middle of the night the two Sikh leaders, Bakhtawar Singh and Bhag Singh, were woken and told the column must start to move immediately. They protested and were instantly bayoneted. The column was roused and started off again.

They had not gone far when they heard the sound of firing ahead. They were told it was armed Hurs, the Hurs being a fanatical group of bandits who were known to operate along the border. The women needed to be separated for safety. They were then taken away to be divided up among the escort while the men, older women and children were told to make a run for it to the border. As they set off they were mown down by half the escort who had gone on ahead to ambush them and who had been responsible for the earlier alleged Hur firing. Running, terrified, through the desert, they were nearly all killed. Some did survive to reach Jaisalmer. Camels and search parties were sent out and managed to recover any wounded who were treated in hospital in Jodhpur but most of the 2,000 who had set off died in the desert.

Inevitably the arrival of truckloads of loot and abducted women caused a stir when the escort returned. Moon and Gurmani managed to extract the whole story from an assistant police commissioner who had been present. The commanding officer was immediately arrested but within a couple of days he had escaped and made his way to Multan where he was beyond their reach.[29]

News of such massacres caused an inevitable reaction on the Indian side of the border, making Kirpalani's task all the more urgent. After the Jassar massacre, a crowd of 10,000 Sikhs tried to storm the Muslim refugee staging camp at the cattle ground outside Amritsar. The Indian troops on duty behaved well and turned them away.

Slowly the refugee ministry began to produce results. The Military Evacuation Organisation was now beginning to work better but one unforeseen consequence was that the refugee columns were becoming unmanageably large. One group, which originated around Lyallpur, was ninety miles long and contained over one million people by the time it reached Lahore. Kirpalani went to see it. 'It was a seething mass of humanity interspersed with bullock-carts, cattle, horses, camels, donkeys and bicycles. At night the convoy halted for refreshment and rest. The peasants had brought along quantities of grain and flour. They collected brushwood, lit fires and cooked camp rations. Wayside pools, puddles and ponds provided water for cooking and drinking.' Kirpalani became very concerned about cholera. A call went out across India for vaccine and 'Operation Needle' produced an amazing response, not enough to vaccinate that whole column but a vaccination programme was in place in Indian camps by October.

The convoy marched for five days without mishap; there were sporadic attacks but they were beaten off by the accompanying Indian escort. On the sixth day, by which time they had covered about half the distance to the border, the heavens opened. The rain was at first welcome but then it became torrential. The refugees couldn't light fires and so could not cook. They were already on a subsistence diet and now there was no food.

A call went out on the radio. Indians should make chapattis by the million and deliver them to Palam airfield in Delhi. The response was overwhelming. The air force was holding planes in waiting and the plan was to air-drop sacks of these flat loaves to the waiting refugees. But the plan hit an unforeseen snag in that, as the military pointed out, sacks of chapattis dropped from a height would be lethal and, with so many people around, it would be impossible to find clear space. One of the new Indian Air Force's first experimental missions thus became how to deliver chapattis safely by air. When they dropped the loaves without sacks from normal parachute height they found they had disintegrated by the time they reached the ground. The ingenious method they ultimately arrived at was to open the sacks, then fly low over the column dispensing them so that the chapattis arrived in a widespread shower. The convoy duly arrived safely in Ferozepore, where it took over a week for all the refugees to cross the border and disperse to camps.

Another huge column, over 1.5 million strong, was organised to take Muslims from Gurgaon, where there had been so much violence in May and June, and the surrounding areas near Delhi, into Pakistan. With so many people on the move there was always the danger of columns meeting. One evening a signal came through that two huge columns, one of Hindus from Sargodha in Pakistan and the other of Muslims from Hoshiarpur in India were, due to an error in coordinating timing, going to meet head on. The authorities braced themselves for a bloodbath. Kirpalani lay awake all night, dreading the news the next day. To his amazement, although both columns did meet, the refugees greeted each other and asked their opposite numbers to take care of property and animals left behind.

Other measures were also slowly beginning to help. The United Provinces had taken on the task of providing lorries for the Military Evacuation Organisation. By October the redoubtable Pandit Pant had sent 2,000, making a significant difference to escorting refugees to the staging camps. Later that month the Indian government approached the British Overseas Airways Corporation, BOAC, one of the forerunners of today's British Airways, asking whether they could help collect the scattered Hindu groups from deep inside Pakistan. They agreed to provide twenty-five Dakota DC3s. The seats were stripped out so that an aircraft that was designed to take twenty-two passengers could take over a hundred. They were dispatched, in close cooperation with the Pakistani authorities, to remote airfields. There were pathetic scenes as there was never enough room to take everyone who was waiting, with people clinging onto wings and tailplanes rather as they had done to trains, arguing that they were not taking up any space. The air operation continued for ten weeks, rescuing close to 200,000 refugees.

Distribution of refugee property was itself becoming a major political issue. There was a supposition among refugees, given that most had lost everything when they fled, that the new governments would compensate them by allocating property that had belonged to families who had fled the other way. Nehru, backed by Maulana Azad as the leading Congress Muslim voice, had, however, decreed that property should remain under the protection of a Custodian of Refugee Property until it could be determined whether the owners were ever coming back. Nehru remained determined that Congress should speak for all Indians, and he still saw Pakistan as a temporary aberration. Moveable property was considered too difficult to monitor and police but the custodian took over the care of Muslim houses in Delhi, many of which were very valuable. The custodian could allocate empty property but only if he was sure that the government's condition had been met and there was no chance that the owner might return, obviously a very difficult fact to establish. Secondly, there was not nearly enough property to go round and there was the inevitable corruption with people trying to get possession. Outside Delhi it was more of a free for all, with Muslim property in the Punjab villages looted and occupied, with a very similar situation in Pakistan. Commandeering of the best houses in cities like Karachi and Dacca left many Hindus badly affected and was one of the most contentious issues in trying to establish Jinnah's society where all people enjoyed equal rights.

The Pakistani refugee organisation more or less mirrored Neogy and Kirpalani's Ministry of Relief and Rehabilitation. On 11 September West Punjab had established a Rehabilitation Commissioner; by mid-October his office had become a Refugee Council, presided over by Liaquat in person. Similar councils were then set up in Sind and the North West Frontier Province. Jinnah led the public appeal for support much as Nehru was doing in India. 'Let every man and woman resolve from this day to live henceforth strictly on an austerity basis in respect of foodstuffs, clothing.' What they saved should be 'Brought to the common pool for the relief of the stricken',[30] he announced as he launched the *Quaid-i-Azam* Relief Fund. Refugee camps were set up initially across the Punjab; the first was in Lahore Boy Scout camp and the scout staff were drafted in to run it. Each camp held 42,000 people in six blocks of 7,000 each, and soon there were more operating across the country. An appeal for quilts to be knitted as some protection against the coming cold produced 35,000 in Lahore alone. Liaquat received a huge response to his calls to Muslim countries to donate clothes and to his appeal in London for volunteers to help run the camps.

Local cooperation remained good for the first three weeks of the month. Mohindar Singh Chopra, now promoted to brigadier, was posted to Amritsar in October to assume command of an infantry brigade. His daughter sat in the front of the army truck carrying their possessions as they travelled to their new home. She had been through quite a lot in the last few months, moving from Ambala to Assam, then back to Delhi lying on the floor of the train to avoid being shot, and now was on the move again. As they crossed the River Beas, nearing Amritsar, the first thing she noticed was the 'awful stench – that of the dead, both human and animal, with trees devoid of leaves, no grass, only a terrible stillness. A slowly moving snake of humanity was going towards Amritsar, carrying children and the infirm, slowly trudging through the dust and haze'. As they crossed the bridge over the Beas they saw a large and agitated crowd. An old man had been thrown into the river as he was too slow to keep up. Beyond the Beas the scenes became even worse, with 'mile upon mile of devastation, a desolate and arid vista of animal carcasses and leafless trees, bringing to mind just what hell must look like'.[31]

In Amritsar, Singh Chopra, who knew the city of old, was horrified. It was a 'shambles and overrun by refugees'. What upset his daughter most was the 'Recovered Women's' camp. Their situation was particularly pathetic. They had, they said, been abandoned by their men and left to the Muslims. 'Now that we have been ravaged and allocated places in their homes, you want to once again uproot us and for what . . . will our families accept us after all this?' Many would not. Some of the women were defiant and angry but others just seemed 'dejected and mentally disturbed. They sat in the corner with their faces covered and shrieked or fainted whenever the shadow of a man fell on them.' One day she also saw a train at Amritsar station that had crossed the recently reopened border full of dead. It had 'Qatil Karna Hamse Seeko' (which roughly translates as 'Learn to kill Sikhs!') scrawled all over it. A few days later she saw a train full of massacred Muslims being dispatched to Pakistan with 'Qatil Karna Seekhliya' (roughly 'The Sikhs have learned to kill') scrawled on it in return.[32]

There was still an occasional act of mercy to lighten the overall sense of gloom, albeit few happy endings. Singh Chopra received a letter from Kehar Singh, an elderly Sikh from Tarn Taran, a small town just south of Amritsar with an important gurdwara. He had taken pity on a Muslim girl who was about to be killed by a *jatha*. Her husband and all her family had been killed and she had nothing left. Kehar Singh paid the *jatha* leader 350 rupees for her. He fell in love with her, she converted to Sikhism, became known as Pritam Kaur, and they duly married. She was happy and did not want to go to Pakistan. One day, walking through the town, the police seized her to send her off to a refugee camp. She broke down in tears, insisting that she wanted to stay with Kehar, but the police ignored her. Could the brigadier please help? Kehar pleaded but it was too late.

Kharaiti Lal was determined to do what she could to rescue abducted women. She attached herself, with an army truck, to those Indian Army units still operating inside Pakistan to escort non-Muslim refugees. She took a Muslim name, so she could move more freely inside Pakistan, and when refugee columns were being assembled she went to local police stations demanding to be taken to the villages where people had told her women were being hidden. Sometimes the women didn't want to come, terrified again as to how their families would react to having them back, but the majority did. She found one house belonging to a bad-tempered old Muslim man. There was a large pot on top of what was evidently a hole in the ground in his farmyard. Kharaiti asked him what was in there. Pigeons, he replied, and told her not to disturb them as they would fly away. Unperturbed she lifted the pot and found three terrified young girls. The old man produced an ancient revolver and threatened to shoot her. She told him he wouldn't hit her even if he did shoot and he threw the weapon down in a fury. Inside his house they found another six girls. It was a brave campaign. 'The women were all helpless', she recalled. 'They used to weep. God alone knows the things I have seen in those days. Some women's hands had been chopped off, some ears, some arms.'[33]

The plight of women was as bad on both sides; overall it is thought about one hundred thousand disappeared, forced into marriage which usually involved forced conversion, used or just murdered. Sometimes they were taken during the raids on villages, at other times kidnapped from refugee columns when they lagged behind. Young teenage girls were at the most risk. Even once they reached India or Pakistan they were still vulnerable, especially as so many had lost parents. Khorshed Nehta was a welfare worker who met refugee trains at Delhi station. She reckoned that half the women she saw had been assaulted. There was also a major problem with Delhi brothel owners waiting on the station to trap the wretched and confused young girls. The story of a Sikh woman from West Punjab, Parkashwanti, was typical. Muslim *goondas* attacked her village. Her husband rushed her and her young son to the safety of the local rice mill but the *goondas* pursued them. Thinking she was sure to be raped, her husband tried to kill her. He slashed her with his sword but only succeeded in inflicting a deep gash in her jaw. She passed out. When she came round her husband and son had been sliced up and she had been routinely raped. Some months later she gave birth to a daughter.[34]

One of Singh Chopra's tasks as brigade commander in Amritsar was to demarcate the border. Even as late as mid-October there was no physical barrier or even a sign to indicate where India stopped and Pakistan began. Local people knew where the Amritsar–Lahore district border crossed the Grand Trunk Road at Wagah, that artery of empire running from Delhi to Peshawar; it was this district border that was the line Radcliffe had followed. It was not clear to the refugees when they had actually reached their respective promised lands, the flat land with scattered brushwood and villages looked much the same on either side. On 11 October, Singh Chopra installed a joint checkpoint with his Pakistani counterpart, using some whitewashed oil drums and some stones swept into a low berm. Both sides erected tents and left a small guard there; a small swing gate was installed to regulate traffic. Finally they both erected flagpoles and together unveiled a small brass plaque to commemorate the event. It is still there today, despite the savage fighting of 1965, although the Wagah Crossing now looks like Fort Knox and bears little resemblance to that early informality.

More seriously, on 18 October the Indian and Pakistani armies exchanged fire with each other across the border, not far from the village where Kehar Singh had rescued his Muslim wife. There had been small incidents for some time, linked to attacks on refugee columns or cattle raiding, but this was the first time that formed bodies of troops had actually fought a skirmish. They fired at each other, fairly ineffectively, for most of the afternoon, with the Pakistanis sustaining four killed and six wounded. Singh Chopra signalled his opposite number in Lahore, Brigadier Nazir Ahmed. They knew each other well; both had served in the same battalion of the Frontier Force Rifles. The two commanders met in 'the most friendly and cordial atmosphere' at their newly installed border post. Nazir Ahmed later sent Singh Chopra a copy of the article that had appeared in the *Civil and Military Gazette*, Kipling's old paper, which was a Lahore daily, with a letter saying 'we hope and pray that we both now live up to the expectations we built up that day and also that of the public'.[35] Very soon such pleasantries, and the spirit of cooperation that still existed in mid-October, would be gone.

On 15 August three Princely states – Hyderabad, Kashmir and Junagadh – had not acceded either to India or Pakistan. The Nawab of Bhopal had signed sealed papers, which he entrusted personally to Mountbatten on the understanding that they were not to be opened without his agreement. By the end of August he still hesitated. The nawab, Hamidullah Khan, emerges as one of the more sympathetic and tragic figures of the story of 1947. He felt he and his fellow princes had been badly let down by the British. Equally he realised that he must, for the good of his state, and he was among the most committed and conscientious of rulers, decide soon whether it would join India or Pakistan. He had ambitions to play a leading role in the future of Muslim India, and he was afraid that Jinnah would condemn him should he opt for India. On the other hand it made little sense for his important state, deep in central India, to join Pakistan. He flew to Karachi to consult with Jinnah. The *Quaid* was magnanimous. Bhopal duly acceded to India and swore to serve his new nation well. 'If only', recorded Hodson, the Reforms Commissioner before Menon and able chronicler of the period, 'the rulers of the

three [remaining] big apples had been like the Nawab of Bhopal!'
Instead 'all three were weak, eccentric and devious'.[36]

Junagadh would prove altogether more complicated. It was a
low-lying, seaboard state, south of Pakistan with a population of
700,000 who were mostly Hindu. It was important to Hindus, being
where Lord Krishna had died and it was also home to the celebrated
Hindu shrine at Somnath, desecrated by Mahmud of Ghazni in his
violent conquest of 1024. However, its ruler was Muslim, Nawab
Mohammad Mahabat Khanji III, the man who was besotted with
dogs. Junagadh was geographically complicated. It contained parts
of other states, had two vassal states, Mangrol and Barbariawad,
irregular borders which protruded into Baroda and was generally regarded as being an indivisible part of the Kathiawar states,
dominated by the Jam Sahib, the Maharajah of Nawanagar. The
assumption had been that it would, along with the other Kathiawar
states, accede to India. However, in May 1947, Sir Shah Nawaz
Bhutto had staged a palace coup and taken over as the nawab's
dewan. He was a passionate supporter of Pakistan.

On 15 August Junagadh had subsequently acceded to Pakistan
and the nawab had fled to Karachi, although in such a hurry that he
left his baby behind at the airport. His decision, although technically
perfectly legal, was seen by Nehru and Patel as illogical and unreasonable. They argued, correctly, that both Mangrol and Barbariawad
had acceded to India, and that the Kathiawar states as a whole were
an indivisible part of India. His accession left them, however, in
a difficult position. Should India ultimately accept the nawab's
decision to take a Hindu majority state into Pakistan, it would set
a precedent for the much more important state of Hyderabad. If
on the other hand they refused to acknowledge the nawab's choice
and threatened to intervene by force in the interests of the majority
Hindu population, they were likewise setting a dangerous precedent
for Kashmir, where Pakistan could argue it was entitled to do the
same thing. Even if they insisted on a plebiscite, which would have
decided overwhelmingly in favour of India, they were establishing
an equally difficult precedent for themselves in Kashmir.

The arguments raged backwards and forwards throughout September and October. Initially Nehru and Patel were for taking military action. Indian troops were instructed to surround Junagadh and the dewan told to remove his state forces from Barbariawad. Mountbatten managed to calm them both down, pointing out that India did not want to appear to the world as an aggressor. On 6 October Nehru put out a statement calling for a plebiscite: 'the fate of any territory', he wrote, 'should be decided by a referendum or plebiscite of the people concerned'.[37] It was a far cry from his reaction to Caroe's call for a plebiscite in the North West Frontier Province in April and they were words that he would come to regret in Kashmir.

By 21 October no progress had been made and as the refugee crisis seemed to be coming more under control, Delhi returned to the issue of Junagadh. Patel, impatient as always, a Gujurati from the local area, and with his sights firmly set on Hyderabad, argued that they were being weak and that as there had been no reaction to the 6 October announcement, they should take military action. He prevailed and on 1 November Indian troops moved into Barbariawad and Mangrol; there was no resistance and India peacefully took over the government. The situation in Junagadh itself was meanwhile slowly deteriorating. Bhutto wrote to Jinnah on 27 October that the Indian blockade meant that there was no communication with the outside world, food was becoming short and there was no revenue from the railways. What support there had been for joining Pakistan was waning. He asked Jinnah to hold a conference to find a peaceful solution but received no response. On 5 November the Junagadh State Council met and decided that they should have a 'reorientation of state policy'.[38] While the nawab, the state treasury and the dogs remained in Karachi, Bhutto asked India to accede, saying that they wanted to 'save the State from complete administrative breakdown'.[39] Indian forces moved in on 9 November. It would not be the last time that the Bhutto family would feature prominently in Pakistani politics.

The move elicited a furious response from Liaquat who demanded their immediate withdrawal. India's action was a direct act of hostility, an invasion of Pakistani territory and violated international law. But India had set a precedent and even as this war of telegrams raged between Karachi and Delhi, both nations were faced with a much more serious challenge and one that would destroy any remaining willingness to cooperate. Whereas the bitterness of the suffering on both sides in the Punjab had done very serious damage to an already acrimonious relationship, it would still have been possible for Indian and Pakistani relations to recover. Liaquat was still travelling regularly to Delhi throughout October, lunching with Nehru, and, despite arguments such as that over Junagadh, conducting joint business. The relationship, which in June many thought would be similar to that enjoyed between the different countries in the United Kingdom, was certainly not broken beyond repair. By the end of October it would be.

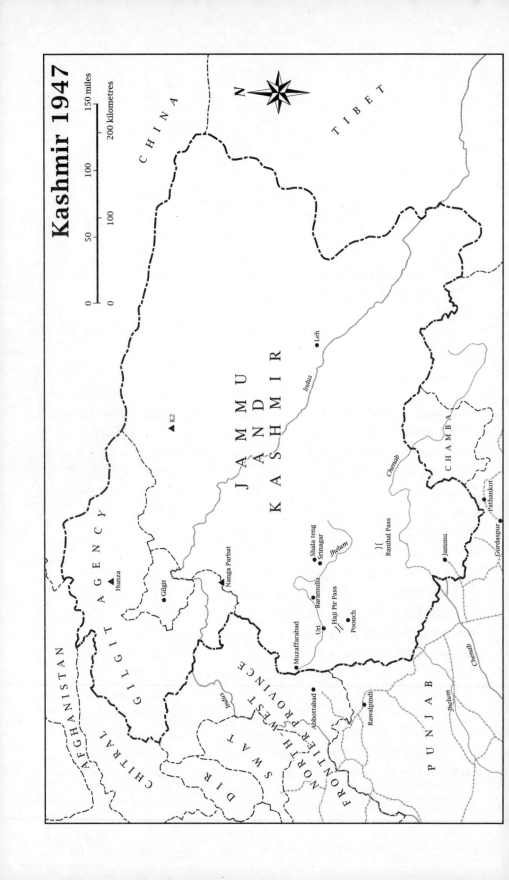

Kashmir 1947

150 miles

200 kilometres

0   50   100

0   100

EIUS RELIGIO

*'The situation was already so bad there was little
that could happen that to make it worse'*

(JINNAH)

On Sunday 2 November, Nehru broadcast to the Indian nation. 'I
want to speak to you tonight about Kashmir. Not about the beauty
of that famous valley but about the horror it has had to face.'[1] The
events of late October and November in Kashmir would lead to tens
of thousands – there is no accurate count – more deaths, another
huge influx of refugees to Pakistan and cause the final breakdown
of relations between the two countries. The extraordinary beauty
of Kashmir seems to heighten the tragedy of its fate. Situated about
five thousand feet up, a fertile and well-watered stretch of green in
the lower ranges of the Karakoram and Hindu Kush, both contrib-
utory ranges to the Himalaya, the Vale of Kashmir is one of the
most scenic and attractive places in the world. Srinagar, the summer
capital, situated on the Jhelum river and beside Dal Lake, combined
the rough charm of a mountain village with the elegance of a city
made fashionable by tourism. A holiday on a Kashmiri houseboat
was one of the 'must dos' of anyone in India who could afford it.
Surrounded by mountains, and yet with a climate that reached 30
degrees in the summer and which allowed gardens to flourish, it was
not surprising that for centuries it had offered an idyllic retreat from

the plains. In 1947, 400 retired British officials and businessmen were living there.

Since Gandhi's and Mountbatten's visits in the summer, and with attention in both Delhi and Karachi firmly fixed on the Punjab, the situation in Kashmir had not been their priority. Maharajah Hari Singh still had not given any indication which way he would go and in October he remained undecided. As a Hindu ruler, supported by a privileged Hindu elite, his tendency might have been to India. However, he knew that accession to India would not be popular among his majority Muslim population and he had no love for Congress. He saw Nehru as a dangerous socialist, committed to democracy, who would have no use for the Dogra dynasty. Accession to Pakistan would have been in many ways the more obvious choice. Kashmir was geographically linked to Pakistan more closely than it was to India. Communications to Jammu and Srinagar, the respective winter and summer capitals, ran north-east from Rawalpindi and the Pakistani Punjab. There was no tarmac road to India, the only route being a dirt track that ran south from Srinagar over the mountains to Jammu and then on to Pathankot and Gurdaspur, against whose final inclusion in India Liaquat had protested so strongly.

The three great rivers that irrigated Pakistan, the Indus, the Jhelum and the Chenab, all had their headwaters in Kashmir. Timber, Kashmir's main export, was largely carried down the Jhelum. Under the August Standstill Agreement, Pakistan continued to provide Kashmir's post and telegraph services. Jinnah was likely to be more tolerant of the maharajah's status and leave him with more authority than if he was cast to the mercy of Patel's States Department. There would also have been little that India could have done about it, other than for Nehru to be personally devastated. It was the maharajah's decision, which would be seen internationally as legitimate and, given his overwhelming Muslim majority, logical.

Yet accession to Pakistan would have been an anathema to Hari Singh. He could not bring himself to submit to Muslim majority rule and, however tolerant Jinnah might be, ultimately he saw his family being forced out by a Muslim government; he was probably correct

in this. He argued, not particularly convincingly, that the strength
of Kashmir was that it was a state in which all religions flourished
and all citizens were equal, free and could worship as they pleased.
This was manifestly untrue. His rule was

> autocratic and despotic. The incidence of land revenue was triple
> that in the Punjab. The sale of grain was a state monopoly. There
> was a tax on every sheep, every hearth and every wife, and a
> professional tax on butchers, bakers, carpenters, boatmen and
> even prostitutes. There was differential treatment of Muslims
> and Hindus. A Muslim, not a Hindu, had to have a gun licence.
> A Hindu on conversion to Islam forfeited all interests in inherited
> property. The Muslims were beef eaters but cow slaughter was
> punishable by a ten-year jail sentence.[2]

Neither were Kashmiri politics straightforward. The main opposition to the maharajah's rule, and that of his unpopular prime
minister, Mehr Chand Mahajan, previously one of Congress' nom-
inations for the Punjab Boundary Commission, who had replaced
the even more unpopular Pandit Kak, was Congress led by the
Muslim Sheikh Mohammed Abdullah, a close confidant and strong
supporter of Nehru. He was therefore, rather like Dr Khan Sahib
had been in the North West Frontier Province, a living example of
Congress' claim that it spoke for all Indian people regardless of religion. Abdullah, like Nehru, saw the situation in Kashmir as one of
democracy versus autocracy and of the need for social and economic
development in the face of oppressive feudal government. A product
of Aligarh, he was, again like Nehru, a well-heeled socialist. He
was married to Akbar Jahan, a daughter of Harry Nedou, from the
family that owned Srinagar's top Swiss hotel. His party, originally
called the Muslim Conference, had changed its name to the National
Conference to broaden its appeal; its flag was a white plough on a
red background, proudly displaying its social agenda. By October
Abdullah was finally, after sixteen months, out of prison, the maharajah having given in to Nehru's demands to release him. He made

a series of journeys to Delhi to consult with Nehru and Patel. On 17 October the *Hindustan Times* carried a front-page photograph of these two Kashmiris side by side.[3]

Not all Muslims supported Sheikh Abdullah. Pitched against him was the League's Kashmiri wing, confusingly also called the Muslim Conference, and led by Choudhury Ghulam Abbas, who increasingly became the focus of the pro-Pakistan lobby. While Indian pressure had secured Sheikh Abdullah's release, Ghulam Abbas remained incarcerated, something on which the League's *Dawn* newspaper was quick to comment. On the fringes of the League were those tribal leaders, part mystic, part bandit whom Kashmir and the Frontier produced generation after generation. They had the ability to combine religious fanaticism with tribal interest to inspire their Pathan tribesmen, men like the Fakir of Ipi who had tied down the Indian Army for so long in the 1930s. In 1947 the Fakir was not reconciled to the idea of Pakistan but others were; of these the most influential was the Pir of Manki Sharif, who claimed a following of 200,000. They would soon answer his call. He was assisted by a shadowy adventurer, Khurshid Anwar, who had once been a major in the army and had since been active in the League's National Guards.

By mid-October neither Abdullah nor Ghulam Abbas had publicly declared their position on accession. It was generally, and reasonably, assumed that they would of course declare for India and Pakistan respectively but there was also a strong belief among Kashmiris in general that it might be possible, rather as the Nizam in Hyderabad was hoping, for their state to remain independent. Although Hari Singh must have known that this was highly unlikely, and that his mountain kingdom would be heavily dependent on its powerful neighbours for its economic survival, it gave him an excuse to prevaricate. His ambition was 'to make Kashmir the Switzerland of the East – a State that is completely neutral. As much of our living depends on visitors, we must think of them. Visitors will not come to a state which is beset with communal problems', announced the deputy prime minister, Ram Lal Batra, as late as mid-October.[4] This was one area where the maharajah was, for once, in touch with popular opinion. Major General Scott, the British officer who had recently retired after eleven years heading the maharajah's fairly incompetent state forces, briefed that the 'vast majority of Kashmiris have no strong bias for either India or Pakistan and prefer to remain independent of either Dominion and free to earn their living'.[5]

Part of the problem in Kashmir was the personality of Hari Singh himself. His Dogra family who, it will be remembered, had effectively purchased Kashmir from the British in 1846, were seen as interlopers. They could not command the sort of respect that rulers like Rajput princes could, families who had grown from their own kin and ruled them for centuries in what was perceived to be their common interest. Even his own son was strongly critical of the way he handled the coming crisis. His father could not, Karan Singh thought, ever accept that the British were going. He was 'very insulated from the rest of India. One of the problems of feudalism is that you tend to get isolated'.[6] Hari Singh's trick when he didn't want to do something or see someone was to feign illness, as Mountbatten and Ismay had discovered. The notion of an independent Kashmir allowed an indecisive man an excuse not to accede to either India or Pakistan.

Communal trouble had started in Kashmir in September in the district of Poonch, south and east of Srinagar, a particularly beautiful and remote area of lakes and hills where the mountain ranges start to give way to the plains. It was a strongly Muslim area with a long military tradition; estimates vary but it is thought Poonch contributed between 40,000 and 60,000 troops to the Indian Army in the Second World War. This meant that there was a considerable degree of residual military expertise. In late August and early September there were a series of Muslim protest meetings demanding that Kashmir join Pakistan. When the maharajah's state forces tried to break these up on 26 August there was rioting and they began firing on the crowds, causing a furious reaction. By mid-September Poonch was in open revolt, the Muslim community were organised under an Azad Kashmir party, literally 'Free Kashmir', led by local barrister Sardar Mohammed Ibrahim, and the state forces were expelled apart from a besieged garrison in Poonch town itself. The

Muslim irregular forces were led by a young landowner, Abdul Qayyum Khan, whose troops were around 75 per cent ex-regular soldiers and whose job was made easier by the state forces' indiscriminate atrocities. Their motivation, Qayyum said, 'was not so much to join Pakistan as to get rid of the Dogra monarchy'.[7] At the same time there were atrocities against the non-Muslim population.

The situation was reversed in Jammu, with its Hindu majority, where Sikh and Hindu refugees from West Punjab had been heading since mid-August. Here the local Muslim population was less well organised. Tens of thousands were rounded up by the maharajah's forces and told to start moving towards Sialkot in Pakistan. The resultant refugee columns were attacked, their property looted and their houses and farms taken over by Punjabi incomers. There was some cross-border support from Pakistan for the Muslim irregulars in both Poonch and Jammu, with stories of armed groups of up to three hundred men coming to their assistance and there was some sporadic assistance from the Pakistan Army. Pakistan had deployed troops into the border area to prevent raids by the maharajah's forces into the Pakistani district of Gujrat. 11th Cavalry, a Pakistani armoured car regiment, for example, assisted Azad forces in taking Mirpur where they were besieging the Dogra garrison. Yet this fell far short of full intervention; Pakistan was simply not organised enough nationally to have effected this. Mostly these were sympathetic local groups coming to help their threatened Muslim comrades.

The more serious trouble, which was to lead to the coming crisis, started on 20 October. There was a well-established annual migration of tribesmen from the North West Frontier and the Afghan borderlands south at the end of the hot weather to find winter employment in the plains. This year they were driven on by the rumours of loot to be had as a result of the communal fighting, and also by stories circulated by men such as the Pir of Manki that Muslims were being massacred by non-Muslims. A large group of assorted tribesmen, known as a *lashkar*, had gathered near Abbottabad, capital of the Hazara tribal region and an important staging post north of Rawalpindi on the Srinagar road; it was named after Major

James Abbott who had been the local British commissioner after the annexation of the Punjab. Initially it was estimated that there were about a thousand Hazara tribesmen, around five hundred Afridis and some Muslim League National Guards, although this number would soon swell to nearer seven thousand. They were travelling in a fleet of lorries and had a plentiful supply of arms and ammunition.

Instead of heading south into the plains, the *lashkar*, under Khurshid Anwar's loose direction, turned north and east. On 22 October they sacked Muzaffarabad, wrecking and looting non-Muslim property, then headed due east across the River Jhelum to the small Kashmiri town of Uri which they reached on 23 October. Here they came up against an advance party of the maharajah's forces, led by Brigadier Rajendra Singh, who had replaced Scott as the maharajah's chief of staff. The Kashmiri forces were no match for the tribesmen, who significantly outnumbered them. Sydney Smith of the *Daily Express* was forward with Rajendra Singh and reported them covering the last few miles into the town in

one hour of non-stop gunfire. Houses on the route of their advance went up in flames and thick black smoke blanketed the valley. The raiders mopped up any Sikhs and Hindus who stayed behind in a desperate attempt to shoot it out. Then the firing died as looting began. Through field glasses I watched mobs of black-turbaned and blanketed figures rushing through Uri's bazaar street. The raiders went on shooting up the town for three hours.[8]

Rajendra Singh sensibly withdrew his outnumbered force back east, down the road to Srinagar, now littered with refugees and the detritus of their flight. On 25 October the *lashkar* had reached Mahura, the site of Kashmir's main hydroelectric power station. The same day Rajendra Singh was killed and, with the majority of their number still committed in Poonch and Jammu, the maharajah's forces became militarily ineffective. The road to Srinagar now lay open.

Maharajah Hari Singh and Prime Minister Mahajan had been

away in Jammu and arrived back in Srinagar on 23 October to be told of the invasion. Immediately they sent Deputy Prime Minister Ram Lal Batra to Delhi where he arrived the next evening. Nehru and Mountbatten were giving a dinner party for a visiting delegation from Siam when they were interrupted by the news. The new Indian Defence Council met the next morning. This body, recently established, was, like the Refugee Committee, chaired by Mountbatten at Nehru's request. Nehru and Patel appear to have been rattled at the military failure in the Punjab and Congress' lack of military experience was becoming evident to them. It was a providential choice as Mountbatten was, again, in his element, and in a position to offer the Indian Cabinet direct advice.

The Defence Council meeting on 25 October decided to rush arms and ammunition to the Kashmir state forces, ignorant of the fact that they had collapsed. There was much discussion as to whether India could intervene if Kashmir had not acceded; it was generally agreed that they could. Nehru was afraid that Jinnah had set Junagadh as a trap. If India had threatened armed intervention there to help a majority Hindu population, Pakistan would justify intervention in Kashmir on the same basis. They also decided to send that inveterate troubleshooter of all Indian problems in 1947, V. P. Menon, to Kashmir that day to find out exactly what was happening. An aeroplane was found and Menon, accompanied by a small army and air force delegation, duly took off.

They arrived at a deserted Srinagar airfield with no sign of any troops. Making their way to the modern and rather utilitarian summer palace beside Dal Lake, they found Hari Singh in a state of panic and about to flee. He had been holding some sort of durbar, an important 'bi-annual event when he sat on a golden throne and everybody paid him homage', remembered Karan Singh, who was in a wheelchair having hurt his hip. Suddenly Srinagar was plunged into darkness as the *lashkar* cut off the power supply. Then 'there was this terrible cacophony of jackals, howling in the darkness. It was a really a very eerie, sort of weird moment'. Hari Singh said he expected the tribesmen in Srinagar within twenty-four hours and that he would do anything India might ask in order to save his throne. Lieutenant Colonel Sam Manekshaw, one of Menon's party, had 'never seen such disorganization in my life. The Maharajah was running around from one room to the other. I have never seen so much jewellery ... pearl necklaces, ruby things, lying in one room; packing here, there and everywhere. There was a convoy of vehicles' outside. The court had commandeered what transport there was and left for Jammu. 'All through that dreadful night we drove', continued Karan Singh, 'slowly, haltingly, as if reluctant to leave the beautiful valley that our ancestors had ruled for generations. Our convoy crawled over the 9,000 foot Banihal Pass just as first light was beginning to break'. His father travelled in stony silence. When they arrived next evening at the palace in Jammu he uttered one single sentence, 'We have lost Kashmir'.[9]

Menon realised that Hari Singh had gone off his head. He also appreciated that there was now nothing to stop the *lashkar* occupying the capital and the vale, thus effectively denying Kashmir to India. He went to the government rest house to try to get some sleep; it was deserted, with nothing to eat or drink and no bedding. He decided to head back to the airport where the pilot said it was too dangerous to take off in such mountainous country until first light. He had a point; Srinagar airfield was basic in the extreme with just a grass strip and windsock. Menon also found the place now packed with desperate Hindu refugees clamouring to be taken out. A middle-aged Hindu lady approached him sobbing, begging him to take her two teenage daughters with him, pointing out in graphic detail, interspersed with shrieks and groans, what the tribesmen were sure to do to them were they to be captured. The kind-hearted Menon found space for the girls but their crying all the way to Delhi denied him the chance of catching any sleep on the flight. He arrived back exhausted to report to the Defence Council on 26 October.[10]

The situation that now confronted India was delicate. If they did not send troops then Kashmir would fall to the tribesmen, there would be much looting and killing and it would ultimately become part of Pakistan. However, if they did send troops then, given that Kashmir had not acceded to India, they were creating a dangerous precedent. They decided on a compromise. Troops would be sent but on the basis that they were there temporarily to save life and pending a plebiscite that would be held as soon as conditions allowed. In the meantime the maharajah should be asked whether he wanted to accede.

While the military started preparations, Menon was sent back again, this time to Jammu. When he arrived he found the situation even more chaotic than it had been in Srinagar. Hari Singh was fast asleep in his Winter Palace, a 'Scottish baronial meets Hollywood Gothic' building even uglier than the Summer Palace in Srinagar. Menon had him woken up. The maharajah said he was ready to accede at once. He then signed both an Instrument of Accession that Menon had prepared and a letter to India asking for military help. He told Menon that he had arrived just in time. Before he went to bed he had left instructions with his ADC that he was only to be woken if Menon returned from Delhi as that would mean India was coming to his aid; if he failed to return then the ADC had instructions to shoot him in his sleep. It is not clear which outcome the perplexed Menon might have thought the most advantageous.

Back in Delhi, at a third meeting of the Defence Council, the Indian government decided to accept the Instrument of Accession and confirmed the dispatch of troops. The military situation was, however, as delicate as the political, both practically and in terms of relations with Pakistan. General Lockhart, commander of the Indian forces, recommended sending a battalion of Gurkhas. The Defence Council did not think Gurkhas were appropriate; Nehru had a particular dislike for the Gurkhas. Lockhart then said there was a battalion of Sikhs in Gurgaon who could go. He pointed out 'the extreme hazards of flying in troops' on such an operation.[11] Mountbatten supported him. There was no way of knowing whether Srinagar airfield was still secure, the troops could only take limited heavy weapons and no transport, resupply would be very difficult and Gurgaon would be left without any troops. The Cabinet were, however, determined and instructions were issued to Lieutenant Colonel Ranjit Rai and the 1st Sikhs. His orders were a model of brevity, if a little ambitious. He was told to 'secure Srinagar airport, drive away the tribesmen and maintain law and order in Srinagar'.[12]

Major Ferris, who went with the battalion, thought the whole move was a nightmare. There was no information of any sort and nobody knew what was going on. They could only fit seventeen troops into each of the military Dakotas available, with the soldiers squatting on the back decks. Dakotas, the military DC3 that was ubiquitous in Asia after the Second World War, were the only aircraft that could land on Srinagar's airfield. The air force didn't have enough aircraft so they pressed civilian planes into service, ripping out 'the luxury fittings and comfortable chairs' and cramming in as many soldiers and equipment as they could. Many were flown by British and Australian pilots. Finally, with the 1st Sikhs crammed in, they taxied and took off north from Palam airport at first light on 27 October.

As hazardous as the military operation was thought to be in itself, it also posed a huge risk in relations with Pakistan. Nehru and the Indian Defence Committee were sure that the tribesmen's invasion was inspired and supported by the Pakistan military. 'It must', he told his colleagues, 'have the full assistance of the Pakistan authorities'. He said that he had information, the source of which was never forthcoming, that the invasion had been planned a fortnight previously at a meeting in Rawalpindi. What was happening in Junagadh was 'intended as a screen for Pakistan's operations against Kashmir'.[13] In fact, although the Pakistan Army undoubtedly knew about what was happening, and Cunningham had got wind of it in Peshawar, they had not actually organised it. It is difficult to overemphasise the teething problems that Pakistan was having as a nation; to organise and plan an invasion of a neighbouring state by an irregular force, to equip it and direct it, was simply beyond their existing capability. Individual Pakistani officers, like Brigadier Akbar Khan, in charge of weapons and equipment in the new Pakistan Army headquarters, did undoubtedly assist, by sending the *lashkar* four hundred rifles intended for the Punjab police, and 11th Cavalry, the armoured car regiment which was already deployed along the border in Gujrat to the south, was sent to relay reports of the *lashkar's* progress and, later, to cover their withdrawal but there was no full-scale structured support from the government as such.[14] What Pakistan could have done, as Jinnah would later tell Mountbatten, is to have made it very difficult for the tribesmen to continue by sending 'large forces along their lines of communication'.[15] This did not happen as Jinnah's reaction was to do something very different.

The conflict also put the high command of both the Indian and Pakistani armies in a difficult position. Both Lockhart, in India, and Messervy, his counterpart in Pakistan, were British officers as were many of their subordinates, although these now comprised a more dwindling component in the Indian Army than in Pakistan's. Both also were theoretically still subject to the Joint Defence Council and Auchinleck as supreme commander; although Nehru had sacked Auchinleck in September, he had not yet gone and the Joint Defence arrangements from June were still in place, much to Patel's fury. Auchinleck's headquarters was, he told Mountbatten, 'throttling the initiative of Headquarters Indian Army and acting as the advance outpost of Pakistan'.[16] Messervy, who was absent on military business in London, had, like Cunningham, thought that something was afoot. Before he left he had seen Liaquat and told him that the authorities should do all they could to disperse the gathering *lashkar*. Lockhart had already had an altercation with Nehru over Junagadh. When the Indian government had first considered military action, Lockhart and his naval and air-force colleagues had written to Nehru stating that they belonged to 'the British fighting services and it would be impossible for any of them to take part in a war between two Dominions or to be the instrument of planning or conveying orders to others should the operations now contemplated result in such a war, or appear likely to do so'.[17]

The Indian government's reaction had been predictably furious. The chiefs of staff were 'invading political ground'. They were in effect saying that if 'a political decision was taken they would not carry it out; this was highly improper and disloyal'.[18] The chiefs had subsequently withdrawn their paper but the core issue remained unresolved. Now up-to-date news of what was happening in Kashmir was coming to Delhi mostly from Pakistan Army headquarters, where General Douglas Gracey was deputising for the absent General Frank Messervy, via Auchinleck's headquarters in Delhi. It was a curious position when India and Pakistan could go to war, but that was exactly why those arrangements had been made. War was not something that was envisaged; the two countries had been intended to be two parts of the same and peaceful whole.

Jinnah flew to Lahore on 26 October, the evening before Colonel Rai's Sikhs took off from Delhi. He would stay with Sir Francis Mudie for three weeks, partly because in Lahore he felt nearer to the Kashmir problem but also because he was too weak to move. He was confined to bed throughout although he 'never, even by a sign, indicated that he would not shortly be alright again', remembered Mudie.[19] Jinnah's reaction to the Indian move was, initially, to meet force with force. He told Mudie to bring Gracey to a conference in Lahore. Pakistani troops were to be sent immediately into Kashmir. The plan was that they would seize the Banihal Pass, through which Hari Singh and his entourage had just laboured, thus cutting the Vale of Kashmir and Srinagar off from Jammu and from India. It was, as a military strategy, rather sensible. By controlling Banihal the Pakistan Army would also have secured Poonch, and would be able to resupply their troops from Rawalpindi. To take it, however, would lead to a direct confrontation with Rai's Sikhs even now en route to Srinagar and war with India.

Gracey refused. He was not, he said, prepared to order any troop movements without the authority of the supreme commander. A similar situation now arose between Jinnah, backed interestingly by Mudie, who seems to have 'gone native' on this point, and Gracey as Lockhart and his fellow chiefs had just been through with Nehru over Junagadh. Gracey stalled and asked Auchinleck to come urgently to Lahore. Mudie was furious with Gracey and called him a 'wind-up merchant' who was out of his depth and had no political sense; this is the traditional reaction of British civil servants when confronted with uncomfortable truths by generals. He had, he said, no business involving Auchinleck. There was also a rumour that Mountbatten had telephoned Gracey and told him that if he did move troops he would not get a knighthood.[20]

Auchinleck arrived the next morning. The old field marshal, who was seen as increasingly pro-Pakistan and anti-India, still had the authority to deliver a clear message. He was at his best that day. If Jinnah insisted on moving Pakistani troops into Kashmir it would mean certain war with India. In those circumstances he would have to withdraw all British officers. Jinnah had no choice but to capitulate; the Pakistan military could not function without its British element. Several senior Pakistanis were subsequently very critical of Auchinleck, arguing that if he had kept out of it then Pakistan would have moved quickly into Srinagar and easily defeated the few Indian troops there. The Kashmir issue would have been resolved in accordance with the wishes of its majority population and the long-running conflict with India could have been prevented. 'This was a political decision and the Auk should have kept out of it', wrote his otherwise strongly supportive ADC, Shahid Hamid.[21] It was a subjective view. The British government would almost certainly have withdrawn its officers, Pakistan was in no position to organise a complicated military operation and war could not have been restricted to Kashmir. There were, it is true, those in Delhi who were lukewarm about Kashmir, not thinking a territory that was home to just 1 per cent of India's population worth the cost in money and blood. Patel, for example, was not a strong supporter of Sheikh Abdullah, whom he saw as too socialist. However, Nehru was determined and even Patel became one of the main agitators for Indian involvement once news of the *lashkar*'s activities started to reach Delhi. The most far-sighted solution would have been for Jinnah to stop the *lashkar* then, if he really could have done so. India would then have had little justification for retaining troops in Kashmir and it may well have been possible to arrange a plebiscite.

Auchinleck also suggested to Jinnah that he should call a round-table conference of himself, Liaquat, Nehru, Mountbatten and Hari Singh. Jinnah agreed. Auchinleck flew back to Delhi where he was congratulated on what he had achieved. Patel was not, though, keen on the idea of a conference whereby Nehru would have to go to Lahore. It could be seen as an admission of guilt. 'For the Prime Minister to go crawling to Mr. Jinnah when we were the stronger side and in the right would never be forgiven by the people of India', he said.[22] Nehru was, however, keen to go, but while he and Patel were arguing Nehru was taken ill. In the end Mountbatten went on his own, as governor general to governor general.

It was a difficult meeting, the two men as strained as ever in each other's company. Jinnah's principal complaint was that no one in Delhi had informed him or his government what was happening. Had the Indian government told him on 24 October that there was a problem and they wished to send in observers then Pakistan would have cooperated and the whole issue would be over by now. Neither had anyone thought to inform him about the dispatch of troops. Nehru had told Mountbatten that Liaquat had been kept informed; if so, Jinnah retorted, correctly, there was no record of it. It was more likely that, as a result of Delhi believing that the invasion had always been a Pakistani government plot, they had deliberately cut communications.

Jinnah then said that both sides should withdraw at once and simultaneously, with him making the comment that he could force the tribesmen to pull back by hitting their supply routes. Mountbatten, aware that he could not deliver an Indian withdrawal, countered by putting his idea for a plebiscite under United Nations' auspices. Jinnah said any plebiscite with Indian troops still in situ would be false as people would be intimidated into voting for Sheikh Abdullah. He would prefer one organised by the two governor generals. Mountbatten said, correctly, this would be impractical. The meeting was inconclusive. Jinnah finished by saying that it was an Indian attempt to strangle Pakistan at birth, rather as he interpreted the massacres in the Punjab. 'The situation was already so bad there was little that could happen to make it worse.'[23] A political solution in Kashmir would still be elusive seventy years later.

*

On 27 October the *lashkar* had reached the prosperous town of Baramulla, thirty miles from Uri and still thirty-five miles from Srinagar. Baramulla had a large Sikh and Hindu population as well as the substantial St Joseph's Convent, part college and part mission hospital, founded by the Mill Hill fathers and with a complement of two priests and sixteen nuns that autumn. News of the coming attack had spread the previous day. There was a mass exodus of non-Muslims towards Srinagar, egged on by local Muslims 'regaling them with lurid accounts of the treatment meted out to Sikhs at Muzaffarabad', noted Father George Shanks, one of the two Mill Hill priests in the mission. 'The hospital had practically emptied en masse that morning ... girls within a few days of their confinement, women half-dead with TB or cancer ... were hurried off their sick-beds by fearful husbands ... the menacing spectre of rape at their heels'.[24] The Muslim reaction was predictably different. When the *lashkar* started to arrive at 10.30 a.m. on the 27 October, 'Hundreds walked several miles down the river to welcome them' those 'who were coming to rid them of the century-old Dogra slavery. Almost the entire male Muslim inhabitants and thousands of others from the countryside had turned up in their choicest clothes to meet the liberators. Major Khurshid Anwar particularly was the centre of attraction. Almost everyone wanted to thank him personally', recalled Muhammad Yusuf Sarat, a local politician who would end up as a judge in Pakistani or Azad Kashmir.[25] But the euphoria would be short-lived as the Pathan tribesmen made it clear that their priority was loot over liberty. For two days they devoted themselves to stealing what they could.

Shanks found his house within the mission compound surrounded by 'fifteen of the most unpleasant hoodlums I have ever seen. Armed to the teeth with rifle, sword, dagger, most of them carrying an axe for business purposes. Untidy black beards, unkempt long hair, dirty black turbans, ragged clothes caked with blood and dirt'. One of them extended his hand. Father Shanks moved to shake it but found instead that the man had dived into his pocket in search of money. They systematically looted every room, every drawer, every cupboard. Shanks could not help but admire the thoroughness of their theft; they left nothing behind.[26] But worse was happening at the hospital. There 'the whole place erupted with shooting, shouting, screaming, yelling'. Within a few minutes six people lay dead, patients slaughtered in their beds, and a young nun and a British officer, Colonel Tom Dykes, who was staying in the mission with his wife and three young children, had been badly wounded. They both died later that day. Tom Dykes's wife had also been killed, leaving the three boys orphans. Later there were accusations that several of the nuns had been raped, although there seems to be no firm evidence to support this. The hospital was also systematically looted.

Yet although the St Joseph's mission outrage was to command international attention, worse was happening in the town itself. There not only was all non-Muslim property looted or destroyed but Hindu and Sikh girls certainly were raped or were carried off as booty. The Balis, a prominent Sikh family, had seen relations from Muzaffarabad and Uri fleeing in the previous days. They simply bolted their house as best they could and fled into the hills, expecting to return once the *lashkar* had moved on. Instead they would spend weeks running for their lives from village to village. Gunwant Kaur's family were less fortunate. Her father and three to four other members of her family were killed. 'In the middle of all this they were taking away lots of youngsters, young women. Taking them to other villages. Abducting them. Many were forcibly married to their abductors.'[27] Altogether it is estimated that twenty-five women were taken, nearly all Sikhs.

The effect of this prolonged looting was that the *lashkar* stayed in Baramulla for two days. Brigadier Akbar Khan, the senior Pakistani officer who had given the tribesmen rifles, described his fury at the state of Baramulla, previously a town of 'orchards, schools, road and river transport stations, shops and restaurants – in short a bright and cheerful looking place' now looked as if 'an earthquake had shaken it. Shops were empty, doors and windows were gone – brick, stone and paper littered the ground'. Yet he was even more enraged that, while the road to Srinagar lay open, unguarded now the maharajah's forces had fled, the *lashkar* didn't move on to take the capital.

Another two hours, he believed, and before them lay Srinagar, 'trembling at their mercy'. It was the greed, greed of the irregulars that was to cost Pakistan dear. Eric Britter, *The Times* correspondent, and who reckoned the *lashkar* now numbered about ten thousand (probably an exaggeration – Cunningham in Peshawar later estimated that the maximum number they reached was seven thousand),[28] said that Khurshid Anwar was simply not strong enough to force the tribal leaders to stop their men looting and get them on the road. When he attempted to stop them he was, it was rumoured, told to mind his own business or he would be killed.[29] It was not until the rotund Pir of Manki Sharif arrived and 'forcefully reminded the tribesmen that plunder was not the primary purpose for which they had entered Kashmir' that they started moving. The pir also visited St Joseph's and had the Dykes boys given 30 rupees in blood money for the death of their parents. 'Aren't you ashamed', demanded one of the nuns, 'to give thirty rupees to the children whose parents your men have killed?' The pir remained silent.[30]

As the tribesmen were looting, and the pir was lecturing, Colonel Rai's 1st Sikhs were landing at Srinagar's grass airstrip in the DC3s. The first aircraft touched down in the early morning of 27 October, to be followed by a gradual build-up but it would take until that evening to get the bulk of the battalion on the ground. The pilot of one of the Dakotas took off again once he had disembarked his troops and flew west along the Baramulla road. He returned to brief Colonel Rai saying that he had seen Baramulla in flames but otherwise no sign of movement along the road, despite the fact that his aircraft was struck by a bullet. Rai decided that he had insufficient men to hold the airstrip, which was by then thronged with non-Muslims desperate to leave, so he decided, acting on the pilot's fairly sketchy reconnaissance, to take what transport he could find and to move with his lead company towards Baramulla. He arrived there late on 27 October, as the tribesmen were ending their first day of determined looting. He occupied the last ridge before the town on the main Srinagar road, about a mile and a half outside the town, where he found a small detachment of the maharajah's cavalry who had got left behind. Rai could tell he was outnumbered and waited for reinforcements.

The next morning his position was spotted by the *lashkar* who started shooting at his men. At first fire was sporadic but during the afternoon the tribesmen opened up with heavy machine guns and small mortars; it is worth pondering where they had managed to lay their hands on these weapons which required a degree of skill and training to operate. By late afternoon Rai decided that he would have to withdraw and told his men to start pulling back. As he did so he fell dead, shot through the head. His soldiers couldn't bring his body back with them so they hid him on the hillside.

His company pulled back to the next tactical position between Baramulla and Srinagar near the small town of Pattan. Here they again occupied a defensive position, from which, now reinforced from the gradual build up at the airfield, they were able to hold off the *lashkar*'s badly organised attacks. They were also assisted by Indian Air Force fighter-bombers flying initially from Ambala and then from Srinagar. The pilots found the conditions chaotic, the airfield packed with equipment and people and no refuelling facilities so they had to take fuel from the Dakotas. They did, however, give the Sikhs a decided advantage; there were, of course, no Pakistani aircraft flying so the Indian pilots had the sky to themselves. Consequently they stopped the *lashkar*'s vehicles moving, at least in daylight, which meant they had to continue the advance into Srinagar on foot.

Conditions in Srinagar were as chaotic as on the airfield and the atmosphere tense. With the departure of the maharajah, his government had effectively stopped. Policing had been taken over by Sheikh Abdullah's National Conference militia, who now patrolled the streets. The sheikh had been 'sworn in' as head of a provisional government on 31 October, amid scenes of much popular support. Thousands rushed to join the militia, which had both an active women's detachment and a children's wing, who drilled with dummy weapons. Muslim League supporters remained in the background, hoping their day to take political power might come when and if the *lashkar* arrived. Food was scarce and power intermittent. As always, the rarest commodity was reliable information and radios were in short supply. A redoubtable English woman, Gwen Burton, described what it was like being trapped in the comparative comfort of Nedou's Hotel, where at least they had access to a 'wet battery' set. People flocked in to hear the news. 'There was a lot of heavy firing and bombing last night', Mrs Burton wrote home to friends in England, evidently hoping that one day her letter might be delivered. 'Not at all pleasant and very nerve racking. Food is beginning to get scarce ... We have', though, she added, 'had lovely weather' for it all 'so far and only hope it goes on'.[31]

Despite the rapid build-up of Indian troops, the *lashkar* still significantly outnumbered them and for the first few days of November the military situation hung in the balance. A large group of tribesmen, who now appeared slightly better organised, got to within a few miles of the airfield; if India lost that its war was effectively over as what troops it had landed would be cut off. On 3 November about one thousand tribesmen attacked an Indian Army position at Badgam, which, had it fallen, would have meant the airfield was vulnerable. 'The fighting went on from mid-afternoon until dusk. By the end of several hours of bitter fighting, the Indian Army had lost an officer, Major Somnath Sharma, and fourteen other men, with a further twenty-six wounded', noted Andrew Whitehead.[32] Although the position held, the Sikhs were too weak to stop any further advance but, unaccountably, for the second time in a week the tribesmen failed to press home their advantage.

Rai had been replaced by the determined Colonel Harbakhsh Singh who now decided, in light of the Badgam attack, that he was in danger of being outflanked and to pull his remaining troops in from Pattan to concentrate on the defence of the perimeter of Srinagar itself. Lacking radios and transport, he transmitted his orders by dropping notes onto their position from a low-flying aircraft. Gathering what local transport they could, mostly tongas (wheeled cabs) which, in Indian Army legend, they pulled themselves, horses being scarce, the remaining Sikhs withdrew.

Badgam was to be the last chance Khurshid Anwar and his *lash-kar* had to bring about a decisive result. On 6 November he made a determined attempt to force an entry through the Indian-held perimeter. 'The city reverberated to the sound of machine-guns and mortar firing. About 1.00 am the invaders made a daring attempt to enter the city about four and a half miles west', wrote *The Times of India* correspondent but the tribesmen could not force their way past the Sikhs' positions. By this stage there were 3,000 Indian troops in the city and, inevitably when irregulars face formed and trained soldiers in an open engagement like that, they will come off worse. The tribesmen withdrew.

On 7 November the *lashkar* gathered near the village of Shalateng, just north-west of Srinagar, possibly intending to make one more attempt to break in. Their morale was now low and for days groups had been leaving, taking their loot and starting the trek back west. The Indian Army spotted the concentration. Reinforced by sixteen armoured cars, which they had succeeded in bringing up, Brigadier Bogey Sen, now in command as the force had grown well beyond battalion size, prepared an assault. He did it well. Surrounding the tribesmen on three sides, and with coordinated air support, he attacked. The *lashkar*, with limited heavy weapons, was decisively defeated. Within twenty minutes they had broken and started running west, leaving, according to Indian sources but unsubstantiated, 472 dead. A further 146 bodies were found on the road to Baramulla as the Indians pursued them; 138 buses and trucks were taken. Afterwards some would claim that Sen had only turned up at the last minute and that it was Harbakhsh Singh who had planned and executed the attack; whoever was responsible, it was decisive. Shalateng secured the Kashmir valley for India. Tribesmen with bolt-action rifles were no match for armoured cars and Spitfires, as disgruntled Pakistani military commentators would lament.

A visitor to the site of the battle some days afterwards described corpses in profusion, most apparently the victims of air strikes than Indian bayonets: 'Dogs and vultures were eating the bodies'.[33] Andrew Whitehead quotes Margaret Parton of the *Herald Tribune* describing 'a huge, red-bearded tribesman lying dead in a ditch by the highway to Baramulla, his hill-made rifle still clutched in his hand'.[34] More tribesmen were taken in Baramulla itself. Parton described them:

> Never have I seen such disgusting, grotesque figures: one of them, a hulking giant with a filthy grey beard through which straggled one protruding yellow tooth, wore blue checked plus fours, khaki puttees, a blue RAF jacket, and torn sandals. An unclosed knife wound lashed across his right eye and part of his cheek, and the blood had dried without any attempt to wash it away. Then there was a little gnome about five feet high and eighty years old, who cackled; a middle-aged tribesman in a bloodstained burnoose, with the flashing eyes of a zealot; and a half-naked monkey in a string of red and blue beads who claimed to be a local 'faquir'.[35]

On 14 November, Indian troops reached Mahura and reconnected the power supply to Srinagar. 'Srinagar gay again after days of panic', said the *New York Times*.[36] The next day they entered Uri. Here they stopped. Instead of continuing their advance west, sweeping up what remained of the *lashkar*, taking the next few miles of road, dominating the crossing over the Jhelum, and then 'liberating' Muzaffarabad, they were told to turn south. While the situation in Kashmir had taken the world's attention, not least because of the large number of foreign correspondents who were either in Srinagar when the raid started or who managed to get themselves up there, an equally serious situation had developed in Poonch. The beleaguered Indian garrison there needed help.

The failure to 'complete the job' in Kashmir has become one of the big arguments of modern Indian history. Had Brigadier Sen and his troops continued they would, it is contended, have been able to dominate western Kashmir preventing future moves by Pakistan and thus ending the 'Kashmir problem' to India's advantage. That may be wishful thinking on India's part. The area beyond the Jhelum bridge was pretty solidly Muslim and any move to Muzaffarabad would have threatened the approaches to Rawalpindi, making actual war with Pakistan more likely. In the north of Kashmir, in the high tribal areas approaching the Karakoram Pass, dominated by the peaks of Nanga Parbat and K2, the enterprising commanding officer of the Gilgit Scouts, Major Willie Brown, had hoisted the Pakistani flag and declared for Pakistan. The Gilgit Scouts were the only effective force in the vast area they controlled, which was now closed to India. Brown had, to the rage of his British superiors, acted entirely on his own initiative. With these proliferating threats on the flanks, there was a strong military argument for India to consolidate what it had gained.

The situation in Poonch was, however, the most demanding problem facing India and her newly arrived general, Kulwant Singh, in Srinagar. Here the Muslims were much better organised and behaved than the tribesmen of Khurshid Anwar's *lashkar*. With their high proportion of ex-military men they had effectively trapped the maharajah's remaining forces in Poonch; India had to relieve them. Sen's men headed south over the Haji Pir Pass to try to do so.

D. K. Palit had recently taken command of 3rd Battalion 9th Gurkhas, his Indian Gurkha battalion. They had been moved into Poonch in the third week of November but were soon surrounded, alongside the rest of the Indian garrison, by the Muslim irregulars, Abdul Qayyum Khan and his Azad Kashmir men. Palit found himself defending a perimeter of two miles; there were 35,000 non-Muslim refugees trapped with them and a serious problem of resupply. There was, when they arrived, no functioning airstrip in the enclave. Another problem was that they were subject to constant mortaring, directed accurately by the ex-regulars, which caused many casualties. They would try to push the perimeter outwards partly to force the mortar crews out of range of the refugees and partly to seize food supplies. As soon as they did they were counter-attacked by, they said, Pakistani troops; in fact they were mostly tribal irregulars who moved backwards and forwards at will although they were helped by elements of the Pakistani force deployed to secure the border. The Indians' main effort was to repair and extend the airstrip to six hundred yards so they could bring supplies in and get the refugees

out. Initially it was four hundred yards, which led to some brave
if hazardous flying by Indian Air Force crews. But by the end of
November it was still a very long way from being ready and Palit
and his men faced a long winter under siege.[37]

While the fighting was intensifying there was some sort of dialogue, albeit a fairly unfriendly one, between Nehru and Liaquat,
who had taken over direction of the Pakistani side from the bedrid-
den Jinnah. Liaquat went to Delhi on 26 November. He had been
ill, under considerable strain, and was 'Obviously tired and weak'.[38]
The meeting started badly. Liaquat said that he had recently visited
Sialkot and heard the most terrible stories about Sikhs in Jammu massacring every Muslim man they found and abducting their women
who they were keeping as sex slaves in a concentration camp. He was
losing support in Pakistan because he refused to commit Pakistani
troops to help the Muslims despite strong public agitation. The only
way forward was for a full Indian withdrawal and establishing an
impartial administration to conduct a plebiscite. He could not resist a
bitter personal attack on Sheikh Abdullah, who he knew was a close
friend of Nehru's, and whom he called a 'Quisling'. Nehru retorted
that the reports of the *lashkar* 'having indulged in the most ghastly
atrocities, including the wholesale murder of non-Muslims and
the selling of Kashmiri girls' were commonplace. Patel and Baldev
Singh had just visited Jammu and brought back terrible stories of
atrocities against non-Muslims there. How could he withdraw all
Indian troops? Even if he could physically get them out he would
be leaving Hindus and Sikhs in Poonch to the mercy of the Azad
Kashmir militias. How could he also fail to help Sheikh Abdullah's
government when it was running the Vale of Kashmir with strong
popular support? Mountbatten presided and suggested that a way
forward was for Ismay to sit down with Menon and Mohammed Ali
for Pakistan to try to find some points of agreement. 'We drafted
and re-drafted for a full three hours', wrote Ismay. 'In the end we
were rather proud of our handiwork but our hopes were dashed.
Both sides thought that our paper was too biased in favour of the
other to merit discussion.'[39] November ended in political stalemate

as the massacre of Muslims in Jammu and non-Muslims in Poonch continued; it is estimated that total casualties by 30 November were 200,000.

However laudable Auchinleck's intervention with Jinnah had been, his next suggestion was less sensible. He now proposed to Mountbatten that he should send British troops into Kashmir to rescue the four hundred-odd British and the several hundred other Europeans who lived in the vale. Mountbatten correctly refused. Auchinleck remonstrated with him, telling him that they 'will be murdered and their blood will be on your head'.[40] Mountbatten replied that it was a responsibility he was willing to take. It was an extraordinary thing for Auchinleck to have asked and says much about his concept of what British troops in India were for. Having strongly opposed deploying British and Gurkha troops into the Punjab, where they would have significantly reduced the slaughter, Auchinleck was now proposing to send them into the middle of a burgeoning conflict between India and Pakistan. Most of the British and Europeans were either people like Mrs Burton, enjoying the weather in Nedou's Hotel, timber merchants, missionaries like the community in Baramulla, or retired Raj officials and Indian Army officers who were mostly safe in their lakeside cottages. It is an interesting reflection on the priorities of a man who had spent his life in an Indian Army that was still the child of the Mutiny. British troops, to Auchinleck, were there to protect British lives, to ensure that there was no repeat of the grisly events of 1857 in Cawnpore and Lucknow and to protect people like poor Miss Hotz who had been so upset to find her Muslim staff butchered outside Wildflower Hall.

On 15 November Auchinleck presided over his last commander-in-chiefs' conference. He told the three service chiefs that there was 'no hope of reconciliation between the two Dominions and that events may lead to war'.[41] It was a depressing finale for a man who had first arrived in India in 1903, who had fought with his Punjabis through Mesopotamia in the First World War, commanded Indian troops on the Frontier, in North Africa and been commander-in-chief during India's herculean efforts in the Second World War. Attlee still wanted to give him a peerage, something Mountbatten continued to press him hard to accept, but Auchinleck refused. Hamid, reflecting the general Pakistani view of Mountbatten, said that he rejected it because it was Mountbatten who had first recommended it and he was 'the person whom the Auk considers has made a mess of things'.

Auchinleck himself, interviewed many years later, offered a more profound reason. He had, he said, 'a great sadness when I left. A sadness of failure at the latter end. A feeling of sorrow. It had to be', he acknowledged, 'it was inevitable' but, 'at the end of a career of forty years, in an army that I loved, I was almost in a state of despair. I felt responsible for what had happened to the Indian Army. I felt it was the destruction of a life's work. I didn't feel it was an achievement that should be celebrated with a peerage'.[42]

Many in India felt he was being hard on himself. They thought he had been badly treated by Nehru and Patel and by Mountbatten. Tributes poured in during his last weeks in Delhi. They came from the predictable sources, from past politicians and viceroys he had served; Wavell, a man who felt he had been treated in a similar way, wrote a particularly charming latter. Yet letters also came from many unexpected people. Amar Nath Jha, chairman of the Public Service Commission in the United Provinces, told him he ranked with Roberts and Kitchener as one of the greatest chiefs and the Begum of Bhopal wrote that he had 'cherished, loved and served' India with 'all his heart and might'. She felt, she concluded, very sad for him. Yet ultimately Auchinleck allowed sentiment to cloud objectivity. Armies exist to serve the needs of the societies that generate them and the governments that represent those societies. They do not have, nor should they have, any pretension to being an independent entity. They must also reflect the changes that society undergoes. Auchinleck's idea of the Indian Army was out of date by 1945, when he established the Willcox Committee; it was out of tune with Congress, when they were clearly the successors to the Raj; it was out of sympathy with India when he objected so strongly to intervention in the Punjab and it was out of order with Mountbatten whom, however much they disliked each other, was his political master. He was a great man in so many ways. He loved India and was loved by Indian soldiers, but as a man who wielded enormous power, power on a scale which few if any British senior officers have exercised since, he could have done so much more to prevent the tragedy of 1947.

Auchinleck refused a valedictory dinner and on 25 November had lunch with Mountbatten as governor general. He left at 8.00 p.m. the next evening, again refusing any farewell parade or even a guard of honour, slipping quietly away to Bombay. Mountbatten wanted his house to be given to the British high commissioner. The Russians said they had already claimed it for their ambassador. In the end Nehru moved in. Today it is a museum on the making of modern India.

A DOUBTFUL LEGACY

*'Is this to be the culmination of British rule in
India and the fulfilment of our great mission?'*

(ISMAY)

John Christie and his family had been cut off in Simla for a month
but 'gradually, with fewer unprotected Muslims left to kill, the situation was brought under control' and 'as the freshness of autumn
began to change to the chill of winter and the cold weather line of
dusty haze hardened over the plains' they moved back to Delhi in
a convoy protected by British soldiers of the Royal Scots Fusiliers.[1]
The coming of the cooler weather seemed to calm the killing across
the Punjab although there were still violent incidents. A party of
184 Sikhs who were being evacuated from Sind, and staying in the
supposed sanctuary of a gurdwara in Karachi, were attacked by a
Muslim mob. Sixty-four were killed and most of the rest wounded.
The mob then set about looting whatever non-Muslim-owned
shops in the city they had so far spared. Jinnah, who returned to
Karachi from Lahore at the beginning of the month, was furious
and horrified; he ordered soldiers onto the streets and gave them
instructions to shoot rioters on sight. Order was quickly restored.[2]
But such attacks were becoming less common. Fewer refugees were
on the move and the problem now became not so much how to protect their struggling columns as to provide for them in the destitute

squalor of the makeshift camps. 'The vast task of resettlement and rehabilitation had just begun.'[3]

The problem that Sandtas Kirpalani and his ministry faced was that the Indian government had no power to control the movement of refugees once they had arrived from Pakistan. As citizens of the new India, they had 'an inalienable right to go anywhere'. Anything was preferable to the camps and people with relations or money made up their own minds. Many West Punjabi Sikhs just wanted to stay in East Punjab as did quite a number of West Punjabi Hindus. Others were determined to make for the United Provinces, considered a wealthy province where they might make a living. There was also a rush for Delhi. The camps set up around the capital were very soon overflowing and people spilled out to live on the pavements and in the alleys. Connaught Circus, the 'erstwhile impeccable and showy shopping centre of New Delhi became home to thousands of pedlars and beggars'.[4] Yet millions had no choice but to stay in the camps that were run by a combination of central and provincial governments. The main Punjab camp, Kurukshetra, twenty miles south of Ambala, and which had nearly one million people, was run centrally. Providing food and clean water remained a huge challenge, as did warm clothing, once the weather cooled. India responded, as had Pakistan, with a mass quilt-making movement. Kirpalani was full of praise for Edwina Mountbatten who chaired a Volunteer Workers Council which brought together the energy and resources of the numerous and well-found Indian voluntary sector. Ultimately twenty-eight bodies worked under her auspices, Kirpalani and Neogy being amazed at her 'enormous organising ability'.[5]

As much of a problem was the mental state of many of the refugees, not just from what they had experienced, but from enforced idleness, particularly among people who had been tradesmen and artisans, many of whom could see little future for themselves. Camp discipline was fragile, and the government was the obvious target for the refugees' rage and hurt. Predictably the army was soon put in charge. Schools were set up for the children but were swamped by the sheer numbers. The urgent problem quickly became not material provision but rehabilitation. The task facing the new Indian government was vast. They could not build millions of new homes quickly and providing new jobs and rehabilitation would inevitably take years. There were several major strands to the programme. The first was simply to give each provincial government an allocation of refugees and tell them to provide for them. It was a crude measure but it did at least serve to disperse people around India. Bombay, India's richest city, agreed to take 1 million, the Central Provinces 500,000, Rajputana 250,000 and so on. There were also centrally organised schemes to provide work. The long-awaited Bhakra-Nangal dam project in northern India was expedited; it would become India's third-largest reservoir and irrigate over ten million acres. When it was finally opened, Nehru, sensitive to the suffering endured by those who had worked on the project, called it, 'A new temple of resurgent India'. Others worked on the new state capital of the East Punjab at Chandigarh or on the somewhat misnamed Green Belt development of residential areas around Delhi, which would begin the transformation of the small capital of the Moghuls and the Raj into the suburban sprawl of the contemporary mega-city. But much of this was in the future, and for most people in the camps that December, the months ahead held little promise other than the shelter of a mud hut or a bustee and the struggle to rebuild their lives having lost almost everything.

Kirpalani was visiting a camp near Bombay when the director told him that one of the refugees had said that he knew him. It turned out to be his old friend Punwani. They had been at school together. Punwani had gone with a Sindhi company to Trinidad where he had done very well for himself. Kirpalani had stayed with him once and marvelled at his very comfortable life. But Punwani said that he had been away from India for thirty years and longed to go home. He sold up everything in Trinidad and bought property in Karachi. Here he was now, huddled with his wife and two children in a tiny room in a mud-hut dormitory no more than ten feet square 'with two hemp-string beds and a reed curtain at the door. He was dry-eyed and articulate. He was grateful that he and his family had escaped unhurt'. Kirpalani could not help but admire such calm amid such massive adversity. He could never get that meeting out of his mind.

On another visit he was approached by an old man with tears streaming from his eyes and emitting a 'blood-chilling low moan'. He was a rural postman from the Jhelum district. His daughter had been abducted by a Muslim mob. Kirpalani must, he insisted, provide him with a plane so he could go back and find her. Kirpalani patiently explained that this was impossible but the distraught old man did not hear what he said, just continuing to moan, 'My daughter! O my daughter'. Later they discovered that the poor girl had committed suicide. Kirpalani's orderly, Kashi Ram, was so affected he took the old man home to care for him but he died a few days later. Kirpalani could not get this image out of his head either. 'For many, many nights the spectre of the old man haunted me and I could hear the dirge of his moaning in the small hours.'

One morning, visiting the hospital in Kurukshetra, he saw a young woman, surprisingly fair, of about thirty. A week before she had given birth to a stillborn baby; 'big tears rolled silently from her limpid brown eyes'. The doctor told Kirpalani that she had been crying for a week but refused to speak. Kirpalani begged her to tell him her name. Eventually she offered that it was Shanti and that she came from the North West Frontier Province. Kirpalani urged her to give her husband's name so that they could try to trace him. 'Don't you understand', she replied, 'I am a Hindu wife. How can you ask me to voice my husband's name?' She would 'not budge from this stance' despite her terrible circumstances. Kirpalani reflected that his own well-educated and articulate wife, to whom he had been happily married for thirty years, had never once 'hailed me by name'. But for him Shanti's adherence to Hindu tradition at such cost merely added to the pathos of a terrible time.[6]

The human cost of partition would be born by a generation of Indians and Pakistanis. So would the physical cost. It is estimated that Indian refugees leaving West Punjab left behind 6.729 million acres of which 4.3 million were canal-irrigated, so productive and valuable. They also left 500,000 urban houses and 12,000 industrial premises. India calculated this as being worth about 8 billion US dollars. Muslim refugees from East Punjab left less: about 4.73 million acres of which 1.32 million were irrigated. For both governments the issue of how to allocate this and how to calculate compensation would take years. An argument developed over the relative values of this abandoned land and assets. Hindus and Sikhs in West Punjab had certainly been richer than Muslims in East Punjab; many were, as we have seen, landowners and businessmen. India reckoned their assets to be worth at least five times those Muslims had left behind in the east. Inevitably Pakistan disagreed. Nehru's laudable aim of not reallocating the property of families who might still return would slowly, as the borders and attitudes hardened, become impractical.[7]

Although Bengal was spared the huge movement of refugees in 1947, and the slaughter of the Punjab, the subsequent steady flow of non-Muslims from east to west would mean that West Bengal continued to have a serious refugee problem up until the 1970s. By 1973, the numbers swelled by the Brahmaputra floods of 1970 and the Pakistani civil war of 1971, 15 per cent of its total population would be refugees from East Bengal. West Bengal never seemed able to deal with this in the way the Punjab had and the issue would remain politically toxic for years. At one point a decision was taken to resettle 25,000 families in the Dandakaranya area, 30,000 square miles of very poor and infertile land in Orissa and Bihar. Its previous inhabitants were the Gond forest dwellers who led the nomadic life that was all the land could support. Described by one official as 'a forest of breathtaking loveliness ... where God manifested himself as Rama', the refugees were initially taken as labour gangs and then settled in 300 new villages. The project was, predictably, a disaster, with families leaving in droves. This was ascribed variously to their love of Bengal, which they couldn't bear to leave, to their low-caste status or to their being work-shy. Ultimately the Bengal government admitted that only 10 per cent of Dandakaranya was in fact cultivatable.[8]

Many East Bengali refugees simply squatted on what vacant land they could find around Calcutta and other West Bengal cities and relied on their own initiative and skills to secure shelter and work. It was a long and hard struggle, the effects of which are still evident in Calcutta today, and shows that, in its own way, the partition of Bengal was as brutal and damaging as that of the Punjab.

In West Punjab, the Pakistani government faced similar pressures to Kirpalani. Despite all the work done to date in setting up the camps, the refugee problem remained enormous. One of the main difficulties was to know when the flow might start to ease up. Wild rumours reached Lahore that Hindu zealots were intent on expelling every Muslim in India. Would a second mass migration, this time from the United Provinces, follow on behind the East Punjabis? Would Pakistan be swamped at birth by a human flood it could not possibly support? How could resettlement start until there was a clearer idea of how many people would actually need supporting? In late November the huge columns still continued to arrive. 'Hundreds of refugees sat day after day by the roadside huddled together, half dead or dying, in squalor, filth, utter wretchedness and dumb despair', noted Moon.[9] By the beginning of December a floating population of about two thousand squatted and defecated near Samasatta railway station. There were an average of six deaths daily, mostly old people and infants. Very soon the mess and filth in the station became indescribable and there was apparently no one to clear it up. Looting of any removable property left behind was widespread. Moon noted that many refugees died from hunger or exhaustion on arrival; 2,000 succumbed in Bahawalpur alone. It was not until early December that it became clear that the stream was slowly beginning to dwindle.

Resettlement work was, however, well under way by December, with an urgency to get people onto the land so that they could plant the *rabi*, the winter crop that would be harvested in the coming May. Land was given to those who had owned and worked land in India. Applicants were required to submit a sworn affidavit stating how much they had owned before and, although there was a certain amount of fraud, the system worked moderately well. The old settlement system had been to give applicants in the irrigated canal zones a 'square' of 25 acres but now there was insufficient land to do this. The average holding allocated was a quarter of a 'square', so 6.25 acres. The land previously owned by the Sikhs was relatively straightforward to reallocate as they had worked it themselves. That which had belonged to Hindus, who had tended to sublet, was more complicated as their Muslim tenants had already taken possession. The legal basis of this process taxed officials until Mudie produced a very simple ordinance for West Punjab which was copied throughout Pakistan. This nominated a Custodian of Refugee Property, much as India had done. He became the sole legal authority for title and allocation with an appeals system operating under him.

The Pakistani government also made a plan to redistribute refugees around the country, principally moving them from West Punjab to Sind and the North West Frontier Province, where there was more available land. One hundred and fifty thousand were selected to make the 125-mile journey on foot from the Punjab to Sind, accompanied by their bullock carts. The route lay through Bahawalpur. Moon and his colleagues were asked to prepare camping grounds and lay on food and water along the way. After several postponements the date was finally fixed but in the event nobody showed up; the refugees had, as in India, refused to leave the Punjab for the arid and foreign Sind.

There were some happier individual stories. Naffese Chohan, still miserable and homesick, was made to marry a man eighteen years older than her and who had been in the army. She did not know him, although she recalled him being in the truck that they had escaped in. She didn't want to marry him but her mother needed her married off and soon after their wedding her new husband went to work in England. In 1948 he came back for her. She did not want to go to England; even at fifteen she had already suffered enough upheaval in her life. 'I was screaming. I was crying. I didn't know him. I didn't like him. I was eighteen days on a ship from Karachi. I never ate and got ill.' When she arrived in England she weighed just five stone. She spent her first five weeks in her new country in hospital. Her husband spent time caring for her and she came to realise that he was actually quite a decent man; later she described him as 'a man in a million'. Naffese's long journey from her happy childhood near Simla ended running a shop in Nottingham but she was, finally, happy.[10] Abdul Haq, the boy who had escaped from the *jatha* in Jullundur in the week after partition came to Leeds in 1961 where he discovered he had a surviving elder brother. He married and enjoyed a happier second half of his life until his wife died in 1997, when the old feelings of loneliness and despair returned.[11]

In the Vale of Kashmir the fighting, which had died down after the Indian Army had retaken Baramulla, flared up again in early December as what remained of the *lashkar* regrouped and counter-attacked Uri. Srinagar appeared to be once more under threat. Political talks continued. Mountbatten refereed a further session between Nehru and Liaquat on 9 December. The same arguments were rehearsed. Both sides agreed to a plebiscite but Pakistan wanted all Indian troops withdrawn before it took place and Sheikh Abdullah to be removed. Nehru again refused. Mountbatten suggested that the UN be approached to organise the plebiscite. Both countries would make a joint request for intervention. Nehru refused, saying it had nothing to do with Pakistan. Grudgingly, he was slowly coaxed into agreeing. However, while the application was being prepared, news came that Uri was about to fall and that the Indian garrison at Jhangar, a town on the Jhelum and close to the border south-west of Poonch, had to be evacuated. Nehru threatened war. 'The only inference to draw from this is that the invasion of Kashmir is not an accidental affair resulting from the fanaticism or exuberance of the tribesmen but a well-organised business with the backing of the state. The present objective is Kashmir.' He continued, 'The next declared objective is Patiala, East Punjab and Delhi. On to Delhi is the cry all over West Punjab'. It was Nehru at his most emotional but threats to invade West Punjab were not made lightly and the Indian military were instructed to prepare plans. Mountbatten asked Attlee to come out urgently and mediate. Attlee refused saying, sensibly, there was very little he could do.

India's application to the UN was now made alone and under Article 35, the one that allows member states to represent against another state threatening international peace. It called on Pakistan to end its aggression against India. Luckily the Indian garrison at Uri held and, as the renewed threat to Srinagar faded, the Indian chiefs of staff put down their planning maps of the Punjab, at least for the time being. The UN's reaction to India's request was not what they had been anticipating; the Security Council favoured the Pakistan position, which was to call for a neutral administration. Senator Warren Austin, the US representative, 'made no bones about his sympathy for the Pakistan case', complained Nehru, 'Mr. Noel Baker, the leader of the United Kingdom Delegation, had been nearly as hostile to India except he had been more polite and had wrapped up his phrases in more careful language'.[12] He now bitterly regretted approaching the UN at all. As December drew to its close there was no material progress towards a solution in Kashmir; there would not be in the lifetime of anyone who took part in those early negotiations. In January 1949 the United Nations would deploy an Observer Mission to Kashmir. It would still be there sixty-eight years later.

The only other state that had not acceded, Hyderabad, continued to prevaricate. Walter Monckton shuttled between the Nizam's court and Delhi. Well paid as he was, his position was not an easy one. Patel was determined that Hyderabad would form part of India. Any idea that such a large and relatively prosperous state with a majority Hindu population in the centre of India should form part of Pakistan was unacceptable. He was, however, prepared to discuss some flexibility in the arrangements under which that integration would happen. The Nizam, on the other hand, remained determined that he would become independent. He was not altogether a free agent and power in Hyderabad was increasingly in the hands of the new president of his council, Mir Laik Ali, and a hard-line Muslim elite. They saw any concession to India as 'spelling the end of their privileged position'.[13] They were supported by an increasingly extreme militia, the Razakars, drawn from the Ittihad-ul-Muslimeen organisation, who demanded that all recruits swear, 'In the name of

Allah, I hereby promise that I will fight to the last to maintain the supremacy of Muslim power in the Deccan'.[14] Laik Ali calculated that the Indian government had its hands too full with Kashmir to take any action against Hyderabad. In December 1947 he was correct. The negotiations dragged on into 1948. They were 'for the most part wearisome, repetitive and frustrating'.[15] They ended in failure and once Nehru and Patel felt Kashmir had stabilised, if only temporarily, they moved. In September 1948, amid riots in Secunderabad and rumours of a gun-running operation from Pakistan, an Indian Army task force under General Chaudhuri conducted the most inappropriately named *Operation Polo* and invaded Hyderabad. There were 800 casualties, mostly among the Nizam's forces. They would have been considerably higher had Chaudhuri's men not captured early on one of the Nizam's officers en route to order the demolition of the bridges they would have to advance across. It was the third time India had used military force to achieve accession.

There was one more development between Patel and the States that December and one which indicated how Indian policy would develop. Patel, with V. P. Menon once more acting as his henchman, determined to start integrating the smaller states into viable administrative units or, more controversially, simply to merge them into their neighbouring provinces. He started with the group known as the Eastern States of Orissa and Chattisgarh, forty-one mostly minor states, which bordered Orissa or the Central Provinces. Only two of these had a population of more than a million – Bastar and Mayurbhanj – and they were mostly poor and undeveloped. On 14 December their rulers were invited to gather at Nagpur. Here, with Menon cajoling them and in direct contradiction of both Patel's own statement of 5 July and Mountbatten's speech to the Chamber of Princes on 25 July, they signed away their independence and all powers of government in exchange for a tax-free privy purse, retention of their personal property and various other privileges. Their territories were now administered by the Indian government.

Patel was also concerned that what had happened in Kashmir might be repeated in the states which bordered East Bengal. The circumstances in Tripura, a state of about half a million people with a Hindu ruler but a large Muslim majority population, were similar. It was almost an island in East Bengal through which all its communications ran. Its population and, interestingly, its Hindu chief minister, wanted to join Pakistan but the maharajah, a thirteen-gun ruler, had acceded to India. Patel wanted to send troops to stop any possible secessionist moves but there were no aircraft to get them there, despite Tripura having a well-established airport at Agartala. The Assam government was asked whether they could provide troops but the Assam Rifles were one of the units that still had mostly British officers so could not be sent. Eventually the trouble calmed down which, for Tuker, still running Eastern Command, was a relief; Agartala was hard against the border of East Bengal and within thirty miles of a large Pakistani garrison.

Tuker was also concerned about Darjeeling, the famous tea-growing area in the hills north of Calcutta, which Liaquat had been so angry had not been assigned to Pakistan. Patel was afraid that the local hill tribes would rise up and take control; again he wanted to send troops but again it proved impossible to get them there. Although the situation remained tense, nothing actually happened and Indian control was not disputed.

Early in 1948 Patel and Menon turned their attention to the west-coast states in a continuing process of integration that would see the eastern states model repeated across India. By May 1948 the princes had lost the power they had been promised they would keep and, in 1971, Nehru's daughter, Indira Gandhi, Indian prime minister, would remove their privy purses and their remaining privileges. It was, to people who thought like Nehru and Patel, inevitable. For them, and the remorseless anti-monarchical rationale of the late-twentieth century, princely power had no place in a democratic India. Many in that older, deeper India, which politicians so often fail to see, were not so convinced. In March 2017 the Maharajah of Patiala was elected with an overwhelming majority as chief minister of the Punjab.

*

India that December was not just a nation reeling from the shock of the tragedy of the Punjab and the breakdown of relations with Pakistan. It was also a country establishing itself uncertainly as a nation. Grumpy ex-Raj types would complain that nothing worked in those early months. Railways ran 'to any time they pleased' and it was quicker to send an internal letter via England than trust the local post.[16] Food prices were worryingly high. The truth was very little had been working properly for some time, as Kirpalani had discovered when he attempted to set up his new ministry in Delhi. The new Indian government was not just confronted with transferring the administration from the British but in many cases actually starting it from scratch.

British attitudes varied sharply. Tuker thought that most British officers who had remained in Indian service were disillusioned by December and felt they were not valued. 'The British officer's greatest enemy was depression', he wrote gloomily. 'This was born of a knowledge of failure – failure to produce anything of permanent value in India – the knowledge of a life wasted, the blank future before him; his own wrecked career and personal difficulties.' The British government was, he felt, unsympathetic and even charged customs duties on what little returning officers possessed. 'It took a very optimistic and determined officer to remain happy and balanced through all his troubles.'[17]

Others took a more positive view. Ann Wright, the daughter of a senior ICS officer and who had been away at school in Europe during the worst of 1947, regarded India as home. It did not occur to her that she might leave. She would always stay on, in Calcutta and Delhi, taking a particular interest in conservation and pioneering game reserves. She remembered her acute embarrassment when a young Indian ICS officer was posted to her father's remote district in the Central Provinces. He came to live in their house. Despite there being only a handful of British around, the poor young man was still refused membership of the local club, effectively cutting him off from all relaxation. For people like her, the post-Raj generation, India is a nation defined by your allegiance rather than what you were born. She still lives in Delhi today.[18]

John Christie enjoyed the new-found freedom and lack of stuffiness. He left the ICS, taking a job running a Chamber of Commerce in Delhi and later as managing director of a company in Cawnpore. For eleven years he and his family would 'taste the freedom of India', enjoying 'happy and stimulating days in Delhi'. He thought that the fact that a few people like him stayed on helped restore some confidence in the British–Indian relationship, which had been so shaken by 'the appalling aftermath of partition'. He was, like many, gratifyingly surprised that there was hardly any anti-British feeling. Delhi, he felt, changed markedly. First, the influx of refugees brought, despite an associated misery and depression, a new group of people to energise a society where the Raj had previously dominated. Secondly, the arrival of a diplomatic corps gave India international exposure and, thirdly, he and his family felt they could now meet and socialise with Indian women, something that had not happened under the Raj. Even the Gymkhana Club, the arch-preserve of the establishment, both British and Indian, admitted women. 'Indian women', Christie noted, 'began to take their rightful place as hostesses and leaders of society in their own capital city whereby we all immeasurably benefitted'.[19]

Christie reckoned that in the years immediately after independence, the number of British in India, excepting the army, rose, which is, in itself, an interesting comment on how thinly the Raj had been spread throughout its time in India and particularly in its final years. The new people were mostly commercial or people like him who were happy to adapt. Others found their changed circumstances more difficult. Norval Mitchell was told he was to be replaced as chief secretary in West Punjab by Dudley de la Fargue, the officer who had spoken so disloyally about Sir Olaf Caroe and his demand for the plebiscite on the Frontier. Mitchell had only been standing in for de la Fargue, so this was not altogether surprising, but it was quite odd given that de la Fargue's outspoken support of Dr Khan Sahib had been in opposition to the League. Jinnah had, however, offered Mitchell another post, carrying the same salary and conditions. It was an attractive offer, particularly given that he faced an uncertain future with four young children, but he refused. 'I was not', he said, 'for one moment tempted.' His reasons were various but mostly because he felt that 'the opportunity of service that had been so inspiring in 1929 was no longer available'. He had, he reflected, spent the last few years being responsible for suppressing unrest, something he was afraid would continue. It had been 'distasteful and exhausting work'. Instead he resigned, doing what all returning British officials and soldiers did when their ships left Bombay, throwing his solar topee, that instantly recognisable badge of the Raj, over the stern of the ship. He did not feel 'grief-stricken', but more numb and 'tried to look forward cheerfully to an ill-defined future'. Once his ship was out of sight of land he immersed himself in books on sheep farming. For ten years he occupied himself in the Scottish borders before returning to colonial service in Northern Rhodesia as it became Zambia.[20]

For some Indian communities the departure of the few British who remained was sad. In Jodhpur they were sorry, however much they felt betrayed by the Raj, to say farewell to

Loch of the Land Revenue Service, Lowrie of the Forestry, Barr of the Judiciary, Beatson of the Lancers, Cocks of the Police, Joscelyne and Home of the Railways, Miss Massey of the First Girls School, Edgar of the Public Works, and those great and good men, the Residents Powlett, Windham, Hewson. Long after Dufferin, Elgin and Curzon, Minto and Hardinge, Irwin and Willingdon, Linlithgow and Mountbatten have been forgotten, these are the 'sahibs' Marwar [the royal house of Jodhpur] will remember.[21]

For many Indians the end of British rule was, once the celebrations were over, something of a non-event. 'One hundred and fifty years would wash off in the first one hundred and fifty minutes', thought Inder Malhotra. In 1954 he went, as a journalist, on a goodwill cruise with the Indian Navy. They called at Port Swettenham in Malaya (now Port Klang in Malaysia) where a dance had been arranged. The Indian sailors happily danced with British girls in a way that seemed completely natural but Malhotra noticed the Malays watching from the sidelines uncomfortably. Indians had, he thought, completely excised any notion of the British being different but in countries like Malaya the old inhibitions remained. In 1961 he was walking his niece along the seafront in Bombay. They paused at the statue of King George V under the India Gate. His niece asked him why there was a statue of a foreign king in India. Malhotra explained. His niece burst out laughing and told him he was making it all up.[22] One poignant reminder for Malhotra came when he was covering an official trip to Pakistan in 1950. The party had stopped at a local station. On the platform he saw one of those eleven Muslim refugees whose lives his father had saved on Independence Day by smuggling them onto a Pakistan-bound train.

But there was pain to come. Kushwant Singh noted, phlegmatically, that after the high of independence, when he had celebrated so enthusiastically in Delhi, and thought that India 'the land of Gandhi' would show the world, 'it was only later that the disillusionment set in – that we realised we were just like everyone else'.[23] A violent and shocking example of that disillusionment occurred on 30 January 1948. Mahatma Gandhi, supported as usual on the shoulders of two female disciples, hobbled out of Birla House in New Delhi, where he was living, to take his daily prayer meeting. Gandhi made full use of Birla's generosity, causing the industrialist to quip one day, 'Have you any idea what it costs to keep you in the poverty to which you are accustomed?' On 12 January Gandhi had started another fast, declaring that he would continue until Hindu–Muslim unity had been restored. He laid down seven conditions that must be fulfilled, mostly concerning the safety of Muslims and their property in Delhi, before he would agree to eat again. After initially greeting his latest intervention with some irritation, and Patel muttering that the only way to improve Hindu–Muslim relations was to remove every Muslim from East Punjab and every non-Muslim from West Punjab, the government formed a committee under Congress President Rajendra Prasad to put his conditions into effect. On 20 January a young extreme Hindu activist threw a bomb at Gandhi as he conducted his prayers. It caused no damage and the Mahatma was unperturbed but as he climbed the steps to his prayer platform on 30 January a Hindu extremist called Nathuram Godse shot him three times in the chest with a revolver at almost point-blank range.

Thirteen days of state mourning were declared. Tributes were paid from across the world. 'Nearly all from India bore tribute to his non-communal outlook and his equal love for the Muslims. The only one of those which in any way struck a jarring note was Mr. Jinnah's – who referred to Mahatma Gandhi as "one of the greatest men produced by the Hindu community and a leader who commanded their universal confidence and respect".'[24] There was, though, general relief that his assassin was a Hindu and not a Muslim. Had he been, then it would have opened up 'a ghastly prospect; next day rivers of blood would flow in India and Pakistan'.[25] In fact the investigation into Gandhi's assassination revealed a widespread plot, masterminded by cells of the RSS and Hindu Mahasabha, to kill more members of the government who were, they felt, not taking a strong enough Hindu and Indian nationalist line. On 3 February the RSS was declared illegal and many of its members arrested. The Hindu Mahasabha went into voluntary suspension. At the same time the leaders of the two extreme Muslim organisations, the League National Guards and the Khaksars, were rounded up as well.

Gandhi, always a Hindu at heart however hybrid his various religious beliefs, was cremated the next day, attended by a crowd of over a million people. Nehru lit the funeral pyre. Mountbatten attended and sat cross-legged on the ground in the front row. Churchill was appalled that the representative of the ex-King-Emperor should be so seen in public; Mountbatten explained that if he hadn't he would have been pushed into the flames by the weight of the crowd pushing forward.

One of the effects of Gandhi's assassination was to cause a temporary improvement in relations between Nehru and Sardar Patel, which had been getting progressively worse. Christie had been amused to hear the audience at a performance of Shakespeare's *Julius Caesar* in Delhi start muttering during the quarrel scene between Caesar and

Cassius 'Where is Jawaharlal? Is Sardarji [the familiar name for Patel] here?'[26] The two leaders had started to make speeches on the same issue at the same time 'without the least reference to each other'.[27] Gandhi had been disturbed, sensing a serious split in Congress at a time when India faced so many critical issues; some believed his last fast had been an attempt to force a reconciliation. Patel had been to see him the day he was killed, asking for his guidance. Should he resign or stay on? Gandhi urged him to stay. Patel remained hugely influential, as deputy prime minister, minister for home affairs and commander-in-chief of the armed forces until 1950 when his weak heart finally got the better of him. He and Nehru continued to spar, over the integration of the states – Nehru felt he did not consult the wider government fully – on Kashmir and Hyderabad, and later over the integration of the remaining Portuguese outpost of Goa, but they avoided an open split. With Patel went V. P. Menon; he had been the most invaluable servant to two masters, the Raj and Patel. Once they had both gone he was sidelined and went into retirement. At least it meant he had time to write his memoirs.

Jinnah was moved from Karachi to a cottage in the hills at Ziarat, above Quetta, in June 1948. He had endured a demanding year, touring East Bengal and the North West Frontier but his health was now giving out. From Ziarat he was moved down to Quetta in August and then back to Government House in Karachi where he died on 11 September. He was buried the next day, the crowds at his funeral rivalling those who attended Gandhi's cremation. Khwaja Nazimuddin, premier of East Bengal, was selected to take over from him as governor general, a wise choice given what was seen as a widening gulf between the two halves of the country. One of the main issues facing Nazimuddin and Liaquat, apart from their problems with India, was money. There had been a long-standing row with India over what share of India's pre-partition cash reserves would be transferred. In August these had amounted to 400 crore rupees, a crore being 10 million rupees, so about £300 million. Pakistan was allocated 75 crore rupees; 20 crore rupees was paid immediately with the balance of 55 crore to follow. During the Kashmir dispute India decided to withhold this second payment and it had taken Gandhi's intervention with Patel, at Mountbatten's suggestion, to release it. Even so Pakistan was very short of cash. By March 1948 they were running a deficit of 24.3 crore rupees and had to raise an emergency loan to which the country responded very positively, with women even pawning their jewellery and clothes. By 1948 things were more under control and the next two budgets even produced a small surplus but there was little for nation-building in a country that had virtually no government facilities.[28] Pakistan established a State Bank in July 1948 and the Pakistani rupee initially maintained parity with its Indian counterpart, both trading at the same rate against sterling. However, in 1949, when sterling was devalued against the US dollar, India followed suit but Pakistan decided not to and the two rupee currencies began to drift apart.

Neither was the passage of democracy in Pakistan straightforward. Liaquat was assassinated while he was giving a speech in Rawalpindi in 1951 by an Afghan but the motive for his murder is obscure. Nazimuddin then took over as prime minister, handing over as governor general to Malik Ghulam Mohammad, the finance minister. Unrest was meanwhile growing in East Bengal. This was partly nationalist, with East Bengalis protesting about the use of Urdu as the official language but largely because they felt ignored by Karachi. Increasingly the key government jobs were being filled by West Pakistanis and Bengalis saw themselves becoming the poor relations of a government that put the interests of the western provinces first. At the same time the population of East Bengal was growing fast so that it was beginning to dwarf the west. In 1955, in an attempt to answer East Bengal's increasingly violent demands for better representation, the country was divided into West Pakistan and East Pakistan, which now had a greater degree of self-government. Suhrawardy, who had declared his undying loyalty to India in 1947, became prime minister of Pakistan but only lasted until 1957.

These challenges proved too much for the young democracy. In 1958 General Iskander Mirza, in the face of serious unrest in both halves of the country, declared martial law. His successor was General Ayub Khan, Mohindar Singh's old colleague from Sandhurst, and Gracey's successor as chief of the army staff. He ruled the country for the next ten years during which Pakistan fought its first, or second if you count Kashmir, war with India. This started in August 1965 over what were portrayed as Pakistani attempts to start an insurgency in Jammu and Kashmir. It was a violent conventional struggle, with mass armoured forces engaged in the biggest tank battle since the Second World War. It ended in stalemate, with India claiming to have the upper hand but little territorial change; casualties were roughly equal despite each army making contradictory claims. Harbakhsh Singh, now a lieutenant general, led India's Western Command, retaking the Haji Pir Pass over which he had so reluctantly led his 1st Sikhs in 1947.

Ayub Khan faced strong opposition. Early in his term Suhrawardy had tried to make a comeback before being exiled. Despite the war, in 1969 Ayub Khan still managed to hand over to another general, Yahya Khan. In November 1970 a terrible cyclone hit East Pakistan, causing widespread flooding, killing up to a quarter of a million people, and sending a further flood of refugees into India. The response of Yahya Khan's government was thought to be inadequate, he himself spending only one day in the country en route to China and, in a replay of the events of 1942–3, failing to send food supplies. In December he was forced to agree to elections. These were won with an overwhelming majority by Sheikh Mujibur Rahman's Aswami League in the East and with a clear majority by Zulfikar Ali Bhutto's People's Party in the West. Rahman, harking back to 1947, now demanded that the central government in Karachi should control only defence, foreign affairs and communications, leaving all other matters to Dacca but Yahya Khan refused. On 25 March 1971 he sent the Pakistan Army, which had been gradually reinforced so it was around sixty thousand, into Dacca to suppress the Aswami League.

The resulting civil war, which was fought during the summer and autumn of 1971, was bloody and widespread, with accusations of atrocities on both sides. It led to a further mass exodus to West Bengal, estimated to have been several million people who placed an unacceptable strain on an economy already struggling to absorb earlier migrations. India initially stood back but then began to start training East Pakistani 'freedom fighters'. Pakistan took this as a hostile act and in December 1971 mounted a surprise attack on India from the west. India countered this and immediately invaded East Pakistan. It was to prove a one-sided contest. Pakistani forces in the East surrendered on 16 December 1971 after just twelve days and Bangladesh was born with Rahman as its first head of state. The military, discredited, were forced out in West Pakistan, which became just Pakistan, where Bhutto's People's Party formed a new government.

The story of these difficult decades showed the near impossibility of making Pakistan work as a country of two halves separated by a thousand miles, by race, by language, by affinity and united only by religion. They also showed that Burrows' prediction in April 1947 was correct and that East Bengal would not be economically viable nor able to feed itself at least under the semi-colonial administration of West Pakistan. Bangladesh's early years as a nation were equally difficult. Severe flooding along the Brahmaputra in 1974 was blamed for the subsequent famine that lasted from January 1974 until January 1975. By the summer of 1974 the price of rice had doubled in the worst affected areas, mostly higher up the river. In Rangpur, 100,000 died and there were significant casualties in Mymensingh and Sylhet. The Bangladeshi government put the subsequent deaths at 27,000; most independent estimates put them at nearer the one million mark. Again debates raged as to whether there was an actual shortage of food or whether the problem was more one of management and distribution. Again the West, in this case the United States, was criticised for withholding food supplies, trying to exert political pressure on Bangladesh not to trade with Cuba.[29] Economic restructuring after 1975 brought about a gradual change so that, with its well-developed garment industry and more productive agriculture, in 2016 Bangladesh recorded its highest-ever growth rate. East Bengal at least has a happier ending, to date, than it had birth.

*

Within twenty-five years of partition, India and Pakistan, two states
with a common heritage that in June 1947 were intended to work
within a shared defence structure, had been engaged in three major
conflicts. Within fifty years both countries had acquired nuclear
weapons. Their rivalry was reflected in their international affiliations. Nehru, a socialist who was always impressed by Russia, looked
increasingly to Moscow. Pakistan, in contrast, looked to Washington
and China; Nehru was irritated at what he saw as unjustified American
support for Pakistan. Both countries, badly in need of money to fund
development and education, spent excessively on their armies. Nehru,
always suspicious of the military, kept his generals well away from
power. Very soon after independence he slashed their salaries and
privileges. Senior Indian officers served for short periods and were
then replaced so they could not build up any individual power base.
The three services were kept apart, with a weak central defence staff.
If Indian politicians were firmly in charge of the military, in Pakistan
the opposite happened. Forged in the tragedy of the Punjab and in
Kashmir, Pakistan relied on its army from its very beginning. It was
one of the few functioning organisations in the new nation and one
which, with Jinnah gone, represented its sense of nationhood. It was,
as in Israel, part of the fabric of what the new country was. The subsequent military governments have come from that tradition.

There has been much ink spilt over who was to blame for partition
and debate about whether it could have been avoided. It is important
first to accept that the events of August to November 1947 were a
tragedy, a terrible tragedy, not just in bloodshed and human misery
but in their consequences. Were they avoidable and who was responsible for them? Some historians will argue it is Britain's fault for
trying to govern India in the first place, rather than just establishing
a trading partnership. There is an obvious truth in that but it is not
necessarily a helpful debate when confronted with the circumstances
of 1947. However, there is a strong case for arguing that Britain
stayed in India well past the time when it was clear that its presence
benefited neither the British nor Indians.

The critical year was 1919. India had made an extraordinarily generous contribution to the British war effort in the First World War, both in the number of men who volunteered and in money. There had been a genuine expectation that after the war she would receive the same sort of self-government as had already been given to Canada, as early as 1861, to South Africa in 1872 and to Australia in 1900, which is sometimes referred to as Dominion status although technically that did not exist until 1931. What it would have meant, in effect, is that India would have stayed as a united nation in the Commonwealth, with a British governor general and a British hand, albeit a light one, in defence and foreign policy but essentially self-governing. Instead the British stayed put. The Rowlatt Acts insulted Indians, Dyer committed his atrocity in Amritsar, the trading advantages declined, the Muslim League grew apart from Congress and the energy started to go out of the Raj, but still Britain would not compromise. It is difficult not to see a racist element in this; colonies with a white business and governing class were granted self-governing status but Indians were not felt to be ready. The early 1920s are a dark and muddled time for Britain. The losses of the First World War seem to have blighted the judgement of a generation who, despite the primacy of domestic interests, continued to treat both Ireland and India in a way that was not only contrary to what they had been led to expect in 1914 but which was to work directly counter to British interests. It was almost as if George III was once again confronting the American colonies rather than negotiating a common future.

It was this refusal to compromise, while not having the resources nor the real willingness to administer and develop India in the way the country so badly needed, that was the main cause of the tragedy in 1947. A Raj that was already paper-thin became even thinner. The year 1935 presented another opportunity when the Government of India Act offered the logical moment to grant Dominion status but again it was missed. The Second World War masked the cracks in the British administrative machine but, once the army started to demobilise in 1945, they would become all too apparent.

By 1947 there was little of the Raj still functioning apart from the army. India was disintegrating. Congress realised this, as did the senior ICS officers, those men like Jenkins who, however fashionable it may now be to discredit them, really understood India. Nehru and Patel came to two conclusions. First, that if they wanted to have a country left to govern they needed to get on with it and, secondly, that they would not share central power with Jinnah. It was too late for that. Had Congress reacted more favourably to Jinnah's approaches in 1937 then things might have turned out differently but their experience in the Interim Government had shown them that they were better without the League. For Congress, it was essential to maintain that strong central government without which they feared they could not keep the country together. They would force Jinnah into a 'moth-eaten' Pakistan, which they knew he did not want, and which they were sure would not last because it was, as Nehru said in his historic broadcast on 4 June, the quickest route to a unified India. For Jinnah, whose vision was a federal India with the League sharing power and exercising control over the Muslim majority provinces on the original Palestine model, this was a bitter blow. He never got what he wanted.

Yet even once partition had happened, India and Pakistan could have worked cooperatively within the loose federal structure, which was what many people had in mind in June. There was nothing inevitable about the slaughter in the Punjab, nothing inevitable about Kashmir or about the subsequent wars. The Joint Defence arrangements could have worked. The relationship could have been as England to Scotland rather than as an armed stand-off. Mountbatten, so heavily criticised for almost everything he did in his four and a half months as viceroy, was absolutely correct to try to become governor general of both new nations, thus providing an overarching structure. Had Jinnah not been dying it is possible he may have succeeded.

The Punjab made future cooperation almost impossible and Kashmir made it completely impossible. Did the slaughter happen because partition was rushed? Many would argue it did and it became fashionable to denigrate Mountbatten for bringing forward the date from 1948 to August 1947. Yet that decision was not Mountbatten's. The problem with Mountbatten is that he pretended he had more influence than he did, particularly later in life when his tendency to exaggerate was more pronounced. He was an important interlocutor, and a good one, but no more than that. Once Attlee had made his historic announcement on 20 February, and given the very strong links between Congress and the Labour government, it was Nehru and Patel who dictated events. It was Nehru who, after the one occasion Mountbatten stood up to him, on the question of the plebiscite in the North West Frontier Province, decided to go for partition. It was Nehru and Patel who decided to get on with it quickly; Nehru even tried in May to get the British to hand over in June. It was Nehru and Patel, working with V. P. Menon, who crafted the final agreement that Mountbatten took back to Attlee.

It was not the rush that caused the slaughter; rather it was an inability by all the key players to foresee it. Nehru should have done, but for him the new India was about socialism not communalism; he did not believe that religion held such sway. Jinnah should have done but he never really understood the Punjab. Mountbatten should have done, but he hardly knew India. Auchinleck should have done but he was too consumed with the heartbreak of dividing his beloved army. The provincial governors should have done, and they did, but were ignored. It was obvious to people who knew the Punjab that the Sikhs would not form a minority in Pakistan. Their enmity against the Muslims was too deep and, after the Rawalpindi massacres, they were determined to carve out their own part of India. They were well organised and had been preparing since March exactly as Jenkins had warned. The Sikhs, with their traditions, organisation and sense of common purpose, would have struck whenever partition had come.

The only way to prevent the slaughter was to police the Punjab properly and that meant, given the inadequacy of the police, to use the army, that jewel in the crown of India, the one remaining part of the machinery of government that still operated effectively and which had sufficient power to subdue the Sikh *jathas* and the Hindu and Muslim *goondas*. There is no excuse for not using British and Gurkha troops and deploying alongside them those non-communal units of Indian troops who would not be affected by local affiliations. It was the way the army in India had operated for generations; why should it make any difference that they were now saving Indian rather than European life? Mountbatten took two pages in his final report to Attlee to explain why British troops were not used, which is in itself revealing. Had they been deployed, he argued, Britain would have 'incurred the odium of both sides'.[30] He then argued that it would have been 'a task of the utmost military difficulty to have maintained a large number of soldiers in the Punjab'. This is disingenuous. There was hardly anything which attracted such 'odium' on Britain than the murder of one million people, and the troops available were grouped in mobile brigades with their own logistics. There was ample time to brief and deploy a force of the size and capability that Jenkins had recommended, with accompanying air power, in July. Armies are good at moving quickly; that is what they are there for, and to protect the citizens who pay for them. They are not there to become, in inelegant but accurate modern British army slang, 'self-licking lollipops'. In August 1947 over half a million servicemen stood idle.

Were 1 million people killed? Some argue it was far less. Mountbatten put the figure first at 100,000 then at 200,000, but he was trying to justify a course of action.[31] Those on the ground, men like Lieutenant Colonel Mitchison of the PBF and the BBC correspondent Wynford Vaughan-Thomas both thought the figure was nearer 1 million as did Ismay. Others have put it at 500,000, at 600,000 and at 800,000.[32] It is impossible to arrive at an objective figure; whatever it was, it represents a shaming loss of life.

Many British officials felt that shame as they left. Sir Reginald Savory, the adjutant general whom Wavell had knighted at that dinner in January, was called in to see Attlee when he arrived back in London. 'Was it too quick?' Attlee asked. Savory didn't answer but he did say, 'Is this to be the culmination of British rule in India and the fulfilment of our great mission?'[33] Ismay, who had given so much of his life to India, could not, as his ship steamed slowly away from Bombay, 'bear to watch that shore fading out of view'. He went to his cabin alone with his memories. 'I thought of two million British graves that dotted the land, and of the devoted service that many generations of countrymen had given it. Would these forefathers of ours think that all their work and sacrifice had been wasted and their trust betrayed by those who came after them?'[34] They would undoubtedly have judged the Bengal famine of 1942–4 as harshly as the events of 1947.

Ismay's sentiment, testimony to that feeling that so many Raj officials had that they were in some way on a 'civilising' mission in India, was part of the problem. The British went to India to make money. They ended up governing the country because it made trade easier but they never resourced the government in a way that allowed any improvement in the lives of Indians, or which developed their health, education and economy. It is often said that the British left India a valuable legacy in a parliamentary democracy, in the railways and infrastructure and in the English language. That does not quite ring true. The Raj did not operate as a democracy and it was Congress who properly instituted it. Many believe that the sheer complexity of India meant that democracy was anyway the only viable form of government. 'In fact, deep down, Indians are not very democratic; rather the reverse. They're very feudal', thought the journalist Romesh Thapar, who wrote for *The Times of India* and who lived through the events of 1947. 'But we have to be democratic to involve all the many different tribes and castes and now our huge middle class. But our system is not a British or a US system, it's an Indian system' and, he added, 'it hasn't worked very well.'[35] Neither can the path of democracy in Pakistan be judged a particular success.

Neither can the railways be said to have been a gift to the Indian nation. They were laid down after the Mutiny to move troops quickly around the country and, as we have seen, they were funded by loans guaranteed a 5 per cent coupon regardless of whether they made any money. The English language, which Indians and Pakistanis love, and which they have so enriched, does act as a unifying force although only a proportion of the populations of both countries speak it.

Rather than try to justify past actions, the British involvement in India should be seen for what it was. In the age of empire, when European nations were using their comparative technological advantage to dominate the world, in which they saw nothing wrong or immoral, it was a successful venture that benefited British commerce and enriched her international standing. It did very little for the Indians. It could have ended so much better, as with British involvement in many other parts of the globe, had it ended when it should have done, when the age of empire was demonstrably over and when subject peoples were demanding self-government. It did not and when it was finally forced to close it did so amid terrible bloodshed, which the British and British Indian armies could have significantly limited if not wholly prevented. We had stayed too long – just as we were doing in Basrah.

GLOSSARY

Ahimsa: Non-violence.
Aman: Summer harvest.
Ashram: A spiritual hermitage; Gandhi's communities were called ashrams.
Aus: Spring harvest.

Baba-i-Qaum: Father of the Nation; term usually applied to Jinnah.
Bapu: Father. Often applied to Gandhi.
Bhagavad Gita: Hindu holy scriptures.
Bania: Moneylenders.
Batta: The extra payments made to soldiers in the Indian Army to compensate them for field conditions.
Boro: Autumn harvest.
Bustee: Slum dwelling.

Dhoti: Loose-fitting Indian male clothing.
Dupatta: Plait.
Durbar: Ceremonial gathering.

Firman: A decree or mandate and also used to describe a pass or permit.

Gurdwara: A Sikh temple.

Goonda: A mob; mostly used to describe the Hindu and Muslim mobs in Calcutta and Western Punjab.
Guru: A holy teacher or leader.

Havildar: Sergeant.

Ittehad-ul-Muslimeen: The Muslim militia in Hyderabad.

Jagirdar: Landlords who charged rent. Similar to a **Zamindar.**
Jatha: A Sikh war band.
Jathedar: The leader of a Sikh war band.
Jirga: A council or meeting of elders.

Khadi: Homepsun cloth.
Khadi Sherwani: The long, buttoned coats of homespun favoured by Nehru.
Kirpan: A Sikh dagger or sword.
Kuchabandi: A protected place.

Lashkar: A tribal band.
Lathi: A bamboo stave typically carried by rioters and also used by the police.

Mahasabha: The Hindu nationalist movement.
Mahout: The person who guides an elephant.
Maidan: An open space or plain; the large open area in the centre of Calcutta is referred to as the Maidan.
Maulana: An honorific title for a Muslim holy man.
Maund: A measurement of weight equal to 82 pounds or 37 kilograms.
Maharajah: A ruler or prince.
Mahatma: Great Father – usually applied to Gandhi.
Maratha: A Hindu warrior clan from the Western Deccan plain.

Naik: Corporal.

Namaz: Muslim prayers.
Nihang: A warrior caste of Sikhs.

Panchayat: Council of village elders.
Patidar: A caste of small landowners from Gujarat.
Pir: A Muslim preacher.
Pashtun: A tribesman from the North West Frontier.
Pashtunwallah: The honour code by which Pashtuns live.

Quaid-i-Azam: Honorific applied to Jinnah.

Rabi: Autumn harvest; the same as boro.

Satyagraha: Non-violent resistance; used to describe Gandhi's
    campaigns of non-cooperation.
Sepoy: Soldier in East India Company's and later the Raj's armies.
Shikaris: Hunters.
Swadeshi: Homemade; used to denote Indian-made products
    which Gandhi exhorted people to buy instead of imported
    British goods.
Swaraj: Home Rule.

Thanedar: An officer, usually a police officer; often used to
    describe a Hindu village leader in the Punjab.
Tahsil: A land division and area used for tax assessment.
Tahsildar: An official responsible for a tahsil.
Thana: A sub-division of a tahsil; often the area controlled by a
    police station and used as the basic unit by Radcliffe for the
    division of Bengal.
Tikka Para: The Raj's system of protecting railways by
    allocating responsibility for the line to the villages near
    which it passed.

Vaishnava: A tradition of Hinduism that regards Lord Vishnu as
    the Supreme Being.

VCO: A Viceroy's Commissioned Officer; a commission given to Indian soldiers prior to 1947.

Zamindar: A landowner, and usually one who lets his land to tenants.

NOTES

ICHR: Indian Council of Historical Research *Towards Freedom* Series
ToP: *Transfer of Power*

Chapter 1: January

1 Schofield, *Wavell*, p.322.
2 Schofield, p.317.
3 Leo Amery, Secretary of State for India, quoting Churchill at a Cabinet Meeting, January 1944, Schofield, p.325.
4 He was commissioned into the Black Watch, the Royal Highland Regiment, a regiment in the British as opposed to the British Indian Army's Order of Battle. He had, however, served regularly in India since 1907.
5 Shahid Hamid, *Disastrous Twilight*, p.123.
6 Schofield, p.364.
7 Bombay, Madras, Orissa and the Central Provinces. *ToP*, vol. ix, No.229, 24 December 1946.
8 *ToP*, vol. ix, No.236, Bevin to Attlee, 1 January 1947.
9 *ToP*, vol. ix, No.236, 1 January 1947.
10 Schofield, p.367.
11 Figures taken from Tuker, *While Memory Serves*, p.164. Tuker, as general officer commanding Eastern Command, was in as good a position to estimate casualty numbers as anyone but even his estimate cannot be taken as accurate.
12 *The Sole Spokesman* is the title of Ayesha Jalal's excellent history of Jinnah and the League from the 1930s until 1947. Jinnah claimed repeatedly that it was he and the League who alone spoke for India's Muslims.
13 Nikhil Chakravarty interviewed, 26 January 1988.
14 *Indian Express*, 1 July 1997. Gopal Mukherjee interviewed by Andrew Whitehead.
15 Tuker, p.163.

16 Quoted by Sengupta in *The Partition of Bengal*, p.41.
17 Naffese Chohan interviewed by BBC Radio Cleveland. British Library C900/01580.
18 *Indian Express*, 20 May 1997. Noakhali Article by Andrew Whitehead.
19 *Indian Express*, 20 May 1997.
20 *Indian Express*, 20 May 1997.
21 *Indian Express*, 20 May 1997.
22 Tuker quoting eyewitnesses, p.198. The Garhmukteswar massacre remains uninvestigated to this day. Pandit Pant, premier of the United Provinces, where the town lies, and one of the people who emerges from the story of 1947 as among the fairest and most even-handed, initiated an enquiry but was unable to see it through.
23 Moon, *Divide and Quit*, p.30.
24 Khan, *The Great Partition*, p.82.
25 *ToP*, vol.ix, No.255, Pethick-Lawrence to Attlee, 6 January 1947.
26 *ToP*, vol.ix, No.236, Bevin to Attlee, 1 January 1947.
27 A copy of the report on Exercise Embrace is in the British Library: L/MIL/17/5/1816.
28 Mason, *The Men Who Ruled India*, p.318.
29 Mason, *A Matter of Honour*, p.387.
30 Spear, *A History of India*, p.153.
31 Mason, *The Men Who Ruled India*, p.315.
32 In its 2016 Radio 4 series on the Deobandis, the BBC estimated that more people attended a Deobandi mosque every week in the United Kingdom than attended a Church of England service.
33 Spear, p.166.
34 Moon, *Strangers in India*, p.35.
35 Moon, *Strangers in India*, p.52.
36 Moon, *Strangers in India*, p.52.
37 Inder Malhotra interviewed in Delhi. BL C63/195/11.
38 Moon, *Strangers in India*, p.36, quoting W. H. Moreland & Atul Chandra Chatterjee's *A Short History of India*. See also Raghbendra Jha's *The Indian Economy Sixty Years After Independence*, p.18, where the figures are laid out in tables.
39 Moreland & Chatterjee, *A Short History of India*, p.527.
40 See A. N. Maini, *Taxation in India 1934*, published in Oxford Gandhi Group's *India Analysed*, vol. 2. p.24.
41 *The Times* Special Report on India, 18 February 1930.
42 Dr P. P. Pillai, *India Analysed*, p.65. Dr Pillai was director of the International Labour Office in Delhi.
43 S. Moolgaonkar interview, IWM 14660-1-1.
44 Note from Dr Anil Seal to the author, 27 July 2016.
45 Mitchell, *The Quiet People of India*, Chapter 3.

46 Spear, p.185.

47 Brown, *Gandhi*, p.123.

48 Churchill, House of Commons, 8 July 1920, Hansard.

49 Quoted in the British Library catalogue Beyond the Frame: India in Britain 1858–1950.

50 *The Times* Special Report on India, 18 February 1930.

51 Edwardes, *Nehru*, p.138.

52 See Sen, *Poverty and Famines*, p.52, and ICHR 1942–42, Part 2, Section viii, 87.

53 Davis, *Late Victorian Holocausts*, p.172.

54 ICHR 1942–43, Part 2, Section viii, 1912.

55 ICHR 1942–43, Part 2, Section viii, 1916.

56 A *maund* is 82 lbs.

57 Sen, p.58; see also Famine Enquiry 1943.

58 ICHR 1942–43, Part 2, Section viii, 1956.

59 ICHR 1942–43, Part 2, Section viiii, 1855, quoting an article in *Independent India*.

60 ICHR 1942–43, Part 2, Section viiii, 1823, quoting the *Daily Worker*.

61 ICHR 1942–43, Part 2, Section viii, 2059. Letter from Sir N. N. Sircar to Viceroy and *ToP*, vol. iv, No.180, Amery Statement to House of Commons, 14 October 1943.

62 ICHR 1942–43 Part 2, Section viii, 1892. Bankin Mukherjee speaking in Bihar.

63 *ToP*, vol. iv, No.199. Wavell's Visit Report, 27 October 1943.

64 ICHR 1942–43 Part 2, section viii, 1889.

65 *ToP*, vol. iv, No.158, Rutherford to Linlithgow, 2 October 1943, after he had taken over from Herbert as Governor of Bengal.

66 ICHR 1942–43 Part 2, Section viiii, 1859, Herbert to Linlithgow, 2 July 1943.

67 ICHR 1942–43 Part 2, section viii, 1865, Linlithgow to Amery, 4 August 1943.

68 ICHR 1942–43 Part 2, section viii, 1873.

69 ICHR 1942–43 Part 2, section viii, 1838.

70 *ToP*, vol iv, No.213, Wavell to Amery, 8 November 1943.

71 *ToP*, vol iv, No.230, Wavell to Amery, 16 November 1943.

72 Major General D. K. Palit interviewed c.4 December 1988 in Delhi, transcript in British Library R193/9; this is an interview that can be quoted from.

73 *ToP*, vol. iv, Nos. 376, 413, 435 and 551.

74 *ToP*, vol. iv, No.208, Rutherford to Wavell, 4 November 1943.

75 *ToP*, vol. iv, No.199, Wavell to Amery, 1 November 1943.

76 *ToP*, vol. iv, No.364, Wavell to Amery, 9 February 1944.

77 ICHR 1942–43, Part 2, section viii, 1912.

78 Saumarez Smith, *A Young Man's Country*, p.2.

79 *ToP*, vol. iv, No.305, Burrows to Pethick-Lawrence, 25 January 1947.

80 *ToP*, vol. iv, No.145, Gandhi to Linlithgow, 27 September 1943.

81 Edwardes, p.142.

82 Edwardes, p.148.

83 Edwardes, p.159.

84 Moon, *Divide and Quit*, p.57.

85 Khan, *The Great Partition*, p.26.

86 Admiral Chatterji interviewed in Delhi, 26 November 1988. The transcript is in the British Library (C63/195/06); copyright restrictions mean it is not possible to quote directly from it.

87 Major General D. K. Palit interviewed in Delhi, 4 December 1988.

88 Tuker, p.40.

89 *ToP*, vol. iv, No.286, Colville to Pethick-Lawrence, 20 January 1947.

90 Mitchell, Chapter 4.

91 Kushwant Singh, radio interview, BBC World Series. British Library C991/13.

92 Mitchell, Chapter 4.

93 Saumarez Smith, p.x.

94 *ToP*, vol. ix, No.281, Wavell to Attlee, 17 January 1947.

95 *ToP*, vol. ix, No.331, Attlee to Wavell, 31 January 1947.

Chapter 2: February

1 Jalal, p.232.

2 V. P. Menon interviewed by Henry Hodson, 12 September 1964. BBC *Indian Tales from the Raj*, No.55. British Library Sound Archive.

3 Edwardes, p.24.

4 Brown, *Gandhi*, p.139.

5 Brown, *Gandhi*, p.353.

6 Collins & Lapierre, *Freedom at Midnight*, p.52.

7 Quoted by Sheela Reddy, *Mr and Mrs Jinnah*, p.58.

8 Brown, *Gandhi*, p.76.

9 Collins & Lapierre, *Freedom at Midnight*, opp. p.310.

10 *ToP*, vol. ix, No.561, Wavell to Mountbatten 25 March 1947

11 *ToP*, vol. x, No.16, Mountbatten's Notes.

12 Brown, *Gandhi*, p.128.

13 Philips, *The Partition of India 1947*, p.6.

14 Edwardes, p.43.

15 Mercado, *The Shadow Warriors of Nakano*, p.73.

16 Philips, p.8.

17 Philips, p.8.

18 A. K. Damodaran interviewed by the BBC 1988.

19 V. P. Menon interviewed by Henry Hodson, 12 September 1964. British Library Audio Library.

20 *ToP*, vol. ix, No.460, Wavell to HM the King, 24 February 1947.
21 *ToP*, vol. ix, No.460, Wavell to HM the King, 24 February 1947.
22 *ToP*, vol. ix, No.561, Wavell to Mountbatten, 25 March 1947.
23 *ToP*, vol. ix, No.460, Wavell to HM the King, 24 February 1947.
24 *ToP*, vol. ix, No.561, Wavell to Mountbatten, 25 March 1947.
25 *ToP*, vol. ix, No.460, Wavell to HM the King, 24 February 1947.
26 *ToP*, vol. ix, No.561, Wavell to Mountbatten, 25 March 1947.
27 *ToP*, vol. ix, No.561, Wavell to Mountbatten, 25 March 1947.
28 *ToP*, vol. ix, No.350, Nehru to Wavell, 5 February 1947.
29 *ToP*, vol. ix, No.337, Wavell to Pethick-Lawrence, 3 February 1947.
30 *ToP*, vol. ix, No.340, Mountbatten to Attlee, 4 February 1947.
31 *ToP*, vol. ix, No.351, Wavell to Attlee , 5 February 1947.
32 *ToP*, vol. ix, No.395, Note by Sir F. Burrows dated 14 February 1947 and No. 410, Wavell to Pethick-Lawrence, 17 February 1947.
33 *ToP*, vol. ix, No.420, Attlee to Wavell, 18 February 1947.
34 *ToP* vol. ix, No.429, Pethick-Lawrence to Wavell, 19 February 1947.
35 Command 7047, published 20 February 1947, replicated in *ToP*, vol. ix, No.438.
36 *Dawn*, 21 February 1947, replicated in *ToP*, vol. ix, No.440, 1947.
37 *Hindustan Times*, 21 February 1947, replicated in *ToP*, vol. ix, No.439.
38 *ToP*, vol. ix, No.452, quoting *Hindustan Times*, 23 February 1947.
39 *ToP*, vol. ix, No.453, statement by Bhopal, 23 February 1947.
40 *ToP*, vol. ix, No.383, Wavell to Pethick-Lawrence, 12 February 1947.
41 Tuker, p.219.
42 Conversations recorded for BBC documentary *India–Pakistan Partition* (2007), edited by Tarun Rajpoot.
43 Bir Bahadur Singh has spoken extensively about his experiences in 1947. In 2007 he was interviewed by the BBC for its documentary on partition; he is also quoted extensively in Urvash Butalia's *The Other Side of Silence*, from where this quote is taken, p.176.
44 *ToP*, vol. ix, No.354, Baldev Singh to Wavell, 6 February 1947.
45 *ToP*, vol. ix, No.366, Jenkins to Pethick-Lawrence, 8 February 1947.
46 *ToP*, vol. ix, No.351, Wavell to Attlee, 5 February 1947.
47 *ToP*, vol. ix, No.417, Mountbatten to Wavell, 18 February 1947.
48 *ToP*, vol. ix, No.392, Wavell to Mountbatten, 14 February 1947.
49 Hamid, *Disastrous Twilight*, p.133.
50 Hamid, *Disastrous Twilight*, p.133.
51 Christie, *Morning Drum*, p.98.
52 Christie, p.95.
53 Schofield, p.377.
54 *ToP*, vol. ix, No.460, Wavell to HM the King, 24 February 1947.

Chapter 3: March

1 The Akalis were Sikhs who believed in reforming their temples, gurdwaras, and should not be confused with the highly militarised *nihangs* who are often referred to as *akalis* in accounts of 1947.

2 *ToP*, vol. x, No.566, Jenkins to Mountbatten, 30 April 1947.

3 *ToP*, vol. ix, No.476, Jenkins to Wavell, 3 March 1947.

4 *ToP*, vol. ix, No.481, Jenkins to Pethick-Lawrence, 4 March 1947.

5 *ToP*, vol. ix, No.490, Jenkins to Wavell, 5 March 1947.

6 *ToP*, vol. ix, No.540, Jenkins to Wavell, 17 March 1947.

7 Urvash Butalia, *The Other Side of Silence*, p.175.

8 *ToP*, vol. ix, No.560, Messervy to Auchinleck, 22 March 1947.

9 *ToP*, vol. ix, No.560, Messervy to Auchinleck, 22 March 1947.

10 Bir Bahadur Singh related this sad story to the BBC for its 2007 documentary; see note 43 for Chapter 2 above. It is also recounted in detail by Urvash Butalia in *The Other Side of Silence*, pp.179–80.

11 *ToP*, vol. ix, No.501, Jenkins to Wavell, 7 March 1947.

12 *ToP*, vol. ix, No.540, Jenkins to Wavell, 17 March 1947.

13 Bristow, *Memories of the British Raj*, p.146.

14 *ToP*, vol. ix, No.513, Jenkins to Wavell, 9 March 1947.

15 *ToP*, vol. ix, No.560, Messervy to Auchinleck, 22 March 1947.

16 *ToP*, vol. ix, No.513, Jenkins to Wavell, 9 March 1947.

17 Seal, *Emergence of Indian Nationalism*, p.302.

18 V. P. Menon interviewed by Henry Hodson, 12 September 1964.

19 *ToP*, vol. x, No.11, Nehru to Mountbatten, 24 March 1947.

20 V. P. Menon interviewed by Henry Hodson, 12 September 1964.

21 Hamid, *Disastrous Twilight*, p.57.

22 Sarojini Naidu, *Mohomed Ali Jinnah: An Ambassador of Unity*, quoted by Sheela Reddy in *Mr and Mrs Jinnah*, p.17.

23 Jalal, *The Sole Spokesman*, p.38.

24 Jalal, p.42.

25 There were 16 annas to one rupee.

26 *ToP*, vol. x, No.11, Nehru to Mountbatten, 24 March 1947.

27 Jalal, p.48.

28 Jalal, p.49.

29 Jalal, p.57.

30 *ToP*, vol. x, No.30, Cabinet Minutes, 28 March 1947.

31 Geoffrey Lamarque, quoted by kind permission of his family. There is a copy of his interview in the *British Voices from South Asia* Series in the T. Harry Williams Centre for Oral History, Louisiana State University.

32 HMSO, Cmnd 6019, 23 May 1939.

33 Spear, p.235.

34 Schofield, p.371.

35 *ToP*, vol. ix, No.559, Wavell's Farewell Broadcast Press Release, 22 March 1947.
36 Hamid, *Disastrous Twilight*, p.150.
37 Lieutenant Colonel Paddy Massey's personal recollections, 'Life of an Indian Cavalry Officer', were given to the author by his son, Colonel Hamon Massey. Paddy Massey was also interviewed in the Imperial War Museum's Oral History series, IWM No.19975.
38 Quoted by Collins & Lapierre in *Freedom at Midnight*, p.94.
39 *ToP*, vol. x, No.8, Mountbatten's swearing-in address, 24 March 1947.
40 *ToP*, vol. ix, No.543, Attlee to Mountbatten, 18 March 1947.
41 *Freedom at Midnight* was first published in the United Kingdom by William Collins in 1975. Mountbatten's subsequent interviews with Collins & Lapierre were published in *Mountbatten and the Partition of India* in 1982.
42 Kushwant Singh interview, BBC World Series. British Library C991/13.
43 Christie, p.98.
44 Christie, p.100.
45 Ismay, *The Memoirs of Lord Ismay*, pp.416–7 and p.435.
46 Christie, p.100.
47 Ismay, p.417.
48 Dr Prem Bhatia interviewed for the BBC, 30 November 1987.
49 *Time* magazine archive, 1962.
50 *ToP*, vol x, No.451, Viceroy's Personal Report No. 7, 15 May 1947.
51 Patel quoted by French in *Liberty or Death*, p.279.
52 Paddy Massey interviewed for the Imperial War Museum's Oral History series, IWM No.19975.
53 *ToP*, vol. x, No.11; Mountbatten's notes of meeting with Nehru, 24 March 1947.
54 Campbell-Johnson, *Mission with Mountbatten*, p.46.
55 V. P. Menon interviewed by Henry Hodson, 12 September 1964.
56 Mountbatten's account of this first meeting is in *ToP*, vol. x, No.37, 31 March 1947.
57 ICHR Part One 1947, No.615, Gandhi to refugees at Pipalwan, 22 March 1947.
58 Patel to Gandhi, 24 March 1947 and quoted by Brown in *Gandhi*, p.369.
59 *ToP*, vol. x, No.47, Mountbatten's meeting with Gandhi, 1 April 1947.
60 *ToP*, vol. x, No.10, Bikaner to Mountbatten, 24 March 1947.
61 *ToP*, vol. x, No.6, Aiyar to Miéville, 23 March 1947.
62 V. P. Menon interviewed by Henry Hodson, 12 September 1964.
63 Auchinleck interviewed by David Dimbleby for the BBC, 21 June 1974.
64 V. P. Menon interviewed by Henry Hodson, 12 September 1964.
65 Hamid, *Disastrous Twilight*, p.152.
66 *ToP* vol. x, No.50, Mountbatten's meeting with Auchinleck, 1 April 1947.

Chapter 4: April

1   Christie, p.63.
2   Minto, diary entry for Thursday 19 April.
3   There is a good description of what a typical District Officer's visit to a village was like in Moon, *Strangers in India*, pp.22–9.
4   Geoffrey Lamarque's comments are reproduced by kind permission of his family.
5   Christie, pp.38–62.
6   Judge H. C. Beaumont interviewed about 1947. Record in British Library C63/89-93. Permission to quote from this interview has been kindly granted by his family.
7   Notes given to the author by J. P. Cross, 1st Battalion King George V's Own Gurkha Rifles (The Malaun Regiment), 24 May 2016.
8   Ismay, p.415.
9   Bew, *Citzen Clem*, p.187.
10 Bew, p.285.
11 Bew, p.436.
12 Bew, p.434.
13 Bew, p.438.
14 *ToP*, vol. x, No.59, Mountbatten's Personal Report, 2 April 1947.
15 ICHR Part One 1947. No.872; *Hindustan Times*, 1 April 1947.
16 *ToP*, vol. x, No.84, notes of Mountbatten's meeting with Jinnah, 5 April 1947.
17 *ToP*, vol. x, No.92; Liaquat's letter is No.94. Both 7 April 1947.
18 *ToP*, vol. x, No.101, Mountbatten and Jinnah's third meeting, 8 April 1947.
19 *ToP*, vol. x, No.87, minutes of the viceroy's staff meeting, 6 April 1947.
20 *ToP*, vol. x, No.119, minutes of the viceroy's staff meeting, 11 April 1947.
21 *ToP*, vol. x, No.124, Miéville notes on meeting with Jinnah, 11 April 1947.
22 *ToP*, vol. x, No.126, Mountbatten's meeting with Liaquat, 11 April 1947.
23 *ToP*, vol. x, No.120, Ismay to Menon, 11 April 1947.
24 Ismay, p.425.
25 *ToP*, vol. x, No.139, Covering Note for Governors' Conference, 15 April 1947.
26 Tuker, p.275, which also describes the disturbances in the United Provinces.
27 Figures taken from Erskine-Crum's notes from the viceroy's staff meeting, *ToP*, vol. x, No.195, 20 April 1947.
28 *ToP*, vol. x, No.139, Tyson, 15 April 1947; and *ToP*, vol. x, No. 264, Burrows to Mountbatten, 1 May 1947.
29 *ToP*, vol. x, No.139, Nye to Tyson, 15 April 1947; and *ToP*, vol. x, No.163, Suhrawardy to Shone, 16 April 1947.
30 *ToP*, vol. x, No.163, Shone meeting with Suhrawardy, 16 April 1947.
31 *ToP*, vol. x, No.139, Covering Note for Governors' Conference, 15 April 1947.

32 *ToP*, vol. X, No.160, Jenkins to Mountbatten, 16 April 1947.
33 See Jalal, pp.163–8 for full coverage of the Sind elections.
34 *ToP*, vol. x, No.149, Mountbatten meeting with Mudie, 15 April 1947.
35 *ToP*, vol. x, No.139, Covering Note for Governors' Conference, 15 April 1947.
36 Hodson, *The Great Divide*, p.284.
37 Mitchell's comments, and those that follow, come from his autobiography *The Quiet People of India*, which is available as an audiobook although I cannot find it in print anywhere. The events of April 1947 are at the end of Part Two.
38 N. Mukherji interviewed for Imperial War Museum's Oral History series, IWM No.14661.
39 Edward Behr, *Bearings*, p.44.
40 Behr, pp.39 and 51.
41 Hodson, p.278.
42 The minutes of this meeting are in *ToP*, vol. X, No.171, dated 18 April 1947.
43 *ToP*, vol. x, No.122, Mountbatten's meeting with de la Fargue, 11 April 1947.
44 ICHR 1947, Part One, No.1087.
45 *ToP*, vol. x, No.247, Scott to Abell, 28 April 1947.
46 *ToP*, vol. x, No.250, Mountbatten's report on visit to NWFP, 28 April 1947.
47 Mitchell, see Note 36 above.
48 ICHR 1947, Part One, No.1096, dated 30 April 1947.
49 *ToP*, vol. x, No.138, meeting between Mountbatten and Auchinleck, 14 April 1947.
50 *ToP*, vol. x, No.109, Jenkins to Mountbatten, 9 April 1947.
51 Ismay, p.420.
52 *ToP*, vol. x, No.121, Mountbatten meeting with Rajagopalachari, 11 April 1947.
53 *ToP*, vol. x, No.264, viceroy's staff meeting, 1 May 1947.
54 Ismay, p.417.
55 *ToP*, vol. x, No.159, Jinnah to Shone, 16 April 1947.
56 *ToP*, vol. x, No.221, Jinnah to Mountbatten, 26 April 1947.
57 For a full breakdown of centrally retained powers see Jalal, p.261.
58 Jalal, p.245.
59 Jalal, p.262.

Chapter 5: May

1 *ToP*, vol. x, No.200, Menon to Mountbatten, 22 April 1947.
2 *ToP*, vol. x, No.169, Menon to Mountbatten, 17 April 1947.
3 *ToP*, vol. x, No.211, Mountbatten to Nehru, 24 April 1947.
4 *ToP*, vol. x, No.165, Mountbatten's Personal Report, 16 April 1947.

5 Collins & Lapierre, *Mountbatten and the Partition of India*, p.30.
6 ICHR, Part One, 1947, No.890, Saha to Prasad, 4 May 1947.
7 Tuker, p.282.
8 ICHR, *Towards Freedom*, 1947, Part 1, pp.1266 and 1270.
9 Tuker covers the Gurgaon disturbances in detail; chapter XXVII.
10 *ToP*, vol. x, No.558, Liaquat to Mountbatten, 30 May 1947.
11 ICHR, *Towards Freedom*, 1947, Part 1, p.1266.
12 *ToP*, vol. x, No.222, Ismay to Mountbatten, 25 April 1947.
13 Full details of the plan are in *ToP*, vol. x, No.222, 25 April 1947, and No.260, 30 April 1947.
14 Hodson, p.293.
15 *ToP*, vol. x, No.267, Nehru to Mountbatten, 1 May 1947.
16 *ToP*, vol. x, No.276, Viceroy's Personal Report, 1 May 1947.
17 Figures taken from Wilkinson, *Army and Nation*, p.47.
18 D. K. Palit interviewed for the BBC Sound Archive. British Library R193/9.
19 *The Chatfield Report* is in the British Library IOR/L/MIL/17/5/1802.
20 Figures taken from Wilkinson, p.65.
21 Wilkinson, p.75.
22 Strength Returns of Indian Armed Forces, British Library IOR/L/MIL/175/1801.
23 Wilkinson, p.79, quoting Willcox Committee 1945, Section 157, paras 2–3.
24 Evan Charlton interviewed for *Plain Tales from the Raj*, British Library Sound Archive C1398/1833.
25 Spike Milligan, *Plain Tales from the Raj*, British Library Sound Archive C1398/1833.
26 The report is in the British Library IOR/L/MIL/17/5/1801.
27 *The Chatfield Report*, Appendix III.
28 Lieutenant Colonel Denis de Grouchy Lambert interviewed by Margaret Macdonald, 4 September 1984.
29 Tuker, p.293.
30 Strength Returns of Indian Armed Forces and British Forces in India, 1 July 1947. British Library IOR/L/MIL/17/5/1451.
31 Strength Return of Indian Armed Forces and British Forces in India, 1 July 1947. British Library IOR/L/MIL/17/5/1451.
32 ICHR, *Towards Freedom*, Part 3, 1943–4, Chapter XVI, No.33.
33 ICHR, *Towards Freedom*, Part 3, 1943–4, Chapter XVI, No.40.
34 ICHR, *Towards Freedom*, Part 3, 1943–4, Chapter XVI, No.7.
35 ICHR, *Towards Freedom*, Part 2, 1943–4, Chapter XVI, No.76.
36 ICHR, *Towards Freedom*, Part 3, 1943–4, Chapter XVI, p.2677.
37 D. K. Palit interviewed for the BBC Sound Archive. British Library R193/9.
38 ICHR, *Towards Freedom*, Part 3, 1943–4, Chapter XV, Nos.5 and 29.
39 Gandhi to Wavell, 9 March 1944. ICHR, *Towards Freedom*, Part 3, 1943–4, Chapter XVI, Nos.307 and 417.

40 Nehru, *An Autobiography*, p.159.
41 Wilkinson, pp.101–2.
42 Wilkinson, p.57.
43 Jinnah Papers, National Archive of Pakistan, First Series, vol. 1, Part 1. No.420.
44 Ismay, p.415.
45 Hamid, *Disastrous Twilight*, p.167.
46 The minutes of the Cabinet committee meeting are in *ToP*, vol. x, No.320, 5 May 1947.
47 *ToP*, vol. x, No.290, minutes of the viceroy's staff meeting, 3 May 1947.
48 The minutes of the meeting are in *ToP*, vol. x, No.350, 8 May 1947.
49 Gandhi's letter is in *ToP*, vol. x, No.348, 8 May 1947.
50 Patel's AP interview is in *ToP*, vol. x, No.375.
51 *ToP*, vol. x, No.451, Mountbatten's Personal Report No.7, 15 May 1947.
52 *ToP*, vol. x, No.422, Ismay to Mountbatten, 13 May 1947.
53 Collins & Lapierre, *Mountbatten and the Partition of India*, p.57.
54 *ToP*, vol. x, No.402, Nehru to Mountbatten, 11 May 1947.
55 *ToP*, vol. x, No.414, Minutes of Viceroy's Staff Meeting,12 May 1947.
56 *ToP*, vol. x, No.406, Note by Nehru, 11 May 1947.
57 *ToP*, vol. x, No.431, Ismay to Mountbatten, 14 May 1947.
58 *ToP*, vol x, No.428, Attlee to Mountbatten, 13 May 1947.
59 Suhrawardy's correspondence is in *ToP*, vol. x, Nos.462 and 487, 16 and 19 May 1947.
60 *ToP*, vol. x, No.471, Nehru to Mountbatten, 17 May 1947.
61 *ToP*, vol. x, No.472, Interview Mountbatten, Nehru and Patel, 17 May 1947.
62 Mountbatten's meeting with him is recorded in *ToP*, vol. x, No.513, 22 May 1947.

Chapter 6: June

1 *ToP*, vol. xi, No.11, Liaquat to Mountbatten, 31 May 1947.
2 *ToP*, vol. xi, No.232, Liaquat to Mountbatten, 12 June 1947.
3 *ToP*, vol. xi, No.232, Liaquat to Mountbatten, 12 June 1947, and No.234, Ismay to Ghazanfar Ali Khan, 17 Jun 1947.
4 *ToP*, vol. xi, No.254, Mountbatten to Ismay, 18 June 1947.
5 *ToP*, vol. xi, No.274, Auchinleck to Ismay, 20 June 1947.
6 Tuker describes the Gurgaon troubles in detail, chapter XXVII.
7 *ToP*, vol. xi, No.12, Jenkins to Mountbatten, 31 May 1947.
8 *ToP*, vol. xi, No.300, Nehru to Mountbatten, 22 June 1947.
9 For a full study of the Canal Colonies, which were a fascinating agricultural and social experiment, see Indu Agnihotri's 1996 paper, 'Ecology, Land Use and Colonisation: The Canal Colonies of the Punjab', Centre for Women's Development Studies.

10 Kirpalani, *Fifty Years with the British*, pp.309–10.
11 Ismay, p.422.
12 Ismay, p.422, and *ToP*, vol. xi, No.23, for the full text.
13 Erskine Crum's full minutes of this historic meeting are in *ToP*, vol. xi, No.23, dated 2 June 1947.
14 *ToP*, vol. xi, No.24, Gandhi to Mountbatten, 2 June 1947.
15 V. P. Menon interviewed by Henry Hodson for the BBC 1964.
16 Ismay, p.424.
17 *ToP*, vol. xi, No.28, Administrative Consequences of Partition, 2 June 1947.
18 Mountbatten's broadcast, re-agreed with Downing Street, is in *ToP*, vol. xi, No.44, dated 3 June 1947.
19 Nehru's broadcast is in *ToP*, vol. xi, No.41, and part reproduced by Hodson, p.315.
20 Hamid, *Disastrous Twilight*, p.177.
21 For good coverage of the broadcasts see Hodson, p.315, and *ToP*, vol. xi, Nos.41–8.
22 Tuker, p.583.
23 Tuker, p.302.
24 Christie, p.102.
25 The best account of these tortuous negotiations is in Hodson, pp.318–9. They are less well covered in *ToP*.
26 Lieutenant Colonel Paddy Massey, MC, 'Life of an Indian Cavalry Officer', October 1993, private manuscript.
27 Prem Bhatia interviewed for the BBC, 30 November 1987.
28 A. K. Damodaran interviewed by the BBC, 1988. British Library Sound Archive R193/8.
29 *ToP*, vol. xi, No.164, Attlee to Major Adeane, 12 June 1947.
30 *ToP*, vol. xi, No.182, Listowel to Mountbatten, 13 Jun 1947.
31 Reuters reporting 23 June 1947.
32 The full breakdown of the results is in *ToP*, vol. xi, No.278 for Bengal and No.304 for the Punjab.
33 *ToP*, vol. x, No.547, India Office Paper on the Division of the Armed Forces, 27 May 1947.
34 *ToP*, vol. xi, No.217, Partition Council, 16 June 1947.
35 *ToP*, vol. xi, No.416, Partition Council, dated 30 June 1947 and vol. xii, No.77, dated 11 July 1947.
36 J. G. Pocock, *History of 19th King George V's Own Lancers*, p.92.
37 D. K. Dalit interviewed by the BBC. British Library Sound Archive R193.
38 *ToP*, vol. xi, No.39, Viceroy's Meeting, 3 June 1947, and No.217, Meeting Special Committee of the Indian Cabinet, dated 16 June 1947.
39 *ToP*, vol. xi, No.312, Note by Auchinleck, 23 June 1947.
40 *ToP*, vol. xi, No.369, Viceroy's Personal Report No.10, 27 June 1947.
41 *ToP*, vol. xi, No.312, Auchinleck minute, dated 23 June 1947.

42 Wilkinson, p.9,1 and *ToP*, vol. xi, No.388, Nehru's meeting with Montgomery, 24 June 1947.

43 J. P. Cross, manuscript in possession of the author.

44 *ToP*, vol. xi, No.329, Montgomery's meeting with Jinnah, 24 June 1947.

45 *ToP*, vol. xi, No.358, Auchinleck to Mountbatten, 26 June 1947.

46 *ToP*, vol. xi, No.506, Viceroy's Personal Report, 4 July 1947.

47 *ToP*, vol. xi, No.274, Auchinleck to Ismay, 20 June 1947.

48 *ToP*, vol. xi, No.441, Listowel to Attlee, and No. 445, Churchill to Attlee, dated 1 July 1947.

49 *ToP*, vol. xi, No.450, Vellodi to Nehru, 1 July 1947.

50 *ToP*, vol. xi, No.164, Attlee to HM the King, 12 June 1947.

51 *ToP*, vol. xi, No.387, Mountbatten to Webb, 28 June 1947.

52 *ToP*, vol. xi, No.319, Mountbatten to Nehru, 24 June 1947.

53 *ToP*, vol. xi, No.96, Mountbatten to Caroe, 6 June 1947.

54 *ToP*, vol. xi, No.61, Nehru to Mountbatten, 4 June 1947.

55 *ToP*, vol. xi, No.311, Mountbatten to Jinnah, 23 June 1947.

56 Hodson, p.331.

57 Erskine-Crum's paper is reproduced by Hodson, p.333.

Chapter 7: July

1   Singh Chopra, *1947: A Soldier's Story*, p.15.

2   For a full account of the Sylhet Referendum operation, see Singh Chopra, pp.25–54.

3   *ToP*, vol. xi, No.369, dated 27 June 1947.

4   Moon, *Strangers in India*, p.72.

5   Moon, *Strangers in India*, p.76.

6   Quoted by Moon in *Strangers in India*, p.80.

7   Morrow, *Highness*, p.10.

8   Moon, *Divide and Quit*, p.97. Much of the following information about Bahawalpur comes from Chapter VI.

9   Moon, *Divide and Quit*, p.101.

10 ICHR 1947, Part 2, Chapter 38, No.1.

11 *ToP*, vol. xii, No.234, Press Communique, 25 July 1947.

12 Hodson, p.356.

13 Hodson, p.357.

14 *ToP*, vol. xi, No.369, Viceroy's Personal Report No.10, dated 27 June 1947.

15 *ToP*, vol. xii, No.228, Viceroy's Personal Report No.14, dated 25 July 1947.

16 *ToP*, vol. xii, No.201, Bhopal to Mountbatten, 22 July 1947.

17 *ToP*, vol. xii, No.228, Viceroy's Personal Report No.14, dated 25 July 1947.

18 His accession letter is in *ToP*, vol. xii, No.284, dated 30 July 1947.

19 Hodson, p.376.

20 Copland, *The Princes of India in the Endgame of Empire*, p.229.

21 *ToP*, vol. xii, No.317, Listowel to Mountbatten, 1 August 1947.

22 *ToP*, vol. xii, No.264, Herbert to Mountbatten, 29 July 1947.

23 *ToP*, vol. xi, No.112, Monckton to Mountbatten, 9 June 1947.

24 *ToP*, vol. xii, No.390, Monckton to Churchill, 9 August 1947.

25 The violence in Rampur is described in ICHR, 1947, Part 2, Chapter 43, Nos.1 and 3.

26 Singh, *The House of Marwar*, p.179.

27 Hodson, p.380.

28 Singh, p.181.

29 Recounted to the author by Dhananajaya Singh, Hanwant Singh's descendant, and also recorded in *ToP*, vol. xii, No.489, dated 16 August 1947.

30 For good coverage of the Qalat issue see Dr Yaqoob Khan Bangash, *A Princely Affair: Accession and Integration of Princely States in Pakistan 1947–55*.

31 *ToP*, vol. xii, No.265, Mountbatten to Dholpur, 29 July 1947.

32 ICHR, 1947, Part 2, Chapter 40, No.35, Gandhi addressing a Prayer Meeting on 29 July 1947.

33 Morrow, p.8.

34 Copland, p.236.

35 ICHR, 1947, Part 2, Chapter 38, No.55.

36 ICHR, 1947, Part 2, Chapter 40, No.35, Gandhi addressing a Prayer Meeting on 29 July 1947.

37 *ToP*, vol. xii, No.302, Viceroy's Personal Report, 1 August 1947.

38 *ToP*, vol. xii, No.302, Viceroy's Personal Report, 1 August 1947.

39 *ToP*, vol. xi, No.229, Nehru set out his thoughts on Kashmir in a long memo to the viceroy on 17 June 1947, from which all these quotes are taken.

40 *ToP*, vol. xii, No.262, Minutes by Henderson and Rumbold, 28 July 1947, and No.263, India Office Minute, 28 July 1947.

41 *ToP*, vol. xii, No. 340, Mountbatten to Listowel, 4 August 1947.

42 *ToP*, vol. xi, No.162, Viceroy's Personal Report No.9, dated 12 June 1947.

43 *ToP*, vol. xii, No.272, Jenkins to Mountabtten, 29 July 1947, and No.292, Jenkins to Mountbatten, 30 July 1947.

44 *ToP*, vol. xii, No.148, Auchinleck to Partition Council, 17 July 1947.

45 The Punjab Boundary Force's composition is detailed in Rees's Post Operational Report held by Sussex University Library, SxMs 16 Rees Papers No.1.

46 The Intelligence Summaries are in the British Library IOR/L/MIL/17/5/4276.

47 The order is in *ToP*, vol. xii, No.267, dated 29 July 1947.

48 *ToP*, vol. xii, No.169, Listowel to Mountbatten, dated 18 July 1947.

49 *ToP*, vol. xii, No.302, Viceroy's Personal Report, 1 August 1947.

50 *ToP*, vol. xii, Nos.287, Minutes of Viceroy's Miscellanuous Meeting, 30 July 1947, and No.302, Viceroy's Personal Report No.15, 1 August 1947.

Chapter 8: August

1   Christie, p.63.
2   Christopher Beaumont, 'The Partition of India', private papers in possession of his son.
3   Christopher Beaumont, *A Judge Remembers*, Andrew Roberts, BBC Radio 4, IWM 14577/2/1-2.
4   See Note 2 above.
5   Beaumont interviewed by a luckless Belgian interviewer, whom he treated roughly, for an unknown radio programme. British Library Sound Archive C63/89-93 and quoted by kind permission of the Beaumont family.
6   *ToP*, vol. xii, No.337, Jenkins to Mountbatten, dated 4 August 1947.
7   *ToP*, vol. xii, No.345, Punjab CID Report, dated 5 August 1947.
8   Kirpalani, pp.319-21.
9   Letter, dated 7 August 1947, Rees Papers, Sussex University Library, SxMs 16/2.
10 Report of the Punjab Boundary Force, 15 November 1947. British Library IOR/L/MIL/17/5/4319.
11 Moon, *Divide and Quit*, pp.95-6.
12 *ToP*, vol. xii, No. 459, Jenkins to Mountbatten, 13 August 1947; No.484, dated 13 August 1947; and No.448, dated 12 August 1947.
13 Hawthorn's report is in *ToP*, vol. xii, No.432, dated 11 August 1947.
14 V. P. Menon interviewed by Henry Hodson, BBC Radio, 12 September 1964.
15 Tuker, p.407.
16 The *Daily Telegraph* published an account of this incident in February 1992 based on Beaumont's papers. He wrote two accounts, 'The Partition of India' and 'The Truth of the Partition of the Punjab in August 1947'. Both have been kindly made available to the author by his son, Robert Beaumont. Originally deposited in All Souls, Christopher Beaumont decided to publish when Mountbatten's Private Secretary, Sir George Abell, died in 1989, the only other man whom he thought knew the true story. Beaumont had also made his papers available to his grandson who was reading history at Oxford; he reproduced his grandfather's account in his exam papers only to be marked down. 'It is a mistake', Christopher Beaumont noted, 'to know more about the subject than the examiners.'
17 For fuller public coverage of the Ferozepore issue, listen to Christopher Beaumont, *A Judge Remembers*, Andrew Roberts, BBC Radio 4, IWM 14577/2/1-2.
18 *ToP*, vol. xii, No.489, Viceroy's Personal Report, 16 August 1947.
19 Christie, p.106.
20 Hamid, *Disastrous Twilight*, pp.225-6
21 Hamid, *Disastrous Twilight*, pp.228-9
22 Christie, p.106.

23 *ToP*, vol. xii, No.489, Viceroy's Personal Report, dated 16 August 1947.

24 *The Times*, 15 August 1947.

25 Hamid, *Disastrous Twilight*, p.229.

26 Kushwant Singh interviewed by the BBC World Service British Library Sound Archive C991/13.

27 Kushwant Singh, C991/13.

28 *Daily Telegraph*, 15 August 1947.

29 Collins & Lapierre, *Freedom at Midnight*, p.317.

30 *Daily Telegraph*, 15 August 1947.

31 Ismay, pp.434–5.

32 *ToP*, vol. xii, No.489, Mountbatten to Listowel, 16 August 1947.

33 Tuker, p.413.

34 *Daily Telegraph*, 15 August 1947.

35 *The Times*, 15 August 1947.

36 J. P. Cross's personal reminiscences shared with the author.

37 Behr, pp.54–7.

38 Pocock, p.92.

39 Hamid, *Disastrous Twilight*, pp.220–1.

40 Collins & Lapierre, *Freedom at Midnight*, p.323.

41 The Radcliffe Awards are reproduced in full in *ToP*, vol. xii, No.488, dated 12 August 1947.

42 The minutes of the Boundary Commissions Award Conference are at *ToP*, vol. xii, No.487, dated 16 August 1947.

43 Quoted in BBC documentary *India-Pakistan Partition 1947* (2007), edited by Tarun Rajpoot.

44 See Note 16 above.

45 PBF Post Operation Report, 15 November 1947, p.9. British Library, IOR/L/ MIL/17/5/4319.

46 Bristow, p.153.

47 Abdul Haq talking to BBC Radio 4 in 2000. Imperial War Museum Sound Archive 31490. In 1961 he came to England to find an older brother and ended up living in Leeds.

48 Rees's notes taken at the conference; SxMs16, 15 August 1947.

49 Bristow, p.163.

50 Bristow, p.165.

51 Moon, *Divide and Quit*, pp.134–5.

52 Collins & Lapierre, *Freedom at Midnight*, p.361.

53 Collins & Lapierre, *Freedom at Midnight*, p.363.

54 Taken from Collins & Lapierre, *Freedom at Midnight*, pp.367–8.

55 John Moores talking in BBC documentary *India-Pakistan Partition 1947* (2007).

56 Naffese Chohan, a retired shopkeeper from Nottingham, talking to BBC Radio Cleveland. British Library Sound Archive C900/01580.

57 Kirpalani, p.342.
58 BBC documentary *India-Pakistan Partition 1947* (2007).
59 Rees Papers, SxMs 16, Notebook, 27 August 1947.
60 Rees Papers SxMs 16, Notebook, 25 August 1947.
61 Bristow, p.168.
62 Rees Papers, SxMs16, 25 August 1947.
63 Rees Papers, SxMs 16, 30 August 1947.
64 Rees Papers, SxMs 16, 27 August 1947.
65 Punjab Boundary Force Post Operation Report, 15 November 1947, p.18. British Library IOR/L/MIL/17/5/4319.

Chapter 9: September

1   Tuker, p.427, after talking to employers in Calcutta.
2   Tuker p. 427.
3   *Indian Express*, 1 July 1997, Gopal Mukherjee interviewed by Andrew Whitehead.
4   The 1 September Calcutta riot is well covered by Tuker, pp.424–8, from where these quotes are taken.
5   Singh Chopra, pp.55–6.
6   V. P. Menon quoted by Singh Chopra, p.57.
7   Paddy Massey interview, IWM Sound Archive 19975.
8   Kirpalani, p.330.
9   Kirpalani, p.331.
10 Ismay, pp.434–6.
11 Hamid, *Disastrous Twilight*, p.244.
12 James Cameron interviewed. British Library Sound Archive C1398/1368.
13 Ismay, p.438.
14 Behr, pp.59–63.
15 Hamid, *Disastrous Twilight*, p.246.
16 *Guardian*, 1 September 1947.
17 Christopher Beaumont, *A Judge Remembers*, Andrew Roberts, BBC Radio 4, IWM 14577/2/1-2.
18 Tuker, p.495.
19 Tuker, p.494.
20 Dhillon talking on BBC documentary *India-Pakistan Partition 1947* (2007).
21 Moon, *Divide and Quit*, p.217.
22 Gurdeep Singh interviewed for the Amritsar Partition Museum.
23 Maynard Hastings Pockson, interviewed by Conrad Wood. Imperial War Museum Sound Archive 10632.
24 Kirpalani, pp.328–9.
25 Singh Chopra, p.201.
26 Ismay, p.441.

27 Tuker quoting a Dogra officer, pp.486–7.
28 Bristow, p.182.
29 Ismay, pp.438–9.
30 Lawrence James, *Raj*, p.637.
31 British Library Sound Archive C900/01580.
32 British Library IOR/L/MIL/17/5/4319, p.32.
33 Hamid, *Disastrous Twilight*, p.239, quoting *Hindustan Times*, 27 August 1947.
34 Bristow, p.168, quoting Humphrey Evans's *Thimayya of India: A Soldier's Life*.
35 Auchinleck to Mountbatten, dated 13 September 19. Quoted by Hamid in *Disastrous Twilight*, pp.249–50.
36 Alexander Greenwood, *Field Marshal Auchinleck*.
37 Mountbatten to Auchinleck, 26 September 1947, quoted by Hamid, *Disastrous Twilight*, pp.254–8.
38 Hamid, *Disastrous Twilight*, p.265.
39 Tuker, pp.455–9, quoting press reports.
40 Ismay, p.442.
41 Tuker, p.453.
42 Bolitho, p.200, quoting Messervy.
43 Tuker, p.455.
44 *Hindustan Standard*, 26 September 1947.
45 Hansard, 27 September 1947.

Chapter 10: October

1 Bolitho, *Jinnah*, p.209.
2 Birnie's proper name was Colonel Eugene St John Birnie, Guides Cavalry (Frontier Force), born 1900.
3 Bolitho, p.213. Bolitho's is an engaging account. He was evidently very fond of Jinnah and he does occasionally stray into hagiography.
4 Bolitho, p.197.
5 Bolitho, p.198.
6 Alice Faiz interviewed in Lahore, 11 October 1995, by Andrew Whitehead. SOAS Library, India: A People Partitioned OA3.
7 Saleem Siddiqi interviewed by the BBC. British Library Sound Archive C900.
8 Moon, *Divide and Quit*, pp.228–9.
9 Symonds, *The Making of Pakistan*, pp.99–100.
10 Chatterji, *The Spoils of Partition*, p.159.
11 The most important studies are by Professor Joya Chatterji whose *The Spoils of Partition* (Cambridge, 2007) is the determining work.
12 Hodson, p.420.
13 Ghosh, *The Moments of Bengal Partition*, pp.12 and 27.

14 Exact figures remain hard to determine. Those given here come from the respective Indian and Pakistani censuses of 1951, corroborated by Chatterji, pp.105–6.
15 From Islam, *A Bangladesh Village*.
16 Ghosh, *The Moments of Bengal Partition*, p.186.
17 Chatterji, *The Spoils of Partition*, p.113.
18 Sengupta, p.119.
19 K. N. Dalal, AP, 16 October 1947, quoted by Ghosh, *The Moments of Bengal Partition*, p.42.
20 Chatterji, *The Spoils of Partition*, pp.171–2.
21 Ghosh, *The Moments of Bengal Partition*, p.61.
22 Ghosh, *The Moments of Bengal Partition*, p.75.
23 Tuker, pp.476–7.
24 Symonds, p.145.
25 Symonds, p.153.
26 Nehru quoted by BBC, 27 March 1947.
27 Figures given by Andrew Whitehead, *A Mission in Kashmir*, p.33.
28 Kirpalani, p.339.
29 This story is recounted in much more detail by Moon, *Divide and Quit*, pp.231–7.
30 Jinnah quoted by Hassan, *Impact of Partition*, p.35.
31 Singh Chopra, pp.221–2.
32 Singh Chopra, p.223.
33 Kharaiti Lal interviewed by Andrew Whitehead, 17 March 1997. SOAS Library OA3, India: A People Partitioned.
34 *Indian Express*, 1 August 1997; 'Brutalised and Humiliated' by Andrew Whitehead.
35 Singh Chopra, p.243.
36 Hodson, p.427.
37 Hodson, p.437.
38 Hodson, p.439.
39 Hodson, p.439.

Chapter 11: November

1 Whitehead, p.198.
2 Symonds, p.156.
3 Whitehead, p.34.
4 Whitehead, p.26.
5 Whitehead, p.27.
6 Whitehead, p.23.
7 Whitehead, p.47.
8 Quoted by Whitehead, pp.62–3.

9   Whitehead, p.107.
10 Hodson, pp.450–1.
11 Governor General's Personal Report No.5, dated 7 November 1947.
12 From papers in the Indian Ministry of Defence's 'History of Operations in Jammu and Kashmir 1947–48' and quoted by Whitehead, p.116.
13 Hodson, p.449.
14 Hamid, *At The Forward Edge of Battle*, the history of Pakistan's Armoured Corps. There is a full description of 11th Cavalry's operations on p. 578.
15 Mountbatten quoted by Whitehead, p.138.
16 Hodson, p.507.
17 Hodson, p.432.
18 Hodson, p.433.
19 Bolitho, p.209.
20 Hamid, *Disastrous Twilight*, pp.278–9.
21 Hamid, *Disastrous Twilight*, p.278.
22 Hodson, p.458.
23 Governor general's Personal Report No.5, dated 7 November 1947.
24 Father Shanks's account is taken from *A Mission in Kashmir* by Andrew Whitehead, to whom I am most grateful for his permission to draw so extensively on his research.
25 Quoted by Whitehead, p.76.
26 Whitehead, p.78.
27 Whitehead, p.127.
28 Whitehead, p.197.
29 Whitehead, p.132.
30 Interview by Frank Moraes in 1957, quoted by Whitehead, p.135.
31 Whitehead, p.150.
32 Whitehead, p.161.
33 Whitehead, p.160.
34 Whitehead, p.160.
35 Whitehead, p.187.
36 Whitehead, p.189.
37 Major General D. K. Palit interviewed by BBC British Library Sound Archive R193/9.
38 Mountbatten's Personal Report as governor general, No.6.
39 Ismay, p.445.
40 Hodson, p.453.
41 Hamid, *Disastrous Twilight*, p.282. Hamid was present at the conference.
42 Auchinleck interviewed by David Dimbleby, 21 June 1974.

Chapter 12: December

1 Christie, p.110.
2 Details in Hodson, p.418.
3 Hodson, p.418.
4 Kirpalani, p.439.
5 Kirpalani, p.351.
6 Kirpalani, pp.365–7.
7 Hassan, p.36.
8 Chatterji, *Spoils of Partition*, pp.137–8.
9 Moon, *Divide and Quit*, p.258.
10 British Library Sound Archive C900/01580.
11 Imperial War Museum Sound Archive 31490.
12 Mountbatten's Personal Report as governor general, No.8, quoted by Hodson, p.471.
13 V. P. Menon, *The Integration of the Indian States*, p.369.
14 Hodson, p.475.
15 V. P. Menon quoted by Hodson, p.475.
16 Tuker, p.503.
17 Tuker, p.503.
18 Interview with the author, February 2017.
19 Christie, p.114.
20 Mitchell, Chapter 7. There is no page number as this book was only produced as an audiobook.
21 Singh, *The House of Marwar*, p.183.
22 Inder Malhotra interviewed by the BBC. British Library Sound Archive C63/195/11.
23 Kushwant Singh interviewed by the BBC. British Library Sound Archive C991/13.
24 Mountbatten's Personal Report.
25 K. M. Munshi, *The End of an Era*, p.107.
26 Christie, p.118.
27 Hodson, p.420.
28 Figures from Symonds, p.116.
29 Figures from Sen, Chapter 9.
30 Mountbatten's Report on the Last Viceroyalty, September 1948. Reproduced by Hodson, p.548.
31 Roberts, *Eminent Churchillians*, p.127.
32 Roberts, pp.130–1.
33 James, *Raj*, p.637.
34 Ismay, p.445.
35 R. Thapar interviewed by the BBC in 1986. Imperial War Museum Sound Archive 14678-2-1/2.

Notes on the Sources

There is a wealth of material relating to the events of 1947, both in written and oral form. Given that there are not many people left alive who were intimately involved in the politics, it is fortunate that there are literally hundreds of recorded interviews and libraries full of personal recollections. This makes writing about it both easier, in that there is so much to draw on, but also more difficult as one could easily end up writing ten volumes. The problem, as usual, is what to leave out.

There are some key source documents. First, *The Transfer of Power* is a massive twelve-volume compendium of all official correspondence relating to Indian Independence and partition between 1942–7. Published by the British government between 1970 and 1983, it is a godsend for a historian, gathering as it does all the government documents in one well-edited series. However, the researcher should be aware that because Mountbatten tended not to have anyone taking notes in his meetings, instead debriefing his version of what was said afterwards, some of his records should be treated carefully.

Another key set of publications is the Indian Council of Historical Research's multi-volume *Towards Freedom* series. This covers the years 1937 to 1947 and combines both official correspondence with press articles, letters and other documents and therefore offers a wider field than *The Transfer of Power*. There seems to be some doubt as to whether the whole series was actually completed but certainly the volumes I consulted gave comprehensive coverage of 1947 and were invaluable.

Many British official papers that were not important enough to be included in *The Transfer of Power* are held in the British Library, now home to the India Office Records, or in the Public Record Office. The Army headquarters files in the British Library are particularly revealing and I have listed the key ones below. There are equally many very valuable collections in the National Army Museum, the Imperial War Museum, Sussex (Rees Papers) and Southampton (Mountbatten papers) University libraries. In Amritsar the recently opened Partition Museum looks like becoming a most valuable centre for future research.

The British Library holds an extensive oral archive on Indian Independence although it suffers from being held in several different files. I have listed some of the interviews I found most useful but there are hundreds more. Some are copyright-protected, which means they can be referred to but not quoted from at any length. However, the families I contacted to obtain copyright when I did want to quote directly were always happy to allow it. Confusingly some of the interviews are reproduced elsewhere without any copyright restriction, such as Alice Faiz's. Another key source of interview material is Andrew Whitehead's oral archive in the SOAS Library in London and the University of Louisiana Archive in Baton Rouge; again, some of these interviews are copyright-protected and I am most grateful to Andrew Whitehead for his generosity in allowing me to draw on his material and to the Lamarque family for access to their family records in Baton Rouge.

I am particularly grateful to Robert Beaumont for his very kind permission to quote in full from his father, Christopher Beaumont's, personal papers and for so generously copying these to me. These remain private although they formed the basis of an article in the *Daily Telegraph* on the Ferozepore issue in February 1992. They have been invaluable to my research, as has Robert's kind permission to draw in full on his father's copyright-protected interview in the British Library Sound Archive.

Of the other works that cover 1947, I found Henry Hodson's *The Great Divide* particularly useful. Hodson was Reforms Commissioner before V. P. Menon so consequently had a very good understanding of the issues and personalities. It is not necessarily holiday reading but an impressively complete work of scholarship. Patrick French's *Liberty or Death* is equally good, particularly on the road to Independence in the preceding decades. Collins and Lapierre's *Freedom at Midnight*, which seems to have formed the basis for the film *Viceroy's House* is an exciting read but historically doubtful and was largely based on interviews with Mountbatten when his memory was perhaps beginning to fade.

Pakistan and Bengal have, in general, been written about less than India and the Punjab. I am much indebted to Anil Seal and Ayesha Jalal for their thorough work on Jinnah, *The Sole Spokesman*, and to Joya Chatterji for her authoritative works on the partition of Bengal. There is a particular lack of material on Jinnah. What correspondence of his has been released is dry and one can only hope that somewhere in the archives in Karachi or Islamabad there is a wealth of personal papers awaiting publication.

Lastly, I am especially indebted to Andrew Whitehead for his excellent *A Mission in Kashmir*, which contains so much original interview material and which I used as the basis of November. There can be few better books on the subject.

Bibliography

Published Works

Allen, Charles, *Plain Tales from The Raj* (Futura, 1986)
—— *Soldier Sahibs* (Abacus, 2001)
Allen, Charles, Dwivedi, Sharada, *Lives of the Indian Princes* (Century, 1984)
Azad, Maulana Abul Kalam, *India Wins Freedom* (Orient Longmans, 1959)
Bangash, Dr Yaqoob Khan, *A Princely Affair: Accession and Integration of Princely States in Pakistan 1947–55* (OUP, 2016)
Behr, Edward, *Bearings: A Foreign Correspondent's Life Behind the Lines* (Viking, 1978)
Bew, John, *Citizen Clem: A Biography of Attlee* (Riverrun, 2016)
Bolitho, Hector, *Jinnah* (John Murray, 1954)
Bose, Sisir (with Werth & Ayer), *A Beacon Across Asia: A Biography of Subhas Chandra Bose* (Orient Longman, 1973)
Bourke-White, Margaret, *Witness to Life and Freedom* (Roli Books: New Delhi, 2010)
Branson, Clive, *British Soldier in India* (Communist Party, 1944)
Brass, P., *The Politics of India Since Independence* (CUP, 1990)
Bristow, Brigadier R. C. B, *Memories of the British Raj: Soldier in India* (Johnson, 1974)

Brown, Judith, *Gandhi: Prisoner of Hope* (Yale University Press, 1989)
—— *Nehru: A Political Life* (Yale, 2003)
Butalia, Urvashi, *The Other Side of Silence* (Hurst & Co., 2000)
Campbell-Johnson, Alan, *Mission with Mountbatten* (New Age International, 1972)
Chatterji, Professor Joya, *Bengal Divided* (CUP, 1994)
—— *The Spoils of Partition* (CUP, 2007)
Chopra, Major General Mohindar Singh, *1947: A Soldier's Story* (The Military Studies Convention, 1997)
Christie, John, *Morning Drum* (BACSA, 1983)
Collett, Nigel, *The Butcher of Amritsar: General Reginald Dyer* (Hambledon, 2005)
Collins, Larry & Lapierre, Dominique, *Freedom at Midnight* (William Collins, 1975)
—— *Mountbatten and the Partition of India* (Vikas, 1982)
Connell, John, *Auchinleck: A Critical Biography* (Cassell, 1959)
Copland, Ian, *The Princes of India in the Endgame of Empire* (CUP, 1997)
Dalrymple, William, *City of Djinns: A Year in Delhi* (HarperCollins, 1996)
—— *White Mughals* (HarperCollins, 2004)
—— *The Last Mughal: The Fall of a Dynasty, Delhi 1857* (Bloomsbury, 2007)
Davis, Mike, *Late Victorian Holocausts* (Verso, 2002)
Dogra, Rajiv, *Where Borders Bleed: An Insider's Account of Indo-Pak Relations* (Rupa & Co., 2015)
Dwarkadas, *Ten Years to Freedom* (Popular Prakashan, 1968)
Edwardes, Michael, *Nehru: A Political Biography* (Pelican, 1973)
Evans, Humphrey, *Thimayya of India: A Soldier's Life* (Harcourt Brace, 1960)
Fort, Adrian, *Archibald Wavell: The Life and Times of an Imperial Servant* (Jonathan Cape, 2009)
French, Patrick, *Liberty or Death* (HarperCollins, 1997)
Gallagher, John, *The Decline and Fall of the British Empire* (CUP, 1982)

Ghosh, Arun, *The Moments of Bengal Partition: Selections from the Amrita Bazar Patrika 1947–48* (Seribaan, 2010)

Ghosh, Suniti Kumar, *The Tragic Partition of Bengal* (Indian Academy of Social Sciences, 2002)

Greenwood, Alexander, *Field Marshal Auchinleck* (Pentland, 1990)

Gupta, Partha Sarathi, *Towards Freedom: Documents on the Movement for Independence in India* (Indian Council for Historical Research, OUP, 1997)

Hamid, Major General Shahid, *Disastrous Twilight* (Leo Cooper, 1986)

Hamid, Major General Syed Ali, *At the Forward Edge of Battle: A History of the Pakistan Armoured Corps* (Army Press, 2016)

Hardy, Justine, *In the Valley of the Mist: Kashmir's Long War* (Rider, 2001)

Hassan, Amtul, *Impact of Partition: Refugees in Pakistan* (RCSS Policy Studies, 2006)

Heehs, Peter, *India's Freedom Struggle* (OUP, 1998)

Hodson, H. V., *The Great Divide* (OUP, 1985)

Islam, A. K. M. Aminul, *A Bangladesh Village: Conflict and Cohesion* (Schenkmann, 1974)

Ismay, Lord, *The Memoirs of Lord Ismay* (Heinemann, 1960)

Jalal, Ayesha, *The Sole Spokesman: Jinnah, the Muslim League and the Demand for Pakistan* (CUP, 1985)

James, Lawrence, *Raj* (Little, Brown, 1997)

Jha, Raghbendra, *The Indian Economy Sixty Years After Independence* (Palgrave Macmillan, 2008)

Jinnah, Mohammed Ali, *Quaid-i-Azam Jinnah Papers: First Series, 3 volumes*, editor in chief Z. H. Zaidi (National Archives of Pakistan, 1994)

Karnard, Raghu, *Farthest Field: An Indian Story of the Second World War* (Collins, 2014)

Kaul, Chandrika, *Communications, India and the Imperial Experience* (Palgrave, 2014)

Keay, John, *Into India* (John Murray, 1975)

—— *India: A History* (HarperCollins, 2001)

Kesavan, Mukul, *Looking Through Glass* (Vintage, 1996)

Khan, Yasmin, *The Great Partition: The Making of India and Pakistan* (Yale University Press, 2007)

——*The Raj at War: A People's History of India's Second World War* (Bodley Head, 2015)

Khilnani, Sunil, *The Idea of India* (Hamilton, 1997)

Kirpalani, Santdas, *Fifty Years with the British* (Sangam Books, 1993)

Loyd, Annabel (ed.), *Vicereine: The Indian Journal of Mary Minto* (Amazon, 2014)

Mansergh, Nicholas (ed.), *The Transfer of Power 1942–47* (10 volumes) (HMSO, 1970)

Marston, Daniel, *The Indian Army and the End of the Raj* (CUP, 2014)

Mason, Philip, *A Matter of Honour* (Jonathan Cape, 1974)

——*The Men Who Ruled India* (Pan, 1987)

Mason, Philip, Mayo, Katherine, *Mother India* (Blue Ribbon Books, 1927)

Menon V. P., *Integration of the Indian States* (Orient Black Swan, 2014)

——*The Transfer of Power in India*, reprint (Permanent Black, 2017)

Mercado, Stephen C., *The Shadow Warriors of Nakano* (Potomac, 2002)

Mitchell, Norval, *The Quiet People of India* (Coolbeat Audio Books, 2010)

Moon, Edward Penderel, *Strangers in India* (Faber, 1945)

Moon, Penderel, *Divide and Quit: An Eye-witness Account of the Partition of India* (Chatto & Windus, 1961)

Moreland, W. H. & Chatterjee, Atul Chandra, *A Short History of India* (Longman, Green & Co., 1944)

Moreland, W. H., *The Agrarian System of Moslem India* (Reprinted by Oriental Books, 1968)

Morrow, Ann, *Highness: The Maharajahs of India* (Grafton, 1986)

Munshi, K. M., *The End of an Era* (Bharatiya Vida Bhavan Reprint, 2017)

Naipaul, V. S., *An Area of Darkness* (Penguin, 1968)

Nayar, Kuldip, *Wall at Wagah: India-Pakistan Relations* (Gyan, 2003)

Nayar, Kuldip & Noorani, Asif, *Tales of Two Cities* (Roli Books, 2008)

Nehru, Jawaharlal, *An Autobiography* (OUP, 1991)

Nolan, Peter, 'The Causation and Prevention of Famines: A Critique of A. K. Sen', *Journal of Peasant Studies*, 21:1, 1–28

Oborne, Peter, *Wounded Tiger: A History of Cricket in Pakistan* (Simon & Schuster, 2014)

Ohlmeyer, Jane, 'Ireland, India and the British Empire', Studies in People's History, vol.2, issue 2 (2015) 169–88

Oxford Economic Studies, *South Indian Villages*, Vol.1. Edited by Gilbert Slahel (OUP, 1918)

Oxford University Gandhi Group, *India Analysed* (Victor Gollancz, 1934)

Philips, C. H., *The Partition of India 1947: Montague Burton Lecture on International Relations* (Leeds University Press, 1967)

Pocock, J. G., *History of 19th King George V's Own Lancers* (Gale & Polden, 1962)

Reddy, Sheela, *Mr and Mrs Jinnah* (Penguin, 2017)

Roberts, Andrew, *Eminent Churchillians* (Weidenfeld & Nicolson, 1994)

Roy, Asim, 'The High Politics of India's Partition', *Modern Asian Studies*, 24, 2 (1990)

Royle, Trevor, *The Last Days of the Raj* (Michael Joseph, 1989)

Sarila, Narendra Singh, *The Shadow of the Great Game: The Untold Story of India's Partition* (Constable, 2006)

—— *Once a Prince of Sarila* (I. B. Tauris, 2008)

Sarila, Narendra Singh, Sattar, Abdul, *Pakistan's Foreign Policy 1947–2012*, third edition (OUP Pakistan, 2013)

Schofield, Victoria, *Wavell: Soldier and Statesman* (John Murray, 2006)

Seal, Dr Anil, *The Emergence of Indian Nationalism* (CUP, 1968)

Sen, Amartya, *Poverty and Famines: An Essay on Entitlement and Deprivation* (OUP, 1981)

Sengupta, Debjani, *The Partition of Bengal: Fragile Borders and New Identities* (CUP, 2016)

Singh, Dhananajaya, *The House of Marwar* (Roli Books, 1994)

Singh, Jaswant, *Jinnah: India-Partition-Independence* (Rupa, 2009)

Slim, Field Marshal Viscount, *Defeat Into Victory* (Papermac, 1986)

Smith, W. H. Saumarez, *A Young Man's Country: Letters of a Subdivisional Officer of the Indian Civil Service 1936–1937* (Michael Russell, 1977)

Soherwordi, Syed Hussain Shaheed, 'Punjabisation in the British Indian Army 1857–1947 and the Advent of Military Rule in Pakistan', Edinburgh Papers in South Asian Studies, Number 24 (2010)

Spear, Percival, *A History of India: Vol 2* (Pelican, 1965)

Symonds, Richard, *The Making of Pakistan* (Faber & Faber, 1950)

Von Tuzelmann, Alex, *Indian Summer* (Simon & Schuster, 2007)

Tuker, Lt Gen Sir Francis, *While Memory Serves: The Story of the Last Two Years of British Rule in India* (Cassell, 1950)

Warner, Philip, *Auchinleck: The Lonely Soldier* (Sphere, 1982)

Whitehead, Andrew, *A Mission in Kashmir* (Penguin Viking, 2007)

Wilkinson, Steven, *Army and Nation: The Military and Indian Democracy Since Independence* (Harvard, 2015)

Willasley-Wilsey, Tim, 'The Day the Clocks Stopped: The Peshawar Club and Library': victorianweb.org 2014

Wilson, Jon, *India Conquered* (Simon & Schuster, 2016)

Wolpert, Stanley, *Shameful Flight: The Last Years of the British Empire in India* (OUP, 2006)

Ziegler, Philip, *Mountbatten: The Official Biography* (HarperCollins, 1985)

Official Reports and Documents

The Transfer of Power 1942–47, Volumes 1 to 12 (HMSO, 1970)
Indian Council for Historical Research, *Towards Freedom:
    Documents on the Movement for Independence in India*,
    edited by Partha Sarathi Gupta (OUP, 1997)
Jinnah Papers, National Archive of Pakistan, edited by Z. H. Zaidi

In British Library IOR/MIL/17/5:

Report of the Expert Committee on the Defence of India: the
    Chatfield Report, HMSO, 1939, File 1802
Various Military Reports and Returns June–July 1947 – see notes
    for specific file references. British Library IOR/L/MIL/17/5
Post Exercise Report Exercise 'Embrace' Armed Forces
    Headquarters India 1946. File 1816
Intelligence Summaries, Armed Forces Headquarters India,
    January 1946 to August 1947. File 4276
India Internal Security Instructions 1937, File 4252
List of Units Indian Army and British Forces in India, June 1947,
    File 1127
List of Units Indian Army and British Forces in India, July 1947,
    File 1128
Post Operational Report on Punjab Frontier Force, Major General
    Pete Rees, File 4319
Southern Command Order of Battle, June 1947, File 1610
Strength Return Indian Army and British Forces in India, July
    1947, File 1451
Supreme Commander's Orders, August to December 1947,
    Supreme Headquarters Armed Forces of India and Pakistan,
    British Library, File 300
Model Exercise: Future Organisation of Indian Army, File 1806
Modernisation and Re-Organisation of the Indian Army, 1939,
    Armed Forces Headquarters, India 1939, File 1803
Northern Command Strength Return and Order of Battle, June
    1947, File 1575

In Public Record Office, Kew:

Command of British Troops in India, DEFE 5/5/145
India: Evacuation Plan for Europeans, DEFE 4/9/146
Whistler Report, DEFE/5/7/15
Palestine: Statement of Policy 1939, White Paper, HMSO
    Command 6019, 23 May 1939

Personal Diaries and Records

Major General Peter Rees, University of Sussex GB181 SxMs 16
Colonel Paddy Massey, Private Collection
John Cross, Private Collection
Charles Ouin, Indian Political Intelligence in Wartime
Judge Christopher Beaumont, Private Collection

Oral Interviews

Held in the British Library (with accession number). Several of these interviews are copyright-protected, which means they cannot be quoted from directly. However, they still provide helpful and interesting background. Several of them are also repeats of other interviews held either in the Imperial War Museum Sound Archive or in Andrew Whitehead's oral archive in SOAS Library. When I contacted next of kin to ask for permission to use direct quotes, this was unfailingly granted.

C900: Millenium Memory Bank

00083B Krishna Davi
00083 Hardian Bains
00083 Saleem Siddiqi
01580 Naffese Chohan
03096 C1 Ranjit Bains

C991/13 Kushwant Singh (repeats much of C63/12)

C63/195:

02 Pren Bhatia
03 Dr Bharat Ram
03 Lt Gen Palat Candeth
04 Nikhil Chakravarty
06 Admiral Chatterji
09 Govind Narain (largely repeated in R193/09)
11 Inder Malhorta
12 Kushwant Singh
51 Brian Montgomery
211/08 Leslie Robbins

C63/89-93 Christopher Beaumont (with grateful thanks to Robert Beaumont)

C1398:

Lieutenant Colonel Denis de Grouchy Lambert, 4 September 1984
1368 James Cameron
1833 Evan Charlton

R193:

08 A. K. Damodaran
09 Govind Narain
09 Major General D. K. Palit

Held in the Imperial War Museum (with accession number):

10632 Maynard Hastings Pockson
11748 Mohammed Ismail Khan
14660 S. Moolgaonkar
14661 N. Mukherji
14662 D. K. Palit
14666 F. Rustjani

14667 N. Rustjani
14668 R. Thakar
18781 Ronald Brockman
30563 Nirmal Kaur
30559 Upendra Nath Pathak
31490/30557 Abdul Haq
31492 Dil Mohammed
31492 Mir Bostan

Held in Louisiana State University, Baton Rouge:

Sir Charles and Lady Dalton
Brigadier and Mrs Herbert Dinwiddie
Mr and Mrs Geoffrey Lamarque: quoted by kind permission of
    the Lamarque family.

*Held in the School of Oriental and African Studies, London
University. All conducted by Andrew Whitehead.*

Alice Faiz, 17 June 1995
Amjad Hussain, 11 October 1995
Kharaiti Lal, 17 March 1997

Conducted by the author:

Ann Wright, 25 February 2017
Dhananajaya Singh, 23 February 2017
Hassan Hamid, 25 February 2017
Ali Hamid, 25 February 2017
Abdul Sattar, 25 February 2017
Robin Whiteside, 31 March 2017
Robert Beaumont, 20 April 2017

Film and Broadcast Material

Rajpoot, Tarun, *Indian-Pakistan Partition 1947*, BBC 2007
Seth, Roshan, *The Language of Protest*, BBC Radio 4: series of
five programmes broadcast in May 1986

V. P. Menon, Interviewed by Henry Hodson, 12 September 1964,
BBC Radio 4
Roberts, Andrew, *A Judge Remembers*, BBC Radio 4

Newspaper Articles

*The Times, Telegraph, Guardian, Hindustan Times, Statesman,
    The Times of India, Herald Tribune, New York Times* and
    Dawn throughout 1947
The Times Special India Supplement, 18 February 1930
Indian Express: 8 April, 20 May, 1 July, 1 August 1997

ACKNOWLEDGEMENTS

A lot of very kind people have helped me to write this book. I must start by thanking my indefatigable agent, Michael Sissons, and his assistant Fiona Petheram for their help and support throughout. I am also much indebted to Iain MacGregor at Simon & Schuster in London who gave me the initial inspiration and who has shepherded the project since inception. I am also deeply grateful to Jo Whitford for her tireless work in editing and arranging my ramblings.

I am deeply grateful for all those at Cambridge University for their guidance and mentoring, and in particular to Professor John Davidson of Trinity College for all his introductions and most generous hospitality while visiting.

Of all the many historians and experts whose works I have consulted, I must record special thanks to Andrew Whitehead, not only for his very generous permission to draw on his extensive oral archive in SOAS Library, but also to make full use of his excellent account of the Kashmir conflict.

Many people have been extraordinarily generous in giving me access to family papers and experiences. I am most grateful to Charles Ouin, Colonel Hamon Massey, Major J. P. Cross, Robin Whiteside, William Lamarque, Penelope Denny, Robert Beaumont, Edward Kneale, George Busby, Nick Allan, Barnaby Rogerson, Jane Ohlmeyer and Peter Oborne for all their help.

In India I am much indebted to Dhananajaya Singh, to Ann Wright, to Sir Dominic Asquith, Anuj and Aanchal Bahri, to Melissa van der Klugt and to all the Simon and Schuster staff, particularly to Rahul Srivastava, Yatindra Chaturvedi and Bharti Taneja.

In Pakistan I owe particular thanks to Major General Syed Ali Hamid, to his brother Hassan (who is Auchinleck's godson), to Major General Isfandyhar Pataudi, to Abdul Sattar, ex-Foreign Minister of Pakistan, to Salim Gandapur and to Ahmad Saeed of the eponymous Book Store.

A special thank you to the British Library staff, to Cai Parry-Jones and to Steven Dryden, to the London Library for their endless patience and to the staff at the Sussex University Library and at the National Army and Imperial War Museums.

Lastly a very special thank you to my daughter Florence who patiently read, questioned, amended and improved the manuscript throughout, and to everyone at Simon & Schuster in London who has made the production of this book possible.

Barney White-Spunner
Dorset
April 2017

INDEX